Lecture Notes in Computer Science 4836

Commenced Publication in 1973
Founding and Former Series Editors:
Gerhard Goos, Juris Hartmanis, and Jan van Leeuwen

Haruhisa Ichikawa   We-Duke Cho
Ichiro Satoh   Hee Yong Youn (Eds.)

Ubiquitous Computing Systems

4th International Symposium, UCS 2007
Tokyo, Japan, November 25-28, 2007
Proceedings

 Springer

Volume Editors

Haruhisa Ichikawa
The University of Electro-Communications
Tokyo 182-8585, Japan
E-mail: h.ichikw@hc.uec.ac.jp

We-Duke Cho
UCN/CUS Ajou University
Suwon, 443-749, South Korea
E-mail: chowd@ajou.ac.kr

Ichiro Satoh
National Institute of Informatics
Tokyo 101-8430, Japan
E-mail: ichiro@nii.ac.jp

Hee Yong Youn
Sungkyunkwan University
Suwon, 440-746 South Korea
E-mail: youn@ece.skku.ac.kr

Library of Congress Control Number: 2007938892

CR Subject Classification (1998): C.2, C.3, C.5.3, D.2, D.4, H.4, H.5, K.4, J.7

LNCS Sublibrary: SL 3 – Information Systems and Application, incl. Internet/Web
and HCI

ISSN   0302-9743
ISBN-10   3-540-76771-1 Springer Berlin Heidelberg New York
ISBN-13   978-3-540-76771-8 Springer Berlin Heidelberg New York

Springer is a part of Springer Science+Business Media

springer.com

© Springer-Verlag Berlin Heidelberg 2007
Printed in Germany

Typesetting: Camera-ready by author, data conversion by Scientific Publishing Services, Chennai, India
Printed on acid-free paper   SPIN: 12191024   06/3180   5 4 3 2 1 0

Preface

We cordially welcome you to the proceedings of the 2007 International Symposium on Ubiquitous Computing Systems (UCS) held at Akihabara, Tokyo, Japan. UCS has become a symposium for the dissemination of state-of-the-art research and engineering practices in ubiquitous computing with particular emphasis on systems and software. UCS 2007 was the fourth of this series of international symposia. This was the year for the Next Generation Network (NGN) to be commercially launched so that the Internet could become the infrastructure for communications and computing substituting the NGN in telephone networks. The maturity of the Internet encourages the research and development of the next computing systems, where ubiquitous computing is recognized as one of the most promising computing paradigms.

This symposium was organized by IPSJ SIGUBI, IEICE USN and UCN, Korea, in cooperation with the IEEE Tokyo Section, IPSJ SIGEMB, IEICE Smart Info-media Systems Technical Group, and Human Interface Society. It was also sponsored by Ubiquitous Networking Forum, Nokia, NTT, SCAT, IISF and TAF.

This year, we had 96 submissions from 18 countries. The Program Committee reviewed all the papers carefully and then selected 16 full papers and 8 short papers. The very low acceptance rate of about 22.6% clearly demonstrates the high quality of the conference, and this tradition will continue in the upcoming conferences. Two distinguished speakers were also invited for keynote speeches, who enlightened the audience on ubiquitous computing and applications.

The high-quality technical program of UCS 2007 depends very much on the precise and stringent review process. The Technical Program Committee consisted of 62 excellent members. Most reviews ware almost of journal paper review quality, and the paper selection was very serious and strict.

Along with the symposium, we also offered a workshop and a poster session. This was for providing the researchers and engineers with opportunities to share their ideas and solutions for a broad range of challenging problems in this area.

As General Co-chairs and Program Co-chairs, we would like to express our appreciation to all the volunteers working hard for the symposium: members of the Steering Committee, the Organizing Committee, the Program Committee, the authors and the reviewers. Special thanks go to Yoshito Tobe and Jin Nakazawa.

November 2007

Haruhisa Ichikawa
We-Duke Cho
Ichiro Satoh
Hee Yong Youn

Organization

Executive Committee

General Co-chairs	Haruhisa Ichikawa (NTT Corporation, Japan)
	We-Duke Cho (UCN, Ajou University, Korea)
Program Co-chairs	Ichiro Satoh (National Institute of Informatics, Japan)
	Hee Yong Youn (Sungkyunkwan University, Korea)
Local Arrangements Chair	Jin Nakazawa (Keio University, Japan)
Treasurer	Masashi Toda (Future University-Hakodate, Japan)
Publication Co-chairs	Kazunori Takashio (Keio University, Japan)
	Marc Langheinrich (ETH Zurich, Switzerland)
	Young Ik Eom (Sungkyunkwan University, Korea)
Publicity Co-chairs	Sozo Inoue (Kyushu University, Japan)
	Matthias Kranz (Technische Universität Braunschweig, Germany)
	Moon Hyun Kim (Sungkyunkwan University, Korea)
Industrial Liaison Chair	Yoshito Tobe (Tokyo Denki University, Japan)
Workshops Chair	Masayoshi Ohashi (KDDI Corporation, Japan)
Posters Chair	Masateru Minami (Shibaura Institute of Technology, Japan)
	Charles Perkins (Nokia, USA)
Demonstrations Chair	Kazushige Ouchi (Toshiba Corporation, Japan)
Secretariat	Kaori Fujinami (Tokyo University of Agriculture and Technology, Japan)
	Masayasu Yamaguchi (NTT Corporation, Japan)
Steering Committee	Tomonori Aoyama (Keio University, Japan)
	We-Duke Cho (UCN, Korea)
	Hyeon-Kon Kim (NCA, Korea)
	Tei-Wei Kuo (National Taiwan University, Taiwan)
	Hideyuki Nakashima (Future University-Hakodate, Japan)
	Joseph Kee-Yin Ng (Hong Kong Baptist University, Hong Kong)
	Ramakoti Sadananda (Rangsit University, Thailand)
	Sang-Chul Shin (NCA, Korea)
	Hideyuki Tokuda (Keio University, Japan)

Program Committee

Jörg Baus (Saarland University, Germany)
Christian Becker (Universität Mannheim, Germany)
Michael Beigl (Technische Universität Braunschweig, Germany)
Roy Campbell (University of Illinois at Urbana-Champaign, USA)
K. Selcuk Candan (Arizona State University, USA)
Diane Cook (The University of Texas at Arlington, USA)
Antonio Coronato (ICAR-CNR, Italy)
Christian Decker (University of Karlsruhe, Germany)
Alois Ferscha (University of Linz, Austria)
Kaori Fujinami (Tokyo University of Agriculture and Technology, Japan)
Hani Hagras (University of Essex, UK)
Mikio Hasegawa (Tokyo University of Science, Japan)
Lars Erik Holmquist (Viktoria Institute, Sweden)
Liviu Iftode (Rutgers University, USA)
Michita Imai (Keio University, Japan)
Sozo Inoue (Kyushu University, Japan)
Susumu Ishihara (Shizuoka University, Japan)
Jihong Jeung (Kookmin University, Korea)
Yoshihiro Kawahara (The University of Tokyo, Japan)
Takahiro Kawamura (TOSHIBA Corp., Japan)
Hideki Koike (University of Electro-Communications, Japan)
Mohan Kumar (The University of Texas at Arlington, USA)
Koichi Kurumatani (AIST, Japan)
Fusako Kusunoki (Tama Art University, Japan)
Marc Langheinrich (ETH Zurich, Switzerland)
Frederic Le Mouel (INRIA / INSA Lyon, France)
Dongman Lee (Information and Communications University, Korea)
Wonjun Lee (Korea University, Korea)
Claudia Linnhoff-Popien (University of Munich, Germany)
Cristina Videira Lopes (University of California Irvine, USA)
Javier Lopez-Munoz (University of Malaga, Spain)
Paul Lukowicz (University of Passau, Germany)
Fabio Martinelli (CNR-IIT, Italy)
Kazuhiro Minami (University of Illinois at Urbana-Champaign, USA)
Masateru Minami (Shibaura Institute of Technology, Japan)
Hiroyuki Morikawa (The University of Tokyo, Japan)
Jin Nakazawa (Keio University, Japan)
Sotiris Nikoletseas (University of Patras and Computer Technology Institute,
    Greece)
Kazushi Nishimoto (JAIST, Japan)
Paddy Nixon (University College Dublin, Ireland)
Melek Önen (Institut EURECOM, France)

Kazushige Ouchi (Toshiba Corporation, Japan)
Susanna Pirttikangas (University of Oulu, Finland)
Jukka Riekki (University of Oulu, Finland)
Yves Roudier (Institut EURECOM, France)
Umar Saif (MIT, USA)
Aruna Seneviratne (University of New South Wales, Australia)
Mukesh Singhal (University of Kentucky, USA)
Joshua Smith (Intel Research Seattle, USA)
Toshio Soumiya (FUJITSU LABS. LTD., Japan)
Yasuyuki Sumi (Kyoto University, Japan)
Yasuo Tan (JAIST, Japan)
Hiroyuki Tarumi (Kagawa University, Japan)
Tsutomu Terada (Osaka University, Japan)
Yoshito Tobe (Tokyo Denki University, Japan)
Tonouchi Toshio (NEC, Japan)
Anand Tripathi (University of Minnesota, USA)
Kristof Van Laerhoven (Darmstadt University of Technology, Germany)
Xin Wang (Stony Brook University, USA)
Steven Willmott (Universitat Politecnica de Catalunya, Spain)
Woontack Woo (GIST, Korea)
Keiichi Yasumoto (Nara Institute of Science and Technology, Japan)

Reviewers

Ioannis Aekaterinidis (University of Patras, Greece)
Martin Berchtold (University of Karlsruhe, Germany)
Shinsuke Hara (Osaka City University, Japan)
Mattias Jacobsson (Viktoria Institute, Sweden)
Antonis Kalis (AIT - Athens Information Technology, Greece)
Athanasios Kinalis (University of Patras and Computer Technology Institute,
    Greece)
Tomoya Kitani (Nara Institute of Science and Technology, Japan)
Mihai Marin-Perianu (University of Twente, The Netherlands)
Nishkam Ravi (Rutgers University, USA)
Till Riedel (TecO & University of Karlsruhe, Germany)
Mattias Rost (Viktoria Institute, Sweden)
Gregor Schiele (University of Mannheim, Germany)
Pravin Shankar (Rutgers University, USA)
Naoki Shibata (Shiga University, Japan)
Kenichi Takizawa (National Institute of Information and Communications
    Technology, Japan)
Morihiko Tamai (Nara Institute of Science and Technology, Japan)
Tadahiro Wada (Shizuoka University, Japan)

Sponsoring Institutions

Ubiquitous Networking Forum
Nokia
NTT
Support Center for Advanced Telecommunications Technology Research,
    Foundation
International Information Science Foundation
The Telecommunications Advancement Foundation

Supporting Societies

UCS2007 was organized by IPSJ SIGUBI, IEICE USN, and UCN (Korea) in
cooperation with the IEEE Tokyo Section, IPSJ SIGEMB, IEICE Smart Info-
media Systems Technical Group, and Human Interface Society.

Table of Contents

Middleware

Modeling and Social Aspects

Smart Devices

Network

RFID Privacy Using Spatially Distributed Shared Secrets

Marc Langheinrich[1] and Remo Marti[2]

[1] Inst. for Pervasive Computing
ETH Zurich, 8092 Zurich, Switzerland
langheinrich@inf.ethz.ch
[2] Ergon Informatik AG
8008 Zurich, Switzerland
remo.marti@ergon.ch

Abstract. Many of today's proposed RFID privacy schemes rely on the encryption of tag IDs with user-chosen keys. However, password management quickly becomes a bottleneck in such proposals, rendering them infeasible in situations where tagged items are repeatedly exchanged in informal (i.e., personal) situations, in particular outside industrial supply-chains or supermarket checkout lanes. An alternative to explicit access control management are RFID privacy systems that provides access to tag IDs *over time*, i.e., only after prolonged and detailed reading of an item. Such themes can minimize the risk of unwanted exposure through accidental read-outs, or offer protection during brief encounters with strangers. This paper describes a spatially distributed ID-disclosure scheme that uses a (potentially large) set of miniature RFID tags to distribute the true ID of an item across the entire product surface. We introduce the underlying mechanism of our spatially distributed RFID privacy system and report on initial performance results.

1 Introduction

Today's best protection from unwanted RFID readouts is to completely disable the tag – either by executing a *kill-command* [1] at checkout that renders the tag silent to all reader requests, or by physically clipping the tag antenna [2]. In the future, however, additional services such as warranty returns and repairs, smart laundry machines, automated inventories, or electronically augmented everyday appliances [3] may offer tangible consumer benefits for RFID-tagged items beyond the supply chain, which would force consumers to choose between these novel services and their privacy.

Short of killing tags completely, so far only password-based methods have seemed feasible for protecting RFID tags from unwanted readouts [4,5,6].[1] While their general principle is easy enough for implementation on a tiny RFID tag,

---

[1] An excellent overview of RFID privacy methods can be found in [7].

H. Ichikawa et al. (Eds.): UCS 2007, LNCS 4836, pp. 1–16, 2007.

the practical use of such schemes is often challenging. In order to facilitate the exchange, sale, or return of tagged items, all involved parties must own and operate reasonably sophisticated information infrastructures that can pass and receive the individual passwords for each tagged item. In principle, NFC-enabled smartphones could easily receive such passwords as an integral part of a mobile phone based payment procedure, but in reality, it will still take many years before a majority of shoppers will own, carry, and use such phones. Equally unlikely is the fast spread of corresponding NFC-enabled point-of-sales systems, as retail-chains would need to add costly upgrades to their systems without clear benefits to their bottom line, while smaller outlets such as kiosks or newsstands would need to upgrade their entire procurement, inventory, and sales operations at costs that could easily dwarf their yearly profits.

A number of password-less alternatives for RFID privacy have since been proposed, such as Juels et al.'s *blocker tag* [8], where a specifically engineered RFID tag causes signal collisions with all regular RFID tags in its vicinity, effectively preventing their readout. While simple in use, the need for carrying a blocker tag puts the burden of privacy protection on the user, who looses this protection should she forget to carry it. Blocker tags are also subject to the same reliability concerns as ordinary tags, i.e., a suboptimal position in the reader's field might not sufficiently power the tag, thus allowing full access to all other RFID tags. In order to limit the types of deactivated tags, e.g., to only those belonging to the user, a password management scheme is again needed that allows configuring regular RFID tags to be protected by a particular blocker tag. Fishkin et al. [9] instead propose a simple but intuitive *distance-based* access control scheme, where tags reply with different levels of detail depending on their distance to the reader. Apart from the increased costs for the required on-tag circuitry to reliably detect signal strength, distance-based authentication might not always yield the desired functionality, e.g., when passing narrow passageways or small store entrances.

In an earlier paper [10], we have proposed a third alternative, called a *Shamir Tag*, which neither require costly password management nor error-prone distance measurements. Using the cryptographic principle of *secret shares* [11], Shamir Tags yield virtually no information to casual "hit-and-run" attackers, but only reveal their true ID after continuous and undisturbed reading from up-close – something that can hardly go unnoticed by an item's owner. At the same time, however, the system allows tag owners to use *caching* for speeding-up this process, effectively preserving instant item identification in home-automation or supply-chain applications.

In order to prevent secret long-range scanning with powerful antennas, Shamir Tags' antennas will need to be constructed with limited read-out ranges, potentially yielding only a few centimeters of distance for systems operating within the allowed power levels. This in turn might complicate the readout process also for tag owners, as tagged items need to be positioned more carefully with respect to the antenna. This paper presents a *multi-tag* extension to Shamir Tags, allowing the use of dozens, if not hundreds of miniature tags on the same product, thus alleviating positioning problems without the need for increased read ranges. Our approach is based on the idea of *super-distributed RFID tag-infrastructures* (SDRI) [12], where tiny RFID chips are brought out in large numbers, e.g., mixed into wall paint, woven into carpets or clothing, or sprinkled into an item's plastic casing. Thus, instead of having a single RFID tag per item, we envision items that feature several hundreds of tags, with the item's ID being *spread out* across all tags. Given appropriate communication protocols and antenna sizes, reading that many tags at once will be infeasible, instead requiring readers to scan small areas sequentially. While clearly not yet a reality, we believe that current[2] trends in RFID miniaturization, such as Hitachi's μ-chip,[2] offer ample potential for actually deploying such simple but reliable RFID privacy systems in the future.

The remainder of this paper is structured as follows. Section 2 will briefly describe our previously proposed Shamir Tags and their underlying principles, Shamir's *secret sharing* scheme and *bit-throttling*, as well as outline a distributed, multi-tag variant. Section 3 then presents two extensions that we developed for using distributed Shamir Tags concurrently, i.e., in a multi-item scenario. Section 4 will briefly outline the prototype system we built for evaluating our approach, before we report on the results of initial experiments in section 5.

2   Shamir Tags

Shamir Tags use two principles to protect the true ID of an item (e.g., its EPC-code) [10]. Firstly, data readout is performed in two stages using a *bit-by-bit* strategy. Initially, a Shamir Tag discloses a small subset (e.g., 5%) of bits to a reader, which allows owners to quickly identify the entire bit-string from a small list (cache) of personal items. This is then followed by a steady "trickle" of bits that reveals the entire ID to the reader only after prolonged reading, e.g., several minutes. This allows anybody to eventually identify an item, yet forces them to stay close enough to the tag during the entire time. This process is called *bit-throttling*, and it makes tag-tracking difficult.

However, since industrial code-schemes are often heavily structured, even releasing only a few bits might already disclose sensitive data. E.g., an EPC-header featuring the combination 10 at the third and fourth position uniquely identifies items tagged by the U.S. Department of Defense [13]. To prevent such data disclosure, Shamir Tags are additionally *encoded* using *shared secrets*. The process of creating a shared secret basically re-encodes the tag's true ID into n seemingly unrelated numbers. Only by combining all n numbers, the original ID can be (trivially) reconstructed. Section 2.1 will give some more background information on this process – for now it suffices to know that this encoding step basically protects our Shamir Tag from inadvertently disclosing meaningful bits.

---

[2] Hitachi's current generation μ-chip has a size of less than 0.2 mm^2, its next generation will have only about 0.02 mm^2. Also see `www.hitachi.co.jp/Prod/mu-chip`

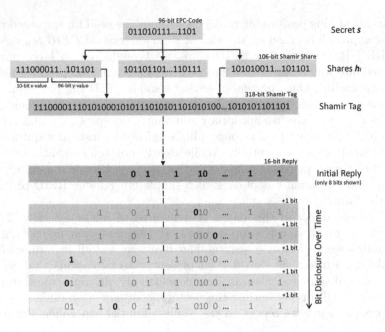

Fig. 1. *Principal Construction of a Shamir Tag* (from [10]). Based on the tag's "true" ID, e.g., its EPC-code, multiple Shamir shares are concatenated to form the tag's new ID, which is then stored on the tag. Upon reader inquiry, an initial set of random bits is released, with subsequent throttled single-bit releases.

Only after all bits have been read (which, due to bit-throttling, may take up to several minutes) they can be combined into the true ID.[3]

Figure 1 shows the principal construction of a Shamir Tag from a 96-bit EPC. In our previous work [10], we have shown that Shamir Tags provide an effective and cheap protection from unwanted and inadvertent tag readouts. Item owners can use simple caching strategies to ensure instantaneous identification of their own tags, while foreign readers will need to have continuous access to the tag for prolonged amounts of time, in order to read a sufficiently large percentage of bits from the tag that allows reconstructing the Shamir-encoded true ID. However, a critical factor of this protection is the effective read range of such tags – if the read range is too large, attackers can read out tags from several meters away whenever their owners are not moving fast enough, e.g., in public transport, or while waiting in line. Reducing the read range by limiting tag antenna sizes helps to prevent such attacks, yet at the same time complicates tag readout for legitimate owners, as they will also need to position their antennas very close to

---

[3] Note that if x bits are missing, rogue readers can of course try out all possible 2^x combinations to compute 2^x potential true IDs, and then use knowledge about valid EPC values (e.g., allowed manufacturer IDs, or known product IDs) to discard invalid IDs.

the tag. In industrial settings, or when the exact location of an embedded tag is not known, this might significantly hamper legitimate tag use.

Our solution to this is – as outlined in the introduction – straightforward: instead of using a single Shamir Tag with a reasonable antenna range that simplifies tag detection at the expense of long-range scanning protection, we use dozens, if not hundreds of miniature Shamir Tags, woven into the garment of clothing, or mixed into the plastic casing of products, that have a much shorter antenna range but which distribute the item's (protected) ID more or less evenly across the entire product surface. However, this approach offers new challenges for ID reconstruction, which are outlined in section 3 below. But first, we will briefly give some background on the construction of shared secrets using Shamir's scheme in the following section.

2.1 Shamir's Secret Sharing Scheme

In a secret sharing scheme, each participant receives a *share* that is a part of a secret. The secret can only be recovered if enough participants cooperate in recombining their shares. Schemes that allow a reconstruction of the secret with only t out of n participants involved are called *(t,n)-threshold schemes*. They fulfill the following two properties: Firstly, no subset of participants smaller than a threshold t can gain information on the secret s, even when cooperating with each other. Secondly, any subset equal to or larger than a threshold t can reconstruct the secret s at any time.

One of the most famous (t,n)-threshold schemes was introduced by Shamir in 1979 [11]. It is based on polynomials, and in particular on the observation that a polynomial of degree $t - 1$ is defined by t coordinate-pairs (x_i, y_i). To encode a secret s for n participants with a threshold t, one chooses a random polynomial of degree $t - 1$ that crosses the y-axis at s. The n participants are each given exactly one point on the polynomial's curve, thus allowing any t members to compute the exact polynomial and thus the y-intercept s.

The reconstruction of the secret is essentially a polynomial interpolation based on the *Lagrange* formula. Since only the y-intercept is of interest, it can be simplified to the following formula (with k being the number of tags read):[4]

$$s = q(0) = \sum_{i=1}^{k} y_i \prod_{1 \leq j \leq k, i \neq j} \frac{x_j}{x_j - x_i} \tag{1}$$

In practice, computing the secret s given large numbers of shares (e.g., thousands) quickly becomes infeasible. Calculations are therefore carried out in a finite field modulo p (written as $\mathbb{Z}_p$)[5], with p being a large prime number. Not only does this reduce the size of exponents, but it also removes the need for floating point operations (thus limiting numerical errors).

---

[4] Obviously, computing s with $k < t$ shares is not possible.
[5] $\mathbb{Z}_p$ designates the set $\{0, 1, ..., p - 1\}$.

A comprehensive discussion of this topic is beyond the scope of this paper, but an excellent introduction, as well as efficient algorithms for solving (1) in $\mathbb{Z}_p$, can be found in [14]. Operating a secret sharing scheme within $\mathbb{Z}_p$ not only makes reconstruction of the secret s (e.g., its Electronic Product Code/EPC) feasible, but also helps with the practical problem of resolving multiple secrets concurrently. This will be described in section 3 below.

2.2 A Spatially Distributed Shamir Tag

A straightforward implementation of a distributed Shamir Tag would simply put the individual shares not just on a single tag, but distribute them among *multiple* tags on (or in) an item. As Shamir's scheme allows the reconstruction of the secret irrespective of the order of the shares, no special order would need to be observed when reading shares off the individual tags. Bit-throttling could also still be used, as each tag would choose a random temporary ID during readout, allowing a reader to group bits from the same share properly together. In order to make use of *caching* [10], however, bits would need to be continously numbered across all tags, in order to have a defined order. Note that this would *not* decrease the level of protection compared to a single Shamir Tag, as this simply orders the distributed bits just as in the non-distributed (i.e., single-tag) version – this would simply increase per-tag storage requirements, as each distributed share would need to also store its original position within the Shamir Tag.

By properly adjusting the threshold parameter t, defective or detuned tags could be tolerated. This also adds flexibility to the readout process, as only part of an item's surface would need to be scanned.[6] Just like in the single-tag case, a reader would gradually assemble the set of tags and their IDs in an item and repeatedly compute the secret s until a stable y-intercept had been found. Obviously, the overall disclosure-delay of a single tag could be significantly shortened, as the spatial distribution of the shares combined with the shortened read range of individual tags introduces an additional delay during readout.

3   Distributed Multi-item Identification

The approach described in section 2.2 above works well as long as only a single item/ID at a time needs to be reconstructed. However, once multiple items are within the reading range of the antenna, interpolation points from two or more polynomials would get mixed together that would never converge on a stable s value (nor yield multiple values for the different items). Since the Shamir scheme has no means of differentiating points from different polynomials, we will need to extend it if we want it to support decoding two or more secrets concurrently.

---

[6] The ratio between t and n could be adjusted individually for different products, depending on the envisioned privacy degree: a threshold t close to n requires many tags to be read, a small t allows the reconstruction of the secret s already with a small subset of tags.

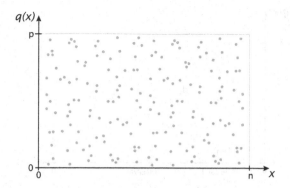

Fig. 2. *Distribution of Interpolation Points in* $\mathbb{Z}_p$. The sampling points on the polynomial $q(x)$ *mod* p appear evenly distributed in the Shamir Space $n \times p$. This allows us to choose a subset n' of points that fulfill certain geometric requirements, thus facilitating item discrimination. Note that the drawing is not to scale, as typically $p \gg n$.

A naïve idea to discriminate between different set of interpolation points would be to use a common prefix for all tags of a single item, thus allowing a reader to compute multiple s-values for different items concurrently. Obviously, such a prefix would constitute just another fixed, trackable pseudonym, rendering the benefits of the entire sharing scheme void. Instead, we will need a method similar to our initial approach, i.e., a discrimination system that works well once a certain threshold of points have been assembled, but which does not work if only few interpolation points have been read.

The following sections describe two such discrimination methods that we have developed, both based on the geometric distribution of interpolation points: *cluster-based discrimination* and *line-based discrimination*. They both make use of the fact that the n interpolation points on the polynomial $q(x)$ *mod* p (i.e., within $\mathbb{Z}_p$) are spread in a seemingly uniform way in the "Shamir Space" $n \times p$ (see figure 2). The basic idea is to oversample $q(x)$ with much more points than needed for item integration. We then have the choice of carefully selecting n' out of the n generated points, based on the specific geometric requirements of our discrimination method, and use only those n' points as our tags.[7] During item detection, we can then use the discrimination method to properly distinguish tags from different items.

3.1   Cluster-Based Item Discrimination

For the *clustering method*, we select the n' points in the shape of several clusters, all of them similar in size and laid out on a regular grid. This allows our cluster-based discrimination algorithm to determine which tag-IDs belong to the same item, according to cluster size and cluster position. Figure 3 illustrates the selection of IDs for one item during tag generation. In addition to the previously discussed parameters (i.e., the total number n' of tags on the item, the

---

[7] Note that $n \gg n' > t$ holds, i.e., the secret can still be computed with only t tags.

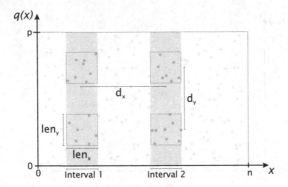

Fig. 3. *Cluster-Based Selection of n'.* Given a choice of individual item parameters d_x and d_y, $c = 4$ clusters of approximately the same size (in an area of $len_x \times len_y$) are randomly selected from a regular grid.

encoded secret ID s, and the threshold of tags t that need to be read), each item gets assigned a random number c of clusters and a corresponding cluster size[8] (len_x and len_y). Given a system-wide, fixed cluster grid size (d_x and d_y) and the Shamir Space dimensions n and p, the tag-ID generation algorithm simply chooses a random origin and then proceeds to place the c clusters randomly on a rectangular grid. Note that instead of sampling the polynomial for all n x_i, it suffices to compute the y_i within the intervals where the actual clusters lie, thus greatly speeding up share generation. These intervals are also shown in figure 3.

Once we have generated the tag-IDs according to the above steps, *item detection* can then proceed in three phases: cluster detection, item discrimination, and secret reconstruction. In the first phase, all found tag-IDs are analyzed by means of a clustering algorithm in order to identify cluster centers. We have found the *subtractive clustering* algorithm [15] to be very efficient for our purposes. Note that an appropriate distance measure must be chosen in order to account for the stretched space with its elongated clusters. Once the clusters have been returned by the algorithm, phase two groups clusters with similar size (i.e., number of associated points) and position (i.e., with the cluster center near a node on the same grid) together. Since tags for different items are generated independently, cluster collisions can occur if two items in the reading range have tags residing in the same area. Such a scenario is depicted in figure 4. Collisions result in larger clusters and are discarded by the detection algorithm as they do not match any other cluster either with regard to size, position, or both. However, in most cases this will still leave enough points for reconstruction, as

---

[8] The cluster dimensions have to be chosen in such a way that the expected sum of all points contained therein matches or slightly exceeds n'. Under the assumption of regular point distribution, cluster length and width can be calculated as $len_x = \sqrt{\frac{n'}{n \cdot c}} \cdot n$ and $len_y = \sqrt{\frac{n'}{n \cdot c}} \cdot p$. Also note that p is usually much larger than n, resulting in a massively stretched Shamir Space. In account with this stretch, len_x and len_y are chosen such that the ratio $\frac{len_x}{len_y}$ equals $\frac{n}{p}$.

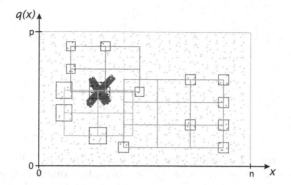

Fig. 4. *Cluster-Based Item Detection in the Shamir Space.* The example shows clusters from three different items. A collision between two clusters occurs that can be identified due to the unusual size and position of the resulting collision-cluster.

t out of n' tags already suffice. Phase three finally reconstructs the secrets s_i separately for all identified items I_i by means of (1) within $\mathbb{Z}_p$.

3.2 Line-Based Discrimination

The *line-based method* locates the subset of n' tags per item along lines of different origin and slope within the oversampled Shamir Space. In order to facilitate detection, we restrict lines to a number of four predefined slopes $m \in \{0, 1, -1, \pm\infty\}$[9]. While the slope m of an item's line is selected randomly, the line's respective y-intercept b depends on m, as shown in table 1. A third parameter, the line width d (i.e., the maximal allowed distance of a point from the line), is used to regulate the number of points available along a line, as we eventually need to select n' tags per item, irrespective of line slope and origin.[10]

In contrast to the cluster-based detection, the line width parameters d^i (i.e., one for each possible value of m) must be chosen and fixed in advance for all items in the system, irrespective of an item's number of shares n'. This is because during detection, we otherwise have no way of bounding our search along these lines. Given the set of four slopes and y-intercepts shown in table 1, the following

---

[9] Since $p \gg n$ holds, we actually use $m \in \{0, \frac{p}{n}, -\frac{p}{n}, \pm\infty\}$, as the slopes ± 1 and 0 can hardly be distinguished.

[10] This is necessary as different slopes and different origins result in widely different numbers of available points. A horizontal line ($m = 0$) has a length of only n, while a vertical line ($m = \pm\infty$) extends over p units (recall that $p \gg n$). Their respective widths d^h_{max} and d^v_{max} must compensate for their difference in length in order for both to select n' points. Diagonal lines ($m = \pm\frac{p}{n}$) differ greatly based on their origin: The more centered they are in the Shamir Space, the more points are selected. The closer they are to the corners, the fewer points are available. However, we cannot always choose lines in the center, as this would cause different lines to collide with high probability, rendering item detection almost impossible.

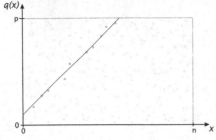 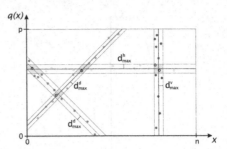

(a) *Selection.* n' tags are selected randomly along lines with slope m, width d, and y-intercept b.

(b) *Item Detection.* The example shows lines from four different items. Tags in the intersecting areas are discarded.

Fig. 5. *Line-Based Item Discrimination.* Lines representing items cross the Shamir Space with predefined slopes.

widths guarantee that all types of lines select at least n'_{max} tags[11] in the Shamir Space:[12]

$$d^v_{max} = tolerance, \quad d^h_{max} = \frac{p}{n} \cdot tolerance, \quad d^d_{max} \geq \frac{p \cdot tolerance}{\sqrt{\left(\frac{p}{2}\right)^2 + \left(\frac{n}{2}\right)^2}},$$

$$\text{with} \quad tolerance = \frac{n'_{max}}{2} \tag{2}$$

Knowing the system-wide *tolerance* parameter, item discrimination is fairly straightforward. After acquiring the point cloud of all tags in the reading range, the detection algorithm selects a random point and searches for close-by values in all possible directions (i.e., horizontal, vertical and diagonal). Should the number of detected points in the four directions not differ significantly, the starting point most likely lies in an intersection of two or more lines, which prompts the algorithm to choose another random point and start over. As the starting point might reside near the edge of a line, the four directions are explored with a distance of $2d_{max}$[13] (see figure 5(b)). A pruning step then discard points that have wrongly been assigned due to this increased search range. For diagonal lines, this is done by trying to estimate the real line using a *linear least squares* fit and rejecting points in a distance larger than d^d_{max}. For horizontal and vertical lines, simply averaging over the points' (x,y)-coordinates results in the estimated line. Points with a distance larger than d^h_{max} or d^v_{max}, respectively, are discarded.

All remaining points after the pruning step are considered valid points of an item, and are subsequently removed from the point cloud before the algorithm

---

[11] If a smaller amount than n'_{max} is desired, points can be discarded randomly, effectively *thinning* the line.

[12] In equation 2, n'_{max} designates the largest n' of all items ever to be generated.

[13] That is, $2d^h_{max}$ for horizontal, $2d^v_{max}$ for vertical and $2d^d_{max}$ for diagonal lines.

Table 1. *Parameter Choices for Line-Based Detection.* Depending on a line's slope m, different y-intercepts b are chosen.

Slope m	0	$\frac{p}{n}$	$-\frac{p}{n}$	$\pm\infty$
y-intercept b	$[d^h_{max}, p - 1 - d^h_{max}]$	$[-\frac{1}{2}p, \frac{1}{2}p]$	$[\frac{1}{2}p, \frac{3}{2}p]$	$[d^v_{max}, n - d^v_{max}]$

is restarted for detecting another item among the remaining points. Once all points have been assigned to items this way, the algorithm finally checks for intersections. Points in the area of an intersection will be removed from the corresponding items' sets, as they might have been wrongly assigned to an item. A final phase reconstructs the s_i by means of (1) within $\mathbb{Z}_p$ for all items.

4 Prototype System

In order to evaluate our proposed time-delayed identification method, we created a Java application that could both simulate tag generation and item detection for arbitrarily large item and tag populations, as well as drive an actual hardware reader (using Hitachi's μ-Chips)[14] to read out SDRI-tagged items. Figure 6 shows the main program interface, as well as an actual set of SDRI-tagged items (baby clothing) that can be read out using a regular reader.[15]

The SDRI-Privacy Demonstrator allows manual and automated generation of tag-sets, i.e., the encoding of arbitrary IDs s_i (e.g., an EPC) onto arbitrary numbers of tags n_i with a chosen threshold t_i. To simplify the operation of our initial prototype, we have not implemented the bit-throttling feature of the Shamir tags – upon readout, each tag reveals the entire Shamir share stored on the tag. The generated shares can be assigned to simulated tags (for simulated items), or linked to real RFID-tags (that are affixed to real items) in the form of a translation table, which translates the fixed ID of a read-only RFID-tag into one of the m_i Shamir shares of the Shamir polynomial.[16]

A built-in simulator can be used to automate the process of repeatedly reading out RFID-tags from the generated item sets, keeping track of successful item identification under various conditions. The results presented in section 5 below are based on such simulations. For demonstration purposes, a small number of tags can also be read directly using a conventional RFID reader. Due to their small size, short range, and restricted anti-collision capabilities, a few dozen Hitachi μ-Chips were incorporated into a small set of baby clothes (see figure 6(b)[17]), demonstrating

---

[14] See www.hitachi.co.jp/Prod/mu-chip

[15] While both the *clustering* and the *line* method were prototypically implemented in MATLAB, the demonstrator currently supports only the clustering method.

[16] Ideally, the shares on a tag (representing interpolation points on its item's polynomial) are set during the manufacturing process, e.g., using write-once tags. However, as the RFID tags we were using were not writable, their fixed IDs are mapped to coordinates in Shamir space by means of a translation table that is maintained in the demonstrator software.

[17] The skirt is pictured inside out, showing the affixed μ-chip tags.

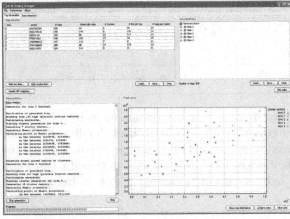

(a) Screenshot of Main Program Interface   (b) Setup in Hardware Mode

Fig. 6. *The SDRI-Privacy Demonstrator.* A prototypical implementation demonstrates the feasibility of the SDRI-privacy approach and allows performance measurements.

the envisioned interaction concept: only by sweeping the reader back and forth over the items, the individual IDs of each clothing can be reassembled.[18]

5   Analysis

This section will evaluate the performance of our proposed spatially distributed Shamir Tags in terms of *detection rates* and *traceability.* Ideally, we want our tagged items to be difficult to trace, yet reliably detectable for authorized readers.[19]

Detection might be hampered by the bit-throttling of each individual tag, as well as due to our multi-item discrimination algorithms (i.e., the cluster-based and line-based methods described in section 3). While we have not yet implemented bit-throttling in our prototype, the general performance aspects of our previously proposed *single-tag* solution [10] should still hold. Table 2 (reprinted from [10]) shows the discriminatory power of a certain number of bits in a cached population. Using this, we can conclude that a set of 10 distributed tags each releasing only 1-2 bits upon initial readout (thus yielding about 15 bits total) would already allow the identification of an item from a list of some 30 000 items (see row 15 and interpolate the values between column 10 000 and 100 000). This of course requires unique bit-positions among all tags on an item, in order to allow for this kind of lookup table to work. Note, however, that this does not imply that tags would be *traceable* using these 15 bits: it is only if a tag owner

---

[18] Note that the short antenna sizes on the RFID chips and the lack of an anti-collision protocol are central to our approach, as they prevent malicious readers from quickly scanning all available tags on a person, potentially from a large distance.

[19] As we do not use passwords, "authorized" in our case means a reader that is able to read a majority of the tags (which should take considerable effort).

Table 2. Number of Items Identified by Bit-Strings of Different Lengths (from [10])

Bits ↓ Items →	100	1 000	10 000	100 000	1 000 000	10 000 000	100 000 000	1 000 000 000	10 000 000 000
1	50	500	5 000	50 000	500 000	5 000 000	50 000 000	500 000 000	5 000 000 000
2	25	250	2 500	25 000	250 000	2 500 000	25 000 000	250 000 000	2 500 000 000
3	13	125	1 250	12 500	125 000	1 250 000	12 500 000	125 000 000	1 250 000 000
4	6	63	625	6 250	62 500	625 000	6 250 000	62 500 000	625 000 000
5	3	31	313	3 125	31 250	312 500	3 125 000	31 250 000	312 500 000
6	2	16	156	1 563	15 625	156 250	1 562 500	15 625 000	156 250 000
7	0.78	8	78	781	7 813	78 125	781 250	7 812 500	78 125 000
8	0.39	4	39	391	3 906	39 063	390 625	3 906 250	39 062 500
9	0.20	2	20	195	1 953	19 531	195 313	1 953 125	19 531 250
10	0.10	0.98	10	98	977	9 766	97 656	976 563	9 765 625
11	0.05	0.49	5	49	488	4 883	48 828	488 281	4 882 813
12	0.02	0.24	2	24	244	2 441	24 414	244 141	2 441 406
13	0.01	0.12	1	12	122	1 221	12 207	122 070	1 220 703
14	0.01	0.06	0.61	6	61	610	6 104	61 035	610 352
15	0.00	0.03	0.31	3	31	305	3 052	30 518	305 176
16	0.00	0.02	0.15	2	15	153	1 526	15 259	152 588
17	0.00	0.01	0.08	0.76	8	76	763	7 629	76 294
18	0.00	0.00	0.04	0.38	4	38	381	3 815	38 147
19	0.00	0.00	0.02	0.19	2	19	191	1 907	19 073
20	0.00	0.00	0.01	0.10	0.95	10	95	954	9 537

knows the entire set of Shamir shares that this lookup works – simply knowing 15 bits of an item obviously does not allow identification without knowing *all* bits.

This leaves us to evaluate our multi-item discrimination algorithms, which might not be able to properly separate shares/points from multiple items. We also need to analyze how the discrimination algorithms affect traceability. This is done in the following two sections.

5.1   Detection Rates

Since the math behind Shamir's secret sharing *guarantees* that we can successfully identify a single item once t or more pieces have been read (i.e., more than an item's threshold), we do not need to evaluate the chances for identifying a single-item, once t or more shares have been read. With multiple items, however, it is up to our discrimination algorithms presented in section 3 to properly group the individual tags into separate items. If only a single tag is accidentally assigned to the wrong item, detection will fail.[20] How often does this, on average, happen? We used our Java simulator and ran 100 iterations of the following experiment:

- Generate between 1 and i items (i being 20 or 10), each having between $0.5n'$ and n' tags (n' being 800 or 600) with a random threshold t between $0.4n'$ and $0.8n'$.
- From all generated tags, read a random fraction of f tags ($f = 0.8, 0.9, 1.0$).
- Identify items and record percentage of items identified.[21]

---

[20] Note that it is easy to verify whether we have assembled the right item ID, as removing a single tag from the set should not change the retrieved secret value s (unless we have collected exactly t or even fewer tags).

[21] Note that we do not have false positives, i.e., we will never wrongly identify a non-existent item (see previous footnote).

Table 3. *Detection Rates.* Simulation results for the *clustering* and *line* methods with three different setups. While the cluster-based method achieved high item discrimination rates, the line-based method is limited by a much smaller Shamir Space.

Percentage of Tags Read	Detection Rate Clustering	Lines	System Setup
100%	99.36%	95.12%	up to 20 items, each $\leq$ 800 tags
90%	97.38%	93.81%	
80%	94.67%	91.10%	
100%	99.66%	95.32%	up to 20 items, each $\leq$ 600 tags
90%	98.06%	94.91%	
80%	94.60%	94.15%	
100%	99.89%	98.33%	up to 10 items, each $\leq$ 800 tags
90%	99.11%	97.90%	
80%	96.20%	97.57%	

Table 3 shows the detection rates of both the *cluster-based* and the *line-based* method. The tests for the cluster-based method were performed with our simulator, using $n = 10\,000\,000$ and $p = 3\,037\,000\,493$. The line-based method, in contrast, uses a much smaller value of $n = 120\,000$ (but the same value for p), as otherwise the sampling of horizontal or diagonal lines across the entire Shamir Space proved to be too costly. This, in turn, has a direct effect on the detection rates, as the much smaller Shamir Space in our line-based simulation results in more overlaps, where conflicting tags must be removed (and thus cannot help with item identification).

The three different test cases shown in table 3 demonstrate that detection rates are better if fewer items are within reading range. Lowering the number of tags per item only yields marginal improvements, however. This is because fewer tags only "thin out" our clusters/lines, while fewer items translate directly into fewer clusters/lines, thus reducing the number of collisions (this effect, however, is much more significant when using the line-based method, see table 3).

5.2 Traceability

One might argue that due to our clustering methods, repeated readouts might show re-identifiable cluster patterns. Figure 7 shows a set of four readouts from a person carrying 15 items, each containing up to 800 tags (totaling 9032 tags). Each read detects a random subset of 0.5% of all tags. Due to the setup of the cluster-based method, a random subset of tags is typically scattered widely across the whole Shamir space. When reading only a small subset of all integrated tags, clusters are hardly visible. This changes, however, if the system's Shamir Space (i.e., $n \times p$) is very large. Under such conditions, tags of a single cluster are grouped relatively close together, which in turn makes cluster differentiation across multiple readout simple. This is an inherent trade-off between good detection rates and the prevention of traceability in this method.

A visual inspection of the line-based method exhibits similar results. With very small subsets, the alignment of the tags along lines is no longer visible and

Fig. 7. *Tracking Items Without Overlapping IDs.* With no direct ID overlap, tracking people requires identifying patterns in the clustering algorithm. The above plots show three subsequent readouts of ≈45 tags each, based on 15 items with ≈800 tags.

they seem to be randomly spread across the Shamir Space. With large values of n, however, the increased space separates the lines more clearly, resulting in a visibility of the individual items even in small tag subsets. Surprisingly though, the line-based method seems to outperform the cluster-based method in terms of traceability protection. Since a large n causes clusters to be very small, one single tag ID can easily give the position of a whole cluster away. This is different with the line-based method, as tags can, in principle, appear anywhere within the Shamir Space.

6   Conclusions

In this paper, we have extended our previously proposed alternative access control method [10] to allow for a *spatial distribution* of tags. This allows us to further limit read ranges of individual tags without making finding the tag (for readout) impossible. Instead, the surface of an item could be covered with dozens or even hundreds of tags featuring very short read ranges, thus making secret long-range readouts practically impossible.

We have extended the existing scheme based on shared secrets with support for concurrently resolving *multiple* secrets. This is achieved by means of geometric discrimination functions, two of which have been proposed in this paper: a cluster-based, and a line-based method. Simulations have demonstrated the ability of these methods to properly distinguish multiple items, while at the same time offering reasonable protection against unwanted tracking.

We envision that the continuing trend in miniaturization will one day render RFID chips the very first "smart dust" that can be cheaply woven into garments, integrated into plastic casings, or mixed into wall paint. Write-once tags might then be easily initialized during production using our methods described above and provide an implicit privacy protection without preventing any of the envisioned future uses of RFID-enabled items.

Acknowledgements

This work has been partially funded by Hitachi Systems Development Laboratories (SDL), Japan, who also provided the μ-chip RFID equipment.

References

1. EPCglobal: Class-1 generation-2 UHF RFID protocol for communications at 860 MHz–960 MHz, version 1.0.9. EPC radio-frequency identity protocols (2005), See http://www.epcglobalinc.org/standards/Class_1_Generation_2_UHF_Air_Interface_Protocol_Standard_Version_1.0.9.pdf
2. Karjoth, G., Moskowitz, P.A.: Disabling RFID tags with visible confirmation: clipped tags are silenced. In: Atluri, V., Capitani, D., di Vimercati, S., Dingledine, R. (eds.) WPES 2005. Proceedings of the 2005 ACM Workshop on Privacy in the Electronic Society, pp. 27–30. ACM Press, Alexandria, VA (2005)
3. Roduner, C., Langheinrich, M., Floerkemeier, C., Schwarzentrub, B.: Operating appliances with mobile phones – strengths and limits of a universal interaction device. In: Proceedings of Pervasive 2007, Toronto, Canada, May 13-16, 2007. LNCS, vol. 4480, Springer, Heidelberg (2007)
4. Weis, S.A., Sarma, S.E., Rivest, R.L., Engels, D.W.: Security and privacy aspects of low-cost radio frequency identification systems. In: Hutter, D., Müller, G., Stephan, W., Ullmann, M. (eds.) Security in Pervasive Computing. LNCS, vol. 2802, pp. 201–212. Springer, Heidelberg (2004)
5. Ohkubo, M., Suzuki, K., Kinoshita, S.: Cryptographic approach to privacy-friendly tags. In: Garfinkel, S., Rosenberg, B. (eds.) RFID: Applications, Security, and Privacy, Addison-Wesley, Reading (2005)
6. Henrici, D., Müller, P.: Tackling security and privacy issues in radio frequency identification devices. In: Ferscha, A., Mattern, F. (eds.) PERVASIVE 2004. LNCS, vol. 3001, pp. 219–224. Springer, Heidelberg (2004)
7. Juels, A.: RFID security and privacy: A research survey. IEEE Journal on Selected Areas in Communications 24(2), 381–394 (2006)
8. Juels, A., Rivest, R.L., Szydlo, M.: The blocker tag: Selective blocking of RFID tags for consumer privacy. In: Jajodia, S., Atluri, V., Jaeger, T. (eds.) Proceedings of the 10th ACM Conference on Computer and Communication Security, pp. 103–111. ACM Press, Washington, D.C. (2003)
9. Fishkin, K., Roy, S., Jiang, B.: Some methods for privacy in RFID communication. In: Castelluccia, C., Hartenstein, H., Paar, C., Westhoff, D. (eds.) ESAS 2004. LNCS, vol. 3313, pp. 42–53. Springer, Heidelberg (2005)
10. Langheinrich, M., Marti, R.: Practical minimalist cryptography for RFID privacy. Submitted for publication (2007), Available online at http://www.vs.inf.ethz.ch/publ/papers/shamirtags07.pdf
11. Shamir, A.: How to share a secret. Comm. of the ACM 22(11), 612–613 (1979)
12. Bohn, J., Mattern, F.: Super-distributed RFID tag infrastructures. In: Markopoulos, P., Eggen, B., Aarts, E., Crowley, J.L. (eds.) EUSAI 2004. LNCS, vol. 3295, pp. 1–12. Springer, Heidelberg (2004)
13. EPCglobal: EPC tag data specification 1.1. EPCglobal Standard (2003)
14. Menezes, A.J., van Oorschot, P.C., Vanstone, S.A.: Handbook of applied cryptography. CRC Press, Boca Raton, Florida (1996)
15. Chiu, S.L.: Fuzzy model identification based on cluster estimation. Journal of Intelligent and Fuzzy Systems 2(3), 267–278 (1994)

Context Adapted Certificate Using Morph Template Signature for Pervasive Environments

Rachid Saadi[1], Jean Marc Pierson[2], and Lionel Brunie[1]

[1] LIRIS lab, INSA de Lyon, France
{rachid.saadi,lionel.brunie}@liris.cnrs.fr
[2] IRIT lab, University Paul Sabatier Toulouse, France
jean-marc.pierson@irit.fr

Abstract. In distributed systems, especially in pervasive and ubiquitous environments, mobile users gather certificates providing them rights to access unknown and trusted environments. Such a certificate embeds increasing number of information that leads the certificate provider to adapt existing standards to its requirements. In this paper, we propose a new model of certification called X316[1] to set up an XML certificates with a contextual morph capability. This morph characteristic enables each certificate owner to disclose and to blind some sensitive certificate parts according to surrounding context. The usability of the X316 is illustrated with the "Chameleon" architecture offering users such a possible access if they appear with trusted certificates. These certificates may be gathered during their roaming in the pervasive environment, and they offer direct or transitive access to foreign sites, based on trust relationships.

1 Introduction

Ubiquitous environments (especially pervasive environments) are an emerging field of research which enables large access to information for any user, dynamically with respect to different constraints of the user's context such as position, device capabilities and network conditions. The increasing interest for the related technologies (wireless networks, lighter devices) introduces hard security challenges providing a wide range of certificates and credentials to enable user authentication and to perform a decentralized access control policy.

Indeed in pervasive environments, each nomadic user roams among various sites in order to interact with surrounding users and resources. To gain an access in this environment, a user must prove her rights by using credentials or certificates. However existing models of certification must be modified and improved to satisfy the requirements of pervasive environment such as: contextual adaptation, multi-user devices, mobility etc.

To extend the certification policy scope, the trust paradigm seems to be the most flexible approach. Indeed in the vision of ubiquitous computing [1] especially the pervasive environment, using trust model is the most suitable solution to extend users access scope.

---

[1] X316: [13]Morph [1]Access [16]Pass. "A" is the first letter of the alphabet...

H. Ichikawa et al. (Eds.): UCS 2007, LNCS 4836, pp. 17–32, 2007.
© Springer-Verlag Berlin Heidelberg 2007

In this paper we define a trust architecture called Chameleon using a new model and mechanism of certification called X316. This model provides the site administrator a general formalism enabling to express and customize a certificate according to members rights and users' device capabilities. Moreover, a new method of signature is defined allowing the certificate owner to adapt it freely according to its context by selecting only the relevant information in the X316.

This paper is organized as follows. In section 2 we introduce our approach that delineates the Chameleon Architecture and show its implementation in the pervasive environment using the X316 certificate. Then we describe the X316 in section 3. In section for we introduce the X316 signature with the morph template. Next section 4 presents the related works of our proposal. In section 5 we discuss benefits and the scalability of our certification model with experiments. Finally, we draw some conclusions, and suggest some directions for future work as well.

2   The CHAMELEON Architecture

The main characteristic of a pervasive environment is mobility. The user roams inside the environment and tries to access or use surrounding resources and services. The question is: *How the local site policy can control and authenticate these unknown guests?*

To extend the access scope of the users and enhance the access control policy, our architecture works as a front-end of each site which provides an authority on its resources. It is called "**Chameleon**" similar to the animal chameleon which has the capability to fit into its environment. Therefore, when the user gets to the proximity of each site she becomes like a local user.

To set up this architecture we define four modules:

2.1   TMM Trust Manager Module

Each mobile user belongs to one or many sites. To recognize this user anywhere, the TMM works between sites and enables them to communicate and to share some information about their members. Each site X builds its trust set. It is composed of the sites that X trusts, which we call: "trusted sites". Then, to evaluate the trusted sites' trustworthiness, X assigns to each one of them a corresponding degree using a trust function called t^0 [14]. In this manner, the environment can be seen as a graph, and we note $T_g(S, E)$ a valued and directed graph such that:

- The nodes of the graph represent the sites of S.
- Each trust relation between two sites is represented by a directed edge e. The set of edges is consequently identified with the set of relations E.
- Each edge is valued by the trust degree [14] between the sites represented by the source and destination nodes of this edge.

TMM module uses this trust graph to decide wether a "foreign" user can access the local site (i.e. to decide if a user who does not own an account of the system can get logged in the system).

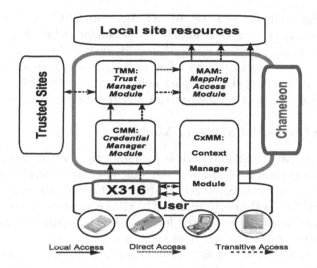

Fig. 1. Chameleon Architecture

We will consider three types of access: *local access, direct access and transitive access.*

- Local access: It is provided by the home site to all registered users (i.e. where they have their accounts and can authenticate themselves).
- Direct access: It is provided by the TMM module of local site to all users registered in trusted sites. This direct access is valued by the trust degree between the local and the trusted site.
- Transitive access: It can be provided by a local site X to a user who does not belong to its trust set, under a condition that a valid trust chain between one of the user's home sites and trusted site exists in the graph. This transitive access is valued by the trust propagation degree between these two sites (as before, in case of the existence of several possible chains, the TMM is responsible for choosing the reference chain). To manage the users' access, each site has to define thresholds beyond which access is not allowed.

2.2   MAM: Mapping Access Module

This module defines a mapping policy which is defined between the local and the trusted users' profiles. When a user is allowed to access a site X, the MAM module attributes to her a new profile using a mapping policy. This profile defines the user's rights inside the site X and is called: "A-profile" (Analogue profile).

A mapping policy can be simply implemented by creating a mapping table to store the correspondences between foreign profiles of trusted sites and their analogue profiles, for example: The user Alice has, in her home site B, a profile equal to level 3, Alice wants to access site A, this site trusts B. Then, A applies a mapping policy and maps from her original profile "Level 3" into a local profile corresponding to "STUDENT role". The mapping policy can be fulfilled between various policy models e.g. RBAC, MAC or DAC. However, it should be applied among sites which generally use a similar policy. For example: In a medical community, it is probable that roles such as "Doctor", "Nurse" or "Patient" exist in all organizations, allowing for an easy mapping through the community. Furthermore, this mapping policy can be enhanced by looking for user's capabilities, such as delegation right and resources access, etc.

2.3   CMM: Credential Manager Module

The main objective of our approach is to allow any user to roam and access various sites freely from the site where she is member (home site). Consequently, each site fulfils a policy based on certification mechanism, allowing its members to prove their rights in the environment. The CIM constitutes the module which has the responsibility to manage the local certification policy; it can give and generate certificates to its members or trust users.

Existing certification models have some drawbacks. In fact, on one hand, once confronted with an unexpected situation the user must contact her home site to retrieve a corresponding certificate; on the other hand, she must manage several certificates.

Our approach consists of using a unique certificate that contains all user's privileges in her home site/trusted site. It is attractive, because the user manages only one certificate by site and adapts it according to context.

2.4   CxMM: Context Manager Module

In the pervasive environment, the context paradigm is critical. The user device policy must be convenient to contexts such as: device type, user practice, environment etc. This module describes the context of the user (User Context) and undertakes discovering the surrounding environment (Environment Context). In fact, when the user wants to access a target site, her device should mainly perform two actions:

- Select the corresponding certificate which helps the user to gain a maximum access in the target site.
- Select the corresponding certificate subparts which are essential for this access, according to the context, and hide others.

3   X316: Morph Access Pass Certificate

In this paper, we define a new certificate structure called X316: Morph Access Pass Certificate. This format enables creating any sort of certificates or credentials e.g. Attribute certificate, Role certificate etc. The "X316" can be seen as a passkey, allowing its owner to roam and gain access in the environment.

Our contribution has an objective to define a very flexible model of certification. It is inspirited by the W3C standards: "XML Digital signature" (XMLDSig). The X316 is designed for a nomadic user. Indeed, unlike other certification systems, the same X316 certificate can be used and authenticated from various devices with different capability and characteristics, and can be generated dynamically along a user trip. In fact, by defining specific tags to delimit the dynamic parts, this certificate acquires the capability to transform and to morph easily its content according to context, situation, and environment.

Therefor, the X316 fulfills three properties: Generic structure, Multi authentication and Contextual adaptation.

The X316 certificate is composed of four parts: Header, Right, Authentication and Signature.

The X316 could be obtained in three different ways (see figure 2):

– Each site gives a Home Certificate or **H316**, to all its members.
– Each site gives a Roam certificate or **R316**, to a passing user, when it trusts her Home Site. This certificate allows the user to extend her access scope along her trip. The R-316 does not provide access, it proves the user rights. This credential type is generated dynamically without user authentication.
– Each site gives a Trust certificate or **T316**, to a guest, when it trusts her Home Site. Instead of the R-316 the T-316 provides an access inside the target site and needs user authentication.

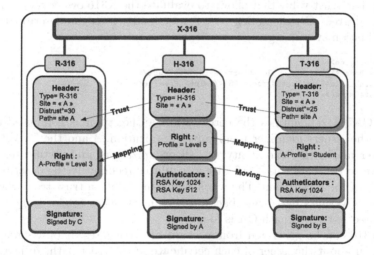

Fig. 2. The X316 type

In the rest of the paper we use this syntax definition to describe each of the X316 parts, where "?" denotes zero or one occurrence; "+" denotes one or more occurrences and "*" denotes zero or more occurrences.

3.1 The HEADER Part

This part identifies the certificate. In fact, it is composed of some fields which define the certificate's identity, such as: the CA (Certification Authority), The time of validity, The user owner, etc.

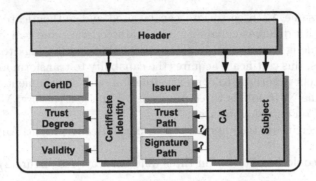

Fig. 3. The X316 Header

The header part describes mainly three items: the identity of certificate, the certification authority(issuers), and the user(subject).

The certificate identity defines the Identifier of the X316 ("CertificateID"), the certificate type and the period within the certificate is valid ("Validity"). In pervasive system, the relation between actors is generally valuated by a trust function. The trust value that allows to evaluate the X316 owner represents the certificate degree "CertificateDegree". The defined syntax can describe different trust evaluation system e.g.

```
<CertificateDegree>
 <ComputeMethode Algorithm=....X316MCert/degree#Distrust/>
 <Values> <Value id="DistrustDegree"> 45 </Value> </Values>
</CertificateDegree>
```

The "CA" part identifies the certification authority, it is composed of two sections: the issuers identifier (company, organization...) and the "TrustPart". This latter marks the traceability, i.e. all organizations and certificates which contribute to generate this X316. It encapsulates recursively the description of each node of the trust chain. The whole structure is like a trust tree, where the certificate is verified by tracing backward from its issuer to the issuer's issuer until a directly trusted path CA is found.

The X316 can be generated from a chain of certificates. It only embeds the information about the issuer of each certificate in the trust path. In fact, when an entity trusts each certificate issuer, it does not need to check all trust path actors. However, The "SignaturePath" can be defined allowing each node of the original certificate trust path to sign its link with its public key. To reduce the generated signature trace, recent works explore some algorithms to involve a sequential aggregation signature [16]. Therefore, unlike all certification systems paths that load into the credential all certificates chain, the X316 enables to aggregate all chain sites' signatures in only one.

Finally, the "Subject" part describes the certificate owner: user identifier, user name...

3.2 The RIGHT Part

It is a variable part of the certificate that depends on the issuer's policy. This part contains information about the user's rights within each company. Unlike other systems of certification that certify access to particular resources, this one certifies the user's rights that represent all authorized accesses to the organization resources.

This part is divided into two sections:

- **Subject profile:** it contains a specific profile such as the user's status or access level in certificate issuer.
- **Subject Attributes:** this part is variable, it mainly contains the user's authorized resources, and defines some capabilities.

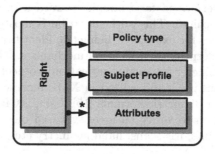

Fig. 4. The X316 Right

Example: It defines the role of the user(line 04), and her capability to delegate (line 25) the access to the PrinterID(line 18).

```
00 <RIGHT>                                        17      <AttributeValue DataType="">
01 <PolicyType> RBAC </PolicyType>                18        PrinterID
02  <Profiles>                                    19      </AttributeValue>
03   <Profile>                                    20     </ResourceMatch>
04    <ProfileID> Student </ProfileID>            21    </Resource></Resources>
05    <Descritpion>...</Description>              22    <Actions><Action>
06   </Profile>                                   23     <ActionMatch MatchId="">
07  </Profiles>                                   24      <AttributeValue DataType="">
08  <Attributes>                                  25        Delegate
09   <Attribute Format="XACML 1.0">               26      </AttributeValue>
10    <Rule xmlns="...:xacml:1.0:policy"          27     </ActionMatch>
11      ...RuleId="" Effect="Permit">             28    </Action></Actions>
12     <Description>...</Description>              29   </Target>
13     <Target>                                   30  </Rule>
14      <Subjects><Subject></Subject></Subjects>  31  </Attribute>
15      <Resources><Resource>                     32 </Attributes>
16       <ResourceMatch MatchId="">               33 </RIGHT>
```

3.3 The IDENTIFICATION Part

This part allows to identify and authenticate the owner of the X316. Identifier are numerous, and related to the variety of devices (PDA, mobile phone, terminals).

Thus, facilitating certificates management could be fulfilled by embedding some identifiers according to the device's capabilities and the organization's security policy.

Two ways of Authentication have been identified, remote and local authentication.

1) Remote authentication: This one is used with any system of communication, in general if the authentication procedure is fulfilled through an open communication(e.g. Wireless). The most important system is a challenge response authentication. It uses a public key as identifier. The X316 can embed one or several keys depending on the user's devices capabilities e.g. "512bits RSA public key" for a small device like a PDA, and "2048 RSA public" key for a laptop device.

2) Local authentication: This authentication is used if the authentication procedure is locally performed for example: toward a terminal like the ATM (Automated Teller Machine). This authentication is mostly specified to derive with specific capabilities for example a biometric identification. Recently, some devices integrate a fingerprint identification mechanism. This can be defined in the certificate as a parameter for an authentication protocol. The majority of the biometric identifications are standardized in XML representation called XCBF (OASIS XML Common Biometric Format) [15]. Using XCBF, our certificate can describe any information to verify an identity based on human characteristics such as DNA, fingerprints, iris scans, hand geometry etc.

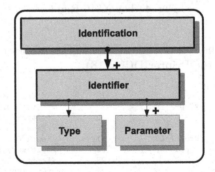

Fig. 5. The X316 Identifier

The Identification part contains one or more identifier. Each Identifier is composed of:

- "Authenticator type" defines the sort of Authentication: Local or remote.
- "Parameters" defines the needed parameters to each authentication method. The definition of these parameters is expressed in standard languages namely: W3C(public key) and XCBF (fingerprint).

Example

```
00 <IDENTIFICATION>                        09            vmJ2k9b3JrDhG5LQ8uFFg9h1NO=
01   <Authenticator Type="....#Remote">    10            </ds:Modulus>
02    <AuthenticationMethod Protocol=       11            <ds:Exponent>AQAB</ds:Exponent>
03           ...#Challenge_Response">       12          </ds:RSAKeyValue>
04     <Parameters>                        13        </ParameterValue>
05      <Parameter Id="512RSAPubKey">       14      </Parameter>
06        <ParameterValue>                  15     </Parameters>
07        <ds:RSAKeyValue>                  16   </Authenticator>
08          <ds:Modulus>                    17 </AUTHENTICATION>
```

This example describes a remote authenticator(line 01). It defines a challenge response protocol(lines 02-03) using a 512 RSA public key(lines 05-15) as a parameter(user identifier).

3.4 The SIGNATURE Part

This part is divided into two sections:

- The FloatSignature part. (Described in next section)
- The BodySignature part.

The signature part contains the information about the used key and the result of the certificate's signature.

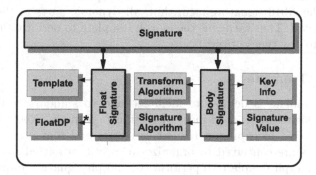

Fig. 6. The X316 Signature

The "Body Signature" defines the signature of the certificate. This part is composed of:

- "Transforms" defines the X316 morph signature algorithm to fulfill a right checking signature. (see next section)
- "SignatureMethod Algorithm" informs the algorithms to compute the signature namely the hash algorithm (e.g. SHA) and the public key algorithm (e.g. RSA), it uses the W3C notation.
- "KeyInfo" defines the public key value as W3C key definition.
- "SignatureValue" defines the the computed value of the signature algorithm as W3C definition.

4   X316 Signature (The Morph Capability)

All standards (e.g. X509 and PGP) use a hash algorithm to obtain a residual value from the certificate data. This value is signed by a private key of the certification authority. Consequently if the content of the certificate is modified, the residual result will be erroneous. Thus, the user is not able to adapt her certificate by blinding any information inside.

In our solution, we use a single certificate that mainly contains the user profile, all user access rights and some authentication systems. Yet we define in this model a specific signature method, using specific tags. Thus, the user can manage and morph her certificates according to the specific transaction or context. However, some authorized information can be freely masked by the certificate owner far from her home site. In this manner each user extracts a sub-certificate from the original one which only contains needed information for each specific situation.

Thus, the challenge is: how each user can customize her static certificates according to a contextual situation? To solve this problem, we must distinguish The Dynamic Part from the Static Part. **The Static Parts:** is composed of mandatory and non changeable data (ex: the ID of the certificate, the time of validity). These data set up the identity of the certificate. **The Dynamic Part:** provides sensitive information (e.g. the user name profile, telephone...) and a contextual information (e.g. the device capability, security context...). To perform the X316 signature algorithm, all dynamic parts in the certificate must be delimited. Thus we define the morph template to perform this signature specification to any types of certificate.

4.1   Morph Template

The morph template is defined to facilitate and to standardize the creation of the morph signature. Indeed most of certificate formats (X509, PGP, SPKI etc.) are formatted to express a regular structure and semantic contents. All these standards are conceived to organize in a well-formatted manner. Thus, we define the morph template to perform the morph signature process through any certificate formats. The morph template is composed of two sections: The 'Credential Type' and the The 'Dynamic Mask'.

- The credential type: The morph signature should be computed through any type of certificate (XML or ANS). This section tells about the type of the signed document. This information is crucial as it defines how it will be parsed.
- The Dynamic Mask: This section defines the dynamic parts in the signed certificate. For instance, in the X509 certificate, the "extensions" part or "email" parts can be considered as dynamic parts.

Dynamic Mask Syntax
The dynamic Mask enables to define the parts that be allowed to blind. This attribute is expressed by alphanumeric values like any search engine, where:

- The '*': corresponds to any sequence of alphanumeric values.
- The '?': corresponds to one alphanumeric value.
- '(xxx)*': if the * is put to the power apply that the corresponding DP part and all its child parts are considered as a DP parts.

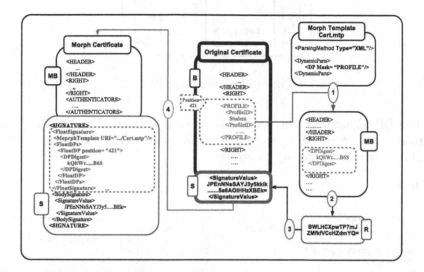

Fig. 7. X316 Signature

As illustrated in figure 7, the morph signature has as inputs the certificate and the corresponding template. The morph signature parses the template to recognize the dynamic parts. Then according to the type of the document, the morph signature algorithm retrieves all defined dynamic parts and replaces them by their corresponding hash values. Finally, the morph document is generated and the signature can be computed. Moreover, each DP can contain some other DP. In this manner, the certificate subject is able to blind all the DP parts or a set of sub-parts inside the DP part. Consequently before computing the global DP part, the digest of all sub DP parts must be computed recursively. For the sake of clarity, these computed parts are moved to the float part in the signature (see figure 7 step 4). To verify the authenticity of each credential, the remaining DP Digest parts are replaced at right position before checking the signature.

4.2   Float Signature

The Float Signature part is composed of three attributes:

- The Morph Template: define the used template to compute the morph signature.
- The "FloatDP": contains all blinded dynamic parts. Each removable part is defined by its corressponding DPDigest value and its position in the original certificate.

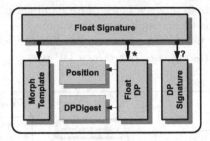

Fig. 8. Float Signature Part

– The DP Signature": This section is optional allowing the certificate owner
to sign the "FloatsDPs" section. This signature permits to check that the
x316 is only generated by its owner.

Example

```
00  <FloatSignature>                              09                    ...xmldsig#rsa-sha1"/>
01  <MoprphTemplate URI=".../X316DP.mtp"/>        10    <KeyInfo>
02  <FloatDPs>                                    11      <KeyValue URI="#512RSAPubKey">
03    <FloatDP position="421">                    12    </KeyInfo>
04      <DPDigest>.KQitWc...B6S</DPDigest>        13    <ds:SignatureValue>
05    </FloatDP>                                  14        KU6t7...BFh= </ds:SignatureValue>
06  </FloatDPs>                                   15  </DPSignature>
07  <DPSignature>                                 16  </FloatSignature>
08    <ds:SignatureMethod Algorithm="
```

This example describes the float signature(lines 01-15) with subject signature
using the "512RSAPubKey" (line 11) held in the last authentication example.

5   Related Works

5.1   Certification Mechanism

The Certification mechanism is a service based on digital signature. It uses the
concept of Public Key Infrastructure (PKI) to provide a security privilege based
on the trust accorded to the signatory. This mechanism is implemented to authenticate contents of the certificate and to implement a distributed system
based on trust.

In the literature, some certification models are standardized and formalized
e.g. PGP(Pretty Good Privacy) [2], SPKI [3], Sygn [4], X509 [5], Akenti [6].

X509 is the most used standard. However, it has first been designed as an
identity certificate, and its last extension proposed to extend its scope to attribute certificate. Unfortunately, the usability of the new extension is deemed
to be too complex and requires adaptations (depending on security policies e.g.
RBAC), like in PRIMA [12] and PERMIS [11] which adapt the X509 attribute
format to extend its capabilities.

SPKI was proposed to become an alternative to X509, SPKI focuses on authorization certificates more than identity certificates. The objective of SPKI is simplicity. Unlike the X509, which is based on ASN 1.0 [7] format, SPKI certificate is described in S-expression [17] offering more flexibility and readability.

These last models of certification have some drawbacks. In fact, all of them identify one user only with her public key using a challenge-response mechanism [18]. But, each nomadic user owns multiple devices with different capacity (computing power) and capabilities (biometric identification,...). One certificate should embed more than one identification offering to user different means to authenticate her certificates. Furthermore, on one hand, the certificate contains more and more information (sensitive or public) and, on the other hand the context is very important in new environment framework. The certificate contents should be adapted according to context.

5.2   Morph Mechanism

We define the morph mechanism to perform the certification contextual adaptation. It represents the ability to hide some attributes on a signed message according to context. Steinfeld and al [19] define this property as CES (Content Extraction Signature): "*A Content Extraction Signature should allow anyone, given a signed document, to extract a publicly verifiable extracted signature for a specified subdocument of a signed document, without interaction with the signer of the original document*".

The most used approach divides the messages into fragments, then signs each one separately. Micaly and Rivest [8] is the first work which introduces the concept of transitive signature. In their algorithm, giving a signature on two graph edges Sig(x,y) and Sig(y,z) (where x, y and z represent subdocuments), a valid signature Sig(x,z) can be computed to hide "y" without accessing the secrete key. Johanson and al [9] have introduced some improvements by enabling a homomorphic signature. Let a signature Sig(x). Anyone can compute a signature Sig(w) on any subpart w of x obtained by rubbing out some position of x.

[10] is the first work which uses homomorphic function property to define a new signature algorithm for morphing certificates.

All previous approaches have a drawback; they define a new algorithm to perform the certificate adaptability, instead of using the existing standard.

[19] exposes a modification of the RSA computing algorithm. Their approach is based on the homomorphic property of RSA, i.e. $h_1^d h_2^d modN = (h_1 h_2)^d modN$. This algorithm multiplies the RSA sub-messages$_i$ signatures ($h_i^d modN$), and checks whether the result is the signature of the hash values products. Their approaches are very useful. However, they are based on mathematical proprieties that address only a specific class of signature algorithm. This constraint reduces the usability scope.

The World Wide Web Consortium "W3C" standard: "XML Digital signature"(XMLDSig) [13] offers the capability to sign different parts of documents. [20] add some elements to the XMLSignature standard to perform the certificate adaptability. These last methods are very attractive, but it is not appropriate in a certificate model. They treat certificates as any documents, where each one is decomposed into several sub-documents. Consequently, the user is free to disclose or blind any part(e.g certificate identifier). In the contrary, credential or certificate does not consist of distinct parts, but composed of a single bloc, which contains two sort of fields: **Static field** (e.g. certificate identifier, issuer identity, time of validity...) and **Dynamic field** (e.g. user name, user rights...).

6   Discussion

The X316 presents a number of advantages. Indeed, on one hand, a unique certificate is able to manage many devices and to express and to integrate a wide range of certificate model. On the other hand, the new computing signature algorithm and the morph characteristic gives to the certificate the ability to be adapted to context.

The X316 chain might be seen as a problem due to the chain of certificates. Nevertheless, the X316 "Path" expresses the traceability of the trust chain. The target site may check the Trust path, and deny access if it does not trust any site in this chain, or if the degree becomes greater than a given threshold (leading to high distrust in the guest).

In our approach we advise, as possible, using a single certificate per site. Even this constraint could be criticized. However it mainly improves the user identification and the certificate management and revocation.

The new technology arise several types of device with different capacities and capabilities. A standard system of certification allows the certificate owner to identify himself, using a simple public key. So, each user possesses a multitude of devices, thus the identification must be adequate with the used one. In our proposal, in a unique certificate, we embed some user's identifications (fingerprint, photo, public keys with different size etc) instead of generating one certificate per device.

Furthermore, along the time the user will acquire and manage an increasing number of certificates. When she want to access a site, where a valid certificate must be selected from the repository, the research task become harder according to certificates amount. Therefore, gathering all user attributes inside single certificate for each site reduces the search space. Moreover, the revocation process is crucial in certification systems. Indeed, each authority of certification AC has the responsibility to generate and to revoke its local certificates. When a user is revoked, the AC must cancel all user's certificates and inform all the community. So, if the user owns a single certificate, the revocation process is more efficient, since revoking one certificate is easier than revoking multiple ones. Some tests were implemented to verify the scalability of the X316 morph characteristic. We used an XML file of 20KByte, and computed the elapsed time to verify the signature by varying the number of dynamic parts (DPs) from 0 to 200. For these tests we have used three devices: a smartphone: SPV m3000 (195MHZ CPU), PDA HP4700 (624MHZ), and a PC (3GHZ), even the SPV M3000 can compute the X316 signature within less than 1 second.

7   Conclusion and Future Work

The certification model is the basis of the authentication in ubiquitous computing. In this paper, we define a new model of certification(X316) which allows a broad user access when this latter is roaming. The X316 presents a number of advantages (see table 1).

Table 1. Signature method comparison

	Traceability	Signature aggregation	Trust evaluation	Multi authentication	Context Adaptation
X509	yes	no	no	no	no
SPKI	yes	no	no	no	no
XmlDSig & CES	-	no	-	no	≈yes
Homomorphic signature	-	yes	-	-	≈yes
X316	yes	yes	yes	yes	yes

Indeed the X316 is able to describe a chain of certificates with including a new mechanism of aggregation signature to minimize the certificate size. Furthermore the user can enter unknown sites with various user interfaces (devices) using the same certificate. We have also introduced a new computing method signature to enrich the certificate adaptability with respect to a contextual situation.

One of pervasive environments challenges is the fluency of the interaction between the environment and the user. As future work, we will integrate the description of context to X316 giving the user device the capacity to manage and adapt the certificate dynamically with respect to context without soliciting any user intervention.

References

1. Shankar, N., Arbaugh, W.: On Trust for Ubiquitous Computing. In: Workshop on Security in Ubiquitous Computing (September 2004)
2. Zimmermann, P.R.: The Official PGP User's Guide. MIT Press, Cambridge, MA (1995)
3. ITU-T Simple public key infrastructure (SPKI) charter, http://www.ietf.org/html.charters/OLD/spki-charter.html
4. Seitz, L., Pierson, J.M., Brunie, L.: Semantic Access Control for Medical Applications in Grid Environments. In: A International Conference on Parallel and Distributed Computing, pp. 374–383 (August 2003)
5. ITU-T Rec. X.509, ISO/IEC 9594-8 The Directory: Authentication Framework (2000)
6. Thompson, M.R., Essiari, A., Mudumbai, S.: Certificate-based authorization policy in a PKI environment. ACM Trans. Inf. Syst. Secur. 6(4), 566–588 (2003)
7. ITU-T Rec. X.680, ISO/IEC 8824-1:2002 (2002), http://asn1.elibel.tm.fr/en/standards/index.htm

8. Micali, S., Rivest, L.R.: Transitive Signature Schemes. In: Preneel, B. (ed.) CT-RSA 2002. LNCS, vol. 2271, pp. 236–243. Springer, Heidelberg (2002)
9. Johnson, R., Molnar, D., Song, D., Wagner, D.: Homomorphic signature schemes. In: Preneel, B. (ed.) CT-RSA 2002. LNCS, vol. 2271, pp. 244–262. Springer, Heidelberg (2002)
10. Brands, S.: A technical Overview of Digital Credentials. Research Report (February 2002)
11. Chadwick, D., Otenko, A.: The PERMIS X.509 Role Based Privilege Management Infrastructure. In: Proceedings of the 7th ACM Symposium on Access Control Models and Technologies, pp. 135–140. ACM Press, New York (2002)
12. Lorch, M., Adams, D., Kafura, D., et al.: The PRIMA System for Privilege Management, Authorization and Enforcement. In: Proceedings of the 4th International Workshop on Grid Computing (November 2003)
13. Bartel, M., Boyer, J., Fox, B., LaMacchia, B., Simon, E.: XML-encryption syntax and processing. In: W3C Recommendation (February 2002), http://www.w3.org/TR/2002/REC-xmldsig-core-20020212/
14. Saadi, R., Pierson, J.M., Brunie, L.: (Dis)trust Certification Model for Large Access in Pervasive Environment. JPCC International Journal of Pervasive Computing and Communications 1(4), 289–299 (2005)
15. XCBF 1.1, OASIS Standard, (approved August 2003), http://www.oasis-open.org/committees/xcbf/
16. Zhao, M., Smith, S.W., Nicol, D.M.: Aggregated path authentication for efficient BGP security. In: CCS 2005. Proceedings of the 12th ACM Conference on Computer and Communications Security, pp. 128–138 (November 2005)
17. Orri, X., Mas, J.M.: SPKI-XML Certificate Structure Internet-Draft, Octalis SA (November 2001), http://www.ietf.org/internetdrafts/draft-orri-spki-xml-cert-struc-00.txt
18. Challenge-response authentication From Wikipedia, the free encyclopedia, http://en.wikipedia.org/wiki/Challenge-response_authentication
19. Steinfeld, R., Bull, L., Zheng, Y.: Content Extraction Signatures. In: Proceedings of 4th International Conference of Information Security and Cryptology, pp. 285–2004 (December 2001)
20. Bull, L., Stanski, P., Squire, D.M.: Content extraction signatures using XML digital signatures and custom transforms on-demand. In: Proceedings of the 12th international Conference on World Wide Web, pp. 170–177 (May 2003)

Handling Spatio-temporal Sensor Data in Global Geographical Context with SENSORD

Takeshi Ikeda, Yutaka Inoue, Akio Sashima, and Koichi Kurumatani

National Institute of Advanced Industrial Science and Technology (AIST)
CREST, JST
2-41-6, Aomi, Koto, Tokyo 135-0064, Japan
{ikeda-takeshi, yutaka.inoue, sashima-akio, k.kurumatani}@aist.go.jp

Abstract. It is important to manage sensors' locations and their attributes in a coordinated manner to realize context-aware services based on sensing data. A coordinated means of management is also necessary for middleware providing various information services. We have been developing Sensor-Event-Driven Service Coordination Middleware (SENSORD) to realize uniform management of various sensors, their locations and their attributes and higher-level service. It provides sensor locations for users using a unified view with region-specific geographical information, so SENSORD provides data access interfaces like GIS. Sensor locations are a component of that spatial information. Therefore, it is effective to aggregate them into geographical information. In this paper, we first describe SENSORD. Second, we explain methods of managing spatial information and the computational flow of acquiring sensor location information. Moreover, we show an application of SENSORD: an indoor emergency response system in our laboratories.

Keywords: sensor, sensor event, middleware, context-awareness, spatio-temporal element.

1 Introduction

In the context of ubiquitous computing, it is important to recognize the context in which users exist and to provide suitable context-aware services. Many studies have developed sensory devices that are suitable for ubiquitous computing and have analyzed large amounts of sensory data [1] [2] [3]. On the other hand, many studies have combined sensing data from various devices in the environment with recognition of users' contexts. In this study, we approach the issue of context awareness and service cooperation by developing sensor middleware for multiple sensors. We have proposed Sensor-Event-Driven Service Coordination Middleware (SENSORD) to realize uniform management of various sensors and higher-level services [4]. A salient functionality of SENSORD is that it stores obtained multiple sensor data in shared memory (in-memory database); it provides SENSORDScript for invoking suitable services when current sensor data satisfy a certain condition that is given as a predefined rule that includes conditions and action-activations. In addition, it provides

H. Ichikawa et al. (Eds.): UCS 2007, LNCS 4836, pp. 33–44, 2007.

management of synthetic geographic information view and user interface (spatial information) related to sensor located areas.

Sensor locations are used in various applications. In particular, sensor locations are important information for use in analyzing obtained sensing data. The system provides sensor locative information in a consistent manner with geographical information to realize facilities that manage sensor-location information. For acquiring sensor information, we prepare a GUI in the same way as querying spatial objects. An application developer can handle sensor location information without using individual sensor information that is of the same level as geographical object.

In this paper, we first describe an overview of SENSORD. Second, we propose a handling mechanism of spatial information including sensor information. Finally, we present an application using SENSORD: an indoor emergency response system.

2 Sensor-Event-Driven Service Coordination Middleware

2.1 Overview

In SENSORD, we intend to provide middleware that integrates three features of context-aware service: (1) various sensor data and interface handling, (2) spatio-temporal sensor data management, and (3) real-time sensor data analysis. SENSORD manages synthetic sensor data from various sensor devices and analyzes the obtained sensing data. It also provides information services in relation with the user's context. In practice, SENSORD provides an API that can be accessed for querying spatio-temporal information, and storage and analysis of sensor data. Another important functionality of SENSORD is the provision of SENSORDScript, which is a service framework based on rule description. Actually, SENSORD is implemented with JAVA (JDK1.5).

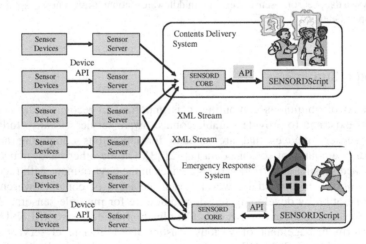

Fig. 1. SENSORD Software Modules for Implementing Application Program

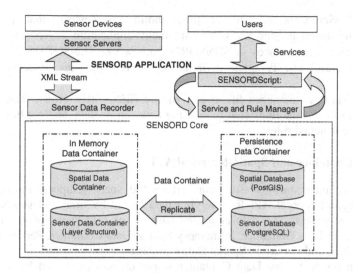

Fig. 2. Software Architecture and Modules of SENSORD

Cooperatively, SENSORD functions with other software modules, hardware modules, and end-user application programs (GUI). A typical application with SENSORD is constructed as the following four modules: sensor devices, sensor servers, SENSORD core, and SENSORDScript (Figs. 1 and 2). Application developers can implement various applications by combining such SENSORD modules.

In SENSORD, the following sensors are assumed to be handled: thermometers, hygrometers, accelerometers, vision sensors with tracked humans, and microphone arrays. New kinds of sensor devices can be added easily to SENSORD by implementing a corresponding sensor server that is described in the following section. These devices are assumed to have a communication interface with SENSORD by some kind of network (TCP/IP, ad-hoc wireless, infrared, etc.) to send obtained data to other systems and to receive control commands from the others.

The sensor server functionality is to access sensor devices, receive sensor data, and send control commands to the devices. A sensor server communicates with SENSORD using the original protocol "SENSORD Protocol" via XML-Stream (TCP/IP). The SENSORD Protocol is developed for uniform handling of various representations of sensor data and a control command suitable for the sensor devices.

A SENSORD Core obtains and stores sensing data received from the sensor servers; it stores the data into in-memory data container. The in-memory data container serves as the buffer in memory. It works as a database system to realize rapid analysis of the obtained data. Using spatio-temporal API, users can seamlessly receive not only real-time data, but also past data recorded in the database. SENSORD can store various types of data, such as html contents and images along with regular sensing data type, i.e. real numbers. A sensor recorder records the sensor data obtained from a sensor server. Sensor recorders usually work in multi-threaded processes of JAVA. They can acquire multiple types of data simultaneously.

SENSORDScript is a kind of programming framework that provides a programming language for users to implement application logics as a pair of conditions and consequences in SENSORD framework. SENSORDScript provides the following abilities: Template definition of service plug-ins, Execution control API.

Service Manager manages life cycles of the SENSORDScripts. Rule manager repeatedly evaluates the registered rules using new sensor data, and notifies the client scripts of the matched rules.

2.2 Data Container and Spatio-temporal API

The data container stores sensor data and related spatio-temporal information; it provides spatio-temporal API for querying data keyed by time and geometry from application programs. The data container consists of four types of container: In-memory Sensor Data Container, In-memory Spatial Data Container, Persistent Sensor Data Container, and Persistent Spatial Data Container.

The In-memory Sensor Data Container stores objects converted by sensor data recorder. The container is instantiated for each sensor device. The In-memory Data Container stores it in time-order in the In-memory Sensor Data container when SENSORD receives sensor data from the sensor recorder. The container has a ring buffer; sensor data are stored at a constant frequency. The ring buffer is divided into blocks, and to delete previous periodic sensor data, so it prevents mixture past periodic sensor data. The index in the buffer is assigned by time and its position is unique. For those reasons, temporal queries are processed rapidly.

The In-memory Spatial Data Container stores spatial and geometric information such as location of human, sensor devices and geo-features. The indoor and outdoor locations are represented in the form of a widely used geographic coordinate system WGS84. A container has a layered structure that enables SENSORD to store many kinds of spatial objects into suitable layers, e.g., a sensor device layer, an indoor layer, and a building equipment layer. Using the mechanism, we can obtain a specific type of object by selecting a proper layer. Actually, SENSORD does not distinguish sensor spatial objects from other general spatial objects when analyzing sensing data.

Persistent Sensor/Spatial Data Containers are copies of the In-memory Sensor or Spatial Data Containers. The data container-manager replicates the data in In-Memory data containers to the persistent data containers. To store the sensor data for a long time, we have implemented the persistent data containers by PostgreSQL [5]. Spatial queries for data in the containers are processed using PostGIS [6], which is a plug-in of the PostgreSQL.

3 Spatial Objects

3.1 In-Memory Spatial Data Container

To maintain sensing data properly in middleware, it is crucial to represent the geometric and topological attributes of entities in a uniform and coordinated way.

Such entities include sensors and their surrounding properties, e.g., building components, furnishings, and so on. In SENSORD, spatial objects and entities are represented and handled in the In-Memory Spatial Data Container component to satisfy such requirement. The following objects are handled in the In-Memory Spatial Data Container:

- Sensor Objects
- Indoor Objects
- Outdoor Objects
- Topology Objects

The sensor object in SENSORD represents a sensor device installed in the environment. A kind of spatial object attribute called the "geometric value" represents the real coordinate values of the sensor location. The indoor object represents furnishings in the environment such as walls, doors, tables, and so on. Outdoor objects represent some specific or distinguished special areas such as roads, parks, railways, and so on. Outdoor objects correspond to map objects in usual GIS systems. Topology objects are not actual physical objects. It is prepared to represent abstract spatial objects such as graph structures and their attributes (e.g., nodes and links, path names, walking costs) to represent human and object flows in the environment.

Using such a coordinated means of representing and handling spatial objects in SENSORD, querying spatial objects can be done independently from the classify-cation of objects such as indoor or outdoor classification, which enables seamless viewing GUI in the SENSORD user interfaces presented in Fig. 3.

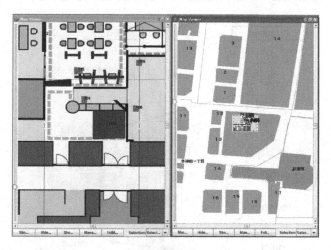

Fig. 3. Example of seamless viewing GUI that is independent from the spatial magnitude (smooth view change from indoor to outdoor)

The layer structure is prepared as the internal data model of In-Memory Spatial Container (Fig. 4). SENSORD users can exploit the layer structure to classify spatial objects and to store them in the proper selected layers. For instance, users can classify pre-defined data such as the building structure and furnishings in a certain layer, and classify additional sensor devices in another type of layer. Users can select not only a certain layer but also all the layers simultaneously when querying and viewing such spatial objects.

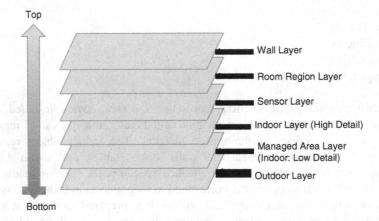

Fig. 4. Layer Structure as a Data Model in the In-Memory Spatial Data Container

3.2 Definition of Spatial Objects

The primary definition of spatial object is a 'primitive shape' such as point, line, rectangle, polygon, and so on. Additional attributes can be added to spatial objects.

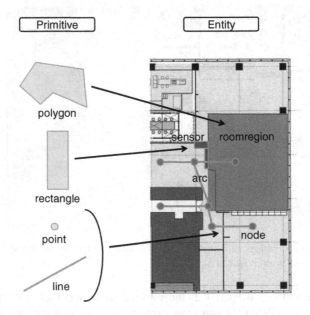

Fig. 5. Spatial Object Definition – Primitive Shape and Entity

For instance, an additional attribute called 'name,' e.g. "sensor" or "wall," is definable for the primary definition of a point or line, respectively. An additional attribute such as "sensor type (camera)" or "wall thickness" can be added to the objects. Such an additional attribute is called an 'entity' in SENSORD (Fig. 5). In other words, a spatial object is defined as 1) a single primary attribute that represents its shape (point, line, rectangle, etc.), and 2) (possibly multi-numbers of) entity(es) that represents additional attribute(s). Using the 'entity' field of spatial objects, users can choose a specific class of spatial objects such as "sensor," "wall," "desk," and so on, instead of specifying the locations and geometry of the objects stored in the SENSORD system.

From the computational point of view, a spatial object is defined as the set of the following elements:

1. Object Name
2. Entity (e.g., sensor, wall, desk)
3. Set of Vertex Coordinate Values
4. Attribute Name and Value

All coordinate values are represented in the WGS84 coordination system. 'Attribute' is different from the 'Entity' field. In contrast to an entity field, users can describe more detailed attributes and their values in the attribute field. Examples of the principal attribute type are shown in Table 1. Second and third attributes are also prepared.

Table 1. Principal Attribute Type in SENSORD

Attribute	Means
type	Type of Object
walkcost	Walkness Cost
passflow	Walkable Direction
uri	URI
id	Object ID
line_color, fill_color	Draw Color of Object

An example of an external data format of spatial object in SENSORD is shown in the following. The first example shows a wall, and the second one shows a sensor.

```
ObjectName;Entity(Vertex,...);Attribute=Value;…
```

```
Example 1:

Wall1;wall(139.77194969512195
35.699446341463414,139.77195274390243
35.699446341463414,139.77195274390243
35.69915792682927,139.77194908536586
35.69915792682927);type=partition;cost=100;...
```

Example 2:

```
SensorP400;sensor(139.77228430582335
35.69933366443411,139.77228823407725
35.69933366443411,139.77228823407725
35.6993145843437,139.77228486700247
35.6993145843437);id=400;type=passcounter;uri=http://ww
w.consorts.org/sensor/dai-
bldg/10f/passercounter/400;...
```

The sensor shown in the second example is "Passer Counter," as described in the 'type' attribute. The specified spatial region in this example represents the reaction-region (sensible-region) of the sensor. This object also has a URI field by which users can access the sensor via TCP/IP.

Users can query about spatial objects included in a specific rectangle or polygon, by sending the corresponding rectangle or polygon object to SENSORD middleware (Fig. 6). The SENSORD middleware memorizes already queried regions; it can thereby avoid redundant data transmissions.

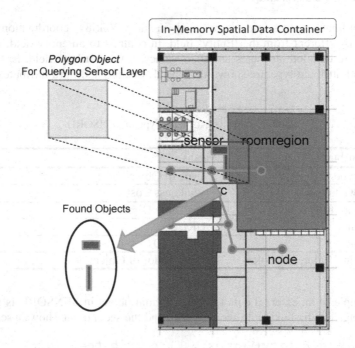

Fig. 6. Query about Spatial Objects Process

Figure 7 shows the computational process of a sensing data query. First, a client issues a query related to spatial objects by specifying a region in which desired spatial objects exist. Users can exploit the layer structure to suppress unnecessary queries in this step. Second, the SENSORD system returns the list of spatial objects included in

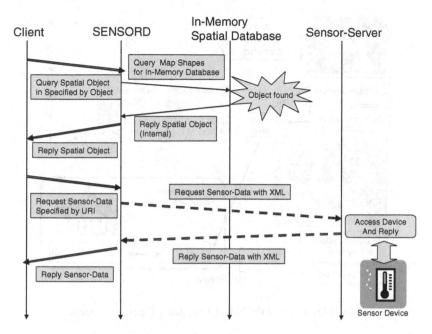

Fig. 7. Computation Process of Sensor Data Query

the specified region. Users can analyze the sensor's URI from attributes in the returned objects, and can access the sensor using the URI.

4 An Example: Indoor Emergency Response Systems

Using SENSORD middleware, we have been developing a software application called an "Indoor Emergency Response System" at our laboratory [7]. The emergency response system has been prepared to detect emergency situations and to provide evacuation signals. It manages sensor devices (e.g., thermometers, hygrometers, video surveillance systems, microphone arrays) and monitors the entire space along with its environmental status to detect abnormal events such as fire emergencies. It also monitors the number of humans remaining in a specific area, such as a floor of a building or a room, to provide basic information for evacuation.

Overview of the system developed for a floor of our laboratory building is shown in Fig. 8. The monitored area of the floor is about 700 m^2. There are 20 thermometers and hygrometers[1], and 9 video surveillance camera systems that count the number of humans who cross predefined border lines in the monitoring area. We use three video surveillance systems: Vitracom SiteView EP[2], Ubiquitous Stereo Vision System (USV) [8] [9], and IBS Counter[3].

---

[1] T&D Corporation TR-72W: http://english.tandd.com/product/tr_7w/tr_7w_01feature.html
[2] Vitracom SiteView EP: http://wwwvitracom.de/downloads/site-view-st-ep-en.pdf
[3] CED System, Inc. IBS Counter: http://www.ced.co.jp/IBS_CT_CAT.pdf

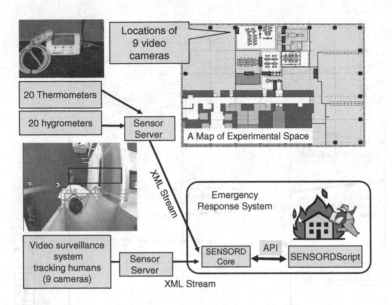

Fig. 8. Overview of the Indoor Emergency Response System

The SENSORD system communicates with these sensors, receives the sensor-event (e.g. the event detecting passers cross a predefined line), and infers the status of the environment (e.g. the number of people staying in a closed areas) by analyzing the sensor events.

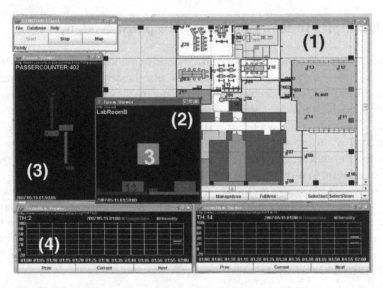

Fig. 9. Indoor Emergency Response System snapshot: three humans are present in LabRoomB

In this example, the SENSORD system counts the number of people staying at four different rooms such as "LabRoomB." A snapshot of a GUI of the system is shown in Fig. 9. It displays four window types: (1) a map of a monitoring area, (2) the number of humans staying in a closed area (LabRoomB), (3) the number of humans who cross a predefined border line in the monitoring area for a camera system (PASSERCOUNTER:402), and (4) a graph of sensing values of a sensor device (temperature and humidity in LabRoomB). Users can interactively select graphical sensor object in the map window (1). The map image is assembled automatically from various object layers stored in the SENSORD system. For that reason, users can develop each object layer independently without considering spatial relations of the layers. Using URI contained in a "sensor" spatial object, the implementation of lunching monitoring window is also simple.

Moreover, this system can launch graph window (4) simultaneously, which shows sensor values of the sensor devices in a region specified by the user. To realize this feature, it is necessary to determine the types and locations of sensor devices in the region. The user must query the sensor devices by its device-name if it is not supported by SENSORD. However, using SENSORD, the user needs only to specify a region such as a polygon.

5 Related Work

In the field of database research, various types of database are proposed. Some studies have been made of databases that manage spatio-temporal information [10] [11] [12]. Some middleware intended to handle sensor-events, such as GEM [13], MASTAQ [14], and DSWare [15], has been proposed. In contrast to those systems, SENSORD is a middleware that unifies context-aware services and spatio-temporal information framework. Moreover, SENSORD can manage and process all spatial information including sensor locations and attributes in a uniform manner.

6 Conclusion

In this paper, we have described SENSORD, spatio-temporal in-memory sensor data management middleware, which can uniformly manage various kinds of sensors and can unify such sensing data with higher-level information services. We have examined the method of handling spatial information on SENSORD, by implementing an Indoor Emergency Response System. To implement sensor-event-based applications, SENSORD can radically strengthen spatio-temporal information processing. Consequently, users can readily implement client software. Future work will include the extension of SENSORD for flexible handling of radiowave sensing data such as RFID and ad-hoc sensor networks.

References

1. Abowd, G.D., Atkeson, C.G., Hong, J., Long, S., Kooper, R., Pinkerton, M.: Cyberguide: a mobile context-aware tour guide. Wireless Network 3(5), 421–433 (1997)
2. Addlesee, M., Curwen, R., Hodges, S., Newman, J., Steggles, P., Ward, A., Hopper, A.: Implementing a sentient computing system. IEEE Computer Magazine (8), 50–56 (2001)

3. Krumm, J., Horvitz, E.: Predestinations: Inferring destinations from partial trajectories. In: Eighth International Conference on Ubiquitous Computing, pp. 243–260. ACM Press, New York (2006)
4. Sashima, A., Inoue, Y., Kurumatani, K.: Spatio-Temporal Sensor Data Management for Context-Aware Services. In: ADPUC 2006. Proc. of the International Workshop on Advanced Data Processing in Ubiquitous Computing (2006)
5. PostgreSQL, http://wwww.postgresql.org
6. PostGIS, http://www.postgis.org
7. Inoue, Y., Sashima, A., Kurumatani, K.: Indoor navigation system for emergency evacuation in ubiquitous environment. In: Eighth International Conference on Ubiquitous Computing, CD-ROM, ACM Press, New York (2006)
8. Yoda, I., Hosotani, D., Sakaue, K.: Ubiquitous strep vision for controlling safety on platforms in railroad stations. In: ACCV 2004. Proc. of the Sixth Asian Conference on Computer Vision, vol. 2, pp. 770–775 (2004)
9. Yoda, I., Sakaue, K.: Concept of ubiquitous streo vision and applications for human sensing. In: CIRA 2003. Proc. 2003 IEEE International Symposium on Computational Intelligence in Robotics and Automation, pp. 1251–1257. IEEE Computer Society Press, Los Alamitos (2003)
10. Al-Taha, K.K., Snodgrass, R.T., Soo, M.D.: Biblography on spatiotemporal databases. SIGMOD Rec. 22(1), 59–67 (1993)
11. Kim, D.H., Ryu, K.H., Park, C.H.: Design and implementation of spatiotemporal database query processing system. Journal of Systems and Software 60(1), 37–49 (2002)
12. Wolfson, O., Xu, B., Chamberlain, S., Jiang, L.: Moving objects database: Issues and solutions. In: Proc. of the 10th International Conference on Scientific and Statistical Database Management, pp. 111–122 (1998)
13. Jiao, B., Son, S.H., Stankovic, J.: GEM: Generic event service middleware for wireless sensor networks. In: INSS 2005. Proc. of the 2nd International Workshop on Networked Sensing Systems (June 2005)
14. Hwang, I., Han, Q., Miasra, A.: MASTAQ: A middleware architecture for sensor applications with statistical quality constraints. In: PERCOMW 2005: Proc. of the Third IEEE International Conference on Pervasive Computing and Communications Workshops, pp. 390–395. IEEE Computer Society, Washington, DC (2005)
15. Li, S., Son, S.H., Stankovic, J.A.: Event detection services using data service middleware in distributed sensor networks. In: Zhao, F., Guibas, L.J. (eds.) IPSN 2003. LNCS, vol. 2634, pp. 502–517. Springer, Heidelberg (2003)

Context Awareness by Case-Based Reasoning in a Music Recommendation System

Jae Sik Lee[1] and Jin Chun Lee[2]

[1] Division of e-Business, School of Business Administration, Ajou University
San 5, Wonchun-Dong, Youngtong-Gu, Suwon 443-749, Korea
leejsk@ajou.ac.kr
[2] Ubiquitous Convergence Research Institute
San 5, Wonchun-Dong, Youngtong-Gu, Suwon 443-749, Korea
giny777@empal.com

Abstract. The recommendation system is one of the core technologies for implementing personalization services. Recommendation systems in ubiquitous computing environment should have the capability of context-awareness. In this research, we developed a music recommendation system, which we shall call C^2_Music, which utilizes not only the user's demographics and behavioral patterns but also the user's context. For a specific user in a specific context, the C^2_Music recommends the music that the similar users listened most in the similar context. In evaluating the performance of C^2_Music using a real world data, it outperforms the comparative system that utilizes the user's demographics and behavioral patterns only.

Keywords: Music Recommendation System, Context-Awareness, Case-based Reasoning, Ubiquitous Data Mining, Personalization.

1 Introduction

In ubiquitous computing environment, various types of data will be obtained through various types of devices in any time and any place. Enormous amount of data generated from our everyday life will be collected by sensors and computers, and will be used to provide us with intelligent services.

The problem that we will be confronted with in this ubiquitous computing environment is 'information overload.' Therefore, we need some systems that alleviate this information overload problem effectively and efficiently, that is, recommendation systems. Recommendation can be defined as "the process of utilizing the opinions of a community of customers to help individuals in that community more effectively identify content of interest from a potentially overwhelming set of choices" [21]. Effective recommendation reduces the user's effort and time in making decisions. Researches on recommendation systems have been performed actively both in academy and practice. However, in making recommendation, most of the existing researches have focused on using the user's

H. Ichikawa et al. (Eds.): UCS 2007, LNCS 4836, pp. 45–58, 2007.

preference and/or transaction data. They rarely considered such information as user's context at the time of making recommendation.

Suppose a customer at his thirties visits a department store. Traditional recommendation systems will recommend the items that he might be interested in by analyzing his past purchase history and preferences. If he comes to the department store for the purpose of buying some items for himself, then the recommended items by the traditional systems would be appropriate. However, if his purpose is to buy some presents for his wife for their wedding anniversary, then anniversary items or ladies' accessories should be recommended. In other words, the items must be recommended considering the situation the customer is placed in, i.e., the customer's context.

In this research, we developed a music recommendation system that utilizes not only the user's demographics and behavioral patterns but also his/her context at the time of making recommendation. The underlying algorithm of our proposed system is case-based reasoning. The rest of the paper is organized as follows: The next section provides a brief overview of the related work, i.e., context, context-awareness, recommendation systems and case-based reasoning. Section 3 provides an overall structure of our proposed music recommendation system. Section 4 describes the implementation process of our proposed system. Section 5 presents the performance evaluation of the proposed system. The final section provides concluding remarks and directions for further research.

2 Related Work

2.1 Context and Context-Awareness

Context-awareness is to use information about the circumstances that the application is running in, to provide relevant information and/or services to the user [5]. The term 'context-awareness' was introduced by Schilit and Theimer [24]. Context awareness is a term that describes the ability of the computer to sense and act upon information about its environment, such as location, time, temperature or user identity [22].

Schilit and Theimer [24] defined 'context' through giving a number of examples of context, i.e., location, identities of nearby people and objects, and changes to those objects. The term context, however, has been defined by many researchers in various ways. Schmidt et al. [25] defined it using three dimensions: physical environment, human factors and time. Benerecetti et al. [2] classified context into physical context and cultural context. Physical context is a set of features of the environment while cultural context includes user information, the social environment and beliefs. Dey and Abowd [7] defined context as "any information that can be used to characterize the situation of an entity, where an entity can be a person, place, physical or computational object that is considered relevant to the interaction between a user and an application, including the user and the application themselves". Dey [6] presented four types of context, i.e., location, identity, time and activity, and provided a framework for defining a context by giving values to these four types.

By sensing context information, context-aware applications can present context information to users, or modify their behavior according to changes in the environment [23]. Dey [6] defined context-aware application as "a system is context-aware if it uses context to provide relevant information and/or services to the user, where relevancy depends on the user's task." Three important context awareness behaviors are the presentation of information and services to a user, automatic execution of a service, and tagging of context to information for later retrieval [7].

Early investigations on context-aware application were carried out at the Olivetti Research Lab with development of the active badge system [27][29], sensing locality of mobile users to adapt applications to people's whereabouts. Another research can be found at Xerox PARC with the ubiquitous computing experiment, from which a first general consideration of context-aware mobile computing emerged [22]. Dey *et al.* developed the Conference Assistant, a prototype context-aware application for assisting conference attendees and presenters [8]. The capabilities of this system is to help users decide which activities to attend, to provide awareness of the activities of colleagues, to enhance interactions between users and the environment, to assist users in taking notes on presentations and to aid in the retrieval of conference information after the conference concludes. Dey *et al.* [9] also developed a context toolkit to support rapid prototyping of certain types of context-aware applications. Many researchers have adopted this toolkit approach [11][12], while others have been developing a middleware infrastructure [16].

2.2 Music Recommendation Systems

The recommendation systems are to recommend items that users may be interested in based on their predefined preferences or access histories [4]. Many of the leading companies such as Amazon, Google, CDNOW, LA Times and eBay, are already using personalized recommendation systems to help their customers find products to purchase.

Ringo is a pioneer music recommendation system using collaborative filtering [26]. In Ringo, each user is requested to make ratings for music objects. These ratings constitute the personal profiles. For collaborative recommendation, only the ratings of the users whose profiles are similar to the target user are considered. Whether a music objects will be recommended is then based on the weighted average of the ratings considered.

Kuo and Shan [18] developed a content-based music recommendation system. In their system, the users' preferences are learned by mining the melody patterns, i.e., the pitch information, of the music they listened. Chen and Chen [4] proposed a music recommendation system that employed three recommendation mechanisms, i.e., content-based method, collaborative filtering and statistics-based method, for different users' needs. In their system, music objects are grouped according to the properties such as pitch, duration and loudness, and users are grouped according to their interests and behaviors derived from the access histories.

Celma *et al.* [3] proposed a music recommendation system called 'Foafing the Music'. The Friend of a Friend (FOAF) project is about creating a Web of machine-readable homepages describing people, the things they create and do, their interests and the links between them. The 'Foafing the Music' system uses this FOAF information and the Rich Site Summary that publishes new releases or artists' related news, for recommending music to a user, depending on his/her musical tastes.

Park *et al.* [20] proposed a context-aware music recommendation system that employs fuzzy system, Bayesian networks and utility theory. Kim *et al.* [13] designed a music recommendation system that makes recommendation using user information such as sex, age and pulsation, and surrounding contexts such as weather, temperature and location. The profiles of music, not music listeners, are prepared using these factors and stored in Music Content Information Database. Then, suitable music is selected using a statistical filtering method.

2.3 Case-Based Reasoning

Case-based reasoning (CBR), a well-known artificial intelligence technique, has already proven its effectiveness in numerous domains. The fundamental concept in CBR is that similar problems will have similar solutions. CBR is a method of solving a new problem by analyzing the solutions to previous, similar problems [15][28][30]. Since CBR can provide answers just using accumulated previous cases, i.e., case base, it can be applied to complicated and unstructured problems relatively easily. The most distinguished advantage of CBR is that it can learn continuously by just adding new cases to the case base.

As shown in Figure 1, CBR is typically described as a cyclical process comprising the four REs [1]: (1) REtrieve the most similar case or cases, (2) REuse the information and knowledge in that case to attempt to solve the problem, (3) REvise the proposed solution if necessary, and (4) REtain the parts of this experience likely to be useful for future problem solving.

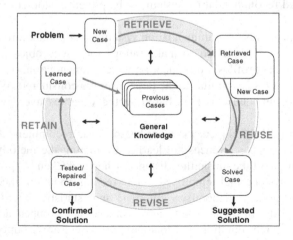

Fig. 1. Problem Solving Cycle of CBR

CBR is basically based on the k-Nearest Neighbors (NN) algorithm. Therefore, in order to build the CBR model, we need to define the similarity function that will be used to find k previous cases similar to the new case. The similarity score between a new case N and a previous case C is calculated using the Equation (1) in general,

$$Similarity\ (N,C) = \frac{\sum_{i=1}^{n} f(N_i, C_i) \times W_i}{\sum_{i=1}^{n} W_i} \qquad (1)$$

where N_i is the ith feature value of the new case, C_i is the ith feature value of the old case, n is the number of features, $f(N_i, C_i)$ is the distance function between N_i and C_i, and W_i is the weight of ith feature. The value of similarity score is between 0 and 1. The more the two cases N and C are similar, the more similarity score becomes close to 1.

Recently, CBR became applied to the development of context-aware applications. Kofod-Petersen and Aamodt [14] incorporated context information as cases in CBR for user situation assessment in a mobile context-aware system. Kumar et al. [17] proposed a context enabled Multi-CBR approach. It consisted of two CBRs, i.e., user context CBR and product context CBR, for aiding the recommendation engine in retrieving appropriate information for e-commerce applications. Leake et al. [19] presented three potential areas in which the use of CBR may provide benefits for context-aware applications, especially in smart homes, i.e., supporting personalization, supporting interactive adjustment of the system by the user, and facilitating customization and knowledge acquisition by the developer.

3   A Case-Based Context-Aware Music Recommendation System

In this section, we describe the structure and the components of the proposed system, we shall call C^2_Music. Let us think about the following scenario:

> "The user A is a white-collar worker at his early thirties who enjoys listening to music. It is Friday and has been raining from morning, and it is chilly for a day in late June. When he enters his room after returning home from work, his audio system is turned on automatically and plays the Creedence Clearwater Revival's 'Who'll Stop the Rain' that he usually listened on a day like today. Even though Rod Stewart revived the song recently, the user A prefers the original song by CCR back in 1970."

In the above scenario, the music is selected by C^2_Music. The C^2_Music consists of three layers, i.e., Interface Layer, Application Layer and Repository Layer as depicted in Figure 2.

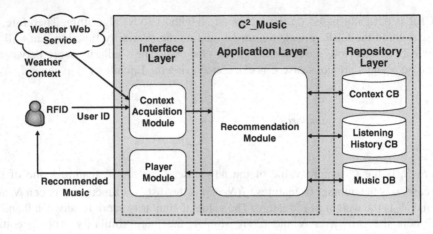

Fig. 2. The Structure of C^2_Music

The Interface Layer is to identify the user, to collect the context data and to deliver the recommended music to the user. The Application Layer is to select the music for recommendation. The Repository Layer is to store relevant cases and data. The detailed roles and functions of the three layers and their modules will be explained as we describe the music recommendation process of C^2_Music in section 4.2. Figure 3 shows the entity-relationship diagram of the cases and data stored in the Repository Layer that consists of Context Case Base (CB), Listening History CB and Music Data Base (DB).

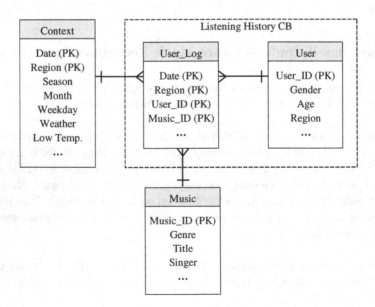

Fig. 3. ERD for the Repository Layer

4 Implementation of C^2_Music

4.1 Data Description

The data used in this research are listening history data set and weather data set. The listening history data set was obtained from a streaming music service company in Korea, and it contains the list of songs listened by 659 customers for 6 months. Table 1 shows the features of user's characteristics stored in the Listening History CB. The weather data set was obtained from the Weather Bureau. Table 2 shows the weather data stored in the Context CB.

Table 1. Features of User's Characteristics Stored in Listening History CB

Feature Name	Description	Type
User_ID	User's ID Number	Categorical
X1	Gender	Categorical
X2	Age	Numerical
X3	Region	Categorical
X4	Number of Listening Days for Last One Month	Numerical
X5	Number of Listening Times for Last One Month	Numerical
X6	Number of Listened Songs for Last One Month	Numerical
....	....	....
X12	Ratio of Rock and Metal Songs for Last One Month	Numerical
X13	Ratio of Korean Trot Songs for Last One Month	Numerical

Table 2. Features Stored in Context CB

Feature Name	Description	Type
Date	Music Listening Date	Categorical
Region	Residence Area of User	Categorical
Season	Spring, Summer, Fall, Winter	Categorical
Month	January, February, March, April, May, June, July, August, September, October, November, December	Categorical
Weekday	Monday, Tuesday, Wednesday, Thursday, Friday, Saturday, Sunday	Categorical
Weather	Sunny, Partly Cloudy, Mostly Cloudy, Cloudy, Rainy, Snow	Categorical
Avg_Temp	Average Temperature During a Day (Unit: Celsius)	Numeric
High_Temp	Highest Temperature During a Day (Unit: Celsius)	Numeric
Low_Temp	Lowest Temperature During a Day (Unit: Celsius)	Numeric

4.2 Implementation of the Recommendation Module

The C^2_Music recommends the music to the user in the following four steps:

Step 1: Identify the user and collect the context data

The Context Acquisition Module identifies the user A using the RFID sensor, and collects the weather data from web service. The collected weather data includes 'season,' 'month,' 'day of the week,' 'atmospheric condition,' 'the lowest temperature,' 'the highest temperature' and 'the average temperature' of the corresponding date. The Context Acquisition Module constructs an input case using these collected data and delivers it to the Recommendation Module. This constructed case is stored in the Context CB for later use.

The following steps, i.e., steps 2, 3 and 4 performed by the Recommendation Module are simply depicted in Figure 4.

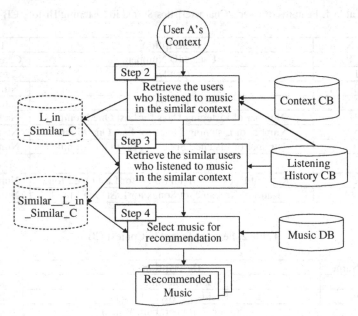

Fig. 4. The Music Recommendation Process of C^2_Music

Step 2: Retrieve the users who listened to music in the similar context

The Recommendation Module retrieves the top k past contexts similar to the user A's present context from the Context CB, and identifies the dates that correspond to the retrieved contexts. Input features for CBR model are presented in Table 2. Then, it retrieves the users who listened to music on these dates from the Listening History CB and makes a temporary case base named 'L_in_Similar_C' (meaning 'Listeners in the Similar Context'). In other words, in this step, we retrieve the users who listened to music in the context similar to the user A's present context from the Listening History CB.

In calculating the similarity scores for finding similar contexts, Equation (2) is used for numerical features.

$$f(N_i, C_i) = \begin{cases} 1-d & if \ 0 \le d \le 1 \\ 0 & if \ d > 1 \end{cases} \tag{2}$$

where,

$$d = \frac{|N_i - C_i|}{Max - Min}$$

Max: maximum value among i^{th} feature values for all cases in case base.
Min: minimum value among i^{th} feature values for all cases in case base.

For categorical features, a partial matching scheme is devised using the domain knowledge as shown in Table 3.

Table 3. Similarity Score Metrics for Categorical Features

Feature	Similarity Score Metrics				
Season					
	Old Case \ New Case	Spring	Summer	Fall	Winter
	Spring	1	0.2	0.5	0.2
	Summer	0.2	1	0.2	0
	Fall	0.5	0.2	1	0.2
	Winter	0.2	0	0.2	1
Month					
	Similarity Value	Condition			
	1	$N_i = C_i$			
	0.5	Distance Between N_i and C_i = 1 Month			
	0.2	Distance Between N_i and C_i = 2 Months			
	0	Otherwise			
....	....				
....	....				

Step 3: Retrieve the similar users who listened to music in the similar context

The Recommendation Module retrieves the top k users whose demographics and behavioral patterns are similar to those of the user A from 'L_in_Similar_C', and makes a temporary case base named 'Similar_L_in_Similar_C' (meaning 'Similar Listeners in the Similar Context'). Input features for CBR model are presented in Table 1.

In calculating the similarity scores for finding similar contexts, Equation (2) is used for numerical features. For categorical features, an exact matching scheme is used. Similarity score 1 is assigned if two features have the same values, 0 is assigned otherwise.

Step 4: Select music for recommendation

The Recommendation Module first retrieves the songs listened by the users in 'Similar_L_in_Similar_C' from the Listening History CB and composes the candidates set for recommendation. Before selecting the songs for recommendation from the candidates set, we need to determine the selection criterion and the number of songs to be recommended. In this research, we select songs on the basis of frequency and recency. Therefore, we sort the candidate songs in the descending order of the listening frequencies by similar listeners and the last dates when they are listened. Since the number of songs normally contained in one CD is 15, we select 15 songs for recommendation.

In other words, the Recommendation Module selects the top 15 songs that the users in 'Similar_L_in_Similar_C' listened most and recently, from the Listening History CB. Then, it retrieves the corresponding music files from Music DB and provides them for the user A through the Player Module.

5   Performance Evaluation of C^2_Music

In order to evaluate the performance of C^2_Music, we implemented a comparative system. The comparative system is C_Music (meaning conventional Case-Based Music Recommendation System) that employs CBR technique and makes recommendations using the other users' listening histories stored in the Listening History CB. In other words, while the input features of C^2_Music are the features presented in Tables 1and 2, the input features of C_Music are the features in Table 1 only. The two systems were implemented using Microsoft Visual Basic 6.0 on PC.

For performance evaluation of the two systems, we performed 10-fold cross validation. The 10-fold data sets were prepared as shown in Figure 5. In each fold, we divided the data set into the training data set and the test data set in the ratio of 6 and 4.The training data set was used for constructing the case base and optimizing the CBR models. The test data set was used for evaluating the performances of the two final systems.

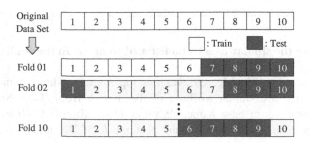

Fig. 5. Configuration of 10-Fold Data Sets

CBR is basically based on the k-NN algorithm. Therefore the performance of CBR model is affected by the value of k. Another factor that affects the performance of

CBR is the weight vector of the input features. For implementing the best model, we first generated hundred weight vectors, and then experimented with the resulting CBR model by varying the value of k from 10 to 100 at the increment of 5 for each weight vector.

Evaluation metrics are essential in order to judge the quality and performance of recommendation systems. There has been considerable research in the area of recommendation systems evaluation [10]. In this research, we use Precision calculated using Equation (3) as our choice of evaluation measure because the number of recommended songs is fixed as 15 and our research focus is to improve the accuracy of the recommendation system [4].

$$\text{Pr} \, ecision \;\; = \;\; \frac{R^L}{R} \tag{3}$$

where,

R^L : the number of songs, among the recommended songs, actually listened.

R : the number of songs recommended by the recommendation system.

Table 4 shows the precisions of the two systems, i.e., C_Music and C^2_Music on the test data set.

Table 4. Precision Comparison of C_Music and C^2_Music on Test Data Sets

Fold	C_Music	C^2_Music
Fold 01	0.464	0.534
Fold 02	0.493	0.533
Fold 03	0.481	0.595
Fold 04	0.470	0.572
Fold 05	0.420	0.490
Fold 06	0.410	0.500
Fold 07	0.480	0.551
Fold 08	0.467	0.545
Fold 09	0.457	0.559
Fold 10	0.465	0.548
Average	0.461	0.542

As shown in Table 4, on average, the precision of C^2_Music is 0.542 that is 8% point higher than the precision of C_Music, 0.461. In order to examine if our results are statistically significant, the Wilcoxon Signed Rank Sum Test is performed.

Table 5. Wilcoxon Signed Rank Sum Test of C_Music and C^2_Music

Comparison	z-Statistic[*]
C_Music – C^2_Music	−2.806[*]

*: Significant at 5% level

As shown in Table 5, C^2_Music outperforms C_Music at the 5% significance level. This fact shows that the precision of recommendation can be increased by utilizing the environmental context data.

6 Conclusion

In ubiquitous computing environment, the need for context-aware recommendation systems that provides the users with personalized services using various contextual information will be increased. In this research, we developed a context-aware music recommendation system using case-based reasoning, that we shall call C^2_Music. The distinguished features of C^2_Music are twofold. First, for selecting the music for recommendation, it utilizes not only the user's demographics and behavioral patterns but also his/her context at the time of making recommendation. Secondly, it employs 2-step case-based reasoning, i.e., the first step for retrieving the similar contexts and the second step for retrieving the similar users.

The C^2_Music consists of three layers, i.e., Interface Layer, Application Layer and Repository Layer. The Interface Layer is to identify the user, to collect the context data and to deliver the recommended music to the user. The Application Layer is to select the music for recommendation. The Repository Layer that consists of Context Case Base, Listening History Case Base and Music Data Base is to store relevant cases and data.

In order to evaluate the performance of C^2_Music, we implemented a comparative system C_Music that also employs case-based reasoning technique but does not utilize the user's context. As a result of 10-fold cross validation with a real world data, the average precision of C^2_Music is 0.542 that is 8% point higher than the average precision of C_Music, 0.461. This result shows that the precision of recommendation can be increased by utilizing the context data.

For further research, we plan to continue our study on the following issues: First, we will consider and collect more features that can represent the user's context, and then select the appropriate features by feature selection process. Secondly, we need to compare our proposed system with other context-aware recommendation systems that employ some techniques other than case-based reasoning, such as ontology. Finally, we will do our research on the methods for speeding up the recommendation system, because in ubiquitous computing environment, not only accuracy but also speed of the recommendation is important.

Acknowledgments. This research is supported by the Ubiquitous Autonomic Computing and Network Project, the Ministry of Information and Communication (MIC), 21st Century Frontier R&D Program in Korea.

References

1. Aamodt, A., Plaza, E.: Case-based Reasoning: Fundamental Issues, Methodological Variations, and System Approaches. Artificial Intelligence Communication 7, 39–59 (1994)
2. Benerecetti, M., Bouquet, P., Bonifacio, M.: Distributed Context-Aware System. Human-Computer Interaction 16, 213–228 (2000)

3. Celma, O., Ramírez, M., Herrera, P.: Foafing the Music: A Music Recommendation System based on RSS Feeds and User Preferences. In: Proceedings: 6th International Conference on Music Information Retrieval, London, UK (2005)
4. Chen, H.C., Chen, A.P.: A Music Recommendation System Based on Music and User Grouping. Journal of Intelligent Information Systems 24, 113–132 (2005)
5. Cuddy, S., Katchabaw, M., Lutfiyya, H.: Context-Aware Service Selection based on Dynamic and Static Service Attributes. In: Wireless and Mobile Computing, Networking and Communications, IEEE International Conference (2005)
6. Dey, A.K.: Understanding and Using Context. Personal and Ubiquitous Computing 5, 4–7 (2001)
7. Dey, A.K., Abowd, G.D.: Towards a Better Understanding of Context and Context-Awareness. In: Proceedings of CHI 2000 Workshop on the What, Who, Where, When, Why, and How of Context-Awareness, The Hague, Netherlands, pp. 1–6 (2000)
8. Dey, A.K., Futakawa, M., Salber, D., Abowd, G.D.: The Conference Assistant: Combining Context-Awareness with Wearable Computing. In: Proceedings Symposium on Wearable Computers, pp. 21–28 (1999)
9. Dey, A.K., Salber, D., Abowd, G.D.: A Conceptual Framework and a Toolkit for Supporting the Rapid Prototyping of Context-Aware Applications. Human-Computer Interaction 16, 97–166 (2001)
10. Herlocker, J., Konstan, J., Tervin, L.G., Riedl, J.: Evaluating Collaborative Filtering Recommender Systems. ACM Transactions on Information Systems 22, 5–53 (2004)
11. Hong, J.: The Context Fabric. Berkeley, USA (2003), http://guir.berkeley.edu/projects/confab/
12. Jang, S., Woo, W.: Ubi-UCAM: A Unified Context-Aware Application Model. In: Proceedings of Context 2003, Stanford, CA, USA (2003)
13. Kim, J.H., Song, C.H., Lim, K.W., Lee, J.H.: Design of Music Recommendation System Using Context Information. In: Shi, Z.-Z., Sadananda, R. (eds.) PRIMA 2006. LNCS (LNAI), vol. 4088, pp. 708–713. Springer, Heidelberg (2006)
14. Kofod-Petersen, A., Aamodt, A.: Case-based Situation Assessment in a Mobile Context-Aware Systems. In: AIMS2003. Workshop on Artificial Intelligence for Mobile Systems, Seattle (October 2003)
15. Kolodner, J.L.: Case-based Reasoning. Morgan Kaufman, San Mateo, CA (1993)
16. Kumar, M., Shirazi, B.A., Das, S.K., Sung, B.Y., Levine, D., Singhal, M.: PICO: a Middleware Framework for Pervasive Computing. IEEE Pervasive Computing 2, 72–79 (2003)
17. Kumar, P., Gopalan, S., Sridhar, V.: Context Enabled Multi-CBR based Recommendation Engine for E-Commerce. In: ICEBE 2005. Proceedings of IEEE International Conference on e-Business Engineering, pp. 237–244. IEEE Computer Society Press, Los Alamitos (2005)
18. Kuo, F.F., Shan, M.K.: A Personalized Music Filtering System Based on Melody Style Classification. In: Proceedings of IEEE international Conference on Data Mining, pp. 649–652. IEEE Computer Society Press, Los Alamitos (2002)
19. Leake, D., Maguitman, A., Reichherzer, T.: Cases, Context, and Comfort: Opportunities for Case-Based Reasoning in Smart Homes. In: Augusto, J.C., Nugent, C.D. (eds.) Designing Smart Homes. LNCS (LNAI), vol. 4008, pp. 109–131. Springer, Heidelberg (2006)
20. Park, H.S., Yoo, J.O., Cho, S.B.: A Context-Aware Music Recommendation System Using Fuzzy Bayesian Networks with Utility Theory. In: Wang, L., Jiao, L., Shi, G., Li, X., Liu, J. (eds.) FSKD 2006. LNCS (LNAI), vol. 4223, pp. 970–979. Springer, Heidelberg (2006)

21. Resnick, P., Varian, H.R.: Recommender Systems. Communications of the ACM 40, 56–58 (1997)
22. Ryan, N.: Mobile Computing in a Fieldwork Environment: Metadata Elements. Project Working Document, Version 0.2 (1997)
23. Salber, D., Dey, A.K., Orr, R.J., Abowd, G.D.: Designing For Ubiquitous Computing: A Case Study in Context Sensing. GVU Technical Report GIT-GVU, 99–129 (1999)
24. Schilit, B., Theimer, M.: Disseminating Active Map Information to Mobile Hosts. IEEE Network 8, 22–32 (1994)
25. Schmidt, A., Beigl, M., Gellersen, H.W.: There is More to Context Than Location. Computers and Graphics 23, 893–901 (1999)
26. Sharadanand, U., Maes, P.: Social Information Filtering: Algorithms for Automating 'Word of Mouth'. In: Proceedings of CHI 1995 Conference on Human Factors in Computing Systems, pp. 210–217 (1995)
27. Want, R., Hopper, A., Falcao, V., Gibbons, J.: The Active Badge Location System. ACM Transactions on Information Systems 10, 91–102 (1992)
28. Wang, H.C., Wang, H.S.: A Hybrid Expert System for Equipment Failure Analysis. Expert Systems with Applications 28, 615–622 (2005)
29. Ward, A., Jones, A., Hopper, A.: A New Location Technique for the Active Office. IEEE Personal Communications 4, 42–47 (1997)
30. Watson, I.: Applying Case-based Reasoning: Techniques for Enterprise System. Morgan Kaufmann, San Francisco, CA (1997)

Developing Intelligent Smart Home by Utilizing Community Computing

Soung Hun You[1], Hui Jung Park[1], Tae Su Kim[1], Jung Wook Park[1],
Uin Burn[1], Jin An Seol[2], and We Duke Cho[1]

[1] Center of Excellence for Ubiquitous System
408 Paldal Hall, Ajou University, Suwon, Korea
{sy05804, joshua, betzzi, bl008, byunja, chowd}@ajou.ac.kr
[2] Home Network Lab, Cvnet
KFTC Bundang Center, Seongnam, Korea
nicolas@cvnet.co.kr

Abstract. In Ubiquitous environment, system makes their own decision without or with minimized user interaction to provide required services to users. To fulfill this requirement the system needs to collect the proper information of surroundings and define how to react to the changes based on found information autonomously. To achieve this process, the system should equipped with three basic components which are sensing infrastructure, context aware or intelligent decision, and smart services. Main purpose of this research is how to enable this process efficiently and suggest the way of developing smart space. In this paper, we present *Community Computing* as the method of developing smart space and three components are briefly described. Also, three applicable scenarios and problems that might be happened at smart home are suggested and how community computing can be utilized to solve these problems is shown.

Keywords: Ubiquitous, Smart Home, Community Computing, Intelligent Service, Sensor Network, Context Aware.

1 Introduction

Since Mark Weiser [1] stated basic concept of Ubiquitous computing in 1990s, great attention has been paid to the implementation of it. Even though in the early concept of his Ubiquitous computing simply states that user can access and utilize computing power anytime and anywhere easily today's definition of Ubiquitous computing has been changed and evolved according to rapid growth of technology. In the smart environment, the deployed system recognizes user's behavior and does its best to fulfill any service request from user by self-decision. Therefore, recent Ubiquitous computing can be newly defined as *"The system figures out users' intention intelligently with minimized interface with user and makes their own decision such as what type of service provide and how to provide to users based on specific situation."* By considering this definition, the main critical factor of implementing

H. Ichikawa et al. (Eds.): UCS 2007, LNCS 4836, pp. 59–71, 2007.

the Ubiquitous computing is that *"Defining Specific Situation and Providing Services Intelligently"* Most all of the services are strongly depend on the situation and only well defined situation enables the system to provide the right services to user. Therefore, finding or defining of current situation plays critical role in Ubiquitous computing environment. The Ubiquitous computing system collects information or context, analyzes the given information, and makes their own decision to provide best services to users with or minimized interaction with them. For that reason, all of the Ubiquitous services are provided based on the situation around users and situation-aware is the starting point of providing services. In the recent year, numerous studies have attempted to find and explore field of situation-aware and situation based services [2][3][4]. To achieve this goal, the system should have or acquire fair amount of rich information in the environment. Since the user interface in the Ubiquitous environment is minimized or even disappeared acquiring user's intention or defining situation is quite limited and not an easy task for the system. However, the system still needs to figure out current situation to make right decision for providing satisfaction to users. To overcome this problems the sensors and sensor network has been researched on broad area [5][6][7][8]. The sensors or sensor network emerged from the question: "How can we collect the accurate information automatically without perception and effort of human?" More to the immediate point, sensing information which collected from sensor network is basic and critical factor of situation-aware. After collecting the environmental information through the sensor network the system should define their own decision that what's the current situation is. As a result, we need stable method of developing smart space and we develop the Community Computing which is new computing paradigm for coming Ubiquitous computing era. This solution provides the method of defining current situation based on the given sensing information and trigger the appropriate services through creating service community. Finally, more advances service is needed to satisfy the requirement of Ubiquitous environment. In this paper, we describe the concept of Community Computing is and how it works. Also, the factors that required developing smart space is suggested in detail such as sensor infrastructure. Finally three problem scenarios of smart home are given and how we solve these problems by utilizing Community Computing are described.

2 Smart Homes and Services Examples

In this section, we introduce two different smart homes briefly and selected services from different organizations.

2.1 House_n Project from MIT (Massachusetts Institute of Technology) [9]

The MIT develops real living test bed for smart home which is called *Place Lab* and conducts research on Ubiquitous services. They developed their own sensing devices and deployed them at their test bed. One of their projects is developing sensor

Fig. 1. The inside of Place lab with the sensing devices

network kits for low cost and easy installation. In this project, any volunteer can join this project and live there for a while and researcher can conduct their study with acquired data through these sensors in the place lab.

They can measure the physical and sedentary activities of user in the place lab through deployed sensor networks. From acquired sensing data, they can define the Activities of Daily Living (ADL) and provide the Ubiquitous services. They also research on way of developing smart home easily and efficiently with industrial construction vendors. Figure 1 shows the inside of place lab and deployed sensor devices at place lab.

2.2 Aware Home Project from GIT (Georgia Institute of Technology) [10]

The GIT also develops its own two stories of smart home which is called Aware Home as the research result of the Aware Home Research Initiative (AHRI). They define four main research categories of smart home "Design for People", "Technology", "Software Engineering", and "Social Implications" They are working on developing smart home services and most of services are based on the context aware technology by utilizing the sensing information. For example, indoor location service, Activity Recognition, Context Aware Computing, Automated Capturing of Live Experience and so on. The test bed (Aware Home) is also living test bed to provide real research data. Figure 2 shows the blueprint of Aware Home with its appearance.

Fig. 2. Picture of Aware Home and Cook's Collage Service

In this smart home, they also equipped with multi-type of sensors. For example, the kitchen has vision sensor and aids the process of cooking with tracking user's behavior as shown in figure 2.

3 Newly Proposed Smart Home

The CUS (Center of Excellence for Ubiquitous System) has also researched on the smart home (hereinafter CUS smart home) since middle of 2003 to provide comfortable and easy wellbeing life to users for coming Ubiquitous era. This chapter mainly focuses on the three components of developing smart home as stated earlier such as sensing infrastructure to get context information, method of making decision with collected sensing information and problems and answers that can be resolved with proposed system.

3.1 Overall Architecture of CUS Smart Home

Overview of CUS Smart Home. The CUS smart home consists of one bed room with one living room. The diverse research result of CUS is installed, deployed and evaluated through this test bed. The main purpose of this smart home is providing wellbeing life to user in Ubiquitous environment through intelligent service which is defined, selected and created by the smart system. To provide Ubiquitous intelligent services, the CUS smart home organizes as three different main components which are sensing infrastructure, intelligent self decision system, and Ubiquitous services. With sensing devices, the smart home is able to collect many different types of context and provide well defined information about home environment. The stable and diverse sensing infrastructure provides basic background knowledge for the intelligent decision making system to able to achieve high quality of situation aware. The intelligent decision making system of smart home which is called Community Computing [11][12] makes its own decisions about *"What the current situation is!"*, *"What type of service should be provided!"* and *"How to provide the services!"* Finally, the digital devices are installed to support the execution and providing of services. Figure 3 shows three steps of proving intelligent service and deployed equipment in the smart home. In this section, we examine three components briefly and suggest the services scenarios that might happen in Ubiquitous smart home.

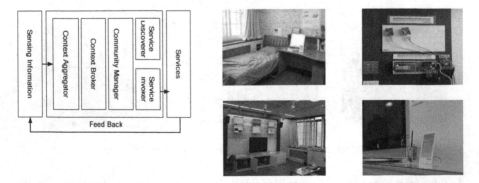

Fig. 3. Three Basic Steps for Implementing CUS Smart Home and Equipped Devices

3.2 Sensing Infrastructure

The sensing infrastructure is basic and inevitable components for Ubiquitous computing and has received much attention in many areas. In this paper, we focus on what type of information is required and how we can get them to support efficient decision through examine CUS smart home. Figure 4 shows the deployed sensors in our smart home.

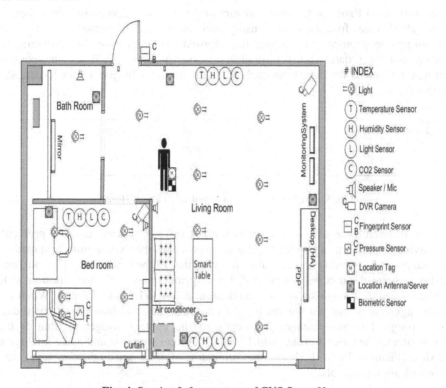

Fig. 4. Sensing Infrastructure of CUS Smart Home

Type of Sensing Information for Smart Home. To define the current situation, the environmental information such as temperature, humidity, light, noise, and quality of air is critical factor in any situation. The CUS smart home deploys these five types of sensing infrastructure and acquires stable information from them. Also, CUS smart home is able to understand the location of each object through two different types of location sensor. The first location system provides area level of location such as bed room, living room or door and the other system provides location of 'cm' level to support more precise information. Also, we deploy the biometric sensing device to get user's current physical state. This device detects user's body temperature, heart rate, blood pressure and so on. For explicit interface with user in the smart home, we develop mobile home pad to control any devices in the home and monitors the state of smart home with much more easy graphical interface. For authentication of user, the finger print device system is installed at the front door and voice recognition system is deployed. Finally, the home has smart bed which equipped with the 12 touch sensors on mattress. With these sensors, the system can figure out if user is sleeping in bed or not. We will go over the logic of defining user's sleeping in detail later. Consequently, we deploy 11 different types of sensing device to collect context information. This might not be enough to provide critical information to support making right decision of smart system. We still struggle to provide many different types of sensing information.

Communication Protocol between Sensors and Context Aggregator. Since there is no standard data formation of sensing information each sensor has its own communication protocol and unique data format. To overcome this problem we develop our own data packet formation as shown figure 5. When the context aggregator receives the data from each sensor it converts to given data format and process them.

1 Byte	1 Byte	1 Byte	1 Byte	1 Byte	7 Bytes	2 Byte
0xC8	Length	Sensor Class	Sensor Type	Sensor Id	Timestamp	Value

Fig. 5. Sensing Data Formation of CUS Smart Home

Also, different type of sensor devices utilizes different communication protocol. The environmental sensors utilize the Zigbee protocol as their communication method and the location sensing system also follows the Zigbee protocol. The pressure sensing system of smart bed, home pad, finger print, and voice information provide their information through socket communication either WLAN or Ethernt. When the context aggregator receives the sensing data it stores the information to its own data base through database manager and sends to the context widget to transfer the information to the context broker which defines current situation and make intelligent decision. Finally, Table 1 shows the summary of each sensing information and communication protocols.

Table 1. Deployed Sensing Type and its Communication Protocols in Smart Home

Category	Type	Communication Protocol	Function
Environment	Temperature Humidity CO2 Light Noise	Zigbee	Environmental Information
Location	Area Level	Zigbee	Location
	cm Level	UWB	Information
Situation	Pressure sensor	LAN	Sleeping Information
Interface	Home Pad	WLAN	Device Control
	Voice Recognition	LAN	
Biometric Information	Heart Rate Blood Pressure	LAN	Biometric Information
Authentication	Finger Print	LAN	Authentication

3.3 Situation-Aware and Creating Service Community by Community Computing

The main and critical factor of smart home is that how to define current situation and way to provide the intelligent services to the users. Our smart home defines the situation by utilizing acquired sensing information through the sensing devices. To define the current situation and select best smart services we develop the ***Community Computing Solution.*** Describing community solution in detail is not a purpose of this paper but we present basic concept of Community Computing briefly. In the Community Computing, the definition of Community can be stated as that *"a community is an abstract unit in developing process and a set of computing entities in execution environment for a fusion service"* which means the Community is that a collection of objects which struggle to provide their capabilities to resolve common problems or required services. Also, Community Template provides basic background of creating community as meta-level. By using Community Template the user or developer is able to define service list for specific situation. To setup the goal or which type of service they provide is closely based on defined situation. We develop the ***Context Broker*** which receives the sensing information from infrastructure, analyzes and defines what the current situation is. After defining current situation, the Context Broker reports the situation to the ***Community Manager.*** The main task of Community Manager is that sets up the service goal and creates community according to the given situation. Each devices, human, or any object can join the community if they are able to provide specific service to resolve common goal. Therefore Community Manager should figure out their capability any time and possibility if they can join the community. By creating community, the Community Manager defines the services that each member should provide for achieving common goal. In this process, the ***Service Discover*** and ***Service Invocator*** methods are implemented. In Community Computing, Community has five states of life cycle as shown at Figure 6 and next section describes the concept of each state briefly,

Fig. 6. Five States of Community Life Cycle

Community Life Cycle
Creation is a process to describe community by system designer or developer. The community is described as a language model which contains a goal description, relation situations, roles or task of members, cooperative methods, and service flows. The community has service types on the creation state and has members as available

services on the organization state. When some physical devices are not available, other devices in same types that can do the same function are recommended.

Organization is similar to instantiation process in the Object Oriented Model. Community manager searches available services which coincide with service types in the community template and admits the service to a member according to policies. After organizing, when new service or new device is discovered, the community may be reconstructed. This organizer can be implemented diverse methods.

Activation/Deactivation is related to achievement of permanent goal. If the permanent goal is fixing indoor temperature, members are not changed frequently. So, Activating/Deactivating community is more effect than organizing community whenever temperature gets out the critical temperature. We describe activation situation and goal situation in community template. When environment situation matches with activation situation, the state of community is activation while members in the community perform required actions. When environment situation matches with goal situation, the community is deactivated. However, higher priority community like emergency community can deactivate other activated community to manage resource even if the environment is not the deactivation situation.

Extermination is a process after achievement of temporal goal. When maintenance of community is not needed after achieving a goal, community is dissolved. Until activation situation becomes again, the community does not exist. The community execution is no more required, the community will be expired. The community no longer has references of community members.

3.4 Service List

Once the service is selected, the Community Manager invokes required service through service invocation method. In our smart home, we expose the service interface through soap protocol to service invocation components. Consequently, any

Table 2. The Service List of CUS Smart Home and Its Communication Protocols

Services	Functions	Communication Protocol
Light	On/Off Dimming Emotional Light	RS 232
Audio	*RCS	IR
TV	RCS	IR
Fan	RCS	IR
Air Cleaner	RCS	IR
Magic Mirror	Display Voice Recognition	IR
Heater/Stove	Heating	IR
Air Condition	Cooling	
Curtain	Open/Close	RS 232
Door	Open/Close	RS 232

*RMC: Remote Control Service

devices or components can implement our supported services. Basically, the automation system is provided with several communication protocols. Table 2 shows current the service list in our smart home as of May 2007 and controlling methods with communication protocols.

4 Intelligent Services for Ubiquitous Smart Home

We have described basic components that Ubiquitous Smart Home should have. In this section, we suggest three different service scenarios and its implementation through our system.

4.1 Replacing Malfunctioning Service

Problem. The air condition runs while a residence is watching TV. However, the air breaks down and can't keep cooling temperature any more.

Solution
Sensing Infrastructure. The system figures out that the user stays at Living room through deployed location sensors. When the user interacts with the mobile home pad to watch TV the signal is transferred to the Community Manager through context broker. With this process the system or community solution figures out the user's intention to watch TV and create TV Community.

Creation of Community. When the residence turns on the TV through mobile home pad, *TV Community* is created by Community Manager. As a result, the TV, emotional light and air join the community as community member and provide their own service to create best environment of TV watching.

Detecting Problem. The digital devices should reports their status periodically if they equip with the home network protocol. We assume any devices are equipped with the home network protocol and the community solution keeps receiving the *"Hello'* packet to figure out if the device works fine. When the air breaks down it can't send the *Hello* packet and the community solution understands one of the members doesn't work correctly.

Service Recovery and Intelligent Decision. When the Community Manager figures out the one of the member doesn't correctly it searches for alternative service through service discoverer which is described as meta-service. In this scenario, the service discoverer finds the fan in the living room and reports to the manager. After all, the manager makes the fan runs through service invocation. In our system, the web service is provided for communication methods between invoker and service provider which send control signal to final end devices.

4.2 Resolving Confliction of Services

Problem. A wife is sleeping while a husband is watching TV. The wife can't sleep well because the TV sound and light from living room.

Solution
Sensing Infrastructure. In the bed room where the wife sleeps at, environmental sensing infrastructure is deployed such as light and noise detection sensors. They keep reports current sensing information to the community solution system. Also, there is pressure sensor on bed and it detects the movement of wife while she stays.

Creation of Community. When a wife went to bed the system figures out that she trying to get sleep. The Community Manager creates *Sleep Community* and sets up the goal such as quiet and dark environment of bed room. Also, when the husband turns on the TV, the TV community is created by Community Manager. As a result, there are two communities in the house and the Community Manager tries to provide best services for both of them.

Detecting Problem. Because of the noise and light from living room the wife can't sleep well and she keeps moving on the bed. The different value pressure sensors are transferred to the system continuously and Community Manager understands that she can't fall asleep well.

Resolving Conflicts and Intelligent Decision. The Community Manager tries to find the reason of this situation through the sensing information. When the manager checks the noise and light sensing information of bed room it figures out the value of information exceeds the limitation of best sleeping environment. Now, the Manager looks for the source of noise and light all over the community currently created and finally finds that the TV sounds and lights of living room cause the problem. It is possible since the Community Manager manages and controls current status of devices in the house or all of the active communities. Since the Manager should provides best service for both of users it controls level of volume and lights little by little until both user are satisfied. So, the level of volume and light are decreased according to amount of movement of wife. We implemented following equation to achieve this situation and the level of them are strongly depends on the movement of wife.

$$\text{Movement} = (\{(\, n(A) - n(A')\,)\,/\,n(A)\,\} * 0.6) + \{(\, n(B)\,/\,(12 - n(A)) * 0.4)\} \quad (1)$$

In this equation, *A* represents the set of touched sensors at the first time, *B* represents the set of touched after moving, and *A'* represents the subset of A and touched after moving. With this equation we can find the amount of movement and the manager can control the lights of living room until she falls asleep.

4.3 Stress Index Based Service

Problem. After work, when the residence comes back home the smart home makes best environment for him to decrease his stress according to current situation index.

Solution. We developed the index based services which is called Wellbeing index based services. To achieve this goal, the system should always figures out about user's information such as biometric, event, and environment information. With utilizing this information, the system defines current situation of user as numerical stress value and provides appropriated service to decrease the stress.

Sensing Infrastructure. In our wellbeing index based system, the smart home needs to understand user's information not only his or her profile but also diverse type of information. Mainly, current system considers three different type of information of each user. First of all, user's biometric information is required. Secondly, the environmental information around user is another critical factor and final information is user's event of current days such as promotion or wedding. For the biometric information we deploy the biometric watch and this device collects the user's biometric information such as blood pressure, heart rate, blood pressure, ECG, in-exhale, and body temperature as long as he wears the watch. Also, the environmental information of home is absolutely considered which are temperature, humidity, noise, CO_2, and lights information. We can collect this information easily with our deployed sensing system. Finally, we have to consider the system should figures out the current event information but we can't detect this information automatically at this time. So we just assume the simulated event data.

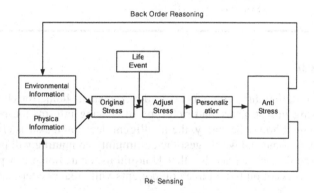

Fig. 7. Wellbeing Index Service Framework

Detecting Problem. Figure 7 shows the method or framework of defining current stress index. This framework utilizes environmental, biometric and life log of user to find the stress index and provides appropriate anti –stress service. This framework defines the original stress index with the found environmental and biometric sensing information as scale between one to three levels. The event score such as score of wedding, score of promotion, score of decease is considered to define the adjust index of stress. After define the final stress index the system personalizes this system based on the survey or feedback from user. As a result, the system always defines the user's current situation as numerical value and defines which service should provide.

Providing Anti-stress Services. After research on the anti-stress services we found the Music, Color, and Air service might help to decrease the stress. We apply this result on our wellbeing system and following tables shows anti-stress services for each stress level. In this scenario, the system plays classical music, emotional light and spray lilac scent.

Table 3. Anti-Stress Service for each Stress Level

Stress Level	Music	Color	Air
0	Slavonic March, Romance, Carmen	Blue, Grey, White, Brown, Green	Peppermint, Lemon Lavender
1	Requiem, Ave Maria, Auferstehung Symponie	Green, Purple, Blue, Red	Peppermint, Lemon Lavender, Rosemary
2	Requiem, Nacht und Traume Wiegenlied	Green, Purple, Blue, Red	Peppermint, Lavender, Rosemary
3	Requiem, Ave Maria, Jardins sous la pluie La Symphonie pastorale	Green, Purple, Blue,	Peppermint, Lavender, Lemon

5 Conclusion

In this paper, we define three components to develop smart home for Ubiquitous era. The smart sensing infrastructure and rich type of sensing information provide basic background of smart home. Secondly, the intelligent decision maker is critical factors and brain of smart home and we suggest the community computing will play this role, final factor is the diverse service list that Ubiquitous smart home can provide. Our research is still working on these three components will create better smart home for near future.

Acknowledgments. This research is supported by the Ubiquitous Computing and Network (UCN) Project, the Ministry of Information and Communication (MIC) 21st Centry Frontier R&D Program in Korea.

References

1. Weiser, M.: The Computer for the Twenty-First Century, Scientific America, pp. 10–94 (September 1991)
2. Yau, S., Karim, F., Wang, Y., Wang, B., Gupta, S.: Reconfigurable Context-Sensitive Middleware for Pervasive Computing. IEEE Pervasive Computing 1(3), 33–40 (2002)
3. In, H.P., Kim, C., Yau, S.: Q-Mar: An Adaptive Qos Management Model for Aware Middleware. In: Yang, L.T., Guo, M., Gao, G.R., Jha, N.K. (eds.) EUC 2004. LNCS, vol. 3207, pp. 972–981. Springer, Heidelberg (2004)

4. Pritchett, A.R., Hansman, R.J.: Use of Testable Responses for Performance based measurement of Situation Awareness. In: International Conference on Experimental Analysis and Measurement of Situation Awareness
5. Mini, R.A.F., Nath, B., Loureiro, A.A.F.: A Probabilistic Approach to Predict the Energy Consumption in Wireless Sensor Networks. In: IV Workshop de Comunicação sem Fio e Computação Móvel, São Paulo, Brazil (October 23-25, 2002)
6. Woo, A., Culler, D.E.: A Transmission Control Scheme for Media Access in Sensor Networks. In: The Seventh annual international conference on Mobile Computing and networking 2001, Rome, Italy, pp. 221–235 (July 16-21, 2001)
7. Shin, E., Cho, S.H., Ickes, N., Min, R., Sinha, A., Wang, A., Chandrakasan, A.: The Seventh annual international conference on Mobile Computing and networking 2001, Rome, Italy, pp. 272–287 (July 16-21, 2001)
8. Sohrabi, K., Gao, J., Ailawadhi, V., Pottie, G.J: Protocols for Self-Organization of a Wireless Sensor Network. IEEE Personal Communications 7(5), 16–27 (2000)
9. Intille, S., Larson, K., Beasudin, J., Munguia Tapia, E., Kaushik, P., Nawyn, J., McLeish, T.J.: The PlaceLab: a Live-in Laboratory for Pervasive Computing Research (viedo). In: Gellersen, H.-W., Want, R., Schmidt, A. (eds.) PERVASIVE 2005. LNCS, vol. 3468, Springer, Heidelberg (2005)
10. Kidd, C.D., Orr, R., Abowd, G.D., Atkeson, C.G., Essa, I.A., MacIntyre, B., Mynatt, E., Starner, T.E., Newstetter, W.: The Aware Home A Living Laboratory for Ubiquitous Computing Research
11. Sim, Y., Kim, H., Kim, M., Cho, W.D.: A Ubiquitous System Architecture based on the Community Computing. In: ICHIT 2006 (2006)

Instant Learning Sound Sensor: Flexible Real-World Event Recognition System for Ubiquitous Computing

Yuya Negishi and Nobuo Kawaguchi

Graduate School of Engineering, Nagoya University
1, Furo-Cho, Chikusa-ku, Nagoya, 464-8601, Japan
negishi@el.itc.nagoya-u.ac.jp, kawaguti@nagoya-u.jp

Abstract. We propose a smart sound sensor for building context-aware systems that instantly learn and detect events from various kinds of everyday sounds and environmental noise by using small and low-cost device. The proposed system automatically analyzes and selects an appropriate sound recognition process, using sample sounds and a parameter templates database in the event learning phase. A user is only required to input target event sounds from a microphone or sound files. Using the proposed sensor, the developer of ubiquitous service can easily utilize real world sounds as event triggers to control appliances or human's activity monitors for presence services without a signal processing programming.

1 Introduction

Context-aware systems are beginning to play an important role in supporting human activities. Various input devices such as accelerometers, pressure and temperature sensors, and GPS are used to input context information into systems. For example, small network devices with these sensors have been developed (MOTE[1] Smart-Its[3]) and used to build a smart room. A health care system that senses a user's actions such as washing hands and taking a shower has been proposed by Jianfeng Chen[6]. Paul Lukowicz[10] proposed an activity sensing system for workshops that uses a microphone and accelerometers worn on the body. There has also been some research on systems that use signal processing with time series data from sensors like microphones and accelerometers that shows this kind of processing is useful in obtaining rich context information[7][8]. However, designing the recognition algorithm for a complex signal pattern is not easy because analyzing feature quantity requires a lot of time, and in the ubiquitous environment, it is assumed that there are many sensing targets.

We propose an instant learning sensor that can learn signal patterns instantly using a small inexpensive device. The proposed sensor can record and learn the time series signal pattern that a user wants to detect as an event. The instant learning sensor has the following three features.

(1) **Instant Learning:** On the sensor installation site, the sensor can instantly learn a signal pattern by user's demonstration of a target event. The

H. Ichikawa et al. (Eds.): UCS 2007, LNCS 4836, pp. 72–85, 2007.

system automatically analyzes the recorded signal and chooses the most appropriate algorithm to extract feature quantity. This enables the user to build context-aware systems without signal processing programming.

(2) Smart Sensor: The sensor can process the signal by itself. It can also cooperate easily with other devices or context-aware systems.

(3) Simple Device: The sensor can be implemented on low-cost devices such as microcontrollers. So, we aim as much as possible at light processing. To make the device simple, we think a sensor only has to be able to recognize a few events and specialize in specific events that reduce the size of the memory and processing power.

We believe our instant learning sensor can simplify building of an advanced ubiquitous service that function as event notifiers. For example, in systems like eBlocks [12], that can easily construct smart environments simply by connecting block devices, instant learning sensors can be used as event triggers for control of appliances. They can be also used for more detailed sensing of peoplesf activities when they are embedded into mobile phones or smart rooms and buildings.

We focus on instant learning and describe the prototype of the instant learning sensor, which can recognize environmental sounds and sounds made by humans and machines. Sound has very rich context information. We designed and implemented an instant learning sound sensor, which we embedded in a PC, and an inexpensive DSP microcontroller using a cheap piezoelectric device as a microphone.

2   Contributions

Obtaining information from the real world is one of the most important issues in ubiquitous computing. Current research on connecting the real and digitized worlds focuses mostly on specialized devices or algorithms for each type of real world event. However, there are an enormous number of types of real world events that must be recognized by these specialized devices or algorithms. It is almost impossible to cover all of these events by studying them one by one.

We propose an instant learning sound sensor built on an inexpensive device. Sound is one of the most rich context media. We believe that most real-world activities such as walking, opening and closing doors, using a vacuum cleaner, watching TV, pouring tea, and bathroom activities can be recognized merely by using the smart sound sensor. Of course, some of these events are easily recognized by sensing devices such as mechanical switches or motion detectors. However, we think it is costly and bothersome to develop a device or method for each event. Our smart sound sensor is a single inexpensive device, is very flexible, and has a wide range of applications, such as do-it-yourself smart spaces and rapid prototyping of context-aware systems.

The main contributions of this paper are summarized as follows.

(1) Proposing a simple sensor, which can only recognize a few sounds. This enables sound recognition in a low-cost device with less processing power and memory. If user wants to recognize several events, just use several sensors.

(2) Consideration of on-site configuration of sensing algorithms and parameters. This enables a single device to be flexibly utilized.

3   Signal Processing

3.1   Light-Weight Sound Recognition Process

In this section, as an example of a light process for everyday sound recognition process, we describe signal processing using DP matching.

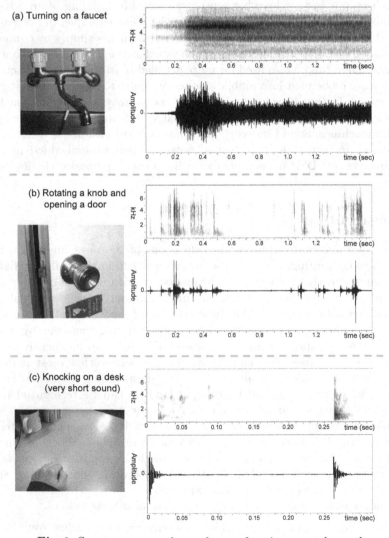

Fig. 1. Spectrograms and waveforms of environmental sound

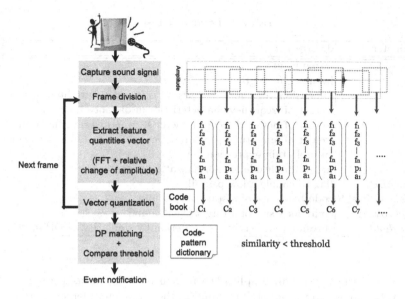

Fig. 2. Basic sound recognition process

A lot of speech recognition system use speech spectra such as mel-cepstrum or liner prediction coefficients (LPC) to extract feature quantities. We use a case study to discuss the signal processing for everyday sound recognition.

Figure 1 shows examples of waveforms and spectrograms of target sounds. First, we considered appropriate feature quantities for recognition of a sound. As can be seen in these figures, there are individual characteristics in each sound. Sound (a) in Figure 1 has a characteristic constant frequency over time. Sound (b) has a characteristic change of amplitude over time. Therefore, we think feature quantity should include not only frequency but amplitude characteristics. It is also be necessary to adjust weights between feature quantities for each target sound.

We designed a basic sound recognition process that calculates the similarity between an input sound and a target event sound using DP matching (dynamic programming matching[5], dynamic time warping[2]) about a change in frequency and amplitude characteristics. The process has some flexibility parameters. It can adjust weights between feature quantities and has options such as whether to enable a low pass filter. Figure 2 shows the overview of a recognition process, and Table 1 shows a list of parameters.

(1) First, it divides inputted waveform into frames. The length of each frame is F_{length} points, and the shift length is F_{shift} points.

(2) Second, in each frame, it extracts feature quantity vectors, calculates power spectra using fast Fourier transform (FFT), divides it equally to N_v sections, calculates the average of each section, and normalizes by maximum power. The range of each element is $0.0 \sim 1.0$. In addition to these N_v elements, it adds an amount of the change of power by the following expression as the $(N_v + 1)$th

Table 1. Parameter List

parameter	description
F_{length}	frame length
F_{shift}	frame shift length
N_v	dimension of frequency characteristics in feature quantity vector
W_f	weight of frequency characteristics in distance function
W_p	weight of power change characteristics in distance function
W_a	weight of amplitude characteristics in distance function
L	variable L in expression (1)
A_{max}	upper amplitude for normalization
$EnableLPF$	flag to enable a low pass filter
$CodebookSize\_S$	code book size of a stationary sound
$CodebookSize\_T$	code book size of a target event sound
$Threshold$	threshold for acceptance criterion by similarity of DP matching

element, and the maximum amplitude value in each frame as the $(N_v + 2)$th element. L is a constant number. The range of the (N_v+1)th element is $0.0 \sim 1.0$, and the range of the $(N_v + 1)$th element is $0.0 \sim 1.0$ using upper value A_{max}. Each feature quantity vector has a total of $N_v + 2$ elements.

$$Vec(N_v + 1) = \frac{Power_{max}(n) - Power_{max}(n-1)}{L} \quad (1)$$

(3) Third, it changes the vectors to code array using vector quantization[11] with a code book of target sound and a following distance function. In the expression, W_f is a weight for frequency characteristic, W_p is a weight for the amount of change in power, and W_a is an amplitude characteristic.

$$dis(v_1, v_2) = W_f \times dist_f(v_1, v_2) + W_p \times dist_p(v_1, v_2) + W_a \times dis_a(v_1, v_2) \quad (2)$$

$$dis_f(v_1, v_2) = \sum_{k=1}^{Nv}(v_1(k) - v_2(k))^2 \quad (3)$$

$$dis_p(v_1, v_2) = (v_1(N_{v+1}) - v_2(N_{v+1}))^2 \quad (4)$$

$$dis_a(v_1, v_2) = (v_1(N_{v+2}) - v_2(N_{v+2}))^2 \quad (5)$$

(4) Finally, using DP matching, it calculates the similarity between the inputted code pattern and one of the target event sounds. Then, it compares the similarity with the threshold for detection judgment.

These are processed in real time every F_{shift} points. The code book and code pattern of the target event sound are made in advance.

3.2   Parameter Configuration

Table 2 shows examples of manual configuration for the sounds in Figure 1. As is the case in Table 2, we think the configurations of the parameters should contain

Table 2. Example of parameter configurations

parameter name	sound (a)	sound (b)	sound (c)
F_{length}	256	128	512
F_{shift}	60	30	120
N_v	16	12	32
W_f	1.0	0.4	0.5
W_p	0	0	0.5
W_a	0	0.6	0
L	-	-	120.0
A_{max}	-	30000	-
$EnableLPF$	false	false	false
$CodebookSize\_S$	2	4	4
$CodebookSize\_T$	4	16	16

fewer vector dimensions and less codebook size for light processing and require less memory.

Our aim is to automatically generate a recognition program for unknown everyday events. This requires a search for specific and appropriate parameter configuration for each target event sounds. Therefore, we designed a method of flexibly configuring the feature quantities to select a proper set for the target sound. In the next section, we describe this flexible configuration method.

4 Design of Instant Learning Sound Sensor

4.1 System Architecture

We designed an instant learning sound sensor to have two modes (Figure 3).

(1) Event Learning Mode: In this mode, the system analyzes a target event sound that is inputted by a user, and automatically selects a specific parameter configuration. Then, it makes a codebook and code pattern dictionary for the target sound.

(2) Event Detection Mode: In this mode, the system monitors a target event sound and notifies other systems via a network if the event is detected.

The proposed system consists of the following two components.

(1) Sensor Configurator: This software supports the event-learning mode and has a function to install the selected recognition process and configuration in sensor devices.

(2) Sound Sensor Device: This is a device that runs the sound recognition process in event detection mode.

To simplify the sensor device, we implemented the sensor configurator in a powerful computer such as a PC.

As a microphone, we chose a piezoelectric device. This device is very cheap small and thin, so it can also be attached to almost any kind of object, for

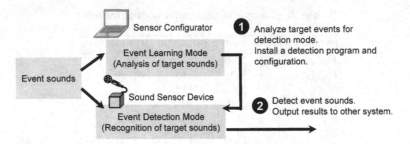

Fig. 3. System Overview

example a wall, a desk, a cup, a faucet, a book, a telephone, or a trash can. Generally, it is said that sound sensing using a microphone is easily disrupted by environmental noise and human speech. However, because a piezoelectric device is a contact sensor, we don't use noise-reduction process in current system.

4.2   Sample Sounds and Parameter Templates Database

In section3.2, we mentioned the need for specific parameter configurations for each event sound. The most naive configuration method is to try all combinations of parameters, but this takes a very long time. Therefore, we collected various environmental and everyday sounds as samples and built a sample sounds database that uses sample sounds and corresponding parameter configurations as templates. The template is an appropriate set of parameters for the light recognition process and is made in advance by such as a full search. In the event learning mode, the sensor configurator utilizes the templates of similar sample sounds with a target event for parameter configurations.

4.3   Instant Learning

The sensor configurator processes the event-learning mode using the sample sounds and parameter templates database. Figure 4 shows the process.

(1) The user inputs a target event sound, then the sensor configurator calculates similarities between sample sound in terms of frequency (sim_f) and amplitude (sim_a) characteristics using the following expressions.

$$sim(s_{sample}, s_{target}) = sim_f(s_{sample}, s_{target}) \times sim_a(s_{sample}, s_{target}) \quad (6)$$

sim_f is the similarity between two N dimension frequency characteristic vectors of amount of change in power on each band in the whole. It uses the vector space model[4].

$$sim_f(s_{sample}, s_{target}) = \frac{\sum_{n=1}^{N} u(n)w(n)}{\sqrt{\sum_{n=1}^{N} u(n)^2 \sum_{n=1}^{N} w(n)^2}} \quad (7)$$

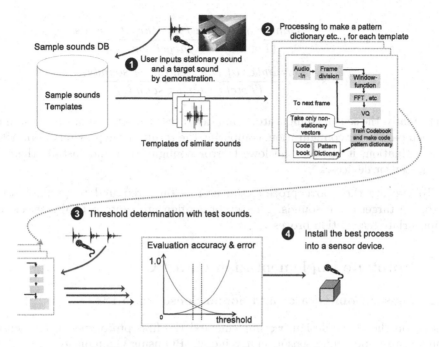

Fig. 4. Process in Event-Learning Mode

sim_a is a similarity between two time series changes of amplitude, using DP matching cost($dtwCost$).

$$sim_a(s_{sample}, s_{target}) = \frac{1}{dtwCost(s_{sample}, s_{target}) + 1} \qquad (8)$$

Both similarities are normalized, so the range of $sim(s_{sample}, s_{target})$ is 0.0 ∼ 1.0. The bigger value means more similar.

(2) Second, the sensor configurator sorts all sample sounds according to their similarities, and selects some templates corresponding to superior sample sounds. Then, based on parameter configurations of selected templates, it makes code books using the LBG algorithm[13] and code pattern dictionaries of target sounds. In the prototype, the sensor configurator tries four templates.

(3) Third, the sensor configurator determines the threshold of cost in DP matching in each parameter configuration. Using target event sounds and non-target sounds, it gets the DP matching set of costs for both target and non-target sounds. The threshold is determined by the following two expressions. $P(S|n)$ is the rate of true detection when non-target sounds are inputted, and $P(N|s)$ is the rate of false detection when target sounds are inputted. The relation between the two expressions and the threshold is shown in Figure 4-(3). As can be seen in Figure 4-(3), the best threshold is estimated at around the point where $P(S|n) = P(N|s)$. For non-target sounds, it uses other sample sounds in the database.

$$P(S|n) = \frac{(Number\ of\ accepted\ non\ target\ sounds)}{(Total\ of\ non\ target\ sounds)} \tag{9}$$

$$P(N|s) = \frac{(Number\ of\ rejected\ target\ sounds)}{(Total\ of\ target\ sounds)} \tag{10}$$

(4) Finally, the sensor configurator evaluates rates of accepted non-target sounds in each parameter configuration, comparing the result of the previous step. After the evaluation, it chooses the lowest error configuration and installs them in sound sensor devices.

To execute the above process, the user is only required to prepare some recorded target event sounds. The sensor configurator automatically selects an appropriate recognition process.

5 Prototype Implementation on a PC

5.1 Sensor Configurator and Sound Sensor on a PC

Based on the above design, we implemented the first prototypes of the sensor configurator and sound sensor on a Windows PC using C language.

Sensor Configurator. Figure 5 is a screenshot of the sensor configurator. The user simply (1) prepare recorded target event sounds as WAVE files, (2) drag & drop them to the sensor configurator, and (3) push the learning button with automatic template selections and evaluations. In this prototyping, the sampling frequency is 12-16 kHz, and there are 16 sampling bits.

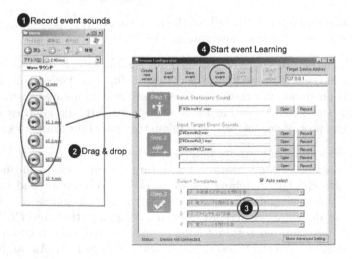

Fig. 5. Screenshot of Sensor Configurator

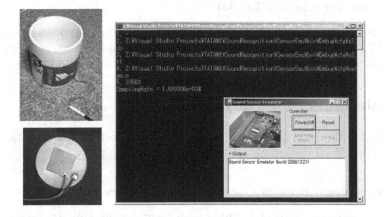

Fig. 6. Screenshot of Sound Sensor on PC

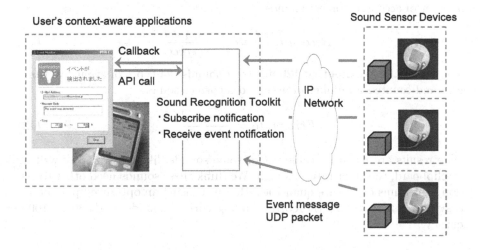

Fig. 7. Example of useage of Sound Recognition Toolkit

For the sample sounds and parameter templates database, we collected 30 events, each with about 50 sounds, for a total of about 1500 sounds. In this implementation, we adjusted parameter templates of sample sounds as light as possible by our hands. As a way of recording sounds, we attached a piezoelectric device to objects like Figure 1 and 6, then we repeated actions and captured event sounds. Table 3 lists examples of recorded sample sounds.

Sound Sensor. Figure 6 is a screenshot of the sound sensor and a photo of an attached piezoelectric device on a coffee cup. On target event detection, it can send notification UDP packets to other systems through an IP network.

5.2 Sound Recognition Toolkit

We also developed a communication API library with the sound sensors on PCs via the Windows DLL IP network. A user's program can receive callback when event sounds are detected. This library can be used as shown in Figure 7.

6 Evaluation of Instant Learning

We evaluated the recognition rate of the proposed instant learning methods, using the prototype system on a PC.

6.1 Recognition Rate of Optimized Parameters in Templates

Before evaluating the instant learning with several event sounds, we evaluated the sound recognition processes with optimized templates as discussed below.

(1) Recognition rate: We inputted about 50 correct event sounds and counted a number of accepted correct sounds.

$$Recognition\ rate = \frac{accepted}{correct} \tag{11}$$

(2) Error rate: We inputted 120 incorrect sounds (24 types of event five times each), and counted a number of accepted incorrect sounds.

$$Error\ rate = \frac{accepted}{incorrect} \tag{12}$$

The results are listed in Table 3. For some sounds, like the sound of writing on a clipboard, the error rate was high. We think these sounds need other recognition algorithms or feature quantities. However, using an optimized parameter, the system can recognize the corresponding correct sounds, with 80 to 100% accuracy.

6.2 Recognition Rate of Unknown Event Sounds

Next, we evaluated the accuracy of the recognition process automatically generated by instant learning system.

(1) Removing four types of sample sounds and templates from the sample sounds database, we inputted those types of event sounds to the sensor configurator and got each recognition process.

(2) Using automatically generated recognition processes, we inputted about 50 correct sounds and 120 incorrect sounds and measured recognition and error rates, as in the previous evaluation.

The results are listed in Table 4. As with the optimized templates, the recognition rates are over 83%, meaning the system can recognize correct events sounds well.

Table 3. Results of evaluation with optimized templates

Event	Recognition rate	Error Rate
1. Turning on a faucet	100.0%	0.0%
2. Closing a sliding door	100.0%	1.7%
3. Closing door of refrigerator	100.0%	2.5%
4. Opening a window shade	100.0%	15.8%
5. Rotating a knob and opening a door	88.9%	0.0%
6. Pouring out tea	86.8 %	5.0%
7. Putting a phone down	86.4%	5.8%
8. Writing on a clipboard	85.6%	65.8%
9. Opening a drawer	83.3%	0.0%
10. Inserting a plug in an outlet	83.3%	0.0%

Table 4. Results for instant learning

Event	Recognition rate	Error Rate
1. Typing on a keyboard	100.0%	35.0%
2. Opening a window shade	96.9%	0.0%
3. Writing on a clipboard	85.6%	35.8%
4. Opening a drawer	83.3%	1.7%

These results show that our proposed method is useful for choosing automatically specific and appropriate parameters for environmental and everyday sounds.

7   Sound Sensor on Small and Low Cost Device

In the next step, we implemented the second prototype sound sensor device on a Microchip dsPIC[9] to evaluate its feasibility on a small inexpensive device.

In this prototype on the DSP microcontroller, we use a Microchip dsPIC30F60 14A with 8 KB Data RAM and a Silicon Laboratories Si3000 codec chip with 12 KHz sampling frequency and 16 sampling bits. We also used a SENA Parani ESD200 Bluetooth communication module for event notification. Figure 8 is a photo of the prototype sensor board. To program target event sound recognition processes to microcontrollers, a user can use codebooks, code pattern dictionaries, and parameter configurations header files for dsPIC C compliers converted by the sensor configurator.

For real-time recognition, the system needs to complete per-frame works within $FrameShiftLength/SamplingFrequency$ (= 5 msec). For example, a specific configuration of the sound recognition process of (a) turning on a faucet, shown in Figure 1, is (a) in Table 2. In this example configuration, we confirmed that per-frame work can be done in an average of $3.49 msec$, with 58.94MHz (14.74MIPS) system clock and 60 code pattern length. The required RAM size can also come to less than 4KB of memory use. The total code size including

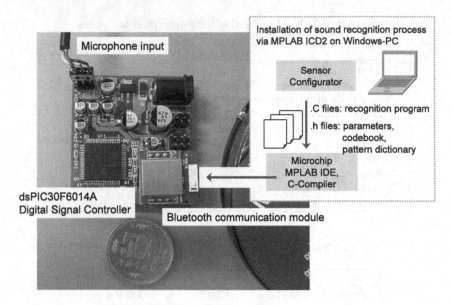

Fig. 8. Prototype of Sound Sensor Device with dsPIC

codebook, and pattern dictionary, is about 10 KB. We also confirmed real-time recognition for the sound of opening a drawer using this device.

This implementation demonstrates the feasibility of the small inexpensive instant learning sound sensor.

8   Conclusion

In this paper, we describe the design and implementation of an instant learning sound sensor that makes it easy to build a context-aware system using sound recognition. The proposed learning sensor can instantly learn and detect target event sounds such as everyday sounds and environmental noise. The sensor configurator automatically analyzes target event sounds and chooses the most appropriate feature quantities and parameter configuration for high recognition rate and light processing using sample sounds and parameter templates DB. Therefore, using the instant learning sensor, a user can build context-aware systems that utilize real world sound as rich context information, without signal processing programming. Users can also easily integrate the sound recognition function with their systems as event notifiers. We have confirmed that the recognition process in this prototype system can run on a small and low cost device.

In future work, we are currently working on design and implementation of small networked instant learning sound sensor devices, and considering a sensor fusion method to treat complicated sounds. We will support more kinds of feature quantities and algorithms for various sounds recognition, and collect more sample sounds and templates. Furthermore, we will extend an instant learning method to the other sensors such as accelerometer.

References

1. Crossbow Technology, MOTE, http://www.xbow.com/
2. Myers, C.S., Rabiner, L.R.: A comparative study of several dynamic time-warping algorithms for connected word recognition. IEEE Trans. on ASSP 26(3), 351–363 (1981)
3. Tapia, E.M., Intille, S.S., Lopez, L., Larson, K.: The design of a portable kit of wireless sensors for naturalistic data collection, Pervasive 2006, pp. 117–134 (2006)
4. Salton, G., Wong, A., Yang, C.S.: A vector space model for automatic indexing. Communications of the ACM 18(11), 613–620 (1975)
5. Sakoe, H., Chiba, S.: A Dynamic Programming Algorithm Optimization for Spoken Word Recognition. IEEE Trans. on ASSP 26(27), 43–49 (1978)
6. Chen, J., Kam, A.H., Zhang, J., Liu, N., Shue, L.: Bathroom Activity Monitoring Based on Sound, Pervasive 2005, pp. 47–61 (2005)
7. Bao, L., Intille, S.S.: Activity Recognition from User-Annotated Acceleration Data, Pervasive 2004, pp. 1–17 (2004)
8. Ma, L., Smith, D., Milner, B.: Environmental Noise Classification for Context-Aware Applications, Database and Expert Systems Applications, pp. 360–370 (2003)
9. Microchip Technology Inc, dsPIC Digital Signal Controllers, http://www.microchip.com
10. Lukowicz, P., Ward, J.A., Junker, H., Stager, M., Troster, G., Atrash, A., Starner, T.: Recognizing Workshop Activity Using Body Worn Microphones and Accelerometers, Pervasive 2004, pp. 18–32 (2004)
11. Gray, R.M.: Vector Quantization. IEEE ASSP Magazine 1, 4–29 (1984)
12. Cotterell, S., Mannion, R., Vahid, F., Hsieh, H.: eBlocks - An Enabling Technology for Basic Sensor Based Systems, IPSN Track on Sensor Platform, Tools and Design Methods for Networked Embedded Systems, SPOTS (2005)
13. Linde, Y., Buzo, A., Gray, R.M.: An Algorithm for Vector Quantizer Design. IEEE Trans. on Comm 28(1), 84–95 (1980)

D-FLER – A Distributed Fuzzy Logic Engine for Rule-Based Wireless Sensor Networks

Mihai Marin-Perianu and Paul Havinga

University of Twente, Enschede, The Netherlands
{m.marinperianu,p.j.m.havinga}@utwente.nl

Abstract. We propose D-FLER, a distributed, general-purpose reasoning engine for WSN. D-FLER uses fuzzy logic for fusing individual and neighborhood observations, in order to produce a more accurate and reliable result. Thorough simulation, we evaluate D-FLER in a fire-detection scenario, using both fire and non-fire input data. D-FLER achieves better detection times, while reducing the false alarm rate. In addition, we implement D-FLER on real sensor nodes and analyze the memory overhead, the numerical accuracy and the execution time.

1 Introduction

Initially perceived as a cost-effective method for monitoring large geographical areas in detail, Wireless Sensor Networks (WSN) exhibit today a rapidly increasing uptake in various industrial and business-related fields [20]. There are two main reasons for this trend. First, the comprehensive set of features (digital I/O, storage and processing, wireless communication) available on current sensor nodes makes the term "intelligent sensor" real to the industrial automation community. Second, WSN are self-organizing, collaborative networks, capable of executing logic in a distributed way, at the point of action. This is a desirable property because it decreases the load on the back-end system [12] and improves the overall reliability and responsiveness. There are, however, several important challenges in this regard. The sensor nodes have limited resources and usually execute only simple logic, such as concise *business rules* [20]. This may lead to erroneous decisions in the presence of inaccurate or faulty sensors. Sensor data fusion techniques can reduce the errors, but also require complex computations that sensor nodes cannot handle, or prior information that is infeasible to obtain practically [15].

In this paper, we explore fuzzy logic as an alternative solution to these problems. The field of fuzzy logic has been developing for more than forty years, with many successful applications in diverse areas as automotive industry, artificial intelligence, medicine, behavioral science, just to mention some [11]. Fuzzy inference systems (FIS) match two of the most challenging requirements of WSN: (1) they are simple and can be executed on limited hardware, and (2) tolerate imprecise, unreliable data. In addition, FIS have several properties that are less mentioned in the WSN literature, but are equally important from a practical point of view. First, fuzzy logic can reduce the development time compared

H. Ichikawa et al. (Eds.): UCS 2007, LNCS 4836, pp. 86–101, 2007.

with other techniques. In Bayesian calculus for example, prior probabilities need to be acquired by means of a statistical analysis requiring massive amounts of data [15]. With fuzzy logic, it is possible to have a running system by using only an intuitive, common-sense description of the problem. Second, fuzzy logic is flexible; it can be built on top of the expert knowledge, mixed with conventional control methods and easy to add or change functionality. Third, FIS are computationally fast [15], which is important because the processing capabilities of sensor nodes are limited. Fourth, FIS can be implemented with little memory overhead, which is a desirable property in WSN because of (1) the limited memory on the sensor nodes and (2) the latency of the network reprogramming. Finally, FIS, potentially combined with neural networks, are adaptive, i.e. can be trained with examples or can learn at runtime from feedback.

To the extent of our knowledge, there is little research effort in the field of WSN that involves fuzzy logic. In this paper, we make a step forward and propose a lightweight, distributed fuzzy logic engine operating with simple IF-THEN rules applied over both the individual sensor readings and the neighborhood observations. We choose event detection (more precisely, fire detection) as an application example to evaluate our approach compared with conventional crisp logic methods. We believe that many other practical WSN applications can benefit from using a distributed inference engine, capable of fusing multi-sensor, multi-node unreliable information, in order to produce a more reliable result.

2 Related Work

Previous research has also considered the idea of reasoning engines for embedded devices. Cooperative Artefacts [23], for example, can autonomously reason about their situation by means of an inference engine based on a Prolog interpreter. The functionality of the interpreter is however limited, since it has to run on resource-poor sensor nodes. An application specific virtual machine, such as Maté [19], offers more flexibility for programming WSN, but at the price of significant overhead. The ubiquitous chip [14] is an event-driven I/O control device based on ECA (Event, Condition, Action) rules. A similar model is used by the business rules for sensor nodes [20], which are designed to express service-oriented business logic in a compact way. Compared to these examples, a fuzzy logic inference engine has the advantage of preserving the simplicity of rule-based logic, while handling unreliable and imprecise numeric information.

3 D-FLER

In this section we describe D-FLER, a distributed rule-based fuzzy logic engine designed for collaborative WSN. We start with a short overview of general fuzzy logic systems and than present the detailed design of D-FLER.

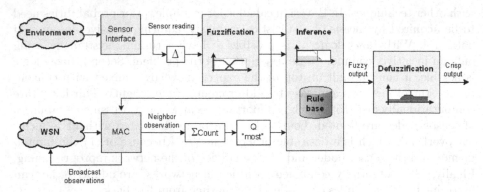

Fig. 1. D-FLER structure

3.1 Overview of Fuzzy Logic

Fuzzy logic systems are in general non-linear input-output mappings [21]. FIS operate with fuzzy sets, which extend the ordinary notion of crisp sets. A fuzzy set F is characterized by a membership function $\mu_F(x)$, which gives the degree of similarity of x to F. An important consequence is that FIS are universal approximators, capable of approximating any continuous function with an arbitrary bound ϵ. In engineering, the most widely used are the rule-based FIS. These systems are composed of four basic components. First, the *fuzzifier* maps crisp inputs into fuzzy sets by using the membership functions. Second, the fuzzified values activate the *rules*, which are provided by experts or extracted from numerical data. The rules are expressed as a collection of IF-THEN statements, having fuzzy propositions as antecedents and consequences. Third, the *fuzzy inference engine* combines the rules to obtain an aggregated fuzzy output. Finally, the *defuzzifier* maps the fuzzy output back to a crisp number that can be used for making decisions or control actions.

3.2 D-FLER Design

WSN usually try to compensate the resource limitations and the lack of reliability through cooperative algorithms, which exploit the high density of nodes deployed. This is why FIS for WSN have to go distributed and embed collaborative mechanisms of reasoning on the observed data and taking decisions or actions in a coordinated manner.

Following this idea, D-FLER uses two types of inputs: individual observations (sensor readings of the current node) and neighborhood observations (fuzzified sensor data from the neighboring nodes). Fig. 1 illustrates how D-FLER fuses these inputs. We distinguish the following main operations:

1. *Fuzzification of individual observations.* D-FLER obtains the sensor readings from the sensor interface of the current node. Both the sensor raw values and

their differential variations Δ are fuzzified through the predefined membership functions. The fuzzified values are scheduled for being broadcast within the local neighborhood by the MAC layer.

2. *Quantification of neighborhood observations.* When receiving neighborhood observations over the radio, the MAC layer forwards them to D-FLER. Then, D-FLER updates the *sigma-count* factor [24], which is formally defined as

$$\sum Count(F) = \sum_i \mu_F(x_i) \qquad (1)$$

where $X = \{x_1, ..., x_n\}$ is the set of neighbors and F is a property of interest related to their observations, e.g. "smoke level is high".

Optionally, the neighborhood observations can be given weighting factors based on the confidence of each neighbor (e.g. given by the precision of its sensors, distance from the event observed, past accuracy computed as false alarm and rejection rates, etc.). In this case, we have a *weighted sigma-count*

$$\sum Count(F; w) = \sum_i w_i \mu_F(x_i) \qquad (2)$$

The neighborhood observations are eventually characterized through a fuzzy majority *quantifier*, such as *most* [18]

$$\mu_{most}\left(\frac{\sum Count(F)}{|X|}\right) = \mu_{most}\left(\frac{\sum_i \mu_F(x_i)}{n}\right) \qquad (3)$$

where

$$\mu_{most}(x) = \begin{cases} 0 & \text{if } x \leq 0.3; \\ 2x - 0.6 & \text{if } 0.3 < x < 0.8; \\ 1 & \text{if } x \geq 0.8. \end{cases} \qquad (4)$$

The *most* quantifier gives a fuzzified indication of the consensual neighborhood opinion that the current node can add to its own observations, in order to take a more accurate decision. However, the decision of the node is not fed back into the neighborhood, in order to avoid an artificial increase of confidence due to ping-pong effects.

3. *Inference.* In addition to conventional fuzzy inference, the D-FLER rules incorporate both the fuzzified individual observations and the quantified neighborhood observations. Such a "distributed" rule has the following structure

$$\text{IF } s_1 \text{ is } F_{i_1} \text{ AND } s_2 \text{ is } F_{i_2} \text{ AND } ... s_p \text{ is } F_{i_p} \text{ AND}$$
$$Q\, n_1 \text{ is } F_{j_1} \text{ AND } Q\, n_2 \text{ is } F_{j_2} \text{ AND}... Q\, n_q \text{ is } F_{j_q}$$
$$\text{THEN } o \text{ is } G \qquad (5)$$

where s_i are fuzzified sensor readings, n_j are neighborhood observations, Q is the majority quantifier, o is the output, F_{i_k, j_l} and G are input and output fuzzy sets, respectively.

Considering the fire detection example (see Sec. 4), a rule can be written as

$$\text{IF } Smoke \text{ is } High \text{ AND } Temp \text{ is } Low \text{ AND}$$
$$most(SmokeNeigh) \text{ is } High \text{ AND } most(TempNeigh) \text{ is } High$$
$$\text{THEN } FireDecision \text{ is } High \qquad (6)$$

During the inference process, several rules are activated and contribute to the combined fuzzy output. Optionally, the combination of rules can be weighted according to the degree of belief to each rule, if such information is available.

4. *Defuzzification.* The last phase, defuzzification, produces a crisp output computed using one of the common methods: maximum, mean of maxima, centroid, etc.

In addition to these operations, D-FLER can be trained and can learn at runtime if feedback is available. To achieve this, two parameters can be adjusted:

- The confidence of each neighbor in the *weighted sigma-count* factor. For example, nodes that constantly report observations in contrast with the right decision will receive a lower weight in the result of the quantification.
- The importance of each rule in the inference process. For example, after training, the rules contributing to correct decisions will be assigned a larger weight in forming the combined fuzzy output.

4   Application Example - Fire Detection

We propose large-scale fire detection as an application example for evaluating D-FLER. The potential usage of WSN for real-time fire detection and firefighting assistance is currently under investigation in several research projects [2,3]. Advanced fire detection algorithms consider distributed sensing as an alternative for improving time to alarm over single-station detectors [6]. In addition, comprehensive experiments show that the use of combined sensors [9] (e.g. smoke and CO) can significantly reduce the false alarm rate, while increasing sensitivity (i.e., decreasing the detection time for real fires). Since fuzzy logic systems can fuse naturally multi-sensor data, they appear as a promising solution for robust fire detection algorithms [7].

In this paper, we show that a distributed FIS, running within the WSN, can improve the overall detection time and reliability, while providing better coverage for monitoring large hazardous areas. We utilize as input data the fire tests carried on by Bukowski et al. [13] to evaluate the performance of modern residential alarms. Both the fire and non-fire (i.e., nuisance alarms) test data is publicly available on the NIST website and well documented. We consider four representative tests: two fire scenarios (flaming mattress and flaming chair) and two nuisance scenarios (fried hamburgers and toasted bagel halves). For the fire scenarios, we follow the temperature and smoke data for approximately one minute after the moment of ignition. Similarly, for the nuisance scenarios, we follow the temperature and smoke data for approximately one minute around the time when the smoke alarms used in the tests reach medium alarm thresholds.

In Fig. 2 we plot two example data sets for a fire and a nuisance scenario, respectively. Fig. 2(a) and 2(b) show the temperature and smoke data for the first fire test used in our simulations (test SDC05 - flaming mattress in bedroom [13]). The ignition takes place at time 0. We notice that the temperature increases much slower than the smoke level, which raises abruptly after 5s and reaches

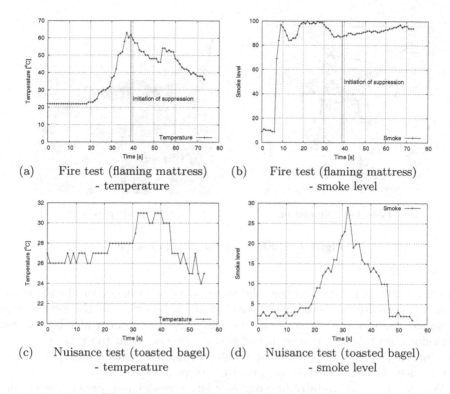

(a)   Fire test (flaming mattress)   (b)   Fire test (flaming mattress)
              - temperature   - smoke level

(c)   Nuisance test (toasted bagel)   (d)   Nuisance test (toasted bagel)
              - temperature   - smoke level

Fig. 2. Example of fire and nuisance test data

a maximum at 9s. However, the temperature has also to be monitored for a reliable detection because smoke can also occur in the case of a failed ignition. The temperature starts to raise quickly after 29s and reaches a maximum at 38s, right before the initiation of suppression.

Fig. 2(c) and 2(d) show the temperature and smoke sample data for the second nuisance test used in our simulations (test MHN20 - two frozen bagel halves toasted [13]). During this test, the frozen bagels were toasted to a medium brown color and did not char significantly. We notice an approximately 5°C rise in temperature, with a peak between 32s and 40s. Similarly, the smoke level increases to a peak level until 32s. After stopping the toaster, the conditions come back to normal at approximately 48s.

The sensor nodes are assumed to sample the temperature and smoke values under two simple fire models:

— *Basic model.* All the nodes deployed on the area measure the same values at the same time, with the variations introduced by their different accuracy and measurement errors.
— *Radial model.* The fire spreads from a central point in circular rings with a specified speed. The nodes therefore measure the fire parameters shifted in time, according to their position on the area.

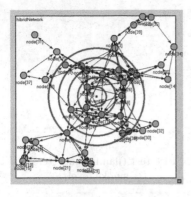 

(a) OMNeT++ simulation   (b) μNode platform

Fig. 3. D-FLER simulation and prototype

In case of fire, it is desirable that the large majority of nodes within the event radius report fire in the shortest possible time. Likewise, in the presence of nuisance conditions, a correct behavior minimizes the number of false alarms. Therefore, we take the percentage of nodes agreeing upon the real event status (fire/non-fire) as a measure of reliability, and the time within which the percentage converges to 100% as a measure of responsiveness.

We are now ready to introduce our simulation model and present the performance results.

5   Simulation

5.1   Simulation Setting

We consider a random deployment of 100 nodes within a rectangular area of 500m x 500m. The radio range is set to 150m. The nodes are considered to be randomly equipped with temperature and/or smoke sensors. The temperature sensor data is expressed in Celsius degrees. The smoke sensor data is derived from the ionization smoke alarm analog output used in the NIST tests, and scaled to 100. The accuracy of the sensors is modeled according to the characteristics of a real sensor [4], by taking into account the linearity, offset and gain errors, plus Gaussian white noise. The overall accuracy lies in the interval ±1–4%.

We implement the following four detection methods in the OMNet++ simulation environment [5] (see Fig. 3(a) for a graphical image of the simulation setting):

1. *Threshold.* Each node decides that a fire occurred when the temperature and smoke values exceed predefined thresholds. The thresholds correspond to the activation time of the medium alarm level in the NIST fire tests.

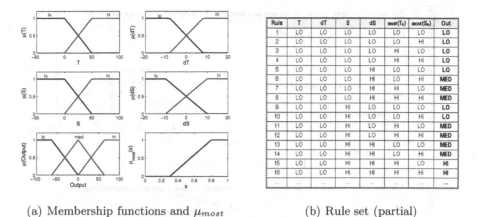

Rule	T	dT	S	dS	most(Tₙ)	most(Sₙ)	Out
1	LO	LO	LO	LO	LO	LO	LO
2	LO	LO	LO	LO	LO	HI	LO
3	LO	LO	LO	LO	HI	LO	LO
4	LO	LO	LO	LO	HI	HI	LO
5	LO	LO	LO	HI	LO	LO	LO
6	LO	LO	LO	HI	LO	HI	MED
7	LO	LO	LO	HI	HI	LO	MED
8	LO	LO	LO	HI	HI	HI	MED
9	LO	LO	HI	LO	LO	LO	LO
10	LO	LO	HI	LO	LO	HI	LO
11	LO	LO	HI	LO	HI	LO	MED
12	LO	LO	HI	LO	HI	HI	MED
13	LO	LO	HI	HI	LO	LO	MED
14	LO	LO	HI	HI	LO	HI	MED
15	LO	LO	HI	HI	HI	LO	HI
16	LO	LO	HI	HI	HI	HI	HI
...	...	...	...	...	...	...	...

(a) Membership functions and μ_{most} (b) Rule set (partial)

Fig. 4. Fuzzy-logic fire detection engine

2. *Average.* A simple distributed mechanism is implemented, where each node takes the mean value between its own samples and the average of the readings reported by its neighbors. The decision it made according to the same thresholds as in the previous case. This method is expected to decrease the false alarm rate in the case of nuisance scenarios, by reducing the effect of individual sensor errors.

3. *Fuzzy.* Each node uses a local fuzzy logic engine. If the node has both temperature and smoke sensors, then four inputs are analyzed: T - temperature, S - smoke level, dT - temperature change (current sample minus previous sample) and dS - smoke level change (current sample minus previous sample). For the nodes with only one sensor, the fuzzy logic engine takes two inputs (T and dT or S and dS). The membership functions are shown in Fig. 4(a). Similar to the first method, no information is exchanged among the nodes.

4. *D-FLER.* As described in Sec. 3, the nodes broadcast their fuzzified temperature and smoke values within the local neighborhood. D-FLER operates with both the inputs mentioned in the previous method (T, S, dT and dS) and the quantified neighborhood observations. The *most* quantifier defined in Eq. 4 is used (see Fig. 4(a)). The rules have the format described in Eq. 5 and 6 and are partially shown in Fig. 4(b).

5.2   Results

The four data sets (fire and nonfire) are input to the four simulated detection methods. We collect the decisions of the nodes at every time step. The results presented in Fig. 5 and 6 are averaged over 10 simulation runs with different random topologies.

In the case of fire, we are interested in a rapid and reliable detection. The more nodes detect the fire, the more reliable is the decision on the average case

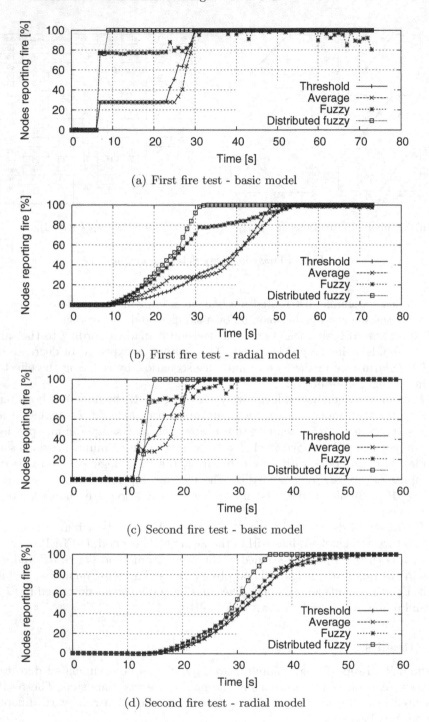

(a) First fire test - basic model

(b) First fire test - radial model

(c) Second fire test - basic model

(d) Second fire test - radial model

Fig. 5. Simulation results of fire tests

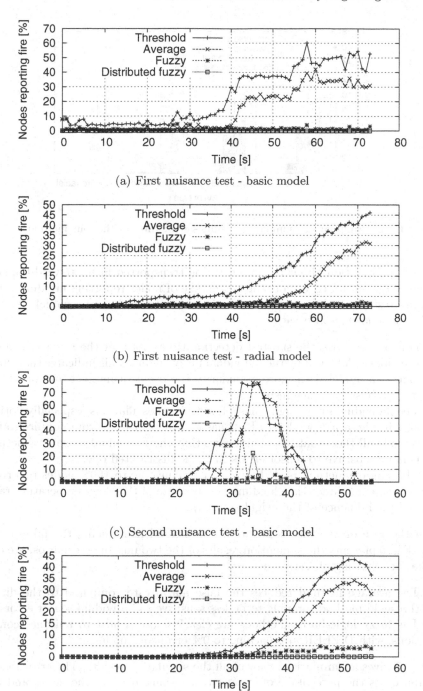

(a) First nuisance test - basic model

(b) First nuisance test - radial model

(c) Second nuisance test - basic model

(d) Second nuisance test - radial model

Fig. 6. Simulation results of nuisance tests

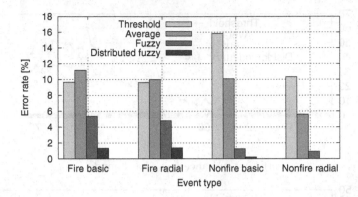

Fig. 7. Summary of simulation results - error rates of the four methods

and the information about the event can be transported faster toward the sink or gateway nodes. Fig. 5 plots the percentage of nodes reporting fire during the two fire tests, considering both the basic and the radial spread model. We can make the following observations:

- D-FLER achieves the shortest detection times both for the basic and radial fire models, followed by the individual fuzzy engine. This indicates that fuzzy logic can model with more granularity the event of interest and provide a more robust inference result.
- The individual fuzzy engine has a few decision oscillations (especially noticeable in Fig. 5(a)), while D-FLER has a clear transition from non-fire to fire state in all the situations. This shows that the individual reasoning method is more sensitive to sensor errors than the distributed one.
- The average method is slightly slower to converge to 100% nodes reporting fire than the direct threshold method because of the slow temperature raise and the influence of the neighbors samples.

In the case of nuisance tests, we are interested in reducing the false alarm rate. Fig. 6 presents the simulation results of the two nuisance scenarios. We can make the following observations:

- The average method reduces the false alarm rate compared to the direct threshold method, proving to be less sensitive to individual sensor errors.
- The fuzzy logic-based methods are clearly more robust to nuisance conditions, with D-FLER approaching to 0% erroneous nodes.

Fig. 7 gives a summarized view of all the simulation results. The error rate is computed as the percentage of erroneous decisions, over all the nodes and the entire simulation duration. The fuzzy logic methods prove to be more reliable than the threshold solutions, D-FLER having an average error rate less than 2% in the case of fire and approaching 0% in the case of nuisance tests.

6   Implementation

We implemented D-FLER on the Ambient μNode 2.0 platform [1] (see Fig. 3(b)), which is based on the MSP430 micro-controller. The μNodes run AmbientRT [16], a real-time multitasking operating system based on publish/subscribe inter-task communication. The publish/subscribe model simplifies the implementation, as D-FLER can abstract from various types of inputs by subscribing only to their data. Similar to our previous work [20], the reasoning engine is decoupled from the *drivers* (custom interfaces giving the sensor readings or radio protocol stack delivering the neighbors messages) that provide the input data. The system is therefore modular and easy to reconfigure over the air.

The following list summarizes the implementation details of the D-FLER components (see also Sec. 3):

1. *Fuzzification.* The local sensor readings are fuzzified according to the user-specified membership functions. D-FLER currently accepts only triangular membership functions. Our implementation of the fuzzification is *computational oriented* [8] due to the small amount of RAM available on the node. To reduce the computational complexity, the maximum fuzzified value is scaled to a power of 2, as recommended by Dannenberg [10].
2. *Quantification of neighborhood observations.* The data from the neighboring nodes is processed through the *sigma-count* factor and μ_{most} operator (see Eq. 1 - 4).
3. *Inference.* The rules are formatted as in Eq. 5, taking into account all the fuzzified inputs. D-FLER uses *max-min* inference for computational simplicity.
4. *Defuzzification.* The aggregated result of the rule evaluation is defuzzified using the *centroid* method.

We evaluate the D-FLER implementation by following three properties of interest: the memory overhead, the numerical accuracy and the execution time.

The code memory footprint amounts to $\approx$1kB FLASH memory (out of 48kB available), leaving thus enough space for the OS kernel, sensor drivers, network stack etc. In addition, D-FLER occupies 20 bytes RAM for static variables and allocates dynamically heap space for the inputs, outputs and rules. To estimate the memory consumption M at runtime, we use the following formula

$$M = I(4m_i + 1) + NIm_i + 2R(Im_i + 1) + O(4m_o + 1) \qquad (7)$$

where I is the number of inputs, each input having m_i membership functions, N is the number of neighbors providing same type of inputs (fuzzified), R is the number of rules and O is the number of outputs, each output having m_o membership functions. An important optimization can be made if every input has two membership functions ($m_i = 2$). In this case, the rules can be represented only as their consequence parts ("*o* is *G*" from Eq. 5). Then, the binary representation of the rule index gives the combination of inputs and fuzzy input sets in the antecedents, e.g. rule number 5 (binary 101) means "i_0 is F_1^0 AND

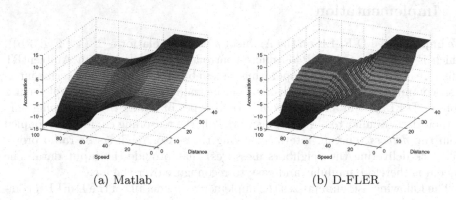

(a) Matlab   (b) D-FLER

Fig. 8. The car control problem

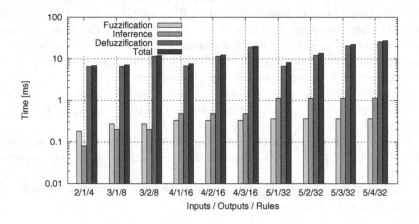

Fig. 9. Performance of D-FLER on μNode platform

i_1 is F_0^1 AND i_2 is F_1^{2}". Using this optimization, a running instance of D-FLER with 5 inputs and 2 outputs allocates 326 bytes RAM out of 10kB available.

D-FLER performs the computations on two-byte signed integers. In order to evaluate the precision error, we run a simple car control problem with two inputs (distance and speed) and one output (acceleration). Fig. 8(a) and 8(b) plot the rule surfaces generated with Matlab and D-FLER, respectively, where the latter is obtained by iterating through the whole input space with unit step. The absolute error of D-FLER (due to integer approximation) is 1% on average, with a maximum of 3.33%.

D-FLER execution time is depicted in Fig. 9 (at logarithmic scale) for different problem complexities, given by the number of inputs, outputs and rules (the number of membership functions is fixed at $m_i = 2$ and $m_o = 3$). For each case, the execution time is computed by averaging over the entire input space, as in the previous example. We can make the following observations:

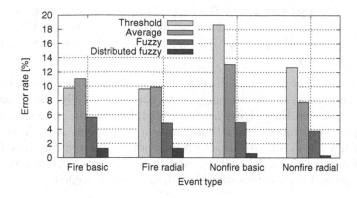

Fig. 10. Error rates for sensors with lower accuracy

- The fuzzification and inference times are in the same range, varying approximately linearly with the number of inputs and rules, respectively. The fuzzification operation takes between 180 and 360μs, while the inference process takes between 80μs and 1.13ms.
- The defuzzification is clearly the most time-consuming operation (between 6.56 and 25.86ms) because of the computation involved in calculating the centroid of the output area. There are several alternatives to reduce the defuzzification time: (1) use rectangular output membership functions [10], (2) use a fast centroid approximation method [22] or (3) use a simpler defuzzification method, e.g. maximum.
- The total execution time is basically given by the defuzzification speed and, consequently, varies linearly with the number of outputs.

7   Discussion

In this section, we briefly discuss the impact of several factors on the performance of D-FLER, pointing out the main advantages and limitations.

Communication. Exchanging the observed data within the one-hop neighborhood increases the communication overhead and, consequently, the energy consumption. On average, each node would send one packet and receive $N\pi r^2/A$ packets per time step, where N is the total number of nodes, A is the area size and r is the radio range. Reducing the duty cycle alleviates the problem, but at the price of increasing the detection time. A better approach is to use cross-layer integration and piggyback the data to the periodic heartbeat messages of the MAC or routing protocols.

Sensing errors. In practical deployments, cheap sensors with low precision may be used due to cost concerns. Likewise, the phenomenon to be detected (e.g. fire) may itself introduce considerable sensing errors. We repeated the simulations from Sec. 5.1 considering sensors with two times lower accuracy (2-8%). The results are shown in Fig. 10. In the case of fire, there is little increase in the detection error rate ($< 0.3\%$). However, for the nuissance scenarios, the false alarm rate grows with up to 3.7% for all the methods except D-FLER, which stays lower the 0.5%.

Computation. The fuzzification using triangular or trapezoidal membership functions and the max-min inference prove computationally fast in our implementation. However, the usage of other membership functions, such as Gaussian, would impose a memory-oriented implementation [8], less suitable for the low amount of RAM typically available on sensor nodes. The centroid-based defuzzification introduces the highest latency and should be optimized or replaced with a simpler method if execution times less than 6ms are needed.

Training and learning. In order to produce optimal results, tedious tuning of the membership functions may be required. In practice, standard methods such as ANFIS [17] and fuzzy clustering are used to build a fuzzy model based on both human knowledge and stipulated input-output data pairs. Since D-FLER is a distributed solution, learning at runtime about the confidence of the neighborhood observations would also be a valuable feature in real-life deployments.

8   Conclusions

In this paper, we described D-FLER, a distributed fuzzy logic reasoning engine for WSN. By combining individual sensor inputs with neighborhood observations, D-FLER produces more accurate results and is more robust to sensor errors. For performance evaluation, we use fire detection as an application scenario. The simulation results show that distributed fuzzy logic is a promising alternative for event detection with WSN, as it improves the detection time, while reducing the false alarm rate. From the implementation point of view, D-FLER proves effective and feasible to run on resource-constrained sensor nodes. As future work, we want to study the impact of WSN communication characteristics (low duty cycle, multihop, high error rates) on the performance of D-FLER. In addition, we plan to conduct an application trial in a real setting for firefighting assistance and distributed coordination.

Acknowledgments

This work has been partially sponsored by the European Commission as part of the AWARE Project (IST-2006-33579).

References

1. Ambient Systems. http://www.ambient-systems.net
2. AWARE project. http://grvc.us.es/aware
3. Fire Information and Rescue Equipment (FIRE). http://fire.me.berkeley.edu

4. National Semiconductor LM92 temperature sensor. http://www.national.com
5. OMNeT++. http://www.omnetpp.org
6. Cleary, T., Notarianni, K.: Distributed sensor fire detection. In: International Conference on Automatic Fire Detection (2001)
7. Cleary, T., Ono, T.: Enhanced residential fire detection by combining smoke and co sensors. In: International Conference on Automatic Fire Detection (2001)
8. Costa, A., De Gloria, A., Giudici, F., Olivieri, M.: Fuzzy logic microcontroller. IEEE Micro 17(1), 66–74 (1997)
9. Roby, R.J., Gottuk, D.T., Peatross, M.J., Beyler, C.L.: Advanced fire detection using multi-signature alarm algorithms. Fire Safety Journal 37, 381–394 (2001)
10. Dannenberg, A.: Fuzzy logic motor control with msp430x14x. Technical Report SLAA235, Texas Instruments (2005)
11. Espinosa, J., Vandewalle, J., Wertz, V.: Fuzzy logic, identification and predictive control. Springer, Heidelberg (2004)
12. Marin-Perianu, M., et al.: Decentralized enterprise systems: A multi-platform wireless sensor networks approach. Technical Report TR-CTIT-07-31, CTIT, University of Twente (2007)
13. Bukowski, R.W., et al.: Performance of home smoke alarms. Technical Report 1455, NIST (2004)
14. Terada, T., et al.: Ubiquitous chip: A rule-based i/o control device for ubiquitous computing. Pervasive, 238–253 (2004)
15. Henkind, S.J., Harrison, M.C.: An analysis of four uncertainty calculi. IEEE Transactions on Systems, Man and Cybernetics 18(5), 700–714 (1988)
16. Hofmeijer, T., Dulman, S., Jansen, P.G., Havinga, P.J.M.: AmbientRT - real time system software support for data centric sensor networks. In: Intelligent Sensors, Sensor Networks and Information Processing (ISSNIP), pp. 61–66 (2004)
17. Roger Jang, J.S.: Anfis: Adaptive-network-based fuzzy inference system. IEEE Transactions on Systems, Man, and Cybernetics 23, 665–684 (1993)
18. Kacprzyk, J.: Group decision making with a fuzzy linguistic majority. Fuzzy Sets and Systems 18(2), 105–118 (1986)
19. Levis, P., Culler, D.: Maté: a tiny virtual machine for sensor networks. In: International Conference on Architectural Support for Programming Languages and Operating Systems, pp. 85–95 (2002)
20. Marin-Perianu, M., Hofmeijer, T.J., Havinga, P.J.M.: Implementing business rules on sensor nodes. In: 11th IEEE International Conference on Emerging Technologies and Factory Automation (ETFA), pp. 292–299. IEEE Computer Society Press, Los Alamitos (2006)
21. Mendel, J.M.: Fuzzy logic systems for engineering: a tutorial. Proceedings of the IEEE 83, 345–377 (1995)
22. Runkler, T.A., Glesner, M.: Decade - fast centroid approximation defuzzification for real time fuzzy control applications. In: SAC 1994. ACM Symposium on Applied Computing, pp. 161–165. ACM Press, New York (1994)
23. Strohbach, M., Gellersen, H.W., Kortuem, G., Kray, C.: Cooperative artefacts: Assessing real world situations with embedded technology. In: Ubicomp, pp. 250–267 (2004)
24. Zadeh, L.A.: A computational approach to fuzzy quantifiers in natural languages. Computers and Mathematics 9, 149–184 (1983)

Secure and Reliable Data Aggregation for Wireless Sensor Networks

Suat Ozdemir

Department of Computer Engineering
Faculty of Engineering and Architecture
Gazi University
Ankara, Turkey, 06570
suatozdemir@gazi.edu.tr

Abstract. This paper presents a data aggregation protocol that ensures security and reliability of aggregated data in the presence of compromised sensor nodes. The proposed protocol relies on a novel trust development algorithm which is used by data aggregators and sensor nodes to ensure the reliability of aggregated data and to select secure and reliable paths. Simulation results show that the proposed protocol improves the security and reliability of aggregated data significantly.

1 Introduction

The emergence of sensor architectures with special capabilities such as the ability to control the activation of different hardware units and the developments in low-power computational components will bring large scale wireless sensor network applications into reality [1]. In such large scale wireless sensor networks, neighboring sensor nodes often have overlapping sensing ranges and therefore they sense the same phenomenon which results in production of large volumes of redundant data. To reduce the amount of data transmission, data redundancy is eliminated at intermediate sensor nodes by performing data aggregation [2].

One unique property of sensor networks is their vulnerability to node compromise attacks [1]. Hence, data aggregation protocols must be able to function securely in the presence of possible compromised nodes within the network. Many existing data aggregation protocols assume that all sensor nodes in the network are trusted [2]. Some other data aggregation protocols that consider compromised nodes rely on pure cryptography [3]. However, cryptographic primitives alone cannot provide a sufficient enough solution as compromised nodes have access to secret keys that are used to secure the data aggregation process [4].

In this paper, we make use of a *web of trust* to overcome shortcomings of cryptography based secure data aggregation solutions. In particular, we propose a *S*ecure and r*EL*iable *D*ata *A*ggregation protocol, called SELDA, which is based on trustworthiness of sensor nodes and data aggregators. The basic idea behind protocol SELDA is that sensor nodes observe actions of their neighboring nodes to develop trust levels for the environment using Beta distribution

H. Ichikawa et al. (Eds.): UCS 2007, LNCS 4836, pp. 102–109, 2007.
© Springer-Verlag Berlin Heidelberg 2007

function [5]. Sensor nodes exchange their trust levels with neighboring nodes to form a web of trust that allows them to determine secure and reliable paths to data aggregators. Based on these trust levels, sensor nodes transmit their data to data aggregator(s) over one or more secure paths. During data aggregation, data aggregators weight the data based on the trust levels of the sender nodes. The simulation results show that protocol SELDA increases the reliability of the aggregated data at the expense of a tolerable communication overhead.

2   Generating the Web of Trust

In protocol SELDA, sensor nodes and data aggregators generate a web of trust by keeping reputation values. The reputation value of a sensor node is computed using *Beta distribution function* [5] of the sensor node's previous actions, namely *sensing, routing,* and *availability*. Sensor nodes and data aggregators monitor their environments periodically to detect the misbehaviors of their neighboring nodes and quantify those observations as reputation values of those nodes. Reputation values are exchanged among sensor nodes to determine reliable data aggregators and secure paths to those data aggregators.

A compromised sensor node may degrade the network's performance by not cooperating with other sensor nodes. Therefore, if a sensor node performs a false active/sleep schedule or do not respond to *hello* messages over a period of time, the reputation value of the node in terms of node *availability* is reduced. In general, to implement media access control mechanisms, sensor nodes are aware of their neighbors' sleep schedules. Therefore, if a sensor node does not response to *hello* messages during its active phase, it is detected by one of its neighbors. In addition, a compromise node may not forward received data packets or misroute them by changing the destination address of the packet. Using one of the existing watchdog mechanisms [6], *routing* misbehaviors can be detected by neighboring nodes. In addition, a compromised node may report false sensor readings to deceive the base station or to distort the aggregated data. However, due to dense deployment requirement of sensor networks, neighboring sensor nodes often have overlapping sensing ranges and data sensed by neighboring sensor nodes are highly correlated. Therefore, a compromised sensor node that reports false sensor readings is detected by its neighboring sensor nodes that sense the same phenomena.

Sensor nodes and data aggregators differ from each other in computing reputation values. A data aggregator computes a reputation value for each neighboring sensor node. On the other hand, to reduce the computational overhead, a sensor node computes a single reputation value for its neighborhood.

Data Aggregator Case: Each data aggregator (A_j) keeps reputation values $(R_{i,j}^{sensing}, R_{i,j}^{routing},$ and $R_{i,j}^{availability})$ for each neighboring node N_i that sends its data to A_j. The reputation value (R_j^i) is computed based on sensor node N_i's previous correct behaviors and misbehaviors. For example, A_j counts the number of correct and false routing actions of N_i for a period of time. Then,

A_j quantifies those values as $R_{i,j}^{routing}$ of N_i using Beta density function. The overall reputation value of N_i is computed by taking the average of $R_{i,j}^{sensing}$, $R_{i,j}^{routing}$, and $R_{i,j}^{availability}$. Before performing data aggregation, A_j use the overall reputation value of N_i to weight the data received from N_i so that the reliability of aggregated data is increased.

Sensor Node Case: A sensor node N_i only keeps a reputation value for its neighborhood $R_i^{environment}$ rather than keeping a reputation value for each neighboring node. Keeping a single reputation value for the environment reduces sensor nodes' computational and storage overhead due to reputation values. To compute $R_i^{environment}$, N_i periodically monitor its neighborhood and keeps a record of correct and false *sensing, routing,* and *availability* actions of its neighboring nodes. Then, N_i converts those correct and false behavior values into $R_i^{environment}$ using Beta density function. N_i uses $R_i^{environment}$ to determine the number of paths that will be used in data transmission to the aggregator.

3 Secure and Reliable Data Aggregation

Protocol SELDA reduces the effect of compromised nodes on aggregated data by using reputation values. The basic rationale behind protocol SELDA is that compromised sensor nodes are likely to have lower reputation values than honest sensor nodes. During the data aggregation process, the data of each sensor node is weighted based on its reputation value with respect to the data aggregator, thereby mitigating the effect of compromised sensor nodes on the aggregated data. This is achieved by running the following Reliable Data Aggregation (RDA) algorithm on each data aggregator A_j in the network.

Algorithm. RDA

Input: Data aggregator A_j, A_j's neighboring nodes $\{N_1, N_2, \cdots, N_i\}$, reputation values $\{R_{1,j}, R_{2,j}, \cdots, R_{i,j}\}$ of neighboring nodes with respect to A_j.
Output: Aggregated data D_{agg}.
Step 1: A_j observers each N_i periodically and updates the number of false and correct actions by N_i.
Step 2: A_j updates $R_{i,j}$ value of each N_i based on the updated number of false and correct actions by N_i.
Step 3: Sensor nodes $\{N_1, N_2, \cdots, N_i\}$ transmit data $(D_1, D_2, \cdots, D_i)$ to A_j.
Step 4: A_j weighs data D_i of each sensor node N_i using the reputation value $R_{i,j}$.
Step 5: A_j aggregates the weighted data to obtain D_{agg}.

The algorithm RDA mitigates the effect of false data sent by the data aggregator's compromised neighboring nodes. However, if the false data is sent by a compromised node which is not a neighboring node of the data aggregator, the algorithm RDA may not able to weight this false data properly. Consider the example presented in Fig. 1-(a) where the compromised node N_c forges the forwarded data and sends the false data to data aggregator A_j through the neighboring node N_n which is not a compromised node. Since N_n forwards N_c's false data, A_j weighs N_c's false data using N_n's high reputation value resulting in corruption of the aggregated data. To detect data forgery by forwarding compromised nodes, in protocol SELDA sensor nodes transmit their data to data aggregators over multiple secure paths.

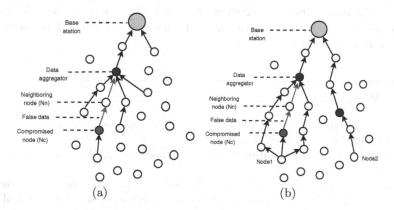

(a)   (b)

Fig. 1. (a) Data forged by compromised node N_c is evaluated by neighboring node N_n's high reputation value resulting in corrupted aggregated data. (b) Multi path data transmission. Node1 sends its data over multiple paths due to the compromised neighboring node. The data aggregator is able to detect the false data by comparing the multiple instances of the same data. On the other hand, Node2 uses only a single path to reach the data aggregator as it completely trusts its neighborhood.

4   Multi Path Data Transmission to Data Aggregators

In addition to data forgery, compromised nodes may also disrupt the network traffic by selectively forwarding or misdirecting packets. In order to prevent forgery and selective forwarding attacks by compromised nodes, we propose a secure multi path data transmission algorithm that ensures secure data delivery to data aggregators. The proposed data transmission algorithm secretly selects some paths based on the reliability of the paths and keeps the quantity and identity of the selected paths secret. Figure 1-(b) shows an example of multi path data transmission. Note that due to relatively short path lengths to data aggregators, it may not be possible to have an enough number of disjoint paths all the time. Hence, paths do not have to be completely disjoint. Sensor node N_i decides the number of paths through which the data are sent based on $R_i^{environment}$ and the paths are selected based on their reliability.

4.1   Multi Path Establishment

In order to perform multi path data transmission, each sensor node N_i discovers the possible paths to reach its data aggregator. Let P denote the path from node N_i to the base station (BS). Also, let node A_j be the first data aggregator on path P between N_i and BS. The disjoint or braided paths from N_i to A_j are called *"local path set"* of node N_i. N_i discovers its local path set using the Local Path Discovery (LPD) algorithm. The algorithm LPD results in n paths that connects sensor node N_i to its data aggregator A_j. Although n paths are established, multi path data transmission is employed when N_i has a low reputation value for its environment which indicates there may be possible compromised nodes in the neighborhood. Whenever this situation arises, N_i first decides the number of paths to send the data, say m, then select m most reliable paths from its local path set.

Algorithm. LPD

Input: Data aggregator A_j, sensor node N_i and N_i's neighboring nodes.
Output: Local path set from N_i to A_j.
Step 1: N_i broadcasts a small route request message M_{rreq} that has destination address A_j.
Step 2: Each one of N_i's neighboring nodes forwards an M_{rreq} message towards A_j after adding its ID to M_{rreq}. A_j receives a number of M_{rreq}s with a list of nodes that relayed the M_{rreq}.
Step 3: A_j replies to each M_{rreq} with an M_{rrep} message along with the ID list of M_{rreq}.
Step 4: Each M_{rrep} message follows the same path of its M_{rreq}. N_i receives each M_{rrep} message along with the ID lists. Each ID list refers to a path N_i to A_j.
Step 5: N_i selects n paths and saves those paths as its *local path set* to data aggregator A_j.

4.2   Reliable Path Selection

Several metrics have been proposed for path selection in sensor networks [7]. However, these metrics do not consider the security aspect of the paths. In order to select reliable paths from its local path set, N_i periodically requests each sensor node N_t on each one of local paths to send its $R_t^{environment}$ value. To reduce the communication overhead, $R_t^{environment}$ values are piggybacked to data and control packets. In terms of security, the metric that is used in selection of the paths is a very important component of the proposed algorithm. Therefore, the proposed path selection metric (ϕ_k) includes $R_t^{environment}$ values of all nodes on path k and a path loss factor (p_k^{loss}) where p_k^{loss} represents the packet loss rate of path k. p_k^{loss} is calculated based on the successful delivery acknowledgement messages of the data aggregator for the path k. Assuming that T is the number of nodes on the path k, N_i computes (ϕ_k) as follows.

$$\phi_k = \left(\sum_{t=1}^{T} \frac{R_t^{environment}}{T} \right) * p_k^{loss}$$

The paths through which the data are transmitted and their quantity should not be revealed to neighboring nodes as they may be compromised. If a compromised node knows that it is the only node that is supposed to forward the data, then it may drop or forge the data without the fear of being caught. Therefore, in the proposed multi path data transmission algorithm, sensor nodes send their data using a special packet header. This special header has n address fields and does not reveal the number of addresses or node IDs of those addresses. Using this header, nodes employ algorithm Secure Multi path Data Transmission (SMDT) for secure data transmission.

Algorithm. SMDT

Input: Sensor node N_i, N_i's local path set, and N_i's reputation value R_i for its environment.

Output: Secure data transmission from N_i to data aggregator A_j.

Step 1: N_i first indexes its neighboring nodes 1 to n, then selects the m most secure paths from its local path set based on its $R_i^{environment}$.

Step 2: For each selected path $Path_k$, N_i encrypts the ID of its neighboring node N_{Path_k} on the path and a nonce using the shared key between N_i and N_{Path_k}.

Step 3: N_i inserts each encrypted node ID of N_{Path_k} and the nonce into one of the address fields based on N_{Path_k}'s index.

Step 4: The empty address fields are filled with dummy bit strings.

Step 5: N_i broadcasts its data using this packet header that has multiple encrypted addresses.

Step 6: Each neighboring node decrypts the address field that corresponds its index number. m neighboring nodes that finds out their IDs in the address fields forward the data to A_j.

In algorithm SMDT, N_i indexes its all neighboring nodes 1 to n, broadcast the indexes of the nodes, and selects m paths based on $R_i^{environment}$. For each selected path $Path_k$, N_i encrypts the ID of the first node on $Path_k$ (N_{Path_k}) using the shared key between N_i and N_{Path_k}. N_i inserts encrypted ID of N_{Path_k} into one of the address fields of the packet header with respect to the index of N_{Path_k}. The empty address fields of the header are filled with dummy bit strings so that the number of selected paths are not known. Data is broadcast using this header to all neighbors but only m neighboring nodes are able to decrypt their address fields and forward the data. Hence, this technique allows sensor nodes to secretly send data to multiple neighbors in one transmission without revealing IDs of those neighbors that forward the data.

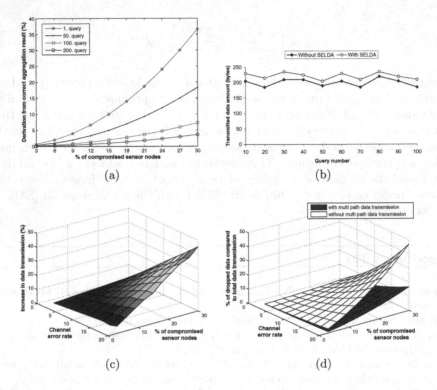

Fig. 2. (a) Reliability of aggregated data. Reliability increases as the number of queries increases. (b) Communication overhead of protocol SELDA due to reputation values. (c) Communication overhead due to multi path data transmission. (d) Reduction in data droppings due to multi path data transmission.

5   Performance Evaluation

Secure data aggregation efficiency of protocol SELDA is evaluated by measuring the deviation from the correct aggregation results under the existence of compromised nodes. Protocol SELDA is implemented in QualNet [8] by considering a cluster based sensor network that monitors the temperature of a terrain. In the simulation scenario, cluster heads act as aggregators. A number of compromised nodes are inserted to each cluster and 200 queries are initiated by the base station. Due to poor radio conditions of sensor networks, a retransmission mechanism is implemented and the retransmission limit is set to 5. The default channel error rate is 10% which is usually accepted as a poor radio condition. Each simulation is run 20 times and results are averaged.

First, we have measured the effect of compromised nodes on aggregation results. As seen from Fig. 2-(a), due to lack of reputation values, when the 1st query is processed compromised nodes are able to deviate the aggregation results by up to 40%. However, after the 100th query is processed, aggregation results are deviated less than 5% because data aggregators weight sensor data based on the reputation values. Second, the communication overhead due to reputation values is evaluated by measuring the total data transmission for each query without including multi path data transmissions. As seen from Fig. 2-(b), despite the reputation value exchange among sensor nodes, communication overhead is increased less than 7%. This is achieved by piggybacking the reputation values to regular data and control packets. Multi path data transmission protocol is also evaluated. In Fig. 2-(c), we show the increase in data transmission due to multi path data transmission protocol for various numbers of compromised nodes in the network. As seen from the figure, if $1/3$ of the network is compromised, then the communication overhead of multi path data transmission is 43%. We also evaluate the efficiency of multi path data transmission against data dropping attacks. The simulation results are shown in Fig. 2-(d). The results show that if the 30% of the sensor nodes are compromised and the channel error rate is 20%, then SMDT algorithm improves the data delivery up to 35%.

6 Conclusion

In this paper, we proposed a secure and reliable data aggregation protocol using trust relations among sensor nodes. The proposed protocol establishes a web of trust based on node misbehaviors. Data aggregators weight collected data using the web of trust to improve the reliability of the aggregated data. Simulation results show that the proposed protocol ensures the reliability of the aggregated data in the presence of compromised nodes. Moreover, the overhead imposed by the proposed protocol is shown to be tolerable.

References

1. Akyildiz, I.F., Su, W., Sankarasubramaniam, Y., Cayirci, E.: A survey on sensor networks. IEEE Communications Magazine 40(8), 102–114 (2002)
2. Intanagonwiwat, C., Estrin, D., Govindan, R., Heidemann, J.: Impact of network density on Data Aggregation in wireless sensor networks. In: Intanagonwiwat, C., Estrin, D., Govindan, R., Heidemann, J. (eds.) Proc. of the 22nd International Conference on Distributed Computing Systems, pp. 575–578 (July 2002)
3. Sang, Y., Shen, H., Inoguchi, Y., Tan, Y., Xiong, N.: Secure Data Aggregation in Wireless Sensor Networks: A Survey. In: Proc of PDCAT 2006, pp. 315–320 (December 2006)
4. Ganeriwal, S., Srivastava, M.B.: Reputation-based framework for high integrity sensor networks. In: Proc. of the 2nd ACM workshop on Security of ad hoc and sensor networks, pp. 66–77. ACM Press, Washington, DC (2004)
5. Casella, G., Berger, R.L.: Statistical Inference. Duxbury Press, Boston, MA (1990)
6. Roman, R., Zhou, J., Lopez, J.: Applying Intrusion Detection Systems to Wireless Sensor Networks. In: Proc. of Consumer Communications and Networking Conference, Las Vegas, pp. 640–644 (January 2006)
7. Chang, J., Tassiulas, L.: Energy conserving routing in wireless ad hoc networks. In: Proc. of IEEE Infocom 2000, pp. 22–31 (2000)
8. QualNet Network Simulator by Scalable Network Technologies, www.scalable-networks.com/

The iNAV Indoor Navigation System

Frank Kargl, Sascha Geßler, and Florian Flerlage

Ulm University, Institute of Media Informatics,
{frank.kargl,sascha.gessler,florian.flerlage}@uni-ulm.de

Abstract. COMPASS is a location framework where location sources
are realized as plugins that contribute probability density functions to
the overall localization result. In addition, COMPASS uses a decentralized location-based service discovery based on Peer-2-Peer distributed
hashtables to retrieve semantical data on the determined position. In
order to demonstrate the usefulness of COMPASS as a localization middleware, we have developed iNAV, an indoor navigation system that
makes extensive use of the previously described mechanisms.

1   Introduction

Mobile nodes often need to determine their current position. Ubiquitous computing applications derive context information from this position, e.g. in order to
determine whether a user is currently at home, at work or on the way in between.
Other applications, like position-based routing or navigation systems rely on position information, too. To support this large demand that applications have for
precise location information, a number of commercial and research projects are
working on this subject (like e.g. [1]. In earlier work [2] we have identified two
major challenges that are not completely resolved yet:

1. Location information from multiple sensors needs to be combined effectively
   in order to present one and only one position to the application. Using only a
   single location sensor has drawbacks in availability and accuracy. So in order
   to provide reliable and pervasive location support, an architecture must use
   multiple sensors, combine their results and present this to the application.
2. Raw coordinates may not really be useful to an application that needs to
   know the position in terms of buildings, rooms, street names etc. So a location system should include an infrastructure to resolve the raw position
   information to some kind of semantic position information.

This lead to the design of COMPASS [2] (short for *COM*mon *P*ositioning
*A*rchitecture for *S*everal *S*ensors) and later to the development of the translator
component[3]. Now we have implemented iNAV, an indoor navigation system
that uses COMPASS as a means for reliable position data and semantic information.

We will first recapitulate the major components of COMPASS before we introduce iNAV and discuss the various advantages and potential drawbacks of
using COMPASS as a localization system. We conclude by comparing related
work and giving an outlook on our ongoing activities.

H. Ichikawa et al. (Eds.): UCS 2007, LNCS 4836, pp. 110–117, 2007.

2   COMPASS Architecture

In COMPASS position information is represented by so called Probability Distribution Functions (PDF) which are based on ideas presented by Angermann, Wendlandt et al. [4]. PDFs are 2- or 3-dimensional probability distributions that represent the measurements of single sensors or a combined measurement of multiple sensors.

Additionally, a PDF contains the origin expressed as WGS-84 coordinates. When multiple sensors output PDFs, these can easily be combined to a joined PDF.

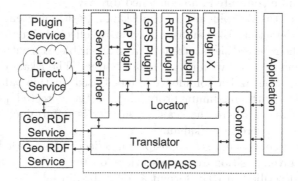

Fig. 1. COMPASS architecture

Figure 1 shows the overall architecture of COMPASS. COMPASS has a plugin-based design. For any source of position information exists a corresponding plugin. The plugins are connected to the so called Locator and deliver a PDF to it on demand. The task of the Locator is to determine the compound PDF of all PDFs supplied by the plugins. Additionally the Locator computes the position of the highest probability.

A plugin may use a service for accessing additional information. Service discovery and access is coordinated by the Service Finder. For this purpose, it uses a location-based directory service that is implemented using a P2P distributed hash table (DHT).

The Translator component accesses external Geo RDF Services (GRS) that can deliver semantic information for the current position in RDF/XML form. GRSs are implemented as SOAP web services. Discovery of suitable GRSs is done via the Service Finder and DHT.

Locator and Translator are controlled by the Control unit which provides the application API. It is also responsible for initialization of all components. The API returns either the compound PDF or the WGS 84 coordinates of the most likely position. Additionally, the application can retrieve the symbolic position information in RDF/XML.

The Locator is responsible for managing plugins, polling for PDFs and delivering the compound PDF of all returned PDFs. The localization quality depends on the selection of available plugins. One plugin that is especially relevant for iNAV is the AP plugin. This module uses WLAN access points as source of position information. It needs a service to resolve the access point's MAC to a geographic position. The service provides the WGS84 coordinates of the AP and optionally a power density spectrum for that AP. Localization can either follow a simple cell-based approach where a PDF is emitted that positions the node inside the covered cell with equal probability. Or the plugin can also take into account the received signal strength measured in the mobile node. From this information the plugin can compute a PDF with respect to properties of the sensor's antenna. If multiple access points are within reach one PDF for each access point can be computed and combined directly.

One variant of the AP plugin uses the Ekahau positioning engine [5] for the actual position detection. Ekahau uses previously collected signal strength maps and compares the received signal strength from all visible APs with these maps to detect the current position with rather high accuracy. The Ekahau API provides the detected position and a confidence value. Based on this value, the plugin generates a PDF with maximum probability at the detected position and a Gaussian distribution where the scale parameter is determined based on the confidence value delivered by Ekahau.

The Translator component is responsible for collecting semantic location information for any given position from the services located in the network. Semantic information is described in RDF format as described in [3].

In order to find the relevant web services that provide semantic information for a given position, we have developed a location-based service discovery mechanism that uses a peer-to-peer distributed hash table for efficient and scalable discovery of semantic information sources [3] based on current node positions. After discovering suitable services, data is retrieved using a SOAP interface.

The COMPASS Location-based Service Discovery (LBSD) is based on Distributed Hash Tables (DHT) which allow the storage and retrieval of arbitrary data in a P2P network. For indexing, a unique key is used that in our case is derived from a space partitioning MX-CIF Quadtrees that is used to map the current location to a unique key.

Again [3] gives more details on this system and also evaluates the performance of the LBSD. The remainder of this paper will now describe the iNAV indoor navigation system that demonstrates how ubiquitous computing applications can use COMPASS for positioning and how they benefit from the architecture.

3   iNAV

Today there is a growing interest for navigation and assistance applications that should operate especially in indoor scenarios like at shopping malls, exhibitions, airports, or in hospitals. Such systems need both position-information and semantic data about their current environment. This is why we choose to implement an indoor navigation system as a first proof-of-concept application that shows the benefits of using COMPASS.

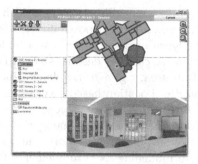

Fig. 2. Several views presenting maps, a compass needle and a panorama viewer

The following sections discuss the special properties of indoor navigation, and how COMPASS can be used to acquire the necessary positioning information, to support orientation in the user near field, and to acquire semantic information for a guided navigation. Finally we introduce the iNAV system, a system architecture for guided indoor navigation. Figure 2 shows the application's graphical user interface.

3.1 Positioning

Indoor Navigation needs an appropriate positioning, that is an adequate accuracy of about 10m with a continuous availability inside of buildings.

Possible candidates for indoor navigation scenarios are positioning systems based on WLAN, ultrasonic, infrared, RFID, and Bluetooth. By embedding these positioning methods in terms of COMPASS plugins, different goals can be achieved. A seamless integration of positioning techniques is provided. No matter what positioning infrastructure is available inside a building, COMPASS can easily adapt by using appropriate plugins. Furthermore there is an enhancement of availability. Often a position source is not available all over the building. COMPASS will simply use the information provided by active plugins and ignore the inactive ones. Additionally overall positioning errors (caused by inaccurate positioning informationen relying on a single plugin) can be reduced. Using multiple plugins, independent errors can cancel each other out. Altogether, COMPASS provides a powerful positioning engine for heterogeneous indoor scenarios.

3.2 User Near Field

Events occurring in a user's nearer environment are especially important to his perception. This is called the user near field. Compared to car navigation scenarios the indoor user near field shows some unique properties. There are no routes in terms of streets. In addition there is a lack of information, e.g. there are typically no routing hints like road signs. Furthermore indoor navigation deals with a far more complex 3-dimensional topography including buildings, floors, and rooms. This allows an extended liberty of action to pedestrians.

A data modelling that deals with such properties has to define several entities. There has to be a possibility to describe *rigid areas* like rooms and corridors. A *logical area*, e.g. a floor or a building, subsumes rigid areas and other logical areas. A *gateway* describes how to enter an area from a nearby area. The form of an area, e.g. a rectangle or a polygon, is defined by a data structure called *validIn*. Location based services may be attached to an area by a *link*.

In a car navigation scenario the user's primary task is to drive the vehicle. Consequently existing navigation systems confine themselves to survey maps, voice output and visual orientation guides like arrows. Supported by the chosen data modelling iNAV implements the mentioned techniques. However, a user in an indoor scenario moves with a larger degree of freedom. Hence the user is in the position to better focus on the system.

This leads to the concept of supporting the user by additional hints describing details of his environment. Using the Translator technology the needed semantic data can be acquired easily. As a side effect, possible changes of data by independent service providers are considered instantly. Furthermore resource restricted mobile devices do not need to permanently store all required data.

3.3   Implementation

The following section describes the implementation of the mentioned ideas. The prototype uses Java SE using a laptop or suitable PDA as client device. The GRSs are implemented as Axis web services backed by an database storing navigation data as RDF/XML-statements.

When a client performs a SOAP query using COMPASS the server has to return relevant semantic data for the given location. For identification of relevant navigation data the server makes use of the *validIn* property of each data record. The *validIn* property of navigation data (e.g. *area* or *rigidArea*) is given by an arbitrary polygon. Points of the polygon are described as WGS84-coordinates. Therefore the decision whether an RDF/XML-statement is relevant can be done by an inclusion test of a WGS84-coordinate with this polygon.

The client architecture follows the *Model-View-Controller* (MVC) design pattern. MVC makes it easy to create different *views* for different application scenarios and devices. In the following these components are described corresponding to the data flow shown in Figure 3. The *controller* acquires positioning and semantic data using COMPASS following a pull strategy. To offer an automatic as well as a manual data acquisition there are two controller components. An automatic controller periodically acquires data to keep the model up-to-date. A manual controller allows the user to retrieve information about remote places. Registered as a listener of the controller the *model* is notified about incoming data, which is given as a combined RDF. To avoid redundant updates the RDF document is splitted into single descriptions, which are compared with the model and translated into an object representation. Data that is simply changed, e.g. by a provider update, results in a replacement of outdated data. New semantic data results in an extension of the model.

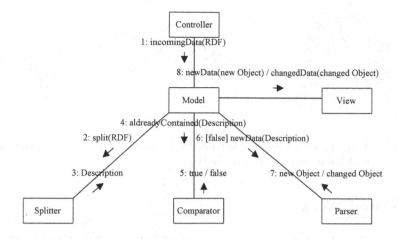

Fig. 3. Overview of the components processing incoming RDF data

Essentially for navigation is the route calculation, which is done using the A*
search algorithm. The necessary graph is created using path data given by the
model. This way typical user movements can be defined by declaring a route
which is simply a set of linked paths.

Based on changes of the current model different kinds of *events* are fired to
inform interested listeners. Typical types of events are related to positioning,
navigation, and user interaction. *Views* register themselves as listener for specific model events. Active views allow an interaction with the system, e.g. for
exploring the user's environment. Passive views assist the user during a navigation with no need of interaction. Beside the mode of operation views differ in
appearance. iNAV implements different visual and auditive views for navigation
and orientation assistance.

Figure 4 shows two orientation maps (user centered or static) which offer
orthogonal and perspective projections. The explorer is a tree view for exploring
the topology of the environment using gateway information. This allows the
user to explore far away areas. A routing planer component adds functionality
for planning and observing a navigation route. In navigation mode additional
information is provided by a compass needle pointing at the route direction.
Different textual and spoken orientation hints give a description of the current
environment. Supportively navigation events are signaled by different kinds of
sounds.

Furthermore simple location based services provide the user with additional
information. For example a viewer for panoramic images can be used to explore
distant navigation targets. A viewer for HTML content may show personal web-
sites or location-specific announcements. In addition messages can be placed and
accessed at certain locations.

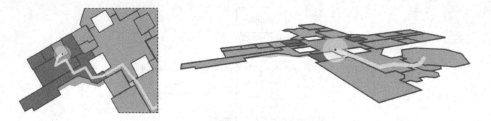

Fig. 4. Two maps in orthogonal and perspective projection showing the current location, the current room, and an overlaid route

4   Related Work

There are different systems that allow an appropriate positioning inside of buildings. Using these techniques a couple of research institutes are dealing with problems given by a multitude of indoor navigation scenarios.

The project presented in [6] focuses on aspects of orientation and guidance for public transport travelers. Using off-the-shelf smart-phones allows a cost effective Bluetooth based positioning solution following a cell-based approach. Routes are pre-calculated on a server. Therefore the user can be guided without needing permanent server access.

SAiMotion [7] provides an information system for trade fair visitors. All phases of navigation are supported, from the planning at home, over situation aware mobile guidance when visiting the exhibition, to the final evaluation of a visit. For positioning purposes a proprietary DECT-based system is used. For application scenarios that need positioning with a higher accuracy other kinds of sensors can be integrated.

5   Summary and Outlook

As we have shown, COMPASS provides a convenient and efficient base for implementing iNAV. Using the provided features, both the selection of positioning methods and the localization itself become almost transparent to the application. At the same time, iNAV can use the mechanisms provided by the translator to store and retrieve map data and other information that assists the user in near-field orientation. This way iNAV is not only a proof-of-concept application for COMPASS, but also represents an advanced indoor navigation system.

On the other hand, there currently also exist some drawbacks, especially in terms of performance. Both some plugins and the translator need to access Geo RDF Services in order to retrieve semantical information like map data. GRS are found using a distributed hash table which might introduce significant delays up to a couple of seconds. As user movements within and between areas might be predicted some time in advance, an intelligent pre-fetching mechanism can lessen this problem significantly.

Combining the different PDFs also imposes a significant calculation load on mobile devices. Our current prototype is based on mobile PCs where this is not too relevant. As our future plans include porting COMPASS and iNAV to other mobile platforms like PDAs, this will become more important then. Some options to handle this problem include changing the granularity of PDFs or identifying relevant parts of the PDFs and combining the PDFs only in these areas.

More problems arise as COMPASS/iNAV assumes constant network connectivity to retrieve necessary navigation data. Here we envision a pre-fetching and caching mechanism that also allows usage in an offline mode similar to the previously mentioned projects [6,7].

Besides addressing the mentioned issues, plans for future work include more tests that quantify the positioning accuracy and performance metrics of COMPASS/iNAV and extending the number of available plugins. Other issues to be addressed include security and authoring tools for data.

The concept of interchangeable localization plugins that complement each other as realized in COMPASS is a very promising approach for future combined in- and outdoor navigation systems and similar applications. Combined with distributed mechanisms to store and retrieve location-based metadata, this allows the efficient implementation of location-based applications as we have demonstrated with the iNAV navigation system.

References

1. Borriello, G., Chalmers, M., LaMarca, A., Nixon, P.: Delivering real-world ubiquitous location systems. Commun. ACM 48, 36–41 (2005)
2. Kargl, F., Bernauer, A.: The compass location system. In: Strang, T., Linnhoff-Popien, C. (eds.) LoCA 2005. LNCS, vol. 3479, Springer, Heidelberg (2005)
3. Kargl, F., Dannhäuser, G., Schlott, S., Nagler-Ihlein, J.: Semantic information retrieval in the compass location system. In: Youn, H.Y., Kim, M., Morikawa, H. (eds.) UCS 2006. LNCS, vol. 4239, Springer, Heidelberg (2006)
4. Wendlandt, K., Ouhmich, A., Angermann, M., Robertson, P.: Implementation of soft location on mobile devices. In: InLoc 2002. International Symposium on Indoor Localisation and Position Finding, Bonn, Germany (2002)
5. Roos, T., Myllymki, P., Tirri, H., Misikangas, P., Sievnen, J.: A Probabilistic Approach to WLAN User Location Estimation. International Journal of Wirelesse Information Networks 9(3), 155–164 (2002)
6. Rehrl, K., Göll, N., Leitinger, S., Bruntsch, S.: Combined indoor/outdoor Smartphone navigation for public transport travellers. In: Proceedings of the 3rd Symposium on LBS & TeleCartography 2005, pp. 235–239 (2005)
7. Schmidt-Belz, B., Hermann, F.: User validation of a nomadic exhibition guide. In: Mobile HCI, pp. 86–97 (2004)

C-ANIS – A Contextual, Automatic and Dynamic Service-Oriented Integration Framework

Noha Ibrahim, Frédéric Le Mouël, and Stéphane Frénot

ARES INRIA / CITI, INSA-Lyon, F-69621, France
{noha.ibrahim,frederic.le-mouel,stephane.frenot}@insa-lyon.fr

Abstract. Ubiquitous computing environments are highly dynamic by nature. Services provided by different devices can appear and disappear as, for example, devices join and leave these environments. This article contributes to the handling of this dynamicity by discussing service integration in the context of service-oriented architectures. We propose C-ANIS: a Contextual, Automatic and dyNamic Integration framework of Services. C-ANIS distinguishes two different approaches to service integration: automatic integration and on-demand integration. Automatic integration automatically extends the capabilities of an existing service S, leaving the interface of S unchanged. On-demand integration builds a new service on request from a list of given services. We have implemented C-ANIS based on the OSGi/Felix framework and thereby demonstrated the feasibility of these two service integration concepts. We have also implemented a toolkit providing two different techniques to realize the automatic and on-demand service integration concepts: Redirection, i.e. calling interfaces and replication, i.e. copying implementations of services[1].

1 Introduction

Ubiquitous computing environments are highly dynamic by nature. Services provided by different devices can appear and disappear as, for example, devices join and leave these environments. This article contributes to the handling of this dynamicity by discussing service integration in the context of service-oriented architectures. We propose to distinguish two different approaches to service integration: automatic integration and on-demand integration. Automatic integration automatically extends the functionality of an existing service S by integrating it with compatible services in the environment, but leaving the interface of S unchanged. This way, the extension in functionality of S can be kept transparent to applications or users employing this service. On-demand integration builds a new service on request from a list of given services. It integrates an existing service S with a list of services in the environment, creating new interfaces. These new interfaces are employed at least by the users or applications which have requested their creation.

---

[1] This work is part of the ongoing European project: IST Amigo-Ambient Intelligence for the Networked Home Environment [1].

H. Ichikawa et al. (Eds.): UCS 2007, LNCS 4836, pp. 118–133, 2007.

In line with the service paradigm, we assume that every relevant context parameter of a ubiquitous computing environment is provided by some service. Consequently, we generally define context as the collection of services available in such an environment. Employing this definition of context, we propose C-ANIS: a Contextual Automatic and dyNamic Integration framework of Services. C-ANIS integrates automatically and on-demand the available services at run time while taking the whole context into account, and if intended, it can also dis-integrate services again.

A use case is described all along the article to motivate, explain and evaluate our two integration approaches.

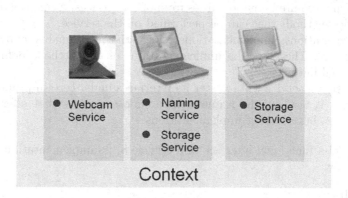

Fig. 1. Use case

The use case defines three services:

- The webcam service: a service that enables to take a photo via a webcam.
- The storage service: a service that enables to store an object on a device. Two different services offer the same functionality. One implementation is for local storage, the other one for remote storage.
- The naming service: a service that execute a naming strategy defined by a user to name his files and objects.

These services are provided by different devices (cf. fig 1) that can join or leave the environment leading these services to appear and disappear at any time.

We have implemented C-ANIS based on the OSGi/Felix framework and thereby demonstrated the feasibility of the two service integration concepts. We have also implemented a toolkit providing two different techniques to realize the automatic and on-demand service integration concepts: Redirection, i.e. calling interfaces and replication, i.e. copying implementations of services.

In the following, we will start by introducing our service model along with our notion of service integration (section 2). This is followed, section 3 and section 4, by the presentation of our two services integration approaches along with their life cycle. In section 5, we discuss the implementation of our concepts, followed by a first evaluation (section 6). In section 7, we will review relevant related work to position our work. Finally, we present conclusions and open issues (section 8).

2   Basic Definitions of Our Service-Integration Approach

2.1   Service Model

A service is composed of three parts:

- interfaces: A service can hold two kinds of interfaces. Provided functional interfaces defining the functional behavior of the service. Required interfaces specifying required functionalities from other services. A functional interface specifies methods that can be performed on the service.
- implementations: Implementations realize the functionality expected from the service. These are the implementations of the methods defined in the functional interfaces.
- properties: a service will register its interfaces under certain properties. The property is used by the framework to choose services that offer the same interfaces, but different implementations.

We model a functional interface of a service S, its implementation and property as follow:

$$Ifc_S \begin{cases} m1(params1) \to r1 \\ \vdots \\ mk(paramsk) \to rk \end{cases}$$

$$Impl_S \begin{cases} Impl1(m1) \\ \vdots \\ Implk(mk) \end{cases}$$

$$property_S : (Ifc_S)_{atomic}$$

Where Ifc_S is one functional interface of the service S, mk the method name, $paramsk$ the list of parameters, rk the return result, and $impl_S(mk)$ the implementation of method mk.

Use case. the use case' services (webcam, storage and naming) are modeled as follows:

$$webcam \begin{cases} Ifc_{webcam} : getSnapShot() \to Image \\ Impl_{webcam} : impl(getSnapShot) \\ prop_{webcam} : webcam_{atomic} \end{cases}$$

$$storage \begin{cases} Ifc_{storage} : save(Object\ obj, String\ ID) \rightarrow void \\[2mm] Impl_{storage} : impl_{local}(save) \\[2mm] prop_{storage} : storagelocal_{atomic} \end{cases}$$

$$storage \begin{cases} Ifc_{storage} : save(Object\ obj, String\ ID) \rightarrow void \\[2mm] Impl_{storage} : impl_{ftp}(save) \\[2mm] prop_{storage} : storageftp_{atomic} \end{cases}$$

$$naming \begin{cases} Ifc_{naming} : getNextName(String\ ID) \rightarrow String \\[2mm] Impl_{naming} : impl(getNextName) \\[2mm] prop_{naming} : naming_{atomic} \end{cases}$$

The property describes the interface implementation and specifies whether this implementation is atomic or integrated (resulting from integration). To execute a service, the framework can choose services' interfaces considering the property they publish. If no property is specified the framework will randomly choose a service' interface implementation.

Two services are considered by users/applications to be the same if they have the same functional interfaces. They indeed provide, externally, the same functionalities. The two storage services are considered to be the same by users. The implementations of these services is kept transparent from the users/applications (cf. fig 2).

Two services are considered by the run-time framework to be the same, if they have not only the same interface but especially the same property. Two services publishing the same interface but under different properties are considered by the framework to be different. The properties describe the implementation of the functional interface and different implementations mean different services. For the run-time framework, the two storage interface are registered under two different properties (storageftp$_{atomic}$ and storagelocal$_{atomic}$) and considered as two different services (cf. fig 2).

Our service model is independent of any implementations and can be applied to EJBs [2], Fractal components [3], OSGi bundles/services [4] or Web Services [5].

2.2 Service Integration Approaches

In ubiquitous computing environments, services provided by different devices can appear and disappear as devices join and leave these environments. These services are employed by users or applications being in the environment. New services only come from new devices joining the environment. The only other way to offer new services in these environments is to respond to an external

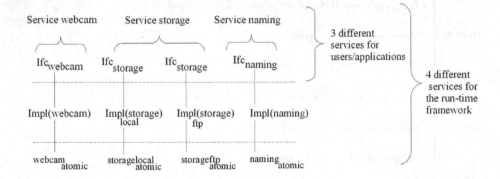

Fig. 2. Different services

demand of integration. If new services are offered, without being requested, they are likely not to be used.

For that, we distinguish on-demand integration that builds new services upon users/applications' requests and automatic integration that extends the functionalities of existing services.

- On-demand service integration: The framework responds to an external demand by providing new services in the environment. This demand comes from users or applications being in the environment. Applications or users tend to use services available everywhere in the context and would like to, whenever it is possible and/or needed, integrate services offered by the context. In particular, if no single service can satisfy the functionality required by the application, combining existing services together should be a possibility in order to fulfill the request [6]. The result of this integration is a new service with new interfaces (new methods), new implementations (new functionalities) and new properties.
- Automatic service integration: The framework selects automatically all the compatible services in the environment and integrates them. The result of these integrations is the same services enriched with new functionalities. The service interfaces and methods do not change, only its functionality and properties change. This way, the extension in functionality can be kept transparent to applications or users employing the services. Once new services are in the environment, the framework automatically compares these services to existent services and if compatible services are found, the automatic integration can take place.

3   On-Demand Service Integration

On-demand integration builds a new service on request from a list of given services. We will first define our compatibility notion, followed by the life-cycle of our on-demand integration approach. Finally, we show its application on our use case example.

3.1 Definition of Compatibility

Two services are compatible if they have two compatible functional interfaces. Two functional interfaces are defined to be compatible if they have at least two compatible methods. Two methods are compatible if the return result of one method is of the same type of one parameter of the other method (cf. fig 3).

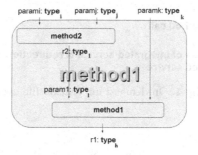

Fig. 3. Combining compatible methods: method1 & method2

Based on the compatibility definition, we define the integration of services as the combination, two by two, of all their compatible functional interfaces, and so of all their compatible methods. The combination of method1 and method2 (cf. fig 3) creates a new method1 with new parameters type corresponding to the parameters of method2 and part of method1' parameters.

3.2 Life Cycle of On-Demand Service Integration

When integrating the services (cf. fig 4), all their methods are listed and only compatible methods are selected. The framework selects the most appropriate service' implementations to create the new service. This selection is context aware and must depend on the users/applications preferences. For now no strategies are defined and the selection is done statically. Once the implementations chosen, the new service is created, with its new interfaces, implementations and properties. The new service is installed, started, monitored and its interfaces published. If services involved in the integration leave the environment, the service newly created, is dis-integrated and a new service is created. For that a contextual selection of new service' implementations is done. In the meanwhile, all the calls to the service are buffered.

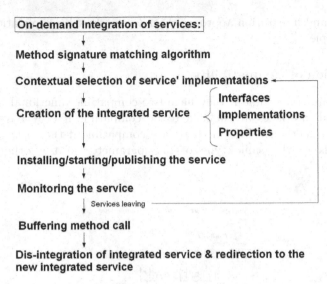

Fig. 4. On-demand integration life cycle

3.3   Example Use Case

An on-demand integration example is the integration of service Webcam and storage (cf. fig 5). The two methods `save` and `getSnapShot` are compatible. Indeed, the return result of `getSnapShot` is of type `Image` which inherits `Object` the type of one parameter of `save`. The two methods can be combined as shown fig 5, and a new method `saveGetSnapShot` can be created. To integrate the two services storage and Webcam, the framework must choose the most appropriate services' implementations. A contextual choice is made upon users/applications preferences. If a user has a constraint device, he will probably prefer to store the image on a remote computer and for that the framework will choose the ftp storage implementation. If the user has a PDA and would like to store the photo on his device, the local storage is selected by the framework. For now, strategies are hard coded and chosen statically.

4   Automatic Service Integration

Automatic integration automatically extends the functionality of an existing service S by integrating it with compatible services in the environment, but leaving the interface of S unchanged. We will first define the modified compatibility definition for automatic integration, followed by its life-cycle. Finally, we show its application on our use case example.

4.1   Definition of Condition-Compatibility

The notion of compatibility is the same as defined for on-demand integration but with additional condition. The automatic integration must remain transparent

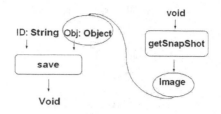

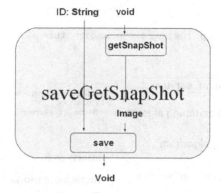

Fig. 5. On-demand service webcam and storage integration

to the users and applications. The new method1 must have the same signature as the initial method1 so that it can be employed by applications and for that some conditions must be fulfilled. Method2 must have only one parameter and of the same type as its return result (cf. fig 6).

The condition that needs to be satisfied in order to have an automatic integration of services without generating new functional interfaces in the context is:

condition. One of the two methods to combine must have only one parameter and this parameter must have the same type as the return result of the method. Two methods are *condition-compatible* if they are compatible and one of the method verifies *condition*. We define the automatic integration of two services as the combination, two by two, of all their *condition-compatible* methods.

4.2   Life Cycle of Automatic Service Integration

Automatic service integration is applied upon each appearance of new services in the context. The integration is contextual because it is very dependent on the services in the context, automatic because it is done by the framework upon each appearance of new services.

For the run-time framework a new service is a service with new functional interfaces or new properties.

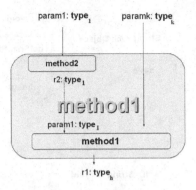

Fig. 6. Keeping the same signature as method1

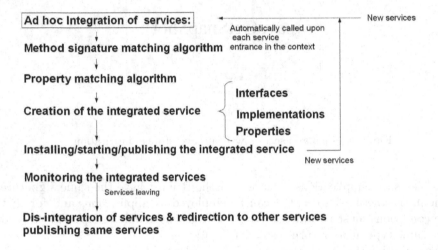

Fig. 7. Automatic integration life cycle

New services appearing: If these services have new interfaces and so new methods, the framework applies the method matching algorithm. This algorithm returns a list of all *condition-compatible* methods. The automatic integration can take place and new services are created (same interfaces, new properties). If the services already exist, the framework do the matching on the property to determine if the services are new in the context, which means new atomic property or new integrated property. In case of new atomic property, the framework verifies if the methods of these services belong to the list of *condition-compatible* methods and if it is the case, automatically integrates these methods and creates new services (same interfaces, new properties). In case of new integrated property, the framework needs to insure that no integration must be done if it involves the same services already integrated. This condition insures the stop of our automatic integration. Indeed, the framework never re-integrates services that were previously integrated. All the new services are installed, published and monitored.

Services disappearing: The framework needs to dis-integrate the integrated services. The call to these services will be automatically redirected to other available services offering same interfaces but with different properties. This redirection is kept transparent to the users and applications.

4.3 Example Use Case

New services: storage, naming and webcam are now available in the context (fig. 1). The framework automatically executes the steps defined in the life-cycle (fig. 7).

These services have all new interfaces. The framework lists all the interfaces available in the context. Once the interfaces known, a list M of all their methods is created (cf. fig 8).

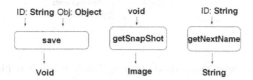

Fig. 8. M: list of all available methods in the context

The framework selects all the methods in this list that has the same parameter and result type. This matching will return a list C of the methods that fulfil the *condition* defined section 3.1 (cf. fig 9).

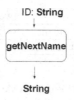

Fig. 9. C: list of methods that has the same parameter and result type

The framework verifies the compatibility of all the methods of M to all the methods of C. The result is a list of all *condition-compatible* methods (cf. fig 10).

The new services are now available in the context and registered under these new properties:

$$\text{storagelocal}_{integrated}(\text{naming}_{atomic}), \text{storageftp}_{integrated}(\text{naming}_{atomic}).$$

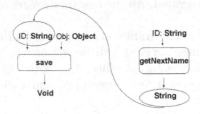

Fig. 10. Compatible methods: save and getNextName

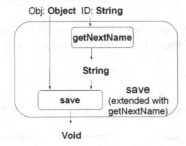

Fig. 11. Same methods signature, different implementations

These new services are reconsidered for a possible re-integration by the framework. As the interfaces are not new, the properties are checked and only non previously integrated services are allowed to integrate (cf. Table 1).

The integrated services resulting from automatic integration are services having the same interfaces (cf. fig 11) but different implementations and properties.

Table 1. Property matching

	webcam$_{atomic}$	naming$_{atomic}$
storagelocal$_{integrated}$(naming$_{atomic}$)	no	no
storageftp$_{integrated}$(naming$_{atomic}$)	no	no

The run-time framework reconsiders these new services for integration, but the property matching algorithm indicates that all the integration possibilities have been already done (cf. Table 1). Indeed, the run-time framework considers two interfaces registered under the same property to be the same.

5   Contextual Service-Integration Toolkit

We developed a toolkit for the C-ANIS framework under Felix/OSGi. The OSGi specifications define a standardized, component oriented, computing environment for networked services. Adding an OSGi Service Platform to a networked device (embedded as well as servers), adds the capability to manage the life cycle of the software components in the device from anywhere in the network. A unit of deployment called bundle offers the services in the framework. We implement our developing framework on Felix which is open source implementation of OSGi framework specification.

The integration call is done by the framework.

– automatic integration call:

```
integrate(context);
```

Listing 1.1. Integrating services of the context

The framework executes this integration call upon each entrance of a new service in the context. The new service is compared to all other services available in the environment.

– on-demand integration: Integrating the specified services is done via an integration call:

```
integrate(webcam,storage);
```

Listing 1.2. Integrating services storage and webcam

In OSGi, creating the service is done by creating the unit of deployment, called bundle. An OSGi bundle is comprised of Java classes and other resources which together can provide functions, services and packages to other bundles. A bundle is distributed as a JAR file. To create a bundle we need to tackle several needs:

– unit of deployment: a bundle to deploy the new integrated service.
– integration glue (Table 2): The java code that do the technical integration. We provide two different techniques: the redirection or interface call, done via method call and RMI, and the replication or implementations copy done via method call to the local replicated implementations.
– needed libraries: in case of replication, the implementations of the replicated services are needed and added to the bundle.
– services dependencies: the new service will have to verify the dependencies of the services involved in the integration.

Table 2. Integration techniques

	unit of deployment	integration glue	needed libraries	services dependencies
Redirection	Bundle (jar)	Method Call or RMI		S1, S2
Replication	Bundle (jar)	Method Call	S1 bundle, S2 bundle	dependencies S1, S2

Once the service created, it is installed, started and its interfaces registered in the context (listing 1.3).

```
Properties props = new Properties();
props.put("StorageIfc", "Storage-integrated(Naming-atomic)");
context.registerService(
            StorageIfc.class.getName(), serv, props);
```

Listing 1.3. Example of a service registration

The run-time framework monitors all the integrated services. For each change in the context involving the integrated services, the framework stops the services and dis-integrates them. For automatic integration, all the calls are redirected to services publishing the same interfaces but with different properties. For on-demand integration, the calls are buffered, for a certain time, while the service is re-created with new services' implementations.

6   Evaluation

To test our prototype we implemented the above described use case employing a Logitech USB webcam (vfw:Microsoft WDM Image Capture (Win32):0), two Dell Latitude D410 laptops (Intel(R) Pentium(R) M, processor 1.73GHz, 0,99Go RAM) running Microsoft Windows XP Professional (version 2002) and Ubuntu 6.06 LTS.

We measured the time of our matching algorithm, service-integration techniques, execution of the services (cf. fig 12) and bundles' size (cf. fig 13).

The time of our integration techniques is about 1 second for integrating two services. One can choose which technique to apply depending on the context. The redirection technique is more appropriate for constraints devices whereas the replication technique is more recommended for integrating services executing on devices that disconnect very often. The contextual choice of the technique will be the subject of another article.

The integrated service has the same execution time as any other atomic service (cf. fig 12).

For n services in the run-time framework, the complexity of our automatic matching algorithm is $O(n)$ upon each entry of a service in the context and $O(n^2)$ if a matching is done between all the services of the context.

The matching algorithm is relatively quick, but the automatic integration time is not scalable for large context. For run-time frameworks with 100 services, if matching only takes 329 ms, the integration time is much slower. Adding to that the time it takes to get distant access between remote run-time frameworks, one can quickly see the limits of the automaticity in large context.

7   Related Work

There has been a lot of work in developing different kinds of pervasive computing environments such as Gaia [7], Oxygen [8], Project Aura [9] and PCOM [10]

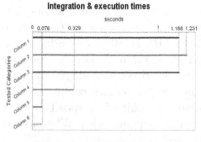

Column 1: Redirection: calling interfaces
Column 2: Replication: copying implementations
Column 3: Redirection and Replication
Column 4: Execution time of matching algorithm on 100 services
Column 5: Execution time of an integrated service
Column 6: Execution time of a normal service

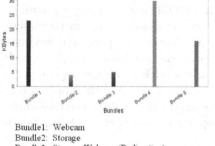

Bundle1: Webcam
Bundle2: Storage
Bundle3: Storage-Webcam (Redirection)
Bundle4: Storage-Webcam (Replication)
Bundle5: Storage-Webcam (Redirection & Replication)

Fig. 12. Average of a 100 test runs

Fig. 13. Bundle size for on-demand integration of webcam and storage services

to cite only these. All these environments try to make life easier for users by deploying various devices and supporting middlewares.

Project Oxygen [8] enables pervasive, human-centered computing through a combination of specific user and system technologies. Oxygen aims to enable pervasive, unobtrusive computing. The project proposes a user-centric support for ubiquitous applications, emphasizing specially the automatic and personalized access to information, adapting applications to users preferences and necessities as they moves through different spaces.

Aura's [9] goal is to provide each user with an invisible halo of computing and information services that persists regardless of location. Meeting this goal will require effort at every level: from the hardware and network layers, through the operating system and middleware, to the user interface and applications. Aura separates the user's intent from the application she uses to satisfy that intent and tries maintain the user's intent as the computing environment changes.

The Gaia system [7] provides a ubiquitous computing infrastructure for active spaces or smart rooms. Pervasive computing required the use of discovery, authentication, events and notification, repositories, location, and trading. Gaia depends on a distributed object, client/server architecture. Gaia adds a level of indirection between traditional applications and input/output resources to enable resource swapping.

These systems structure pervasive applications in terms of tasks and their subtasks, which is a software composition problem. The aim of these systems is to realize users demands. Our approach proposes not only the integration of services on an on-demand basis but also providing an automatic generation of services that can be or not used by the users. It deals more with the proactive property of pervasive environment. Another distinction is that our framework is distributed on the contrary of the previous systems which usually have a star-shaped architecture with central components.

PCOM [10] is a light-weight component system supporting strategy-based adaptation in spontaneous networked pervasive computing environments. Using PCOM, application programmers rely on a component abstraction where interdependencies are contractually specified. PCOM is all about adaptation of applications in pervasive environments and integration is seen as contract dependencies between components. PCOM is not service-oriented. An application is modeled as a tree of components and their dependencies where the root component identifies the application. Components are unit of composition with contractually specified interfaces and explicit context dependencies. Whereas our application and context abstraction are represented as services.

8   Conclusion and Future Work

In this article, we proposed C-ANIS: a Contextual Automatic and dyNamic Integration framework of Services. C-ANIS framework realizes automatically and at runtime the integration of available services in the environment, generating enriched services and new services as described in our two integration approaches. We have implemented C-ANIS based on the OSGi/Felix framework and thereby demonstrated the feasibility of these two service integration concepts.

The contributions of C-ANIS are in its:

- automaticity: Each time a new service is in the framework, a possible integration is done. We distinguished two major integration approaches: automatic integration and on-demand integration.
- context-awareness: Both automatic and on-demand integrations are context-aware. For on-demand integration, The choice of the services' implementations is depending on the context. For automatic integration, the services available in the context define the integration to do.
- dynamicity: Once the integration decided (method matching signature done), the choice of the implementations is done at run-time and can changes with the context changes.

The perspectives of our approach are:

- service model: Our service model do not take into consideration for now the non-functional properties and the state of the services. These two characteristics are important in pervasive environment especially when updating the integration due to context changes.
- generality of the matching algorithm: If a return type of method2 matches several parameters' types of method1, only one match is taken into consideration. Indeed, the properties specify that two services are already integrated and two methods can not be combined more than once. To resolve that issue, we want to describe semantically our services. The matching will be done on semantic description and not only on methods' signature to take all the cases into consideration.
- interoperability: The offered toolkit is only for java technology. We plan to use Amigo interoperable services [1] and extend our toolkit to .Net.

– context-awareness: The context is for now restricted to the set of services available in the environment. Commonly, context also reflects the social context of users and their preferences. We want to define contextual strategies for the run-time framework for choosing the integration techniques (replication or redirection) and services' implementations depending on the context. And for that a new notion of context needs to be defined.

References

1. Georgantas, N. (ed.): Detailed Design of the Amigo Middleware Core: Service Specification, Interoperable Middleware Core. Delivrable D3.1b, IST Amigo project (2005)
2. Monson-Haefel, R.: Entreprise JavaBeans. O'Reilly & Associates (2000)
3. Bruneton, E.: Developing with Fractal. The ObjectWeb Consortium, France Telecom (R&D), version 1.0.3 (2004)
4. OSGIalliance: About the OSGI service platform. Technical report, OSGI alliance, revision 3.0 (2004)
5. Iverson, W.: Real Web services. O'Reilly (2004)
6. Ponnekanti, S.R., Fox, A.: SWORD: A Developer Toolkit for Web Service Composition. In: 11th World Wide Web Conference, Honolulu, USA (2002)
7. Roman, M., Campbell, R.H.: A Middleware-Based Application Framework for Active Space Applications. In: ACM/IFIP/USENIX International Middleware Conference (Middleware 2003) (2003)
8. MIT. Project Oxygen: Pervasive, Human-Centered Computing (2007), http://oxygen.lcs.mit.edu/
9. Garlan, D., Siewiorek, D., Smailagic, A., Steenkiste, P.: Project aura: Towards distraction-free pervasive computing. IEEE Pervasive Computing, special issue on Integrated Pervasive Computing Environments 21(2), 22–31 (2002)
10. Becker, C., Handte, M., Schiele, G., Rothermel, K.: PCOM - A Component System for Pervasive Computing. In: PERCOM 2004. The 2nd IEEE Annual Conference on Pervasive Computing and Communications, IEEE Computer Society, Washington, DC, USA (2004)

Using Auction Based Group Formation for Collaborative Networking in Ubicomp

Christian Decker[1], Emilian Peev[1], Till Riedel[1], Martin Berchtold[1],
Michael Beigl[2], Daniel Roehr[2], and Monty Beuster[2]

[1] Telecooperation Office (TecO), University of Karlsruhe
[2] Distributed and Ubiquitous Computing (DUS), University of Braunschweig
{cdecker,peev,riedel,berch}@teco.edu,
{beigl,roehr,beuster}@ibr.cs.tu-bs.de

Abstract. In many Ubicomp scenarios tiny wireless embedded sensor
devices are used, and devices often collaborate to accomplish a common
goal. This paper presents a group formation method designed for collaboration of devices. The paper analysis requirements for typical application
scenarios, and then presents the general concept of the group formation
process. The proposed formation method is a variant of an auction-based
algorithm. The algorithm works fully distributed and is based on individual, private believes of the devices in the auctioneered item - e.g. a
sensor value. The paper introduces the algorithm and analyses its effects
analytically and in simulation. We show, that fully distributed operation,
high robustness in the case of network failures and extreme low resource
(energy) consumption can be obtained. We introduce an application case
and present results from a real-world implementation.

1 Introduction

The use of tiny battery powered wireless sensor devices is common to many Ubiquitous Computing (Ubicomp) scenarios. Devices as Particles, BTNodes, MITEes
or Berkeley motes enable Ubicomp application to sense object state and surrounding context. Recently, RFID devices are equipped with sensors thus being
able to perform similar functionality at a less complex level. Due to massive price
drop of devices, their potential integration into many (everyday) objects becomes
feasible. A higher density of such networked sensing devices brings in new opportunities for this novel class of computing devices: One example application
is collaborative agreement on redundant sensor measurement which provides
huge improvement in reliability of measured sensor values. Another example is
collaborative group formation of sensor devices to detect critical situations not
detectable by one single sensor system. Furthermore, "group behavior" is common to how human handle real world objects - think of paper files in your shelf!
Thus, group behavior and formation may be seen as a necessary requirement for
appropriate performance of applications in Ubicomp.

The basic concept of collective group behavior, which is the central concept of
this paper, is the **collaborative** achievement of a **common goal**. For instance,

H. Ichikawa et al. (Eds.): UCS 2007, LNCS 4836, pp. 134–149, 2007.
© Springer-Verlag Berlin Heidelberg 2007

several wireless sensor devices, which are attached to objects, work as a collaborative electronic seal [1]. They jointly monitor transport and storage conditions and reason on the common seal's state. Reliability and correct recognition of the seal state is acquired collectively by bringing together information from various types of detection sources from different kind of wireless sensor network devices. This paper presents a novel approach for such robust collective recognition using a specially designed auction algorithm.

The paper starts with a motivating example and requirement analysis followed by an overview over group formation and auction methods. The design of the auction method is presented formally, and its effects are described in theory and based on a performance evaluation. At the end, an application example shows an use case and analysis, how the proposed method helps in that context.

2   Motivation and Requirements Analysis

To informally identify the requirements and constraints for the proposed approach, we depict a motivating example. The example is based on experience collected for a feasibility study from one of our projects [1].

The scenario is taken from an analysis of a notary's office with a large archive containing important paper documents. The archive contains documents that are filed together according to instance or incident. Files are not allowed to be taken apart and documents must not be removed. So far there are only manual countermeasures possible, e.g. supervising each visitor personally while in the archive. The use of technology may be of help, but we learned that there are further restrictions: Not all of the files can be equipped with electronics due to cost reasons, only the important and precious once. Also, it must be possible to take out a archived file to a lawyers desk to allow work on the case, but the system must detect when a single document is removed from the file. No additional manual work should be required to maintain the technical system, such as check in or managing of documents to file order, as this would raise the handling costs. Technical requirements taken from the above example are:

– Autonomous start of the group formation process without user involvement
– Autonomous run of the the detection process
– Infrastructure-less operation: the absence of a document in a file must be detected independent of supporting infrastructure by the involved objects (documents and files). This requires a decentralized, but simple algorithm that could be carried out among the sensor nodes directly.
– For a maintenance free process, minimal energy consumption is required. Minimal energy consumption can be archived by minimizing network time. This impedes the use of existing communication methods and technologies. The exception is the use of superimposing signals as communication technology basis [2] for the algorithm. See discussion at the end of the paper.
– High robustness against miss-detection and performance under inappropriate conditions - e.g. noisy communication channels.

We present in this paper an auction method that is capable of fulfilling the above requirements. The auction algorithm presented is able to collaboratively form a group based on a feature (e.g. a sensor value), or an interval of a feature. In our above example, such characteristic feature (fingerprint) is generated out of movement data. The group is initiated when first bringing in the file into the archive by detecting the same movement fingerprint through the sensors built into each of the documents and the file wrapper. The file wrapper's sensor node is then responsible for holding and comparing the documents belonging to his group and to trigger an alarm when one of the group members leave.

2.1 Potential of Group Formation Algorithms

The above motivation demonstrates only a small part of the potential of the auction based collaborative group formation concept. The proposed method can:

- Set up, supervise and dissolve group membership
- Set up groups according to strict or fuzzy common properties
- Agreement on values (e.g. collective selection of the best sensor reading), similar to voting algorithms. The difference is that auctions algorithms do not require knowledge about the number or identity of participants.
- Epidemic forwarding of agreed values. This is done by successively building up groups that are spread over regional areas.
- Integration of all these processes within a single and minimal communication step, thus greatly minimizing the number of information to be transferred via wireless communication channels. This results in an optimized transmission time and highly reduced power consumptions making the method applicable to low-power sensor networks or passively powered RFID systems.

3   Auction-Based Group Formation

Before we present the group formation method, we shortly introduce auction concepts and auction-based group formation.

3.1 Variants of Auction Methods

Auctions are market-based algorithms, where prices are used to achieve a common coordination. Classical auction methods require an auctioneer that is responsible for starting and closing an auction and one or more bidders communicating bids to the auctioneer.

There are several variants of auction methods known, and the most popular is probably the English auction variant. In an open English auction the auctioneer starts with the lowest price value and increments it step-by-step. Each price is broadcasted to all bidders, which compare it to their private maximum value and accept or close by sending an accept/close message back to the auctioneer. Each bidder follows its own bidding strategy to decide on accepting or closing. All auction participants know all bids. Once the bidder closes the price, she drops out of the next auction step. The auction runs as long as bidders offer bids to the announced price. The final negotiated price is the highest one.

Apart from the above-described English auction, another well-known type is the Dutch auction, where prices are counted downwards. Finally, the Vickrey auction is a closed auction, i.e. only the auctioneer knows the bids. After the start each bidder has exactly one bid and the auctioneer select the second highest bid. Ebay auctions would be Vickrey type auctions, under the condition that all users use the proxy functionality.

3.2 Auction-Based Group Formation Concept

The proposed method is a variant of the English auction type. The difference to the original auction type is twofold: First, there is no dedicated auctioneer. Instead the coordination is distributed among all partners in the auction. Second, there are multiple winners of the auction possible that collectively own the property - i.e. being a member of the group. Sensor nodes take part in the auction based on so-called local belief b. A local belief represents a local and private value of each node stating in how far he believes in the auctioneered item. In the case of a Ubicomp scenario, measured sensor values - e.g. movement fingerprints from the introductionary example - are belief items to be auctioneered. A belief in this case expresses the level of certainty of a sensor sampling or processing result of a reasoning process. The benefit of this approach is, that for example results of context recognition processes such as Bayesian inference processes could be directly used as context believes. Figure 1 shows an example belief function of a sensor node. The belief domain interval is normalized and fixed to $[0; 100]$ in our example. The belief b_n of a node n is surrounded by two border values: b_n^{low} and b_n^{high}. Both values determine the sensor n's local belief interval I_n. The interval expresses the significance of a local belief. A broad interval means that the belief

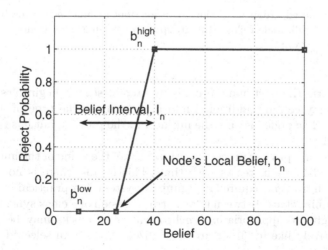

Fig. 1. A node's local auction strategy based on its belief state (example)

b_n is less significant than a very tight interval. For example, if b_n is a context belief, e.g. from a Baysian inference process, then I_n may express the confidence interval around b_n. It suggests how exact the context recognition process is. The more significant, the more exact is the recognition process. As a consequence, the interval around b_n gets tighter. Beliefs outside this interval express then very likely a different context belief than b_n. In relation to the auction algorithm the belief interval defines an auction strategy, i.e. how a node behaves on an offer: A node will at first accept an offer at b_n^{low} and will at latest reject the offer at b_n^{high}. The sensor node may reject even a bit before, as expressed by the growing reject probability between b_n and b_n^{high} in Figure 1.

3.3 Auction-Based Group Formation Algorithm

The group formation takes place using the above described believes as items to be auctioned. Each node starts bidding at the belief point b_n^{low} and ends bidding between b_n and b_n^{high}. The algorithm steps are described below and depicted in Figure 2 for a simple example with two nodes.

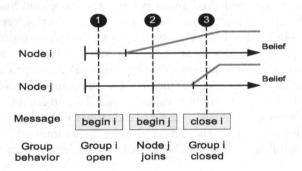

Fig. 2. Auction-based group formation. The auctioneer announces the steps on the belief scale. In step 3, node i closes the group by a close-message. Hence, nodes i and j are in the same group.

1. Node i starts the auctioning process by broadcasting a begin message. The message may contain additional information about the type of item to be auctioned. The node i is only the initiator of the process, but has not further special role.
   - The auctioning process proceeds with time, i.e. the value of the auctioneered item - the belief - increases with time. This means, there is no additional information transfer required in a minimal system. For practical reasons - i.e. to synchronize clocks between nodes - transmission of a clock synchronization signal might be appropriate. Synchronization of clocks may be generated collaboratively like in [3], or are centralized through an selected node, e.g. the initiator.

2. If any node j detects that the belief value reaches b_j^{low}, it enters the auction by broadcasting a begin-message. This way, all participants of the auction group know the identity of all other members of the group.
   - Any node that is member of the auction group checks, if the auctioneered belief value reaches the values b_n. If this is the case, the node computes its current maximal belief b_n^{cur} using the node's belief function shown in figure 1 as input for the probability to end the auction. The node then waits until (and if) the value reaches the computed b_n^{cur} and sends a close-message.
3. If any of the nodes has send a close-message, the group is closed and all other nodes end processing with the previous step. The group members are all nodes that have sent an begin-message, but have not yet seen a close-message so far. The closing node is also a member of this group. Any node, initiator or any other node, is allowed to close a group.

It is important to see, that the above described algorithm could be implemented in a very minimal way, using e.g. short RF signals - not complete packets. An extensive discussion about the features of the proposed algorithm will be presented in the next section.

3.4   Probability of Membership

The above examples are somehow simplified descriptions of the auctioning mechanism presented in this paper. To be more general, the auction may start at any belief point b^{auct} (which was assumed to be 0 in the previous examples) and may end at any value (was 100 in the previous example). For this we are able to give the probability density function. In the algorithm, the auctioneer announces the belief b^{auct} and any node replies with a reject-message according to the belief function in Figure 1. Hence, the probability for a reject message is defined as follows:

$$p(b^{auct}) = \begin{cases} 0 & \text{if } b^{low} < b^{auct} < b \\ \frac{b^{auct}-b}{b^{high}-b} & \text{if } b \le b^{auct} \le b^{high} \\ 1 & \text{if } b^{auct} > b^{high} \end{cases} \quad (1)$$

We denote by $X_i = j$ the membership of node j to group i.

$$\begin{aligned} \forall j \ b_i^{low} \le b_j^{low} \le b_i &\Rightarrow P(X_i = j) = 1 \\ \forall j \ b_i < b_j^{low} \le b_i^{high} &\Rightarrow P(X_i = j) = 1 - p_i(b_j^{low}) \\ \forall j \ b_i^{high} < b_j^{low} &\Rightarrow P(X_i = j) = 0 \end{aligned} \quad (2)$$

This approach can be further extended if the group contains more than just one node. Lets take for example a group containing no less than l members. Node k has sent its begin-message and therewith has opend the group k. The probability that a new node j with a announced believe b_j^{auct} will join this group k can be calculated using:

$$P(X_k = j, l) = \prod_{i=k}^{k+l} \left[1 - p_i(b_j^{auct}) \right] \quad (3)$$

This equation applies when group k has l or more nodes. The probability in (3) states: if there are more nodes within the belief interval I_k of node k, it is less likely for j to join in. The more nodes are within I_k, the more belief functions are ready to trigger a close-message before j has sent its begin-message.

Equation (3) delivers an easy way to calculate the expected value of members in a given group. The approach relies on two conditions. First, the slope in the belief interval, denoted by s, must be the same for all nodes and second all beliefs, which the auctioneer can announce in this interval, must be occupied by the nodes. We begin with the cumulative distribution function (cdf) for a belief slope s given by $\Phi_s(l) = 1 - P(X_k = j, l)$. Because of the monotonic decrease of $P(X_k = j, l)$, we have to apply $1 - P(X_k = j, l)$ in order to get the cdf. The probability density function (pdf) is obtained by the difference quotient Δ, which is the slope in $P(\cdot)$ between l and $l + 1$. We denote $\Delta\Phi_s(l) = \phi_s(l)$. We then proceed to calculating the expected value using the standard formula:

$$E_s[X_k] = \sum_{b_k}^{b_k^{high}} l\phi_s(l) \tag{4}$$

$E_s[X_k]$ denotes the expected number of group member when all nodes have the same slope s and all believes in the belief interval of a group-starting node k are taken by other nodes. The results from our extensive simulations further confirm the validity of the result from equation (4).

3.5   Discussion

This section will discuss primary features of the auction-based group formation algo-rithm and identify advantages of the approach.

Distribution of control, autonomous and infrastructure-free operatoin. The proposed algorithm does not require any dedicated node to drive the auction process, nor any infrastructure support, nor any manual intervention. Although there is an initiator, this role is only defined by this object being the first one to send an open message, and is not distinguished among other nodes. In practical implementation, that initiator may additionally set the initial values and may also define parameters for embedding the algorithm in a concrete application.

Minimized number of communication messages. The number of messages is minimal for the overall process in general. This is because there is only one begin message required from each of the participants - which is minimal because else other group members do not know about the new member. It is also min-imal, because there is only one close message required from one of the node to end the process. Acceptance of group membership for all other nodes is implicit.

Minimized Message complexity. There are only two type of messages re-quired for a minimal process run. Assuming that the communication character-istics are know beforehand, and that the belief interval starts at 0, we would require two simple signals for performing the process. The benefit of such min-imal signaling is twofold: For all types of devices, minimizing signaling greatly reduces energy consumption. Compared to traditional voting algorithms and the required exchange of packets, several magnitudes of gain in energy performance can be expected. The second benefit is the simplicity of the algorithm. Because of this characteristic, the use of the algorithm in extreme simple circuitry - e.g. in ultra-low-cost RFID systems - is possible.

Data compatibility. We see believes as a kind of universal model to express a value and the trust in the value. These values are independent of the used encoding scheme, and thus appropriate for Ubicomp settings with very heterogeneous devices. The analog scheme of the communication process is even capable of including devices that communicate using analog signaling and processing.

Formation control. As presented so far, the group formation algorithm does not include leaving a formed group. Leaving a group can be implemented by a successive group formation runs, where all those nodes that are not willing to believe anymore step out by not bidding. This method has the advantage that a permanent supervision of the group membership takes place and that dynamic changes - e.g. nodes that leave the area or run out of battery or communication link breaks - are automatically taken into account. Dynamicity of the process can be controlled by either setting a fixed time interval for repeated group formation, or by letting any node that wants to propagate information starting the formation process again on demand. The benefit for the latter strategy is the highly reduced power consumption, while the benefit of the first strategy is a highly increased robustness of the process.

Multi-Group Formation. The group formation process can be used to determine group memberships according to various believes by simply successively starting an auction process with different believes. This allows to simply build up interest groups within a large set of sensor nodes.

Privacy. Although nodes are required to uncover their entry point b^{low}, to the members of the group, neither b^{high} nor b are unveiled. For the overall process, other strategies than depicted in figure 1 are thinkable. Different strategies of individual nodes do not disturb the general Auction-based Group Formation Algorithm from section 2. This way a high degree of privacy could be ensured for all participating nodes. As we expect that Ubicomp systems will be used in business and private contexts, this is a must-have property for many applications.

Robustness and Message loss. Loss of messages due to high noise level in the wireless communication channel or to changes in the environment are a common phenomenon in Ubicomp settings. Message loss will bias the auction results for the achieved group size as well as the number of formed groups. But neither a lost begin nor close-message necessarily excludes nodes from a group. When missing a begin-message, other group members joining in will send a begin-message according to the above algorithm thus proving an additional point-of-entry for a node missing a previous begin-message. When missing an close-message, those nodes that are not part of the group yet, may enter the group and thus increase group size - instead of starting their own group. Therefore, close-loss causes less groups, but with more members due to the 'virtually' increased belief interval. In a practical setting there is a simple countermeasure to this problem: Because communication requires only short signaling, repeated run of the algorithm may be feasible even when real-time, low-power communication is required.

4   Performance Evaluation

Group formation depends on a series of parameters such as the belief interval and the number of nodes. In this section we investigate the effects on the parameter choice through simulations. We also investigate the conditions under which the performance of the algorithm declines, but will also show that this happens only under VERY extreme conditions. It should be noted that the group formation is itself a stochastic process, therefore the most results and figures contain average and/or expected values.

4.1   Node Count

The section explores the relation between node count and group formation. We make no assumption on some distinguished beliefs and beliefs are uniformly distributed among the belief scale, here $[0; 100]$. The belief interval for all nodes is equally set to $I = 20$. Figure 3 shows the histogram of the number of groups after 1000 simulations for two cases, 21 and 61 nodes respectively. The group count raises with the introduction of more nodes, which can also be observed for an increasing range of nodes in Figure 4. In the range between 20 and 50 nodes this relation continues almost linearly. However, from point 50 it saturates due to the overpopulation of the belief range with nodes that have overlapping belief intervals. To conclude, for increasing node counts the algorithm may experience saturation, which stops the formation of new groups.

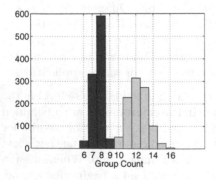
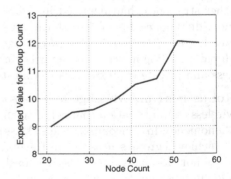

Fig. 3. Distributions of groups with 21 nodes (dark) and 61 nodes (bright)

Fig. 4. Number of formed groups for a given number of nodes

4.2   Robustness and Bias

This section investigates the robustness of the auction-based algorithm in the case of message loss. The message loss probability ranges span across the whole range between 0 (no message loss) and 1 (all messages are lost). Message loss can occur with begin-messages as wells as with close-messages. The loss of messages can have a profound impact on the group formation process and especially on the count of the formed groups. The consequences of a lost close message can lead to a stretching of certain groups and delayed or no formation of groups that follow. Figure 5 shows the change in the formation of new groups in the cases of no

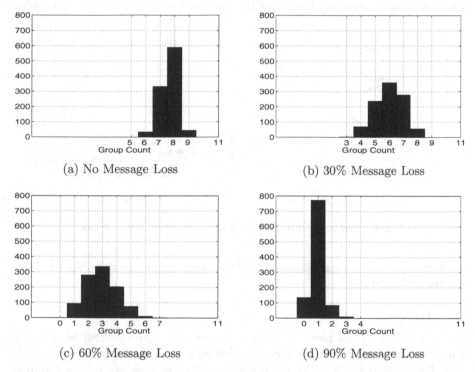

(a) No Message Loss   (b) 30% Message Loss

(c) 60% Message Loss   (d) 90% Message Loss

Fig. 5. Group count distribution for a setting with 21 nodes (1000 simulations)

message loss a), 30% b),60% c) and 90% d) message loss. There exists a tendency of shifting the average group count to the left. As the message loss probability increases the formation of new groups decreases until it reaches a critical point around 90%. From this point forward the auction-based algorithm forms either one large group or no group at all. Figure 6 a) illustrates the distortion in the group count, which is caused by message loss. The relation is approximately linear. An interesting feature is that the form of the function does not change with the increase or decrease of the node count. What changes is the steepness of the almost linear relation. The results found in figure 6 b) show impact of loss of certain messages on average group size. The auction may experience from two types of message loss: loss of begin-messages and loss of close-messages. A typical loss of a begin message must lead to a decrease in current group size. A loss of close-message may lead to an increased group size. To evaluate the impact, we count every begin-loss as a negative distortion on the group size and every close-loss is positively counted. Figure 6b) shows a negative curve indicating that begin-losses causing a dominant distortion on the average group size rather than close-losses. An explanation for such a behavior can be found in the algorithm itself. Every close-message loss can be 'replaced' by a successful close-message from the node that follows, but unsuccessful begin-messages always lead to a decrease in the group size no matter how many members there are in the current group. Another interesting feature of the auction-based algorithm is also shown

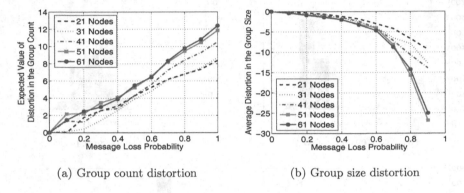

(a) Group count distortion   (b) Group size distortion

Fig. 6. Bias for group count and size caused by message loss

in figure 6b). The average distortion is almost constant up to the point of about 60 Percent for all node counts.

4.3 Accuracy

The accuracy describes how well the auction-based algorithm identifies a single group. We assume that group members follow a normal distribution $\mathcal{N}(b_\mu, \sigma)$ around a given belief b_μ. The parameter σ indicates how strongly a group is stretched. Each group member is assigned to a belief b_n selected from the normal distribution around b_μ. The accuracy depends further on the belief interval I_n of each member. It is further $I_1 = \ldots = I_n = I = const.$ for all members. In this investigation we are interested in the expected number of groups $E_{\sigma,I}[G]$ for a distribution of group counts G found by the auction algorithm. The figure 7 depicts this expected value. It can be seen that the auction-based algorithm works very stable for variances below $\sigma = 1.4$. In these cases, it always forms one single group depicted as a black surface in the figure 7. This is the ideal result. Brighter surfaces in the figure mean group counts larger than 1. The legend at the right side of the graph reflects the expected group counts. We must further note that the parameter σ has a much larger impact on the accuracy of the algorithm than the belief interval I.

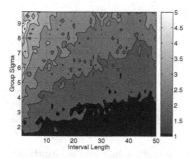
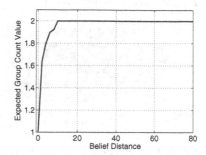

Fig. 7. Accuracy of the auctioning for finding a single group for a belief interval I and a group variance σ (black = single group)

Fig. 8. Selectivity: expected number of groups, when two groups move towards each other (1000 simulations, no loss)

4.4 Selectivity

Selectivity describes the accuracy of separating two groups. We select here two groups, which can be clearly identified as separate groups according to the result from sec. 4.3. Fig. 8 shows the expected value for the number of groups that can be formed using our algorithm. The two groups contain 10 member nodes with beliefs according to a normal distribution with $\sigma = 1.1$ and the interval length of the belief probability function $I = 15$. According to fig. 7, the influence on the accuracy of the algorithm is minimized. The belief distance describes the distance between the centered beliefs values of the two groups on the belief scale. The curve in fig. 8 shows the growing tendency in the selectivity of the algorithm. A critical point is reached at belief distance 10. From that point forward the auction-based method separates the two groups precisely.

5 A Use Case for Collaboration and Group Formation

Within the research project Collaborative Business Items, CoBIs ([4], http://www.cobis-online.de), we explored automatic workplace safety enforcements when handling hazardous chemicals in one of BP's plants. Wireless sensor nodes were attached on chemical drums (figure 9) and collaboratively processed critical information in order to detect hazardous situations like an exceeded storage limit, prohibited storage combinations of materials or an invalid storage area. Alerts were raised visually on the drums for notification of nearby workers. The setting required in-situ, infrastructure-less, real-time detection. CoBIs was implemented on the Particle Computer sensor node platform [5]. The configuration consists of communication board and sensor board in splash water resistant housing: 8bit PIC18LF6720 MCU, RFM TR1001 communciation at 868MHz with 125kbit/s, sensors: light, temperature and acceleration, Actuators: two ultra bright LEDs plus warning light (dedicted nodes only). In [6], we explored an agent-based implementation of auctions on Particle nodes. The auction mechanisms were

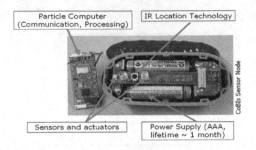

Fig. 9. Left: Particle nodes for CoBIs. Right: Detecting hazardous situations.

implemented on the Particle sensor node using the Particle JavaVM [7]. The auction logic runs independently as a Java agent class on the node. Which node starts the group formation depends on who first detects a situation, e.g. on the detection of a hazardous event. In the implementation the AwareCon TDMA synchronization protocol [3] provides a ultra-low power distributed clock synchronization algorithm for exact high-reliable group formation.

5.1   Collaborative Alerting with Auction-Based Group Formation

In CoBIs, nodes constantly test the current storage conditions such as amount of stored material and dangerous combinations, e.g. inflammable and oxidizing chemicals. Once a violation against pre-defined conditions is found, the nodes raise locally an alert in order to inform nearby workers. Alerts are propagated to other nodes, which also raise an alert and further propagate it. As a result, the alert is flooded through the wireless sensor network. Alerts emitted by the source of the condition violation are so-called *local alerts*, while re-emitted alerts are *remote alerts* (figure 10). Ending an alert situation is more difficult: How can the alert decay or in other words how can the nodes achieve the common state of non-alert? Most nodes are always slightly in a alert situation, also because of their high sensitivity to potential dangerous situations. Hence, remote alerts are sent repeatedly and raise other remote alerts. This motivates a belief model of the alert states as show in figure 11. The alert states are associated with the zones for non-alert, remote alert and local alert on the belief scale. The auction-based group formation detects number of groups and their size. If the alert, e.g. a storage violation is resolved, the local alert group dissolves. This is detected by other groups and the remote alert groups decay their beliefs, e.g. by halving them. Each node does this individually. As a consequence, groups move towards the non-alert zone (see figure 11, lower fig.) similar to the findings in section 4.4, while moving groups are stretched and separated in smaller groups.

We compare the group formation approach with a low pass filter implementation - an application specific implementation for achieving the common non-alert state. The low pass runs on each node and decays the remote alert after a time-out. However, if it receives an alert after it exceeded the timeout, it will start over alerting. Because timeouts are slightly different, an alert will ping-pong

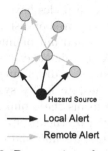

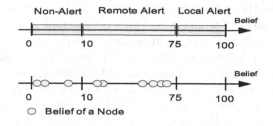

Fig. 10. Propagation of a hazard alert

Fig. 11. Belief scale devided in alert zones (example); lower fig.: beliefs of nodes moving towards the non-alert zone

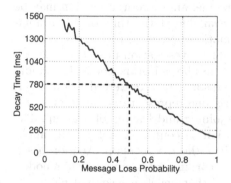

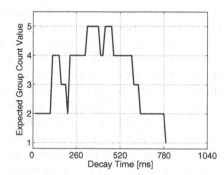

Fig. 12. Alert decay behavior for low pass filter. Message loss behaves causing a low pass effect.

Fig. 13. Group formation behavior when converging to the non-alert zone. After 780ms all nodes achieve the non-alert state.

forever when no message get lost. The degree of message loss determines overall decay time of an alert for the low pass filter (figures 12 , 13). The alert timeout was set to 130ms and blurred for individual nodes to account for slight timeout drifts. For the low pass filter in fig. 12 the message loss corresponds to the decay timeout. For the auction-based group formation the fig. 13 depicts the expected number groups. They finally converge to exactly one group into the non-alert zone at 780ms. We found that as long as the message loss is below approximately 50%, the auction-based approach will outperform the low pass filter. Further, the ping-pong effect is resolved and convergence to the non-alert zone is guaranteed. Decay times are derived based on AwareCon's 13ms TDMA slot. Ideally, if no loss and no time drift occur, the alert will decay in one timeout period of 130ms.

6   Related Work

The XCast approach establishes a distributed shared information space for wireless sensor nodes. Nodes share common information through XCast. It was shown by the authors, that the design can reach a fix point, i.e. all nodes have a consistent view and access on a quantum of shared data. In the area of distributed systems, consensus describes a mechanism to agree on quantum of information between members of a resource population [8]. A prominent example is the Byzantine Agreement (BA), which explores consensus in a distributed voting process [9]. The goal is to agree on a given state despite faulty systems. In contrast to XCast and BA, the auctioning approach forms the group across several belief states. It *agrees on a new value*, represented by the group, which is a compromise for all members. As a consequence, private information has not to be revealed to others. Further, it relaxes the very strict assumptions on message loss and synchronization in case of BA. In the context of CoBIs, a related approach for enabling collaboration is the arteFACT framework [10]. It implements a Prolog interpreter, which uses rules in form of Horn clauses and proves for inconsistencies. Once it discovers one, an appropriate action may be raised. It presumes that all input data is available at the time of rule evaluation. In contrast, auction-based group formation may even proceed to operate when data is missing due to message loss. The investigation in section 4.2 lead even to an estimation of the resulting bias and allows instant corrective action. Finally, group management protocols for sensor networks were developed [11] to organizes them in groups. The group has one representative node and others may join in. The protocols coordinate joining and leaving of a group. The selection of which group is appropriate to join is completely left to the application. Mostly, physical proximity determines the membership. Auction-based group formation builds distributive groups according across a variety of a node's local information. It is automatically ensured that beliefs are compatible.

7   Conclusion and Outlook

We presented an auction-based negotiation mechanism for group formation of networked embedded systems for ubiquitous computing. It exhibits crucial properties for collaborative Ubicomp applications such as data compatibility, robustness against message loss, and privacy. The algorithm runs truly distributed. Auction-based group formation achieves the goal of providing a uniform abstraction layer. Groups are formed across various networked embedded systems and their various local information. The application in the CoBIs use case and the achieved results show that it adds significantly to the performance of collaborative networked embedded systems and outperforms application specific implementations for achieving a common agreement. Future research will analyze effects of node density and large distributed networks. The research question is whether the formation process can be parallelized and local groups can be merged in larger ones. Cooperative transmission was successfully shown to work on sensor nodes [2] and might be an efficient signaling mechanism for the auction. New Ubicomp applications will be based on this group formation and the effects on their performance will be investigated in more detail.

Acknowledgments

The work presented in this paper was partially funded by the EC through the project RELATE (contract no. 4270) and by the Ministry of Economic Affairs of the Netherlands through the project Smart Surroundings (contract no. 03060).

References

1. Decker, C., Beigl, M., Krohn, A., Robinson, P., Kubach, U.: eseal - a system for enhanced electronic assertion of authenticity and integrity. In: Pervasive (2004)
2. Krohn, A.: Optimal non-coherent m-ary energy shift keying for cooperative transmission in sensor networks. In: ICASSP. 31st IEEE International Conference on Acoustics, Speech, and Signal Processing (2006)
3. Krohn, A., Beigl, M., Decker, C., Riedel, T.: Syncob: Collaborative time synchronization in wireless sensor networks. In: INSS. 4th International Conference on Networked Sensing Systems (2007)
4. Decker, C., Riedel, T., Beigl, M., sa de Souza, L.M., Spiess, P., Mueller, J., Haller3, S.: Collaborative business items. In: 3rd IET International Conference on Intelligent Environments (2007)
5. Decker, C., Krohn, A., Beigl, M., Zimmer, T.: The particle computer system. In: IPSN. ACM/IEEE Information Processing in Sensor Networks, pp. 443–448. IEEE Computer Society Press, Los Alamitos (2005)
6. Decker, C., van Dinther, C., Mller, J., Schleyer, M., Peev, E.: Collaborative smart items. In: UbiLog 2007. Workshop for Context-aware and Ubiquitous Applications in Logistics (2007)
7. Riedel, T., Arnold, A., Decker, C.: An oo approach to sensor programming. In: Langendoen, K., Voigt, T. (eds.) EWSN 2007. LNCS, vol. 4373, Springer, Heidelberg (2007)
8. Barborak, M., Dahbura, A., Malek, M.: The consensus problem in fault-tolerant computing. ACM Comput. Surv. 25(2), 171–220 (1993)
9. Lamport, L., Shostak, R., Pease, M.: The byzantine generals problem. ACM Trans. Program. Lang. Syst. 4(3), 382–401 (1982)
10. Strohbach, M., Gellersen, H., Kortuem, G., Kray, C.: Cooperative artefacts: Assessing real world situations with embedded technology. In: Davies, N., Mynatt, E.D., Siio, I. (eds.) UbiComp 2004. LNCS, vol. 3205, Springer, Heidelberg (2004)
11. Vieira, M.S., Rosa, N.S.: A reconfigurable group management middleware service for wireless sensor networks. In: MPAC 2005. Proceedings of the 3rd international workshop on Middleware for pervasive and ad-hoc computing, pp. 1–8. ACM Press, New York (2005)

A Software Architecture for Virtual Device Composition and Its Applications

Jin Wook Lee[1], Su Myeon Kim[1], Hun Lim[1], Mario Schuster[2], and Alexander Domene[2]

[1] Samsung Advanced Institute of Technology (SAIT), Communication & Networking Lab., P.O. Box 111, Suwon, 440-600, Korea
[2] Fraunhofer Institute for Open Communication Systems (FOKUS), Kaiserin-Augusta-Allee 31, 10589, Berlin, Germany

Abstract. In this paper we propose a software architecture enabling a user-centric virtual device which is a composition of partial functions of surrounding devices. Increasingly, new information appliances and mobile personal devices are being equipped with many primitive functions, such as network connectivity, small display, advanced user interface, etc. However, constraints like small screen and tiny keypad impose usage limitations for a user. We focus on the possibility and flexibility of individual functions' unification and separation to create a new user friendly environment with personal and public devices. A software architecture is designed and implemented to show the validation of our proposal.

1 Introduction

Digital convergence has been realized in industry and advanced networking technology has gradually edged closer toward enabling real ubiquitous services. Many innovative devices have been greatly developed and improved recently. However, a number of hardware components is not used fully and freely so that the scope of use of these digital devices is limited. It is challenge to devise a way for a user to be able to exploit more convenient and powerful functions of any surrounding devices for substituting an original function of a device, for instance, switching a keypad of a cell phone to a keyboard of a desktop PC. So far software technology has not been significantly considered as a key inhibitor to the extension of digital device functions whereas hardware design technology has been focused. In this paper we propose a software platform for enabling a user to overcome the limitation or the inconvenience of usage by creating a virtual device integrated with best primitive functions of surrounding devices.

1.1 Concept

The concept and an example of virtual device compositions are illustrated in Fig. 1. At first, devices in the user's vicinity are discovered by a software manager that resides on a user's device (e.g., mobile phone or mobile computer). Discovered devices share the information of their functions, which can be combined by the user on demand to create a virtual device providing rich-input or -output capabilities (e.g., a big display or a keyboard is more suitable to work with the mobile phone). The user selects one or

H. Ichikawa et al. (Eds.): UCS 2007, LNCS 4836, pp. 150–157, 2007.

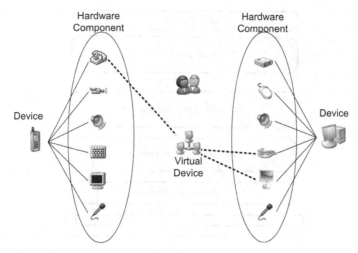

Fig. 1. Concept of Virtual Device Composition. A virtual device is a logical device composed of a collection of multiple device functions. Each function of network connected devices can participate in a virtual device.

multiple device functionalities to form a new virtual device instance within the platform by grouping the chosen hardware components together and connecting matching functions. As shown in Fig. 1, a mobile phone and a desktop PC are connected to wireless network and discovered, for instance. A user may compose a virtual desktop phone by selecting the phone call function of the mobile phone and the keyboard and the display of the desktop PC. This composition provides the user with an enhanced virtual mobile phone which provides the same services as a cell phone but bigger display service and more convenient keyboard service. We developed a modularized solution, called Virtual Device Platform (VDP), consisting of a software manager and a middleware module and a hardware adaptation module on top of Operating System. In the platform, devices can be identified by their function descriptions along with interfaces, which describe device capabilities, and non-functional aspects.

2 Architecture

The abstract architecture of VDP is depicted in Fig. 2 with the block diagram. We believe that, corresponding to virtual device composition, a hierarchy of management responsibilities is needed. The idea behind this architecture is to facilitate the management of software components. The main features of VDP layered architecture may be separated into two abstraction modules, such as hardware adaptation and software abstraction. We envisage more heterogeneous devices will be developed and used in near future. Also more software programming technologies, such as languages will be popularized. It is hence desirable for VDP architecture to be able to accommodate any type of devices and applications. In the platform we propose three different responsibility entities, such as Virtual Device Adaptor, Virtual Device Middleware, and Virtual Device Manager. Virtual Device Adaptor (VDA) is responsible for the adaptation of

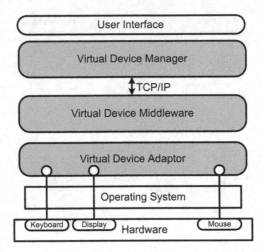

Fig. 2. Architecture of Virtual Device Platform. VDP consists of three function modules, Virtual Device Manager, Virtual Device Middleware, and Virtual Device Adaptor.

hardware and can handle multiple virtual device drivers, which are linked to the device drivers of Operating Systems or to the related system functions of the corresponding runtime environment. Virtual Device Middleware (VDMW) is responsible for overall communications between devices in VDP and adapts native device functionalities to enable sharing functionalities with others. Virtual Device Manager (VDM) is responsible for managing and controlling virtual devices. Above VDM resides a user interface application of the VDM. The first two higher modules (VDA and VDMW) are core and therefore mandatory, which must be installed by all compatible devices that propagate their basic functions to others or to use other services. The remaining two modules (VDM and UI) are optional modules that are more application oriented and are responsible for enabling composition of different services. In the following we introduce VDA, VDMW, and VDM of the VDP software platform.

2.1   Virtual Device Adaptor

Virtual Device Adaptor (VDA) is a software module running in between VDMW and Hardware. VDA manages each hardware component and supports the adaptation of device driver modules. VDA controls and manages Virtual Device Drivers (VDD) associated with general device drivers. A VDD is a wrapping software module of a device driver for each hardware component or functionality. A general device driver acts as a translator between hardware components and software that use the hardware components whereas VDD is an interface module between a general device driver and VDA. A VDD enables hardware components to work as VD enabled function components OS-independently in form of VDD services. A VDD can have several services and a VDD service is a unit in a VD composition. A user composes a VD by selecting multiple VDD services of devices. In other words, a virtual device is a combination of multiple VDDs through the related services. VDA also provides VDMW with the information of the

VDDs of the device. In VDP architecture, VDA contains six sub modules, such as Event Handler, Event Generator, Message Handler, Message Formatter, Message Generator, and VDA Controller. To make hardware components of multiple devices cooperative, it should be possible for events generated by hardware components to exchange between devices through the network. In this work, an event message is defined as a network message whose content is hardware and software events. All hardware and software events should be transferable with event messages. The two key tasks of VDA are to generate event messages responding to events in a self device and to process incoming event messages containing hardware and software events of other devices. During the operation of a VD, VDA monitors hardware components which participate in the VD and fetches hardware and software events of the components. Then, it generates event messages to send out to other devices through a network.

Event Handler. Hardware events are monitored by VDDs and logged by Event Handler. Hardware events trigger general device drivers which embedded in VDDs. VDDs monitor and transform the events into the VDP-compatible event data. For instance, a single keyboard typing generates a hardware event which represents a character. VDD fetches the character input and generates event data. Once Event Handler receives the event data, it forwards the data to Message Formatter in order to adapt the data format for other device. Event Handler collects also software events generated by Event Generator.

Event Generator. Some hardware components, such as a monitor and a disk drive do not generate hardware events because they are passive data processing units. A monitor displays the visual data as an output component. A disk drive works by other components demand. In the case that an update data should be sent from a device to another device, the update data checking is started in response to an explicit request from Event Generator in software manner. Event Generator watches over a hardware component and generates software event as the hardware component generates the event.

Message Formatter. When Event Handler receives an event from a VDD or Event Generator, it forwards the event to Message Formatter. All messages generated in VDs should be understandable by any digital devices. As each device may handle with own data format or size, a message including the data should be transformed to be understandable to other side. The data requiring the transformation are such as Matching display size(Scaling/Scrolling), Image format(GIF), Sound format(RAW/AU), Key mapping, and so on.

Message Generator. Receiving a formatted event data from Message Formatter, Message Generator assorts the event data and provides the address of destination devices. Eventually event messages are generated and queued in Message Generator which sends out the event messages in consideration of the network bandwidth.

Message Handler. When event messages come into VDA, Message Handler catches the messages and opens them to distribute the events into proper VDDs. The VDDs then triggers the action of the hardware components according to the content of the messages.

VDA Controller. VDA Controller manages all VDDs. Loading or unloading VDDs are also the tasks of VDA Controller. During the operation of a VD, VDA Controller monitors the VDDs participated in the VD and reports the states of the VD operation to VDMW regularly or on demand. VDA Controller keeps the information of VDDs and reports them to VDMW which generates service descriptions accordingly.

2.2 Virtual Device Middleware

Virtual Device Middleware (VDMW) is responsible for maintaining Device/Service Description, Device Access Control, and Device Discovery. VDMW also acts like a proxy between VDA and Virtual Device Manager (VDM) for discovery and controlling virtual devices. VDMW enables communication between different VDP instances by managing device to device connection. Brief descriptions of each of these components are described in the followings.

Device/Service Description Module. At bootstrap, VDA scans the VDD states. The raw states are reported by VDA to VDMW. Referencing the states, Device/Service Description module generates the valid device/service descriptions mapping the device/service functions. These device/service descriptions are propagated to the network and are understood by other devices with a VDP runtime environment. These descriptions contain the general meta information about device/service such as vendor, service type, and name as well as the general information about the basic service behavior and the way how the service can be composed with other services.

Device Discovery Module. Device Discovery module advertises the device information such as IP address and general properties of the device by broadcasting device information. As receiving the other devices information, the module collects them and utilizes the presence of devices.

Device Access Control Module. A user uses Device Access Control module to privatize the component of the device. If the device functionality is exclusive and can be used only by one user at a time, then this module locks the functionality to prohibit others from using it at the same time. When a VD composition is activated, this module ensures that all relevant device functionalities are free to use.

Configuration Module. Configuration module controls the behavior of VDMW. The behavior of VDMW is described by its specific attributes (e.g., time interval to send the announcement messages). These attributes can be updated via this module to change how VDMW will function.

Device to Device Connection Module. Device to Device Connection module manages the communication between devices running with VDMW. An advertisement of available devices, a device discovery request, and a request to activate or deactivate a VD composition are sent via this module.

2.3 Virtual Device Manager

Virtual Device Manager (VDM) of VDP architecture is responsible for controlling a virtual device composition and managing the composed virtual device. While the first two modules, VDA and VDMW, are essentially installed in a device to participate in sharing and using device functionalities, VDM in a device is optionally installed and only needed if the device plays a role in creating and managing a virtual device. VDM is an interface module to tell a user of a virtual device composition. VDM uses the interface provided by VDMW to discover available device services and their descriptions and provides an interface that a user interface application can use to manage and control the virtual device composition.

VD Composition Module. VD Composition module is the central component that manages and controls VD compositions. Different sub-components of VD Composition module enable VD Management and Control functionalities. VD management functionality provides interfaces to create a new VD, modify an existing VD, and to remove an existing VD. VD control functionality provides interfaces to activate or deactivate an existing VD.

VD Description Module. Devices, its functionalities and virtual devices are specified in a specified format. VD Description module specifies the structure and provides functionalities to access specific descriptions.

VD Discovery Module. VD Discovery module searches for available devices and their offered functionalities or services. It finds not only the basic device functionalities but also the active virtual devices as a device functionality that can again be used to create a new composition. This component is responsible in maintaining Service Repository.

VD Configuration Module. VD Configuration module is responsible for the configuration of VDM. Through this module the behavior of the VDM can be controlled. VD Configuration module essentially manages different attributes of VDM (e.g., location of the repository, auto or manual service discovery, etc.) and provides the appropriate interfaces to update the configuration. Using the configuration module, a user can adjust the behavior of VDM.

VD Access Control Module. VD Access Control module makes sure whether a user or a virtual device have right to access certain device or services. The module ensures that personal device functionalities are restricted for the owner of a device only and not for public. It also checks if the device functionality is locked before activating a composition for the user.

3 Implementation

To validate the architecture design, we implemented a VDP prototype consisting of VDP architecture, some Virtual Device Drivers (VDDs), and a VDM User Interface for a mobile phone. The implementation is based on several demonstration scenarios to clarify the idea of VDP and to illustrate the benefit of virtual device composition. The reference implementation is realized with Microsoft Operating Systems. Thus, the existing VDP applications are limited to Windows and Windows Mobile at the moment. We decide to focus on this platform due to a rapid prototyping of the envisioned. This does not necessarily mean that VDP only runs under Microsoft based operating systems.

3.1 Discovery

The communication for discovery in the prototype implementation is done using a combination of the Simple Service Discovery Protocol (SSDP) and a proprietary remote invocation implementation based on TCP/IP. SSDP is also part of UPnP and we used the SSDP implementation of the micro UPnP stack from Intel for discovery and service announcement. Therefore, though the architecture does not specify any specific type of network connectivity as obligatory, IP network connectivity is mandatory for running the current VDP implementation.

3.2   Adapted Device Functionalities

Based on the identified demonstration scenarios, several relevant device functionalities have been adapted in the prototype implementation as a virtual service that can be used by others to create a new virtual device. Virtual Device Drivers (VDDs) for display, keyboard, storage, and enhancing phone functionalities have been implemented. VDDs for display and keyboard facilitate sharing display and keyboard function between different devices correspondingly. A VDD for storage functionality enables sharing data storage and the VDD for enhancing mobile phone functionality allows improved user experience for some core mobile phone functionality like SMS receiving and sending.

3.3   An Example of Virtual Device Composition

We set up the demonstration environment that includes three personal devices connected wirelessly, a cell phone, an Ultra Mobile PC (UMPC), and a desktop PC. Windows XP is running on two PCs whereas a cell phone is a Windows Mobile 5.0 device. This section introduces a VD composition in case that a user wants to forward display of a desktop PC to UMPC by composing a virtual device. The following description elaborates how to make an appropriate VD composition for the scenario stated above. Fig. 3 shows all steps of a VD composition.

Fig. 3. GUI for an example of a VD composition

Each composed virtual device is identified by its title and the user interface displays the title and the state of the virtual device. It can be seen that five virtual devices have been composed and a VD, 'I/O by PC', is running. To compose a virtual device, a user clicks 'Composition button'in main menu. Clicking 'Composition button'changes the elements of the top main menu. The composition main menu shows the device function list such as display, keyboard, speaker, microphone, disk, and so on to be selected. For this example, the user selects 'Display service'button. Clicking the service button makes Virtual Device Manager list all discovered display services. The discovered display functions are shown for user interaction. The user makes a display relationship between two devices by clicking input/output choice buttons. After selecting input/output display function devices and clicking 'Add'button finally, the user see the newly added relationship with icons and device titles. The virtual device composition is saved and can be used later on.

4 Conclusion

In this paper we have described a software platform enabling us to conveniently compose a virtual device. We designed and implemented three software modules, such as Virtual Device Manager, Virtual Device Middleware, and Virtual Device Adaptor, to realize the availability of a virtual device composition. We also have developed several applications running on PCs or mobile devices to test the VDP functionality and provide related demonstration scenarios. The notable feature of our architecture is adaptability in that our architecture does not require any hardware modification for a device to be VD-ready. The only software installation is enough to make a digital device VD-ready. In addition, our implementation gives a guidance of the future ubiquitous computing environment as an example. In the future the architecture will be expanded to support developers to write a general application working on top of our architecture.

References

1. Fu, R.Y., Su, H., Fletcher, J.C., Li, W., Liu, X.X., Zhao, S.W., Chi, C.Y.: A framework for device capability on demand and virtual device user experience. IBM Journal Research and Development 48(5/6), 635–648 (2004)
2. Ponnekanti, S.R., Lee, B., Fox, A., Hanrahan, P., Winograd, T.: ICrafter: A Service Framework for Ubiquitous Computing Environments. In: Proceedings of the Third International Conference on Ubiquitous Computing, pp. 56–75 (2001)
3. Thanh, D.V., Jorstad, I.: The Virtual Device - The future mobile phone? Telektronikk Technical Report, vol. 3/4, pp. 165–172 (2005)
4. Brumitt, B., Meyers, B., Krumm, J., Kern, A., Shafer, S.: EasyLiving: Technologies for Intelligent Environments. In: Proceedings of the 2nd International Symposium on Handheld and Ubiquitous Computing, pp. 12–29 (2000)
5. Myers, B.: Pebbles Project: Using PCs and Hand-Held Computers Together; Demonstration Extended Abstract. In: CHI 2000. Proceedings of the ACM Conference on Computer-Human Interaction Human Factors in Computing Systems, pp. 14–15 (2000)
6. Steglich, St., Arbanowski, St.: Middleware for Cooperating Objects. In: SICE 2004. Proceedings of the Society of Instrument and Control Engineers. Annual Conference, Sapporo, Japan (August 4-6, 2004) ISBN: 4907764-22-7

Ubiquitous Communication Services Based on Effective Knowledge Deployment

Shintaro Imai[1,2], Atsushi Takeda[3], Takuo Suganuma[2,4], and Norio Shiratori[2,4]

[1] Research Fellow of the Japan Society for the Promotion of Science
[2] Research Institute of Electrical Communication, Tohoku University
2-1-1 Katahira, Aoba-ku, Sendai, 980-8577, Japan
[3] Department of Computer Science, Tohoku Bunka Gakuen University
6-45-1 Kunimi, Aoba-ku, Sendai, 981-0943, Japan
[4] Graduate School of Information Sciences, Tohoku University
{imashin, atushi, suganuma, norio}@shiratori.riec.tohoku.ac.jp

Abstract. Provisioning high quality communication services in resource-scarce information environments, effective employment of various kinds of knowledge of human users/operators concerning diverse services and continually changing environments is necessary. We have been working on Knowledge Circulation Framework (KCF) to resolve such kind of issue. This framework aims to realize user-oriented and resource-aware services by deploying QoS control knowledge in the network. In this paper, we apply KCF to ubiquitous communication services. We realize KCF by using the concept of knowledge-based multiagent system. We also introduce a similarity metric to compare characteristics of different ubiquitous information environments. We applied KCF to the ubiquitous videoconference system and performed several experiments. The experimental results show that our system can provide better and more stable QoS, by improving the adaptability to the various types of environments.

1 Introduction

In ubiquitous information environments, service provisioning ability of a system is significantly restricted due to the lack of computational power of small devices/sensors and limitations in availability and stability of wireless networks. In these environments, it is difficult to find a suitable mechanism to strategically control the services according to node status and network condition in appropriate manner [1,2,3,4,5].

To resolve this issue, it is essential to effectively acquire, maintain, place and reuse the operational heuristics through the network. To realize this, we have been working on Knowledge Circulation Framework (KCF) [6], a framework that enables sharing of the operational knowledge for effective service provisioning. The main contribution of this paper [6] is to realize flexible service provisioning with adequate QoS, by dynamically replacing the QoS control knowledge, according to the changing resource status of the environments.

In this paper, we propose an extended design and implementation of KCF, targeting the ubiquitous information environments, where computational and

H. Ichikawa et al. (Eds.): UCS 2007, LNCS 4836, pp. 158–165, 2007.

network resources are extremely limited, unstable and drastically changing. To overcome the hurdle in the service provisioning in ubiquitous information environments, to select and reuse the QoS control knowledge acquired in the past operation is a key issue. In this proposed scheme, we introduce a similarity metric to compare characteristics of different ubiquitous information environments. We applied KCF to a bidirectional multimedia communication service for ubiquitous information environments. We developed a ubiquitous videoconferencing system (VCS), and evaluated it through experiments. We verified our proposed system from the users' viewpoints of QoS. From these experimental results, we confirmed that our system can provide better and more stable QoS, improve the adaptability to the various types of environments.

2   Related Works and Problem

2.1   Related Works

There are several previous works dedicated to the adaptive QoS control in application level on best-effort-type networks and systems.

In framework-based approach [1], it provides an infrastructure to address the construction of "network aware" applications. In [2], the QoS control is realized by negotiating QoS among agents based on an arbitrary compromise criterion and QoS trade-off. Moreover, advanced QoS control mechanisms for unstable network environments including wireless networks are considered [3]. In these systems, it is necessary to add the new QoS control model when a new application or a new environment is introduced. Therefore, these works are expected to be extended in adaptability and scalability against various types of applications and environments.

In [4], QoS control is performed based on procedural-type knowledge in agents. This method can cope with drastic changes of the environment by switching the QoS control knowledge. However, the dependency between knowledge components is strong. This makes the addition, change and deletion of knowledge very difficult. Therefore, it is hard to re-write the knowledge according to the change of the environment in run-time.

2.2   Knowledge-Based QoS Control and Its Limitation

To improve upon the previous works described in section 2.1, we proposed Flexible Multimedia Communication Service (FMCS) [5]. In the scheme, service elements are separated from the QoS control function, and the control function is described in rule-type knowledge. The range of QoS control ability is greatly improved by FMCS, compare to the previous works. However, they can only use knowledge given in the design phase of the system. Therefore, it is difficult to adapt sufficiently to the ubiquitous information environment. Consequently, it is necessary to automatically acquire the QoS control knowledge during operation, and to accumulate and reuse the knowledge in the ubiquitous information environment.

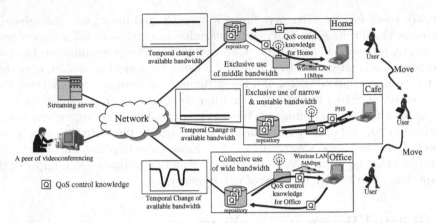

Fig. 1. QoS control knowledge circulated in ubiquitous information environments

3   Agent-Based Design of KCF

3.1   Concept of KCF

Considering the problems described above, in this paper, we propose and develop
Knowledge Circulation Framework (KCF) which enables dynamic circulation of
knowledge in ubiquitous information environments. Fig.1 shows the basic idea
of our framework.

In KCF, the QoS control knowledge is circulated in the network via repository. Using this framework, the knowledge, created during operation, such as
sequence of change on parameters against the typical fluctuation of network resources, can be stored and reused in other similar situations. There are mainly
two distinguished ideas in KCF: (i) Acquisition of knowledge through operation
and (ii) Reuse of the acquired knowledge. KCF consists of three phases of circulation: knowledge acquisition, management, and placement phases. Details of
these phases are described in section 3.2.

3.2   Agent Design of KCF

In order to circulate QoS control knowledge efficiently, KCF uses mobile agent
technology to carry the knowledge. That is, agent plays a role of QoS control
knowledge carrier on the network. Moreover, we introduce agent repository as
a dispatcher and a warehouse of the knowledge. A rule is represented in the
following form.

```
(rule Rule-name Condition-part (If-part)
     --> Action-part (Then-part))
```

If the conditional part is true, the actions described in the action part are performed.

Next, we illustrate the behavior of agents. Agent organization design of KCF
is shown in Fig.2. We circulate the following three types of knowledge: knowledge

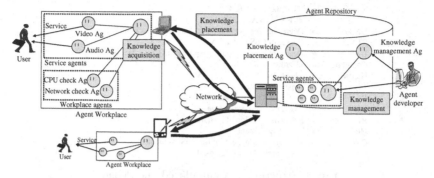

Fig. 2. Agent organization design for KCF

about the environment, history of usage of QoS control knowledge, and heuristics on effects of the applied QoS control knowledge.

(1) Knowledge acquisition phase

(1-a) Knowledge acquisition during service provisioning: Workplace agent permanently resides in Agent Workplace to monitor the status of computational resources, network resources and users. They acquire four kinds of information: they are, type and status of the resource, average of resource usage rate, standard deviation of the resource usage rate, and user requirement.

(1-b) Feed back to agent repository: When the service provisioning ends, Service manager agent, that is one of the Service agents, derives the user requirement achievement level S from the above four kinds of acquired information by the following expressions:

$$S = UNS_{QoS} + STA_{QoS} + UNS_{res}$$

UNS_{QoS}: Degree of user's QoS requirement unsatisfaction
STA_{QoS}: Degree of QoS is stability
UNS_{res}: Degree of user's resource requirement unsatisfaction

As a result, above three kinds of knowledge is acquired for circulation. Moreover, Service manager agent sends the knowledge acquired by Service/Workplace agents to Knowledge management agent.

(2) Knowledge management phase

Knowledge management agent in the Agent Repository classifies and accumulates knowledge is fed back by Service manager agent. This phase includes the following operations:

(2-a) Knowledge association: Knowledge management agent associates the knowledge about user requirement achievement level S and the knowledge about environment with the used QoS control knowledge. Fig.3 represents the structure of the accumulated knowledge.

(2-b) Knowledge integration: Knowledge management agent compares the knowledge that is fed back with existing knowledge about *condition* and *CK*. When

Knowledge	:=	<S, Condition, CK, C>
S	:=	<UNS$_{QoS}$, STA$_{QoS}$, UNS$_{res}$>
UNS$_{QoS}$	:=	Degree of user's QoS requirement unsatisfaction
STA$_{QoS}$	:=	Degree of QoS is stability
UNS$_{res}$	:=	Degree of user's resource requirement unsatisfaction
Condition	:=	<Hardware, R$_{ave}$, R$_{SD}$, UR>
Hardware	:=	<Type, P>
Type	:=	Type of hardware
P	:=	Performance of hardware
R$_{ave}$	:=	Average of resource usage
R$_{SD}$	:=	Standard deviation of resource usage
UR	:=	User Requirement
CK	:=	Control Knowledge used for QoS adjustment
C	:=	Count of the knowledge used

Fig. 3. Structure of accumulated knowledge

Hardware and *CK* match, and R_{ave}, R_{SD} and UR are similar in some measure, Knowledge management agent integrates these knowledge.

(3) Knowledge placement phase

(3-a) Selection of Service agents: When a service is required, the Knowledge placement agent in the Agent Repository determines Service agents to be placed to the Agent Workplace using contract-net protocol.

(3-b) Knowledge hand-over: When Service agents to be placed to Agent Workplace are determined, the Knowledge management agent compares the knowledge about environment that has been accumulated, with the information about environment where the new service will start, in a similar way to (2-b) in Knowledge management phase. Knowledge management agent selects the knowledge that has the highest S and that meets the following conditions: (i) *Hardware* matches, (ii) R_{ave}, R_{SD} and UR are similar in some measure. Knowledge management agent gives the CK to the Service agents.

(3-c) Service initiation: Knowledge is provided to the Service agents and are placed at an Agent Workplace, start to offer the service, and the process returns to (1-a) of Knowledge acquisition phase.

4   Experiments

4.1   Implementation

We implemented KCF based on the design described in section 3.2 using DASH framework [7], a multiagent framework. We developed seven agents: Knowledge management agent, Knowledge placement agent, VideoConference Manager (VCM) agent, Video agent, Netcheck agent, NetcheckVCS agent and UserVCS agent. Each agent has a computational base process (BP) to realize the function described in section 3.2. As for the video transmission/receiving software, we employed Java Media Framework (JMF), and embedded it as a BP in the Video agent.

4.2   Experimental Environment and Conditions

The configuration of experimental environment is shown in Fig.4. This configuration assumes ubiquitous information environment. We installed the agents based

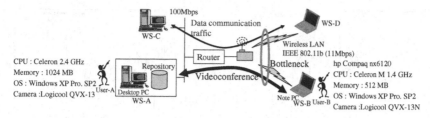

Fig. 4. Experimental environment

on KCF on WS-{A, B} whose specifications are shown in the figure. User-{A, B} receive services on WS-{A, B}. WS-A is connected with 100 Mbps Ethernet. WS-B is connected with 11 Mbps wireless LAN. We also installed an Agent Repository in WS-A.

In this experiment, we assume the average environment that is configured by normal spec PCs and networks. We also assume that the videoconferencing runs with other applications at the same time. Under these conditions, VCS has some restrictions on the resource usage for the other applications. And we fix the user's QoS requirement at fps=20(fps), and network resource availability limitation is available bandwidth rate=75(%). Therefore UNS_{QoS}, STA_{QoS} and UNS_{res} are expressed in the following form:

$$UNS_{QoS} = \text{value of fps / user requirement (20fps)}$$
$$STA_{QoS} = \text{standard variation of fps}$$
$$UNS_{res} = \text{value of available bandwidth / user requirement (75\%)}$$

The VCS had acquired 16 kinds of knowledge by preliminary videoconference operation, and had stored the knowledge in the Repository.

Here, we add some extra traffic load to the wireless link between WS-C and WS-D by data communication. This traffic pattern is a replay of the actual network traffic observed in real networks. We discuss the effectiveness of KCF by observing temporal changes of QoS and resource availability of VCS, comparing the VCS with KCF to the VCS with existing scheme (FMCS [5]).

4.3 Experimental Results and Evaluation

First, we performed the experiment using a network load pattern (pattern-1). The result is shown in Fig.5. After the experiment started, we initiated videoconference and added the extra network load based on the traffic pattern (pattern-1) at point A. As a result, the available network bandwidth was decreased and user's resource requirement was not fulfilled. Here, VCS without KCF corresponded by decreasing QoS to the minimum as shown in Fig.5(a) (point B). After that, when VCS observed that the load of the network became light, it recovered the QoS (point C). On the other hand, VCS with KCF in Fig.5(b), did not reduce QoS to the minimum. In addition, VCS controlled QoS did not adjust frequently, corresponding to the quick change of network resource situation (point D). This behavior is realized by using the knowledge that accumulated beforehand. As a

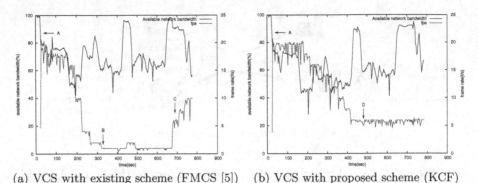

(a) VCS with existing scheme (FMCS [5])   (b) VCS with proposed scheme (KCF)

Fig. 5. QoS control results of VCS against a network traffic pattern (pattern-1)

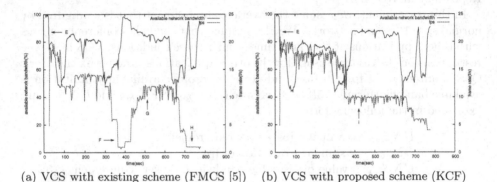

(a) VCS with existing scheme (FMCS [5])   (b) VCS with proposed scheme (KCF)

Fig. 6. QoS control results of VCS against a network traffic pattern (pattern-2)

result, KCF was able to avoid the frequent QoS fluctuation, and provided service with stable quality.

To confirm the reproducibility of the experimental results, we performed the other experiments using another network load pattern (pattern-2). The result is shown in Fig.6. We initiated videoconference and added the network load at point E. VCS without KCF in Fig.6(a) correspond to the adjustment of the QoS (point F). After that, VCS observed the decrease of the network load and recovered QoS (point G). After that, when the network load increased again, it decreased the QoS (point H). As a result, QoS became unstable. On the other hand, VCS with KCF in Fig.6(b), did not decrease the QoS and adjusted it around 10 fps (point I). The above results prove that, can provide stable quality of service than that of without KCF, as shown in Fig.6(a).

We compare operation of VCS without KCF and with KCF, with the experimental results. In Fig.5 and Fig.6, (b) shows that service with KCF was able to improve the QoS and its stability compare to (a) without KCF. This is because VCS with KCF was able to effectively control the QoS, as it has knowledge about the environment. This knowledge was selected by the highest user requirement achievement level S in prior operation. In this case, the QoS control knowledge that suppress the reactive control is selected, considering the rapid changing status of available bandwidth on the target environment. This reduced the excessive control of the QoS, and led the improvement of the stability of QoS. From this experiment, we found that the adaptability of VCS to ubiquitous information environments would be improved by applying the KCF. Moreover, the improvement of adaptability is more effective in the severe condition.

5 Conclusion

In this paper, we proposed a Knowledge Circulation Framework (KCF) that enables sharing knowledge on ubiquitous information environments. This framework supports circulation of knowledge in the network, by a sequence of acquisition, management, and placement of the knowledge to reuse it effectively. We proposed a design of KCF with knowledge-based multiagent system. We also performed experiments by applying the KCF to VCS in the ubiquitous information environment. From the results of the experiments, we concluded that the adaptability of the VCS to the ubiquitous information environments has improved by applying the KCF. In our future work, we will evaluate the KCF by conducting experiments in various actual situations with real network environments.

Acknowledgement. This work has been supported by the Grant-in-Aid for JSPS Fellows No.18-5190 of Japan Society for the Promotion of Science (JSPS).

References

1. Bolliger, J., Gross, T.: A framework-based approach to the development of network-aware applications. IEEE Trans. Software Eng. 24(5), 376–390 (1998)
2. Yamazaki, T., Matsuda, J.: Adaptive QoS management for multimedia applications in heterogeneous environments: A Case Study with Video QoS Mediation. IEICE Trans. Commun. E82-B(11), 1801–1807 (1999)
3. Lei, H., et al.: Adaptive resource allocation for multimedia QoS management in wireless networks. IEEE Trans. on Vehicular Technology 53(2), 547–558 (2004)
4. Suganuma, T., Kinoshita, T., Sugawara, K., Shiratori, N.: Flexible Videoconference System based on ADIPS Framework. In: Proc. PAAM 1998, pp. 83–100 (1998)
5. Suganuma, T., et al.: A Flexible Videoconference System Based on Multiagent Framework. IEEE Trans. on SMC partA 33(5), 633–641 (2003)
6. Imai, S., Suganuma, T., Shiratori, N.: Knowledge Circulation Framework for Flexible Multimedia Communication Services. IEICE Trans. Inf. & Syst. E88-D(9), 2059–2066 (2005)
7. DASH: Distributed Agent System based on Hybrid Architecture,
http://www.agent-town.com/dash/index.html

Detection of User Mode Shift in Home

Hiroyuki Yamahara, Hideyuki Takada, and Hiromitsu Shimakawa

Ritsumeikan University, 1-1-1 Noji-Higashi, Kusatsu, 525-8577 Shiga, Japan
`yama@de.is.ritsumei.ac.jp`

Abstract. A ubiquitous environment enable us to enjoy various services "anytime" "anywhere". However, "everyone" is not realized. We research an intelligent space "everyone" can enjoy services. This paper proposes a method to detect user behavior to provide services according to user context in home. We focus on scenes user's mode significantly changes, such as going out and going to bed. People often have characteristic behavior in these scenes. Our method extracts this characteristic as a behavioral pattern and detects user behavior in these scenes by matching current user behavior online with it. The method characterizes each scene with kind of objects a user touched and the order of them. The method realizes early start of providing services by creating a behavioral pattern from user behavior logs in short duration. The experiment proves the high potency of our method and discusses its weakness at the same time.

Keywords: intelligent space, ubiquitous, context, behavior, RFID.

1 Introduction

A ubiquitous environment enables us to enjoy many kinds of services with information devices such as a cellular phone and information appliances. However, a user must actively access to the environment by operating such devices. It means there are actually a lots of users such as old people who can not enjoy services, because they are unfamiliar with information devices and are not able to use these devices. A variety of intelligent spaces are researched as an environment in which everyone can enjoy services. An intelligent space obtains user position information, user behavior information, information of environment around a user, and so on by a sensor network. The intelligent space can infer user context by using these information and provide services according to user context. Because the environment is active and a user can be passive in the intelligent space, everyone can enjoy services. Some of them provide services at home. The Aware Home[1] aims to provide services in a variety of scenes, such as support of finding objects a user lost and support of taking a medicine. Perkowitz et al. support user's cooking by utilizing recipes got from the internet[2]. Isoda et al. remind a user of the state that had been reached before an interruption of his work when he came back to his work after the interruption[3]. Aoki et al. support solitary old people by detecting their irregular state[4,5]. There are also lots of other researches which aim to infer user context for providing appropriate services[6,7,8,9] These respectively focus on different scenes in daily life.

H. Ichikawa et al. (Eds.): UCS 2007, LNCS 4836, pp. 166–181, 2007.

We focus on scenes in which user's mode significantly changes. In such scenes, an intelligent space can effectively provide services to a user. In daily life, user's mode significantly changes in scenes of going out, coming home, getting up, and going to bed. There are respectively different services to be provided and the timing to be done it on each scene. Our research aims to provide appropriate activity support services according to user intention by detecting user behavior in these scenes with a behavioral pattern extracted from history of objects a user touched in the intelligent space. For example, suppose a user behavior of going out is detected. At that time, a service to warn that a gas valve is open and to close it automatically can be provided. Also a service to notify a user that he does not have something important to go out can be provided. These services improve user amenity, and bring the user relief and safety by preventing danger in advance. These can be provided to a user effectively in user mode shift such as going out, going to bed, and so on. If a user is notified that he does not have his important item after he has gone out of his room, it requires extra time and energy to go back to his room for getting the item. Services should be proactively provided by detecting behavior of his going out before he has gone out. We aim to provide services proactively before user's mode has changed.

To detect user behavior, a behavioral pattern is created by extracting characteristics of behavior of individual user from past behavior logs which are collected as samples in advance per every scene to be detected. User behavior is detected by matching current user behavior log with a behavioral pattern of each scene. For example, a behavior of a user's preparing to go out is different from a behavior of other user's preparing to go out. For providing appropriate services, it is important to recognize user behavior fastly and precisely with a personalized behavioral pattern adapted to individual user. A user is frustrated with inappropriate services provided by mistaken recognition in an intelligent space. In addition, if it costs long time to collect sample behavior logs, services can not start being provided to a user at an early point. Considering practical use, a behavioral pattern must be created with small number of sample behavior logs which can be collected in short duration. If a behavioral pattern is created in short duration, then it is possible to start providing services early. Existing research recognizes user behavior by measuring user motion such as gesture and movement history. This method is efficient to recognize behavior precisely. However, because the method uses probabilistic model such as Hidden Markov Model(HMM), it needs a lot of sample behavior logs to create a behavioral pattern. It can not be applied to a problem of this paper.

This paper proposes a method to detect user behavior in a scene in which user's mode changes. Most people often behave in a set order before his mode shift for not making omission of things to do. The order shows personal characteristics significantly. The proposed method pays attention to not user motion but target objects of user operation. The method records kind of objects which a user touched in order of time as behavior log and creates a behavioral pattern by extracting characteristic habits of the user from small number of behavior logs collected in short duration.

This method can

- individualize user behavior with order of objects a user touches in every scene in which user's mode changes, and
- start providing services to a user by creating a personal adapted behavioral pattern in short duration, and
- detect user behavior without being affected by rare order of user's action.

In this paper, An experiment collected behavior logs of 8 experimental subjects in scenes of going out, coming home, getting up and going to bed. The experiment created a behavioral pattern of each scene only with 5 behavior logs which can be collected in a week in actual life, and then tried detecting user behavior.

2   Providing Service According to Behavior in Home

2.1   Behavior Detection in User Mode Shift

An intelligent space can provide various ubiquitous services to support user activity. We aim to provide services proactively according to user behavior by grasping user intention with the behavior. A user behaves with a variety of intention in a variety of scenes of daily life. However, he does not need services in the all scenes. In general, it is desirable for him to be provided services in special scenes in which his mode significantly changes. For example, suppose a user goes out without closing a gas valve. If he notices the fact after he has gone out of his house, he must waste time and energy to go back to his house to close the gas valve. In such a scene, an intelligent space can improve his amenity by warning that a gas valve is open before he has gone out and closing it automatically. It also means an intelligent space can bring relief and safety to him by preventing danger in advance. There are some scenes in which user's mode significantly changes in daily life. They are scenes of going out, coming home, getting up and going to bed. To provide effective services to a user proactively, we must detect user behavior in these scenes before his mode has changed.

There are respectively different services to be provided and the timing to be done it on each scene. In scenes of going out and going to bed, above mentioned important and urgent services which are able to give relief and safety to a user by preventing danger in advance can be provided. There are definite deadlines to effectively provide services to a user in these scenes. Services in a scene of going out must be provided before a user has gone out through the entrance door. Services in a scene of going to bed should be provided before he has lain down and has slept on the bed. A reminder service is envisioned in a scene of coming home. It reminds a user of things to do in home after his coming home. Similarly, in a scene of getting up, it is envisioned a reminder service reminds him of one day schedule and things to complete by he goes out. For example, a service to inform of urgent message which must be immediately provided after a user comes home should be provided even in a case he only simply comes into his house for a moment. This can be realized only by using a sensor which detects open/close of the entrance door. On the other hand, it is wrong to judge that he came home when he came back into his house to get an umbrella. It is wrong also to judge that he got up when he stood up to go to the toilet in the middle of his sleep. A reminder service based on these wrong judgement makes him uncomfortable. User behavior in these scenes must be precisely detected for providing services. In scenes of coming home and getting up, because services such as a reminder service do not have high urgency, there is no definite deadline to provide services. Nevertheless, services can support him more effectively without making him uncomfortable by providing services before his mode has changed. Consequently, it is adequate to provide services before his mode has changed after a series of regular actions when he comes home or when he gets up. A user often tends to forget something to do in a scene when his mode changes. It is effective to provide assistive services in such a scene. To realize providing advance services effectively, user behavior needs to be detected before his mode has changed.

2.2 Behavioral Pattern

A lot of existing researches recognize user behavior by matching user behavior log with a behavioral pattern. A behavioral pattern is a pattern of characteristic behavior of a user in special scenes. Behavior log is behavior data obtained from observed user behavior. Behavior log is categorized into two kinds. One is a sample behavior log which is used to create a behavioral pattern as sample. The other is a match-target behavior log which is matched with a behavioral pattern to recognize behavior. In advance, specific amount of sample behavior logs are collected in a special scene and a behavioral pattern is created with them. After that, user behavior is recognized by matching a match-target behavior log with the behavioral pattern. A few researches obtain values of floor pressure sensors and open/close sensors as behavior log[3,7,8,10]. In addition, some researches use more varieties of sensors such as infra-red sensors, video cameras, and so on[6,9]. Values of these data are affected by not only a user but also other people and environmental objects. However, it is desirable that behavior log shows individual personal behavior in detail for precise detection of user behavior.

2.3 Problem for Practical Behavior Detection

To detect user behavior precisely, a behavioral pattern must be personalized. Perkowitz et al. aim to provide services according to user behavior with a mannered behavioral pattern such as how to cook, which is automatically extracted from the web[2]. Because this method does not adapt a behavioral pattern to individual, it can not realize providing services according to individual intention.

Considering a practical use, an individual behavioral pattern must be created in short duration to provide services early without giving a user stress in an intelligent space. In existing researches, there are effective methods to recognize user behavior. They use a behavioral pattern created with probabilistic model such as HMM[1,4,5,11,12,13]. These methods regard user behavior as a series of state transition. They judge whether a match-target behavior log meets a behavioral pattern from the result of repeating multiplication of probability according to state transition. Because a behavioral pattern is created with sample behavior logs by a stochastic method, the probability is high while a user behaves in order he frequently behaves. On the other hand, the probability gets low when he behaves in order he rarely behaves. This method can perform reliable behavior recognition based on probabilistic theory. However, because user behavior forms a complex order structure in which regularity and irregularity are mixed, a stochastic method needs a lot of sample behavior logs to create a behavioral pattern which can represent such a complex behavior in daily life. It can not perform reliable probabilistic statistics with small number of sample behavior logs. A behavioral pattern is created in every scene to be recognized. Therefore, a lot of sample behavior logs of each scene must be collected. Suppose a behavioral pattern of a scene a user goes out. Only about 30 sample behavior logs can be collected in a month. Moreover, also behavior logs other than a scene of going out must be collected. Probabilistic statistics are performed by combining these many behavior logs. Consequently, existing methods using probabilistic model need long time till it starts providing services to a user. These method is not adequate to realization of ubiquitous environment under the present circumstances.

In addition, existing methods can not recognize user behavior containing rare actions exceptionally because probability gets low as a result of probabilistic calculation. Even if a few rare actions are contained in user behavior, the behavior is usual for himself. If he can not be provided services which are normally provided, he is dissatisfied. Exceptional rare actions are often weaved into actual user behavior in daily life. Even if user behavior contains rare actions, it must be recognized precisely and appropriate services must be provided for the user.

A problem to solve in this paper is how to create an effective behavioral pattern with collected behavior logs in each scene. A behavioral pattern must satisfy following conditions.

− It is personalized and created in short duration.
− It can recognize behavior containing rare actions.

3   Behavior Detection in Intelligent Space

3.1   Habitual Behavior of Individual User

We are developing the "Tagged World" as an intelligent space to provide services proactively according to user behavior by detecting user behavior in a scene in which user's mode changes. For example, when a user goes out, the intelligent space warns him that a gas valve is open. In another example, the intelligent space calls an elevator to his living floor in a condominium. These services can prevent danger in advance and improve user amenity. In the Tagged World, the RFID tags are embedded in various objects of living space such as a wallet, a cell phone and a doorknob. Because a unique tag-ID is individually stored in a

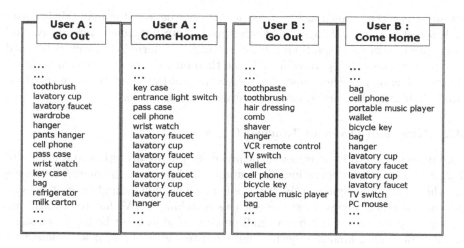

User A : Go Out	User A : Come Home	User B : Go Out	User B : Come Home
...	...	...	...
...	...	...	...
toothbrush	key case	toothpaste	bag
lavatory cup	entrance light switch	toothbrush	cell phone
lavatory faucet	pass case	hair dressing	portable music player
wardrobe	cell phone	comb	wallet
hanger	wrist watch	shaver	bicycle key
pants hanger	lavatory faucet	hanger	bag
cell phone	lavatory cup	VCR remote control	hanger
pass case	lavatory faucet	TV switch	lavatory cup
wrist watch	lavatory cup	wallet	lavatory faucet
key case	lavatory faucet	cell phone	lavatory cup
bag	lavatory cup	bicycle key	lavatory faucet
refrigerator	lavatory faucet	portable music player	TV switch
milk carton	hanger	bag	PC mouse
...	...	...	...
...	...	...	...

Fig. 1. Examples of behavior log

tag, every object can be identified by the tag-ID. A user equips a finger-ring-type RFID reader. The user touches various objects in living space in daily life. When the user touches objects, the RFID reader reads tag-IDs of the objects. Then, a time series of tag-IDs and time stamps which indicate access time are recorded as a behavior log of the user.

A user has some habitual actions in a scene his mode changes. This means the user habitually touches same objects every time in the scene. When a user goes out, for example, there can be habitual actions such as having a wallet, wearing a wristwatch, going to the toilet and having a cell phone. At the same time, accesses to a wallet, a wristwatch, a doorknob of the toilet and a cell phone are recorded as a behavior log in the Tagged World. A time series of stored tag-IDs shows targets of user operation. It details what kind of objects a user uses. It is a behavior log which shows his personal behavior. Some go to the toilet but others do not. Kind and the order of these habitual actions vary with individual user. Thus each scene to provide services to user is characterized by kind of objects and the order of objects which a user touches. These characters indicate his habit. Objects a user touches indicate his intention and his behavior. Their logs are adequate to be used as individual sample behavior logs.

Our research conducted a questionnaire survey. In the questionnaire, answerers recorded kind of objects they touched and the order of objects they touched in 4 scenes of going out, coming home, getting up, and going to bed every day in detail. After that, we had answerers replicate their behaviors in 4 scenes in an experimental space constructed as the Tagged World. Fig. 1 shows examples of behavior logs of two users in scenes of going out and coming home. These are factly collected in the Tagged World. A behavior log is a time series of tag-IDs and time stamps in our research, but this paper shows a time series of objects a user touches as a behavior log for an easy-to-understand explanation. For example, in a scene of going out, habitual actions of user A are different from those of user B as shown in Fig. 1. By looking at the log, it is inferred that user A brushed his teeth, changed his clothes, picked up portable commodities, and brought out a milk carton from a refrigerator. It is inferred that user B brushed his teeth, set his hair, operated a VCR and then picked up portable commodities. These behavior logs show that kind of touched objects and the order of them are individually different among users even in a same scene.

3.2   Kind and Order of Touched Objects

The proposed method detects user behavior by paying attention to touching to target objects of user operation. The number of objects a user touches in a scene in which his mode significantly changes is more than the number of objects he touches in other scenes. In scenes such as watching a TV, having a meal and reading a book, a user touches a small number of objects, or he touches a small number of limited kind of objects. Compared to these scenes, it is obvious that more objects are touched in scenes in which user's mode significantly changes. Thus, it is contemplated that user behavior in his mode shift can be detected by paying attention to target objects of his operation. To detect user behavior, a behavior log is checked with following two points.

1. kind of objects which a user touched
2. order of objects which a user touched

Let us consider a case checking only with kind of objects[15]. Suppose to detect a behavior in a scene of going out. There are differences between the objects touched for going out and the objects touched for cooking or for eating meals. It can be guessed that the behavior of going out has been done with high probability just by evaluating kind of objects. But the behavior can not be identified only with kind of objects, because the objects touched for going out are similar to the objects touched for coming home. In our prior experiment, more than 80% of behavior of going out was precisely detected with a behavioral pattern of going out, which is created by paying attention only to kind of objects. But at the same time, more than 50% of behavior of coming home was mistakenly detected.

Therefore, our method evaluates the behavior log in more detail, paying attention to also the order of touched objects. As shown in Fig. 1, in a scene of coming home, it is inferred that user A put some portable commodities, gargled in the lavatory, and hanged up his clothes. It is inferred that user B put some portable commodities, hanged up his clothes, and gargled in the lavatory. Compared to each user's scene of going out, it is found that in a different scene a user touches different kind of objects or touches same objects in different order. The objects touched for going out are similar to the objects touched for coming home, but the order of them are different. Not a behavior of coming home but only a behavior of going out is detected by checking order. The proposed method evaluates the order of not only successive two objects but also non-successive two objects in a behavior log. In actual user behavior, there is a case which a user finds the door locked after he turned the doorknob to go out through the entrance door. At that time, he turns the doorknob again to go out after he unlocks the door.

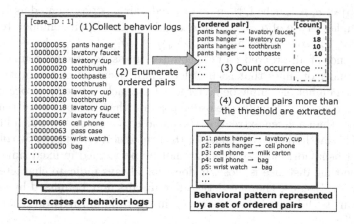

Fig. 2. How to create a behavioral pattern

Such an action is rare for him. By focusing on discrete order, the method can flexibly recognize behavior containing such a rare action.

3.3 Behavior Detection Based on Discrete Ordered Pairs

With sample behavior logs which are histories of objects a user touched, the proposed method creates a behavioral pattern represented by a set of ordered pairs which show the order relation of his access to objects. Using a behavioral pattern in a scene of going out as an example, this paper describes how to create a behavioral pattern with Fig. 2. Generally, existing methods based on probabilistic model such as HMM[4,11] create a behavioral pattern which is high detection performance with both behavior logs in a scene of going out and them of in scenes other than a scene of going out as sample behavior logs. Consider our problems that a behavioral pattern must be created only with a small number of sample behavior logs. Even behavior logs of going out can not be collected a lot. We can not expect to collect behavior logs of other scenes which are proper to make detection performance high. Therefore, a behavioral pattern must be created only with behavior logs of going out. A behavioral pattern is created in a following flow.

1. collect sample behavior logs
2. enumerate ordered pairs in the behavior logs
3. extract ordered pairs which count of occurrence is more than the threshold

First, behavior logs of w cases are collected as sample behavior logs. The time length t_l of a sample behavior log is fixed. If m objects are sequentially touched in a behavior log l, then l is represented as a conjunction $\{o_1, o_2, \ldots, o_i, \ldots, o_m\}$, where, $o_{i-1} \neq o_i (1 < i \leq m)$. Second, all ordered pairs between two objects are enumerated from all of collected sample behavior logs. If an object o_j is touched after an object o_i is touched, then an ordered pair p is represented as $\{o_i \to o_j\}$, which includes a case of $o_i = o_j$. For example, ordered pairs enumerated from a behavior log $\{o_1, o_2, o_3\}$ are $p_1 : \{o_1 \to o_2\} p_2 : \{o_1 \to o_3\} p_3 : \{o_2 \to o_3\}$. Next, the occurrence of all ordered pairs is counted up as occurrence count. It means not the number of times that each ordered pair occurred in a sample behavior log, but the number of sample behavior logs that each ordered pair occurred in w sample behavior logs. Finally, the ordered pairs where ratio of occurrence count to w is more than a given extraction threshold e % are extracted as a behavioral pattern. This method does not consider the time distance between two objects. In actual user behavior, most actions may not be performed in fixed time relation. Even if the time distance is close, it does not always indicate characteristics of user behavior. Because characteristic ordered pairs may be missed by extracting ordered pairs with limited time distance, this method daringly does not consider the time distance.

The Tagged World matches a current behavior log of time length t_l, which is obtained from user behavior online, with a created behavioral pattern π. If more than a given detection threshold d % of ordered pairs composing the behavioral pattern π exist in the current behavior log, user behavior of going out is detected.

3.4 Characteristic of the Proposed Method

The HMM used in the existing methods calculates output probability of an observed symbol sequence by the product of transition probabilities between two successive states and symbol output probability on each state. Thus, if a rare symbol occurs in an observed symbol sequence, the output probability is low. In actual user behavior, there is a case a user finds the door locked after he turned the doorknob to go out through the entrance door. Then he unlocks the door and turns the doorknob again. Because a rare action occurs in a part of the behavior in such a case, the HMM may not be able to detect the user goes out. The proposed method in this paper detects user behavior with paying attention to only occurrence count of ordered pairs which represent characteristic order of actions. The ordered pairs of low occurrence probability are excluded when a behavioral pattern is created. This method can detect user behavior even in a case rare actions occur in the behavior by separating order check from a probabilistic model daringly.

Like the proposed method, Mori et al.[7,8] do not use a probabilistic state transition model such as HMM. They detect user behavior proactively with behavioral patterns created based on characteristics both kind of "events" which happen from several seconds to dozens of seconds before a prediction target behavior and the order of them. Their method defines events as changes of two kinds of sensor. One is a pressure sensor which is set in floor, a chair, a bed, and so on, which are used to detect position of a user. The other is open/close sensor which is set in a refrigerator, chest of drawers, and so on. A sample behavior log is time series of events which happened during several seconds. Their method creates a lot of behavioral patterns by extracting all of possible patterns of order of events from some sample behavior logs. When matching with the behavioral patterns, if time series of events which perfectly meet any of behavioral patterns happen then it is inferred that a prediction target behavior will happen soon. Because all of possible behavioral patterns are extracted, if only behavioral patterns which bring out high prediction performance can be selected from the behavioral patterns, their method can realize precise behavior detection. However, as a matter of fact, it is not easy to select only good behavioral patterns by estimating prediction performance of each behavioral pattern now because there are only a small number of sample behavior logs. Compared with this, our method attempts precise behavior detection by taking the following strategy.

- It creates one behavioral pattern to avoid comparing quality among patterns.
- It represents a variety of behavioral patterns potentially by making a pattern be a set of ordered pairs which means many judgement factors for prediction.
- It extracts more characteristics of user behavior from behavior logs not for dozens of seconds but dozens of minutes as judgement factors.
- It makes every behavior distinct by focusing on history of objects a user touched, which significantly indicates characteristics of his behavior.

Because our method focuses on contact to objects as event, a lot of events occur in a sample behavior log. In addition, it is assumed that length of a sample behavior log is dozens of minutes. This means our method regards several habitual actions as characteristics of user behavior, such as "brush teeth", "go to the toilet" and "pick up a pass case and a key from a drawer" before a user goes out. It can regard also the order of these actions as characteristics, such as "he picks up a pass case and a key from a drawer after he brushes his teeth". If a behavioral pattern is created from sample behavior logs of dozens of seconds, it will increase the chance to mistakenly detect scenes other than going out, because it may regard only one action as characteristic. Our method prevents this mistaken detection by differentiating one behavior and others, using several habitual actions. Inevitably, the number of occurrence of events in our method is more than that of a method in paper[7,8]. Consequently it is impractical to consider all of possible behavioral patterns extracted from sample behavior logs, because there can be vast amounts of possible behavioral patterns. For the reason, our method detects user behavior by partial meeting a behavioral pattern which potentially considers lots of behavioral patterns. Finally, history of user position, open/close information of refrigerator, and so on are used in existing method. They indicate user behavior, however, history of touched objects in our method shows more significant characteristics of user behavior.

4   Performance Evaluation

4.1   Experiment

This paper conducted an experiment to verify whether the proposed method can correctly detect user behavior with a behavioral pattern created only with 5 sample behavior logs which can be collected in a week, with 8 experimental subjects. This experiment set the extraction threshold to 80% and set the time length t_l of a behavior log to 10 minutes.

We collected behavior logs of all experimental subjects for this experiment. They are used as sample behavior logs and match-target behavior logs. Before the experiment, we conducted a questionnaire survey for 2 weeks with 8 subjects. In the questionnaire, subjects recorded complete detail about kind of objects they touched and the order of objects they touched in 4 scenes of going out, coming home, getting up, and going to bed every day. In a scene of going out, subjects recorded for 10 minutes before they touched a doorknob of the entrance door to go out. In a scene of going to bed, subjects recorded for 10 minutes before they had lain down on their bed. In a scene of coming home, subjects recorded for 10 minutes after they touched a doorknob of the entrance door when they came back to their home. In a scene of getting up, subjects recorded for 10 minutes after they got out of their bed when they got up. With the result of questionnaire, we confirmed that many people respectively touch different objects or touch objects in different order in different scenes. We constructed the Tagged World in an experimental space which models actual house. Of course, the experimental space has living, kitchen, entrance, and so on. Also real household goods such as kitchen gas stove, kitchen sink, and electric appliances are set in the space. Experimental subjects can live same as in their own home. We collected behavior logs of actual objects which 8 subjects touch in 4 scenes respectively in the experimental space. Similar to the questionnaire, the time length of a behavior log is ten minutes. They are stored in a database. 70 behavior logs were collected per a subject. In some of collected behavior logs, there are unusual rare actions. For example, a user finds the entrance door locked after he turned the doorknob and unlocks the door. In another example, a user takes an umbrella in rainy day.

Next, we calculated true-positive rate(TPR) and true-negative rate(TNR) per experimental subject by repeatedly creating a behavioral pattern and matching behavior logs with the pattern, using behavior logs in the database. TPR shows the rate which behavior logs in a specific scene is correctly detected with a behavioral pattern of the specific scene. TNR shows the rate which behavior logs in scenes other than a specific scene is correctly neglected with a behavioral pattern of the specific scene. The experiment calculates TPR and TNR by following flow. Matching with a behavioral pattern is executed with all settings of the detection threshold d from 1% to 100%. Here, true case means behavior logs in a scene to be created a behavioral pattern and false case means behavior logs in scenes other than the scene of true case.

1. It selects 5 true cases and creates a behavioral pattern from them.
2. It selects other 1 true case and matches it with the behavioral pattern.
3. It matches all of false cases with the behavioral pattern.
4. It repeats 100 times from step 1 to step 3, with a new behavioral pattern which is created by selecting new combination of 5 true cases every time.

In daily life, a user touches less number and less kinds of objects in scenes other than scenes in which his mode significantly changes. In addition, he touches

Table 1. Result of "Go Out"

subject	TPR(%)	TNR(%)*
A	94	96.02
B	98	85.44
C	78	83.20
D	95	98.00
E	99	98.96
F	96	97.00
G	100	96.36
H	98	95.18
average*	94.75	93.77

Table 2. Result of "Come Home"

subject	TPR(%)	TNR(%)*
A	89	95.93
B	99	98.12
C	81	83.37
D	98	78.40
E	93	99.60
F	99	100.00
G	100	96.80
H	100	98.27
average*	94.88	94.34

different kinds of objects. Considering characteristics of our method, it can distinguish between these scenes. Actually, we conducted a preparatory experiment to demonstrate it. The experiment matched behavior logs of three scenes which are cooking, taking meals and after taking a bath with a behavioral pattern of going out. In the result, any of behavior logs were not detected mistakenly. The proportion of the number of ordered pairs existing both in each behavior log and in a behavioral pattern of going out to the number of ordered pairs composing the behavioral pattern of going out is up to 7%. It is less percentage in most cases. Therefore, these scenes have no chance to be detected by a behavioral pattern of going out. With this result in mind, an experiment of this paper uses behavior logs of scenes of user mode change other than true cases as false cases. It means this experiment evaluate detection performance of our method with severer constraint.

Because this experiment assumes that a small number of behavior logs collected in short duration can be used, a behavioral pattern is created only with true cases. To evaluate detection performance, it is contemplated that we use recall and precision which are used to evaluate retrieval performance. However, this experiment daringly sets only scenes which can be mistakenly detected as false cases without recognizing scenes which can be easily distinguished. Therefore, it does not evaluate with precision. It evaluates with TPR and TNR as recall. Both are desired to be high. The deadline to provide services in a scene of going out is the time a user touches an entrance doorknob to go out. Similarly, in a scene of coming home, the deadline is ten minutes after he touches an entrance doorknob when he comes home. In a scene of getting up, the deadline is ten minutes after he leaves his bed when he gets up. In a scene of going to bed, the deadline is the time he lies down on his bed to sleep. In the experiment, his behavior in each scene must be correctly detected in ten minutes which is length of a match-target behavior log.

4.2 Behavior Detection Performance

From Table 1 to Table 4, four tables show TPR and TNR per a scene. In Tables, values of TNR and average are rounded off in the third decimal place

Table 3. Result of "Get Up"

subject	TPR(%)	TNR(%)*
A	73	99.12
B	90	96.78
C	63	84.35
D	100	99.22
E	64	87.32
F	97	99.68
G	100	74.33
H	56	83.60
average*	80.38	90.55

Table 4. Result of "Go To Bed"

subject	TPR(%)	TNR(%)*
A	62	85.34
B	91	71.84
C	95	96.92
D	78	94.66
E	28	91.24
F	95	99.14
G	98	99.32
H	58	100.00
average*	75.63	92.31

(singed by "*"). A suitable detection threshold is different according to behavior. The experiment calculated suitable detection threshold of each behavior and used it for evaluation. First, TPR and TNR are averaged per experimental subject. Next, the averaged values of all experimental subjects are averaged. Finally, the detection threshold which the value is highest is adopted for evaluation. The detection threshold of each behavior is followed. Going out : 33%, Coming home: 31%, Getting up : 47%, Going to bed : 63%.

As shown in Table 1 and Table 2, more than 90% of behaviors of going out and coming home are correctly detected. Table 3 and Table 4 show about getting up and going to bed. Although part of TPR shows low rates, others result in high rates. These results prove that our method can bring out high detection performance. It means that our method extracted enough characteristics of user behavior to detect from a limited number of sample behavior logs by focusing on habitually touched objects which significantly indicate characteristics of user behavior. Generally, people lives their daily life by a week which is a standard period. Considering two conditions which are to have to create a behavioral pattern in possible short duration and to use an enough variety of behavior logs which are appropriate for sample behavior logs, to collect sample behavior logs and to start providing services to a user within one week are a standard. As a result of the experiment, our method can create an effective behavioral pattern only with five sample behavior logs which can be enough collected within one week. This means that our method is more practical than existing methods which need a lot of sample behavior logs because it can create a personalized behavioral pattern in short duration and start providing services.

4.3 Discussion

Analyzing experimental result and considering characteristics of the method, we discuss causes which our method does not detect some true cases or which our method mistakenly detects false cases. The causes are followed.

1. Some users have few habitual actions
   There is a case which a behavioral pattern is composed of only few ordered pairs because few habitual actions are occurred in sample behavior logs. In

such a case, if those limited ordered pairs just happen also in a false case then our method may detect the false case mistakenly. Also, if those limited ordered pairs do not accidentally occur in a true case, then our method does not detect the true case correctly.

2. Some users have common habitual actions among different scenes

If a user has same actions in same order of them in different scenes, behavioral patterns of the scenes may have same ordered pairs. If same objects are touched in different scenes, most of users touch them in different order. As a result, their behavioral patterns have more ordered pairs which are occurred only in one scene than ordered pairs which are occurred in different scenes in common. But because some users touch same objects in same order in different scenes, for example when going out and when getting up, their behavioral pattern has same ordered pairs in these scenes. It makes recognition accuracy of their behavior worse. In more negative consideration, even if a user touches same objects in different order in different scenes, our method may perform mistaken detection when he behaves in unusual order.

3. Thresholds are not suitable for a user

In this paper, our method set fixed values to an extraction threshold and a detection threshold. However, our analyzation tells suitable thresholds vary among users. Because there are not a lot of sample behavior logs, the setting of thresholds is a delicate problem. If an extraction threshold is too high, our method may not be able to extract enough proper ordered pairs as characteristics of user behavior. If it is too low, a behavioral pattern may include many improper ordered pairs. A proper detection threshold varies among users and behaviors. In our experiment, a proper detection threshold was 30% for some users, and it was 50% or 60% for other users. We must develop a method to set an ideal detection threshold for each user.

4. Infrequently users have greatly unusual actions

Our method detects user behavior based on habitual behavior of each user. Even if a behavioral pattern enough represents characteristics of user habit, it can not detect user behavior in a case which he behaves with greatly unusual actions. Suppose a user hurries up before he goes out. If he omits only a part of his habitual actions, our method can correctly detect his going out. But if he omits most of his habitual actions, our method may not be able to do that.

We must solve these problems in the future. The first and second problems may be solved by adding information other than touched objects into behavior logs. It makes us collect more characteristics of user behavior by combining our method with these information. The existing methods check open/close of refrigerator and drawers, ON/OFF of switches and electric appliances, position of a user, objects around a user, and so on as information[3,7,8,10]. We think these are useful as supplementary information. In this paper, we embedded passive-type RFID tags to objects because it is not realistic to supply electric power to many small objects such as a wallet and a pass case. However, some objects such as an alarm clock, electric appliances and walls of room are already supplied electric power now. We can practically set active device such as a small wireless communication device in these objects. Such devices will give us effective information to improve detection performance. The second problem relates to a constraint that sample behavior logs must be collected in short duration. If sample behavior logs can be collected in long duration, not only more behavior logs as true cases but also proper behavior logs as false cases may be collected. With many false cases and many true cases, we can create more precise behavioral pattern by extracting characteristics which are shown not in false cases and but only in true cases. But we can use only true cases in a constraint of a problem to solve in this paper. Therefore we can extract only "characteristics which are shown in true cases very much" in actual. Our method attempts to overcome its weakness by differentiating user behavior of each scene with information of touched objects which are extremely characteristic of every scene in which user's mode significantly changes. However, some cases detected user behavior mistakenly in the experiment because behavioral patterns of different scenes such as going out and getting up include some same ordered pairs. To solve this problem, it is important to improve an initial behavioral pattren. In addition, after a behavioral pattern mistakenly detected a false case, we need a method to refine the behavioral pattern with the false case to keep the mistake from recurring in a long-term perspective.

Because our research aims to provide services to users, we have a considerable problem of the timing to provide services to users after detection of their behavior. Suppose our method detects that a user goes out when he is brushing his teeth in the lavatory. It is not the best to warn him that a window of his room is open immediately after that. Because he may intend to close the window after his brushing. Instead it will be comfortable for him to warn him immediately before he put his shoes on in the entrance. Too early providing services makes him uncomfortable. In the future, we must develop a method to determine the timing to provide services, using position information of a user.

5   Conclusion

This paper proposed a detection method of user behavior with a behavioral pattern which is created in practical short duration. A behavioral pattern is created with sample behavior logs which are time series of objects a user touches in the Tagged World. An experiment have proved our method can detect user behavior with a behavioral pattern created using only 5 sample behavior logs which can be collected even in a week. In the future, we will consider how to set suitable threshold for individual user.

References

1. Kidd, C.D., Orr, R.J., Abowd, G.D., Atkeson, C.G., Essa, I.A., MacIntyre, B., Mynatt, E., Starner, T.E., Newstetter, W.: The aware home: A living laboratory for ubiquitous computing research. In: Streitz, N.A., Hartkopf, V. (eds.) CoBuild 1999. LNCS, vol. 1670, pp. 191–198. Springer, Heidelberg (1999)

2. Perkowitz, M., Philipose, M., Patterson, D.J., Fishkin, K.: Mining models of human activities from the web. In: WWW 2004. Proc. the 13th International World Wide Web Conference, pp. 573–582 (2004)
3. Isoda, Y., Kurakake, S., Nakano, H.: Ubiquitous sensors based human behavior modeling and recognition using a spatio-temporal representation of user states. In: AINA 2004. Proc. the 18th International Conference on Advanced Information Networking and Applications, pp. 512–517 (2004)
4. Aoki, S., Iwai, Y., Onishi, M., Kojima, A., Fukunaga, K.: Learning and recognizing behavioral patterns using position and posture of human body and its application to detection of irregular state. The Journal of IEICE (D-II) J87-D-II(5), 1083–1093 (2004)
5. Aoki, S., Onishi, M., Kojima, A., Fukunaga, K.: Detection of a solitude senior's irregular states based on learning and recognizing of behavioral patterns. IEEJ Transactions on Sensors and Micromachines 125-E(6), 259–265 (2005)
6. Matsuoka, K.: Smart house understanding human behaviors: who did what, where, and when. In: Proc. the 8th World Multi-Conference on Systems, Cybernetics, and Informatics, pp. 181–185 (2004)
7. Mori, T., Takada, A., Noguchi, H., Sato, T.: Behavior prediction system based on environmental sensor records. In: INSS 2005. Proc. the 2nd International Workshop on Networked Sensing Systems, pp. 197–202 (2005)
8. Mori, T., Takada, A., Noguchi, H., Harada, T., Sato, T.: Behavior prediction based on daily-life record database in distributed sensing space. In: IROS 2005. Proc. the 2005 IEEE/RSJ International Conference on Intelligent Robots and Systems, pp. 1833–1839 (2005)
9. Yamazaki, T.: Ubiquitous home: Real-life testbed for home context-aware service. In: Tridentcom 2005. Proc. the 1st International Conference on Testbeds and Reserch Infrastructures for the DEvelopment of NeTworks and COMmunities, pp. 54–59 (2005)
10. Nakauchi, Y., Noguchi, K., Somwong, P., Matsubara, T., Namatame, A.: Vivid room: Human intention detection and activity support environment for ubiquitous autonomy. In: Proc. the 2003 IEEE/RSJ International Conference on Intelligent Robots and Systems, pp. 773–778 (2003)
11. Aoki, S., Onishi, M., Kojima, A., Fukunaga, K.: Recognition of behavioral pattern based on hmm. The Journal of IEICE (D-II) J85-D-II(7), 1265–1270 (2002)
12. Hara, K., Omori, T., Ueno, R.: Detection of unusual human behavior in intelligent house. In: Proc. Neural Networks for Signal Processing XII - proceedings of the 2002 IEEE Signal Processing Society Workshop - 2002, pp. 697–706. IEEE Computer Society Press, Los Alamitos (2002)
13. Fukuda, T., Nakauchi, Y., Noguchi, K., Matsubara, T.: Time series action support by mobile robot in intelligent environment. In: ICRA 2005. Proc. 2005 IEEE International Conference on Robotics and Automation, pp. 2908–2913. IEEE Computer Society Press, Los Alamitos (2005)
14. Nishida, Y., Kitamura, K., Aizawa, H.: Real world sensorization for observing human behavior and its application to behavior-to-speech. In: IUI 2004. Proc. International Conference on Intelligent User Interface 2004, pp. 289–291 (2004)
15. Kaede, S., Yamahara, H., Noguchi, T., Shimada, Y., Shimakawa, H.: A probabilistic approach to recognize individual behavior from touched objects. IPSJ Journal 48(3) (2007)

Discriminative Temporal Smoothing for Activity Recognition from Wearable Sensors

Jaakko Suutala, Susanna Pirttikangas, and Juha Röning

Intelligent Systems Group, Infotech Oulu
Computer Engineering Laboratory
90014 University of Oulu, Finland
{jaska,msp,jjr}@ee.oulu.fi

Abstract. This paper describes daily life activity recognition using wearable acceleration sensors attached to four different parts of the human body. The experimental data set consisted of signals recorded from 13 different subjects performing 17 daily activities. Furthermore, to attain more general activities, some of the most specific classes were combined for a total of 9 different activities. Simple time domain features were calculated from each sensor device. For the recognition task, we propose a novel sequential learning method that combines discriminative learning of individual input-output mappings using support vector machines (SVM) with generative learning to smooth temporal time-dependent activity sequences with a trained hidden Markov model (HMM) type transition probability matrix. The experiments show that the accuracy of the proposed method is superior to various conventional discriminative and generative methods alone, and it achieved a total recognition rate of 94% and 96% studying 17 and 9 different daily activities, respectively.

1 Introduction

Activity recognition from wearable sensors has become an important research topic in recent years [1], [2], [3]. Successful recognition of basic human activities based on sensing of body posture and motion can be used in different applications, such as health care, child care and elderly care, as well as in personal witness monitoring. In addition, it provides a mechanism for using the activities to control devices around us, for example to provide personalized services to assist those with physical disabilities or cognitive disorders.

In this paper we present a novel method for activity recognition from wearable sensors. It combines ideas from two major categories of supervised machine learning: discriminative and generative learning. Discriminative learning (e.g., kernel methods [4], [5], [6]) provides an effective framework for learning direct input-output mapping from a labeled training data set ($\mathbf{X} = (\mathbf{x}_1, \ldots, \mathbf{x}_n)$ and $\mathbf{y} = (y_1, \ldots, y_n)$, where $\mathbf{x}_i$ presents i:th input feature vector and y_i is i:th target class label) for particular applications, such as classification and regression to predict unknown examples. However, adapting a discriminative framework to more advanced learning problems, such as cases where input or/and output spaces can have a structure (a sequence, for example), is not straightforward.

H. Ichikawa et al. (Eds.): UCS 2007, LNCS 4836, pp. 182–195, 2007.

On the other hand, in generative learning methods, modeling of whole phenomena that generate the data is not efficient, and the discriminative properties are not modeled very powerfully, for example, in classification tasks [7], [8]. However, generative learning is easily extended to a structured domain and it is suitable for activity recognition, as the sequential nature of adjacent class labels can be modeled. Here, the idea that daily activities usually vary smoothly is applied and it is more likely that the same activity as the previous one is detected in a short time period. Moreover, it is useful to handle transitions between activities differently, because some transitions more probably will occur than others.

The most popular model of a generative learning category for sequential data is HMMs [9]. Conventional HMMs are typically trained in a non-discriminative manner, as they are not able to discriminate between different classes very well. Another problem is that multi-dimensional input vectors cannot be used directly and overlapping features are not allowed. The features have to be transformed into a sequence of discrete symbols using some quantization, clustering or static pre-classifier method, or by forming a continuous density model where each observation vector is modeled using some probability distribution, for example a Gaussian mixture [9].

To overcome the problems of discriminative and generative learning, we combine them in a novel way. First, we train a discriminative model (e.g., SVM) to predict confidence of activity labels from individual multi-dimensional input vectors in time-series sequences. Second, we use the conditional posterior probability outputs of a discriminative learning algorithm as the input observation to a generative model. The generative model has a HMM-type structure where observations are the predicted confidence measurements of different classes from the discriminative model. Then, a global transition matrix is trained by the well-known forward-backward (FB) algorithm [9]. Here, the temporal properties of different activities are modeled and individual predictions in sequence are smoothed to remove outliers. For example, in the activity sequence running, running, bicycling, running, the bicycling activity can be detected as an outlier. In the classification stage, the most probable state (i.e., label) sequence is recognized using Viterbi decoding [10]. This paper is an extension of the work [11] where sensor settings, data collection and feature selection along with classification of independent activity examples were studied. We use the same features calculated in the previous study. In addition, we compare our method with the earlier experiments along with other sequential learning methods, such as conventional HMMs and a SVM-HMM combination.

The rest of the paper is organized as follows. Section 2 presents related work in activity recognition by wearable sensors and sequential learning methods and scenarios. Section 3 describes the details of the methods and data set used in this paper and section presents the experimental results. Finally, the conclusions of the work are given in Section 5.

2   Related Work

In ubiquitous computing, activity recognition has been realised using vision, audio, and different environmental and wearable sensing devices [12], [13]. To be able to recognize the actions of an individual person related to everyday tasks, the study of wearable accelerometer sensors has become dominant in the field. Wearable computing provides personalized services [14], which can be utilized by mobile devices or in clothing to assist in health care, fitness or work-related tasks, for example. The use of wearable acceleration sensors provides calm technology that is possibly not as obtrusive for the users compared with vision- and audio-based sensing.

The study of activity recognition using wearable sensors has concentrated on problems from hardware setups and sensor placement to feature extraction and classification methods. Activity recognition using wearable acceleration sensors attached to five different body parts was studied by [1]. Along with comprehensive related work in the field, they present useful features for recognizing everyday activities and the important aspect of the need of user-specific training data for some activities. An 84% accuracy rate for 20 different activities was achieved using user-annotated training data and a decision tree classifier. [15] used cluster analysis to examine which are the best features and time window lengths for discriminating between different activities. According to them, different features, such as Fourier coefficients, mean, and variance as well as different window lengths, are needed in the recognition.

Different features and sensor positions were examined by [16] using a single device with a dual axis accelerometer and a light sensor. They recognized six primary activities: sitting, standing, walking, ascending stairs, descending stairs, and running. To be able to compute features in real time on a wrist watch-like platform, they use only time domain features and feature selection. Wrist position was the best when the subset of features was optimized for it. In multiple sensor recognition, [17] studied the number and placement of devices. Naturally, in recognizing different activities the position of the sensor for a particular activity is important (e.g., lower and upper body motion when walking, upper body when typing with a keyboard).

The sequential nature of activity data has been considered, also. The most popular method is generative HMMs or related methods. Static and dynamic hand gestures of a mobile user were studied by [18] using acceleration sensors with self-organized maps (SOM) and HMMs. [19] combined vision and accelerometers and recognized the gestures of sign language using HMMs. Different daily activities, such as sitting, standing, walking, running, climbing stairs, and bicycling, were recognized by [20]. They combined unsupervised clustering (SOM) with supervised learning (k-nearest neighbors) and sequential modeling (Markov chain). [3] presented methods for recognizing assembly and maintenance work activities by hand motion and activities using an accelerometer and a microphone. Their case study of a wood workshop assembly task uses analysis of sound intensity detection to segment signals, and the classification is performed by the fusion of linear discriminant analysis (sound) and HMMs (acceleration sensors).

In activity recognition, a study most similar to our work is presented in [2]. It uses discriminative learning of multi-dimensional input-output mapping and feature selection of individual examples using boosting, which is then combined with HMMs to capture temporal properties. Compared with our approach, which uses a global transition probability matrix between activities, they trained a single HMM for each activity where a transition matrix models inner-class hidden state variation. They used a single sensor board equipped with an accelerometer, a microphone, two light sensors, barometric pressure, humidity, and temperature sensors, and a compass, and they initially extracted over 600 features. [21] applied another discriminative sequential learning approach to physiological activity data using conditional random fields. In classifying a physical activity (watching TV or sleeping) based on nine different sensor measurements, the method showed more accurate results compared with non-sequential methods, which only use information from individual input vectors. In a different application area [22], support vector machines and temporal smoothing were combined to classify audio sequences, which uses methodology quite similar to ours. However, they only applied it to a binary classification domain to detect speech and non-speech components from a video soundtrack, and they used a more ad-hoc technique to transform SVM outputs into confidence values for temporal modeling compared with our approach.

More generally, the idea of combining discriminative and generative learning has been studied much recently, mostly in the fields of natural language processing and computational biology. [23] give an overview of learning sequential data from simple sliding window techniques to generative methods such as HMMs, as well as discriminative sequential methods, e.g., maximum entropy Markov models and conditional random fields (CRF), which overcome some of the HMM's problems of feature presentation and non-discriminative learning with more expensive training. Additionally, kernel methods have been extended to sequential data through kernel design [24], and structured learning of support vector machines [25] and Gaussian process classification [26], which utilize the idea of HMMs and CRFs in dynamic programming style optimization and inference. Jebara [7] presents a framework for including generative models (e.g., HMMs) in large margin discriminative learning using maximum entropy discrimination.

Fig. 1. Wearable sensor devices used in these experiments

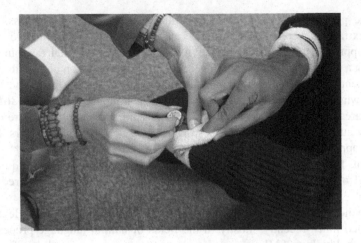

Fig. 2. Attachment of sensor devices to the wrist

3   System for Sequential Learning of Activities

3.1   Activity Data Set and Feature Extraction

In this paper we used the data set collected in [11]. It includes activities recorded from 13 different subjects wearing four sensor nodes, which were attached to different parts of the body: the right thigh and wrist, the left wrist and a necklace. Each sensor node has a triaxial accelerometer that is sampled 64 times at 200 kHz, and the average values are sent every 100 msec to a data collecting terminal. The wearable sensor is presented in Figure 1, and the attachment of the sensor to the wrist is illustrated in Figure 2. The sensor was developed by the Nokia Research Center, Tokyo, in collaboration with the Distributed Computing Laboratory of Waseda University.

As presented in [11], each subject performed a sequence of 17 daily activities and annotated the starting and ending time of each activity using a touch screen or a wearable interface, depending on whether the particular activity was performed inside or outside. Each activity took at least one minute and altogether over 8 hours of data were collected. The 17 activities include *cleaning a whiteboard, reading a newspaper, standing still, sitting and relaxing, drinking, brushing teeth, sitting and watching TV, lying down, typing, vacuum cleaning, walking, climbing stairs, descending stairs, riding an elevator up, riding an elevator down, running,* and *bicycling.* Furthermore, some of the activities were combined into a single class, producing a data set of 9 general activities: *cleaning, standing, sitting, using stairs, brushing teeth, lying down, walking, running,* and *bicycling.* The *drinking* activity was left out because of its multimodal nature (i.e., the subjects were sitting or standing, etc.). Example activities in the data set are shown in Figure 3.

[11] tested different features and time windows and they found out that using a short time window (e.g., 0.7 - 1 second) with simple features (the mean and the standard deviation) gave the most accurate recognition rates. In this study, we also use a 0.7 second window and the mean and the standard deviation calculated from all 3 acceleration

channels of each sensor device, providing a total of 24 features in every time step. The use of such simple features is justified in an application where only limited computational resources are available and a relatively short time window is applied to achieve a real-time response.

(a) Sitting and reading newspaper   (b) Walking

Fig. 3. Example activities performed by the subjects

3.2 Discriminative Learning of Static Examples: SVM Approach

Discriminative learning is a very effective way to train mappings from multidimensional input feature vectors to class labels. Kernel methods in particular have become state-of-the-art, due to their superior performance in many real-world learning problems, clear mathematical foundations and generalization capabilities based on statistical learning theory.

In this study, we use the popular support vector machines (SVM) [27] as base classifiers in our recognition system. The SVM method has many favorable properties such as good generalization by finding the largest margin between classes, the ability to handle non-separable classes via soft-margin criteria, non-linearity modeling via explicit kernel mapping, sparseness by presenting data using only a small number of support vectors, and global convex optimization with given hyperparameters. Fast optimization and a sparse solution are very important in building real-time systems with large-scale data sets. Training can be done effectively, for example by using sequential minimization optimization [28]. After training, an unknown example $f(\mathbf{x})$ in a binary classification case can be labeled as follows,

$$f(\mathbf{x}) = \sum_{i \in SV} y_i \alpha_i k(\mathbf{x}, \mathbf{x}_i) + b \tag{1}$$

where α_i is a non-zero Lagrange multiplier, y_i is the class label of the training set, $k(\mathbf{x}, \mathbf{x}_i)$ is kernel mapping between an unknown example $\mathbf{x}$ and a training example $\mathbf{x}_i$, and b is the bias of the learned solution. SV represents the group of support vectors.

One drawback of SVM is that it is directly applicable only in two-class problems. Thus, there have been different attempts to generalize it to multi-class classification. The simplest and most popular methods are based on multiple binary classifiers using one-vs-one or one-vs-rest approaches as well as error correcting output codes and directed acyclic graphs, to name a few [5]. We apply the one-vs-one strategy due to its simplicity, its good performance in practice, and its capability of extended hard decisions to output confidence values using different post-processing methods. Next, we present algorithms that are able to produce posterior probabilities from binary SVM outputs and combine them into a multiple class classification.

SVM cannot directly give a confidence measurement as an output, but gives only a decision as an unscaled distance from the margin in feature space. However, [29] proposed a very useful method for getting probabilistic outputs by performing another mapping function from the raw outputs to class probabilities. This is calculated through a parametric sigmoid function, as follows

$$P(y = 1|f(\mathbf{x})) = \frac{1}{1 + \exp(Af(\mathbf{x}) + B)} \tag{2}$$

The parameters A and B are found by minimizing the negative log-likelihood of the validation set

$$\min_{A,B} - \sum_{i=1}^{N} (t_i \log(P(y = 1|f(\mathbf{x}_i))) \\ + (1 - t_i) \log(1 - P(y = 1|f(\mathbf{x}_i))))), \tag{3}$$

where

$$t_i = \begin{cases} \frac{N_+ + 1}{N_+ + 2}, & \text{if } y_i = 1 \\ \frac{1}{N_- + 2}, & \text{if } y_i = -1 \end{cases}$$

N_+ is the number of positive class labels and N_- presents the negative ones.

Based on one-vs-one classification, pairwise coupling (PC) is a method of combining multiple two-class probabilities to obtain multi-class estimates for C classes. The method was proposed by [30] and extended by [31]. Let r_{ij} be the probabilistic output of the classifier, obtained, e.g., using Platt's method, and p_i be the probability of the i:th class. Also, let p_i be presented by auxiliary variables $\mu_{ij} = p_i/(p_i + p_j)$. To estimate the values of p_i, the Kullback-Leibler divergence between r_{ij} and μ_{ij} can be determined as follows

$$l(\mathbf{p}) = \sum_{i<j} n_{ij}(r_{ij} \log \frac{r_{ij}}{\mu_{ij}} + (1 + r_{ij}) \log \frac{1 - r_{ij}}{1 - \mu_{ij}}) \tag{4}$$

where the weight n_{ij} is the number of examples of classes i and j in the training set. The weights n_{ij} can be set equal to one if there is no significant difference between class sizes. Minimizing the function in Eq. 4, can be computed using an iterative method [30]. Finally, p_i presents the conditional probability $P(c_i|f(\mathbf{x}))$ of recognizing class i. For example, [32] achieved encouraging multi-class classification results using the methods described above.

3.3 Temporal Smoothing of Sequences

Regardless of SVM's capability of classifying independently and identically distributed (i.i.d) data as presented in the previous subsection, it is not directly applicable to sequential data, such as activities where the data are rather dependent on the neighborhood labels. This subsection presents a general algorithm to train temporal smoothing to the confidence valued outputs of a discriminative (or generative) classifier trained on static independent examples.

The learning of sequential input-output pairs has usually been done with hidden Markov models (HMM) [9], which are generative graphical models with a Markov chain structure. HMMs have some limitations compared with kernel-based methods: they are trained in a generative manner (e.g., one model/class), they have some conditional independence assumptions, they need explicit feature presentation (e.g., suffering from the curse of dimensionality), and they cannot handle overlapping features. To overcome the limitations of HMMs, many discriminative variants have been proposed, including different discriminative training algorithm for HMMs (see section 2 for some of the related approaches).

We propose a simple algorithm that combines discriminative multi-class learning with generative smoothing of activity sequences, named discriminative temporal smoothing (DTS). DTS is a general algorithm in which you can use any base classifier that produces confidence output measurements. However, we applied SVM due to its accurate and efficient sparse solution. Once we have trained the SVM classifiers on the static examples and mapped them to confidence values, we can apply temporal smoothing. First, the probabilistic outputs of the static classifier from the training set is used as an observation input to estimate a global transition probability between class labels. Let $P(c_k|f(\mathbf{x}_1)), P(c_k|f(\mathbf{x}_2)), \ldots, P(c_k|f(\mathbf{x}_t))$ be a sequence of conditional posterior probabilities of class k from the beginning of the sequence to a time step t estimated by SVMs and pairwise coupling. We collect these confidence values from every k class to observation matrix $\mathbf{B}$ as follows

$$
\mathbf{B} = \begin{bmatrix}
P(c_1|f(\mathbf{x}_1)) & P(c_1|f(\mathbf{x}_2)) & \ldots & P(c_1|f(\mathbf{x}_t)) \\
P(c_2|f(\mathbf{x}_1)) & P(c_2|f(\mathbf{x}_2)) & \ldots & P(c_2|f(\mathbf{x}_t)) \\
\vdots & \vdots & \vdots & \vdots \\
P(c_k|f(\mathbf{x}_1)) & P(c_k|f(\mathbf{x}_2)) & \ldots & P(c_k|f(\mathbf{x}_t))
\end{bmatrix}
\tag{5}
$$

Then, a global transition matrix $\mathbf{A}$ with transition coefficients $a_{ij} = P(c_i^t|c_j^{t-1})$ (the probabilities between different classes i and j from the time $t-1$ to t) is calculated. The transition coefficients can be estimated with an iterative forward-backward algorithm, well-known from HMM training [9], over the observation matrix. Finally, an unknown sequence can be labeled from coupled probabilistic SVM confidence outputs with the use of a transition probability matrix and a Viterbi algorithm [10], resulting in smoothed class probabilities $(P_s(c_{1...k}|f(\mathbf{x}_t)) = P_s(c_1|f(\mathbf{x}_t)), P_s(c_2|f(\mathbf{x}_t)), \ldots, P_s(c_k|f(\mathbf{x}_t))$ for example $\mathbf{x}$ at time t). The final classification is made by choosing the most probable class from the smoothed confidence values, i.e., $\mathrm{argmax}[P_s(c_{1...k}|f(\mathbf{x}_t))]$. A diagram of different stages of the proposed activity recognition system based on DTS is presented in Figure 4.

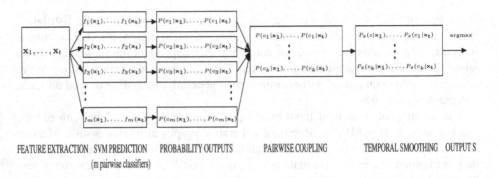

FEATURE EXTRACTION   SVM PREDICTION   PROBABILITY OUTPUTS   PAIRWISE COUPLING   TEMPORAL SMOOTHING   OUTPUT S
(m pairwise classifiers)

Fig. 4. Example diagram of the building blocks of a system for learning to recognize sequential activities

4   Results

This section presents the results of our experiments using the data sets of 17 and 9 activities, respectively. Both data sets consist of the data of 13 subjects. We removed 5 examples (i.e., 3.5 seconds) from the beginning of each activity due to outliers caused by the subject moving from the labeling screen to a spot (e.g., white board) to perform the particular activity. To compare our results with previous work by [11], we use a similar testing scheme, i.e., we presented the test results with four-fold cross-validation (i.e., we used independent test data sets not used for training). In addition, we compare the proposed method with conventional SVM and HMM classifiers as well as a SVM-HMM combination quite similar to the approach presented by [2]. However, they use a different discriminative method (i.e., ADABoost) as the base classifier.

For each data set we trained the ensemble of one-vs-one SVM classifiers (Eq. 1) with radial basis function (RBF) kernels $(K(\mathbf{x}, \mathbf{x}') = exp(-(1/2\sigma^2)||\mathbf{x} - \mathbf{x}'||^2))$. The regularization penalty term $C = \{0.5, 1, 10, 100\}$ and kernel hyperparameter $\sigma = \{0.6, 0.8, 1.0, 1.5, 2\}$ were found using four-fold cross-validation over the training data sets. Furthermore, the parameters of sigmoid mapping (Eq. 2) were estimated by cross-validation of each binary classifier. Pairwise classifiers were finally coupled to give confidence values for each class (Eq. 4). These conditional probabilities were used as an input to different methods: SVM-HMM and DTS, respectively. The structure of HMM (in conventional and SVM-HMM methods) included three hidden states, and the observation probability distributions were presented using a two-component Gaussian mixture model with a diagonal covariance matrix. A single HMM was trained for each class using five consecutive examples in a sliding window, and this sequence was classified as the highest likelihood value among the models. The models were implemented in a Matlab environment. The SVMs were trained using a Spider toolbox [33] with a lib-SVM optimizer [34], and the HMMs were trained using the HMM Matlab toolbox [35].

4.1 Recognition Results

Table 1 presents the total recognition accuracies of 17 activities using different classification methods as well average precision (true positive/(true positive + false positive)) and recall (true positive/(true positive + false negative)) values. The proposed method surpassed all other methods, presenting a 93.6% total recognition rate. Additionally, these experiments show the usefulness of the discriminative SVM classifier, as it gives superior accuracy compared with HMM, which is not able to model a high-dimensional input space accurately. Using the SVM-HMM combination gives a slightly better recognition rate compared with plain HMM, but it is not as effective as presented by [2]. This is related to the fact that besides accelerometers, they used different sensors and features such as audio, which usually includes a lot of temporal dynamics in intra-class variations. In addition, they used a much larger sliding window to extract features in which the usefulness of modeling the hidden dynamics of a single activity is justified. In our experiments, a simple global transition probability smoothing machine works well with simple statistical features and a small sliding window.

Table 1. Total recognition accuracies as well as average precision and recall values of 17 activities using different methods

	SVM	HMM	SVM-HMM	DTS
Accuracy (%)	90.65 (4.53)	84.26 (4.66)	84.39 (5.65)	**93.58 (4.15)**
Precision (%)	88.00 (4.68)	75.69 (3.04)	77.82 (5.36)	**93.88 (3.69)**
Recall (%)	87.74 (3.21)	79.74 (3.76)	81.17 (3.90)	**90.58 (3.55)**

Table 2 presents the total recognition accuracies of 9 activities using different classification methods as well average precision and recall values. Also, in this case the DTS method outperformed the other methods, showing a 96.4% success rate. Similar conclusions can be made with a data set of 17 activities.

Table 2. Total recognition accuracies as well as average precision and recall values of 9 activities using different methods

	SVM	HMM	SVM-HMM	DTS
Accuracy (%)	94.15 (2.62)	88.75 (2.93)	90.42 (4.75)	**96.36 (2.13)**
Precision (%)	92.12 (2.98)	82.32 (4.50)	85.77 (3.14)	**96.76 (2.06)**
Recall (%)	92.10 (1.80)	86.77 (3.74)	87.89 (7.20)	**94.53 (1.05)**

Finally, we examined the individual activities in the data set of 9 activities. Table 3 presents an example confusion matrix of a total number of 4405 test examples of 9 activities performed by 13 subjects recognized by a DTS algorithm. All the activities, except using stairs, are recognized at over a 90% success rate, where the most distinguished ones are: *sitting*, *walking*, *running*, and *bicycling*. The *using stairs* activity is naturally most often confused with *walking*, which is not the case the other way around.

Table 3. Confusion matrix of recognizing 9 different activities with a discriminative temporal smoothing algorithm

%	clean	sit	stand	use stairs	brush teeth	lie down	walk	run	cycle
clean	**94.3**	1.5	1.2	0.0	0.0	0.0	2.4	0.0	0.6
sit	0.0	**99.4**	0.4	0.0	0.0	0.0	0.2	0.0	0.2
stand	3.1	2.6	**94.1**	0.0	0.2	0.0	0.0	0.0	0.0
use stairs	0.0	0.0	0.0	**70.9**	0.0	0.0	29.1	0.0	0.0
brush teeth	1.7	0.7	0.0	0.0	**97.2**	0.4	0.0	0.0	0.0
lie down	3.4	3.4	0.0	0.0	0.0	**92.7**	0.0	0.0	0.5
walk	0.0	0.0	0.0	0.2	0.0	0.0	**99.8**	0.0	0.0
run	0.0	0.0	0.0	0.0	0.0	0.0	0.0	**100.0**	0.0
cycle	0.4	0.0	0.0	0.0	0.0	0.0	0.0	0.0	**99.6**

In comparison, using the same data sets and features, the k-nearest neighbor classifier used by [11] gives total recognition accuracies 89.47% (4.64) for the data set of 17 subjects and 93.02% (2.64) for the data set of 9 subjects, respectively. In both dataset it is more accurate than the HMM and SVM-HMM methods, but DTS also outperforms those methods.

5 Conclusions

We presented a novel approach to activity recognition by wearable sensors. The proposed algorithm combines effective discriminative classification with a smoothing of adjacent class label estimates in an activity sequence. In activity recognition, it is very useful to extend conventional i.i.d data assumption-based classifiers to the sequential learning domain to be able to take advantage of the smoothing changes of the targets and the probabilities of transition between different activities.

We used a SVM classifier to recognize individual activity examples, which were then mapped to class confidence values. At the post-processing stage we trained a global transition probability matrix from the confidence values using a forward-backward algorithm. Final classification was then performed with the confidence values and the transition probability matrix using a Viterbi algorithm.

Using a data set of 13 subject performing 17 daily activities, we were able to achieve a total accuracy of 94%. In addition, we combined some of the most specific classes to present more generic activities, which led to 9 activities. The data set of combined activities gave a recognition rate of 96%. Our results indicate that the proposed algorithm is able take advantage of the sequential nature of activity data, showing superior performance compared with typical non-sequential (standard SVM) and sequential (standard HMM) classifiers. The accurate recognition of human activities can provide useful knowledge for different applications in the ubiquitous computing field.

The method proposed in this paper is general. It is not restricted to SVM-based classifiers but applies to any method that is able to produce probabilistic outputs. For example, Gaussian process classification leads naturally to probabilistic class confidence values compared with the more ad-hoc method used with SVM. In addition, the cross-validation can be replaced by Bayesian model selection strategies. This is one possible direction for future research. Furthermore, in this study we used a data set that was collected in a semi-naturalistic manner, i.e., the subjects performed and labeled the activities in a predefined order to minimize possible disturbance. Using a data set where the activities are performed in a more naturalistic order, e.g., sitting-standing-walking, the sequential method is more advantageous than conventional methods due to its ability to place importance on more probable transitions between activities in real-life sequences.

Acknowledgments

The authors would like to thank K. Fujinami for the sensors and data collection, as well as the voluntary subjects at Waseda University. J.S. would like to thank InfoTech Oulu Graduate school for financial support. Additionally, this work was funded by the Academy of Finland and the Finnish Funding Agency of Technology.

References

1. Bao, L., Intille, S.: Activity recognition from user-annotated acceleration data. In: Ferscha, A., Mattern, F. (eds.) PERVASIVE 2004. LNCS, vol. 3001, pp. 1–17. Springer, Heidelberg (2004)
2. Lester, J., Choudhury, T., Kern, N., Borriello, G., Hannaford, B.: A hybrid discriminative/generative approach for modeling human activities. In: Proceedings of the Nineteenth International Joint Conference on Artificial Intelligence, Edinburgh, Scotland, pp. 766–722 (2005)
3. Ward, J.A., Lukowicz, P., Troster, G., Starner, T.E.: Activity recognition of assembly tasks using body-worn microphones and accelerometers. IEEE Trans. Pattern Anal. Mach. Intell. 28(10), 1553–1567 (2006)
4. Herbrich, R.: Learning Kernel Classifiers. The MIT Press, USA (2002)
5. Schölkopf, B., Smola, A.: Learning with Kernels: Support Vector Machines, Regularization, Optimization, and Beyond. The MIT Press, USA (2001)
6. Shawe-Taylor, J., Cristianini, N.: Kernel Methods for Pattern Analysis. Cambridge University Press, UK (2004)
7. Jebara, T.: Machine Learning: Discriminative and Generative. Kluwer Academic Publishers, Dordrecht (2004)
8. Ng, A.Y., Jordan, M.I.: Classification with hybrid generative/discriminative models. In: NIPS 2001. Advances in Neural Information Processing Systems, vol. 14 (2001)
9. Rabiner, L.R.: A tutorial on hidden markov models and selected applications in speech recognition. Proceedings of the IEEE 77(2), 257–286 (1989)

10. Forney, G.D.: The viterbi algorithm. Proceedings of the IEEE 61, 268–277 (1973)
11. Pirttikangas, S., Fujinami, K., Nakajima, T.: Feature selection and activity recognition from wearable sensors. In: Youn, H.Y., Kim, M., Morikawa, H. (eds.) UCS 2006. LNCS, vol. 4239, pp. 516–527. Springer, Heidelberg (2006)
12. Pentland, A.: Smart rooms. Scientific American 274, 68–76 (1996)
13. Essa, I.A.: Ubiquitous sensing for smart and aware environments: Technologies towards the building of an aware home. IEEE Personal Communications, Special issue on networking the physical world, pp. 47–49 (October 2000)
14. Rhodes, B.J., Minar, N., Weaver, J.: Wearable computing meets ubiquitous computing: reaping the best of both worlds. In: Proc. Third International Symposium on Wearable Computers. Digest of Papers, San Francisco, California, USA, pp. 141–149 (October 18-19, 1999)
15. Huynh, T., Schiele, B.: Analyzing features for activity recognition. In: sOc-EUSAI 2005: Proceedings of the 2005 joint conference on Smart objects and ambient intelligence, pp. 159–163. ACM Press, New York (2005)
16. Maurer, U., Smailagic, A., Siewiorek, D.P., Deisher, M.: Activity recognition and monitoring using multiple sensors on different body positions. In: BSN 2006. Proceedings of the International Workshop on Wearable and Implantable Body Sensor Networks, pp. 113–116. IEEE Computer Society, Washington, DC (2006)
17. Kern, N., Schiele, B.: Multi-sensor activity context detection for wearable computing. In: European Symposium on Ambient Intelligence, Eindhoven, The Netherlands (November 2003)
18. Mäntylä, V.-M., Mäntyjärvi, J., Seppänen, T., Tuulari, E.: Hand gesture recognition of a mobile device user. In: ICME 2000. IEEE International Conference on Multimedia and Expo., New York, USA, vol. 1, pp. 281–284 (2000)
19. Brashear, H., Starner, T., Lukowicz, P., Junker, H.: Using multiple sensors for mobile sign language recognition. In: ISWC 2003. Proceedings of the 7th IEEE International Symposium on Wearable Computers, pp. 45–52. IEEE Computer Society, Washington, DC (2003)
20. Van Laerhoven, K., Cakmakci, O.: What shall we teach our pants? In: ISWC 2000: Proceedings of the 4th IEEE International Symposium on Wearable Computers, p. 77. IEEE Computer Society, Washington, DC (2000)
21. Chieu, H.L., Lee, W.S., Kaelbling, L.P.: Activity recognition from physiological data using conditional random fields. In: Singapore-MIT Alliance Symposium (2006)
22. Naphade, M.R., Wang, R., Huang, T.S.: Classifying motion picture soundtrack for video indexing. In: Proceedings of IEEE International Conference on Multimedia and Expo., pp. 1160–1163. IEEE Computer Society Press, Los Alamitos (2001)
23. Dietterich, T.: Machine learning for sequential data: A review. In: Caelli, T.M., Amin, A., Duin, R.P.W., Kamel, M.S., de Ridder, D. (eds.) SPR 2002 and SSPR 2002. LNCS, vol. 2396, pp. 15–30. Springer, Heidelberg (2002)
24. Jaakkola, T., Haussler, D.: Exploiting generative models in discriminative classifiers. In: NIPS 1998. Advances in Neural Information Processing Systems, vol. 11 (1998)
25. Altun, Y., Tsochantaridis, I., Hofmann, T.: Hidden markov support vector machines. In: ICML 2003. Proceedings of the International Conference of Machine Learning (2003)
26. Altun, Y., Hofmann, T., Smola, A.: Gaussian process classification for segmenting and annotating sequences. In: ICML 2004. Proceedings of the International Conference of Machine Learning (2004)
27. Cristianini, N., Shawe-Taylor, J.: An Introduction to Support Vector Machines and Other Kernel-based Learning Methods. Cambridge University Press, UK (2000)
28. Platt, J.: Fast training of support vector machines using sequential minimal optimization. In: Smola, A., Bartlett, P., Schölkopf, B., Schuurmans, D. (eds.) Advances in Kernel Methods - Support Vector Learning, pp. 185–208. MIT Press, Cambridge (1999)

29. Platt, J.: Probabilistic outputs for support vector machines and comparisons to regularized likelihood methods. In: Smola, A., Bartlett, P., Schölkopf, B., Schuurmans, D. (eds.) Advances in Kernel Methods - Support Vector Learning, pp. 61–74. MIT Press, Cambridge (1999)
30. Hastie, T., Tibshirani, R.: Classification by pairwise coupling. In: Jordan, M.I., Kearns, M.J. (eds.) NIPS 1998. Advances in Neural Information Processing Systems, vol. 10, MIT Press, Cambridge (1998)
31. Wu, T.-F., Lin, C.-J., Weng, R.C.: Probability estimates for multi-class classification by pairwise coupling. Journal of Machine Learning Research 5, 975–1005 (2004)
32. Duan, K.-B., Keerthi, S.: Which is the best multiclass SVM method: An empirical study. In: Oza, N.C., Polikar, R., Kittler, J., Roli, F. (eds.) MCS 2005. LNCS, vol. 3541, pp. 278–285. Springer, Heidelberg (2005)
33. The Spider: Machine learning toolbox for matlab. Software available: http://www.kyb.tuebingen.mpg.de/bs/people/spider/
34. Chang, C.-C., Lin, C.-J.: LIBSVM: A Library for Support Vector Machines, Software available (2001), http://www.csie.ntu.edu.tw/~cjlin/libsvm/
35. Hidden Markov Model (HMM) toolbox for matlab. Software available: http://www.cs.ubc.ca/~murphyk/Software/HMM/hmm.html

Activity Recognition Based on Intra and Extra Manipulation of Everyday Objects

Dipak Surie[1], Fabien Lagriffoul[1], Thomas Pederson[1], and Daniel Sjölie[2]

[1] Department of Computing Science, Umeå University,
S-901 87 Umeå, Sweden
{dipak,fabien,top}@cs.umu.se
[2] VRlab / HPC2N, Umeå University,
S-901 87 Umeå, Sweden
deepone@hpc2n.umu.se

Abstract. Recognizing activities based on an actor's interaction with everyday objects is an important research approach within ubiquitous computing. We present a recognition approach which complement objects grabbed or released information with the object's internal state changes (as an effect of intra manipulation) and the object's external state changes with reference to other objects (as an effect of extra manipulation). The concept of Intra manipulation is inspired by the fact that many everyday objects change their internal state when manipulated by the human actor, while extra manipulation is motivated by the fact that humans commonly rearrange the spatial relations between everyday objects as part of their activities. A detailed evaluation of our prototype activity recognition system in virtual reality (VR) environment is presented as a "proof of concept". We have obtained a recognition precision of 92% on the activity-level and 81% on the action-level among 15 everyday home activities. Virtual reality was used as a test-bed in order to speed up the design process of our activity recognition system, allowing us to compensate for the limitations with currently available sensing technologies and to compare the contributions of intra manipulation and extra manipulation for activity recognition.

Keywords: Activity Recognition, Context Awareness, Ubiquitous Computing, Wearable Computing, Virtual Reality.

1 Introduction

In the recent years, there have been many research efforts that attempt to use computers for supporting human activities performed in the real world [1], [2]. Such systems are not only useful in providing assistance to elderly people and those with cognitive impairments in performing their activities of daily living, but also in other application areas like providing training to newly employed staffs, providing assistance in specialized activities like surgery, etc. Advancements in sensing, processing, communication and storage technologies have played an inspiring role for

H. Ichikawa et al. (Eds.): UCS 2007, LNCS 4836, pp. 196–210, 2007.

such research efforts. To build such systems is a challenging task due to the number and variety of activities performed by human actors in the real world. One interesting challenge is to come up with a general approach for modelling and recognizing human activities with finer-granularity at not only activity level, but also at action and operation level. There have been several attempts in recognizing the actor's current activity based on object manipulation information, in particular based on the objects that are grabbed and released information [3], [4]. This is an interesting approach since most of the physical activities performed by humans in the real world are mediated by objects [5]. We take a similar research stance, but extend this approach to also consider the object's internal state changes and the object's external state changes as an effect of the actor's intra manipulation and extra manipulation respectively for the following reasons:

a) Recognizing activities based on objects grabbed or released information alone is a promising approach, but there are no previous work to our knowledge that has used this information alone in recognize activities at a lower abstraction action level [3], [4], and [6]. However an extension of such an approach has shown promising results at the action level in our previous work [6].

b) Recognizing activities based on objects grabbed or released information alone has also had difficulties in recognizing the activities during the initial phase of an activity, when the activity has just begun[1]. This introduces long temporal delay between the actual starting of an activity and the moment the system makes a guess about the actor's current activity, which we have addressed in this paper.

c) Such an approach has also had difficulties in recognizing the end of an action or an activity due to the unavailability of sharper events that could be generated using intra manipulation and extra manipulation information channels to be discussed later in this paper. This issue is also discussed in [6].

The wearable computing community has investigated activity recognition based on wearable accelerometers [7], [8], [9] microphones [7] and even cameras [10]. Approaches based on accelerometer data are restricted to activity recognition of simple activities like walking, running, etc. that involve the actor's body movements. Approaches using microphones and cameras have had difficulties in extracting high-level features without extensive computation. The ubiquitous computing community has investigated activity recognition using simple state change sensors [11] and using objects grabbed or released information [3], [4]. The approach using objects grabbed or released information is interesting because complex activities like *preparing the table for lunch* or *preparing breakfast* could be recognized with high precision and recall values. However such an approach does not address the three challenges described in a), b) and c). We consider the objects' internal state change data in the context of an actor's interaction with that object concerned (similar to [11]) and also its changed relationships to other objects from a perspective centred on how the actor literally perceives the world. The work within this line of research focus has mainly been driven by currently available sensor technology. In this paper, we introduce a conceptual design platform based on intra and extra manipulation that could survive

---

[1] We need to recognize activities during the initial phase of an activity in order for our activity support application to provide assistance before the activity reaches an irreversible state.

and handle the generations of changes in the field of sensor technology, and present a detailed evaluation of the system as a "proof of concept".

Application Area: Activity Support for People Suffering Dementia. The prototypical activity recognition system discussed in this paper is part of a larger system that aims to provide assistance to people suffering early stages of dementia disease in completing their activities of daily living (ADL) [2]. ADL include getting dressed, preparing breakfast and activities related to personal hygiene. Typical problems include the forgetting of performing an activity or an action within an activity; not being able to get started in the first place; not being able to continue after having been interrupted; or missing some operations that are mandatory for the completion of an activity. A system that could help overcome the above mentioned problems would enable patients to stay in their home for a longer period of time, have a normal independent life, and also reduce the burden on family members and caregivers. The long-term goal is to build a dementia tolerant home environment using ubiquitous and wearable computing technologies[2].

Structuring Human Activities: Activity, Action and Operation. According to activity theory [5], human activities have an objective and are mediated through tools. We consider the objects present in the actor's environment as tools for the actor to accomplish his/her activities. This theory introduces a 3-level hierarchy of activity, action and operation. An activity takes place in several situations, where each situation is comprised of a set of actions under certain conditions like, location, time, etc. An action is a conscious goal-directed process performed by an actor to fulfil an objective and is comprised of a set of operations. Operations are unconscious processes that depend on the structure of the action and the environment in which it takes place. We follow the above mentioned definitions and the 3 levels of granularity in modelling and recognising human activities.

2   Intra and Extra Manipulation of Everyday Objects

Theoretical Background. Distributed Cognition moves the boundary of human cognition outside of the head of an individual to include his/her body parts and the environment as part of a functional system [12]. According to this theory, human cognition is distributed by placing memories, facts, or knowledge in the objects, individuals, and tools in our environment. Within our research, we keep track of the state changes to everyday objects in the actor's environment based on an actor's object manipulation as part of performing an activity. Intra manipulation is inspired by the fact that many everyday objects change their internal state when manipulated by the human actor, while extra manipulation is motivated by the fact that humans commonly arrange and rearrange the spatial relations between everyday objects as

---

[2] We use VR as a test-bed to develop a system that can assist dementia patients in performing their ADL (Fig. 1a.). Dementia patients will not be asked to perform the experiments in a virtual reality environment. Based on our initial results in VR (activity recognition system described in this paper) we are currently developing an actual hardware prototype which will be evaluated by patients suffering early stages of dementia.

part of their activities [13]. For example, a fridge could be considered as a container that contains objects like milk packet, juice bottle, cake box, etc. When the actor removes the milk packet from the fridge, then he/she has actually extra manipulated the milk packet with reference to the fridge and intra manipulated the fridge. Similarly, an actor might turn on the stove, where the actor has intra manipulated the stove by changing its internal state.

2.1 Applying the Concept of Intra and Extra Manipulation

Our operational definition of intra manipulation and extra manipulation is as follows:

- **Intra manipulation (IM).** Any operation that changes the internal state of an object is known as intra manipulation. When an actor interacts with everyday objects, some objects might change their internal state resulting in the following events: <*objectID, {is_grabbed, is_released, is_activated, is_deactivated, is_opened, is_closed}*>. Refer to Fig. 1 (Middle) for all the objects that can change their internal state based on an actor's interaction with it. We consider the *objectID* of all the objects the actor is holding in his/her hands (we do not make a difference between the left hand and the right hand) every 1 sec between their respective *is_grabbed* and *is_released* events. This information is complemented with the everyday objects' internal state information between *is_activated* and *is_deactivated* events or between *is_open* and *is_close* events (when the object is in operation) every 1 sec to obtain what we refer to as the IM information channel.

- **Extra manipulation (EM).** Any operation that changes the external state of an object is known as extra manipulation. When an actor interacts with everyday objects, some objects might change their external state with reference to other objects resulting in the following events: <*objectID, containerID, {has_entered, has_left}*> also referred to as the EM information channel. *ObjectID* refers to the object the actor is currently interacting with, while *containerID* provides information about the object that contained or will contain the object the actor is currently interacting with. Refer to Fig. 1 (Right) for all the objects that can contain other objects. Container objects include fridge, freezer, cupboard, dining table, etc. in our VR simulated home environment. The external state change information includes the relationship change between the object the actor is currently interacting with and the container object in terms of if the object has entered the container or has left the container. The volumes sensitive to extra manipulation are shown in Fig. 1 (Right).[3]

---

[3] In parallel to VR simulation we are currently working on a hardware prototype based on passive RFID technology for sensing EM events. Passive RFID tags are attached to everyday objects, while RFID readers are worn on the actor's wrists for sensing <*objectID,{is_grabbed, is_released}*> events and attached to a selected set of containers for sensing <*objectID, containerID, {has_entered, has_left}*> events in a real home environment used for ubiquitous computing research. Simple state change sensors like on-off switches, light sensors, pressure sensors, temperature sensors, etc. are attached to selected objects in the home environment for sensing <*objectID,{is_activated, is_deactivated, is_opened, is_closed}*> events. Information about EM events and IM events are communicated to a wearable computer using ZigBee communication protocol.

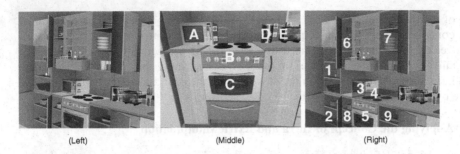

(Left)	(Middle)	(Right)

Internal state change events:

A. *<Microwave Oven, {is_activated, is_deactivated, is_opened, is_closed}>*

B. *<Stove, {is_activated, is_deactivated}>*

C. *<Oven, {is_activated, is_deactivated, is_opened, is_closed}>*

D. *<Coffee Maker, {is_activated, is_deactivated}>*

E. *<Bread Toaster, {is_activated, is_deactivated}>*

F. *<Rice Cooker, {is_activated, is_deactivated}>*

G. *<Tap, {is_activated, is_deactivated}>*

External state change events:

1. *<objectID, Fridge, {has_entered, has_left}>*

2. *<objectID, Freezer, {has_entered, has_left}>*

3. *<objectID, Microwave Oven, {has_entered, has_left}>*

4. *<objectID, Stove, {has_entered, has_left}>*

5. *<objectID, Oven, {has_entered, has_left}>*

6. *<objectID, Cupboard1, {has_entered, has_left}>*

7. *<objectID, Cupboard2, {has_entered, has_left}>*

8. *<objectID, Cupboard3, {has_entered, has_left}>*

9. *<objectID, Cupboard4, {has_entered, has_left}>*

10. *<objectID, Sink, {has_entered, has_left}>*

11. *<objectID, Table, {has_entered, has_left}>*

Fig. 1. VR home environment (Left) with volumes sensitive to extra manipulation marked in red colour (Right) and objects that possess internal states (Middle)

When objects are manipulated by an actor, the following two events *<objectID, {is_grabbed, is_released}>* alone are considered for activity recognition in [3] and [4]. In our previous work [6], we have compared the contributions of such an approach with two other information channels (observable space and manipulable space) and have discussed the limitations of considering an approach based on objects grabbed or released information alone. In this paper we extend such an approach to include IM and EM information channels for recognizing activities with higher precision values and sharper events that are some of the implications for building a system that can provide reliable assistance to people suffering mild dementia in completing their activities of daily living.

3   Activity Recognition System

3.1   Virtual Reality as a "Test-Bed"

VR was used as a test-bed [6] in order to speed up the design process of our activity recognition system, allowing us to compensate for the limitations with currently available sensing technologies and to compare the contributions of intra manipulation information channel and extra manipulation information channel for activity recognition. A VR model, developed using the Colosseum3D real-time physics platform [14] is used to simulate a physical home environment with wearable sensors and sensors embedded on selected everyday objects to capture an actor's intra manipulation (IM) events and extra manipulation (EM) events. Fig. 1 (Left) shows a snapshot of our VR environment. Refer to Fig. 2 for the activity recognition system architecture. We have experimented with 78 object types. Object types include simple object types like *fork, knife, plate* etc. that does not change their internal state, complex object types like *microwave oven, stove, oven, tap*, etc. that can potentially change their internal states and container object types like *fridge, freezer, cupboard, dining table*, etc. that can contain other objects. 7 objects have internal states and 11 objects are container objects. We only consider the *type* of object in recognizing activities, not the identity (e.g. *fork_1* and *fork_2* are both considered as *fork* type).

There are many objects that overlap for several activities. For instance, simple objects like *fork, knife, plate*, etc. are used for several activities like *preparing table for lunch, having lunch, having coffee-break, doing the dishes*, etc. Similarly complex objects like *stove*, oven, *microwave oven*, etc. and container objects like *fridge, freezer, cupboard*, etc. are also used for many activities. This makes the classification problem harder compared to taking an approach where the recognition system is strongly characterised by one or two objects that are unique to the activity. We do have some activities like for instance *preparing_rice*, where the *rice_bag* and the *rice_cooker* are unique objects for this activity. But this does not simplify the classification problem for the following reasons also discussed in [6]: 1) we are not only recognizing the actor's current activity, but also the actor's current action. The *rice_bag* and the *rice_cooker* are not unique objects for all the actions within the activity of *preparing_rice*, but only for some actions; 2) the *rice_bag* manipulation or the *rice_cooker* manipulation might be a noise created by the actor while performing another activity, and 3) the recognition system should recognize the activity and the action before they are actually completed to provide appropriate assistance to the actor. Hence the system cannot wait until the unique object is manipulated to recognize the activity and the action.

3.2 Feature Extraction and Classification

IM and EM information channels consist of sets of events that need to be quantified every second. Our quantification scheme builds $\vec{S}_A$ and $\vec{S}_B$ as shown in Fig. 2, where $\vec{S}_A$ represent the set of distinct *eventID*s calculated using *objectID*s and the object's internal state, while $\vec{S}_B$ represent the set of distinct *eventID*s calculated using *objectID*s, *containerID*s and the object's external state change.

The probabilistic generative framework of hidden-markov model (HMM) [15] is used because of its clear Bayesian semantics, its ability to handle time-varying signals and the availability of efficient algorithms for state and parameter estimation. HMMs reduce the system's configuration space into a number of finite discrete states together with the probabilities for transition between the states. One limitation of HMMs is that the model structure has to be user-defined, which includes the number of states and the connections between the states. The model structure cannot be determined by standard learning methods. This should not pose a major problem since the activities recognized are user-defined (also discussed in [6]). The actor provides ground truth for both activities and actions. Each activity is modelled using a separate

HMM with the number of states corresponding to the number of actions within that activity. Similarly, the transitions between states correspond to the transitions between different actions within that activity. HMMs have shown good results in many activity recognition systems including [16], [17], [18] and [4].

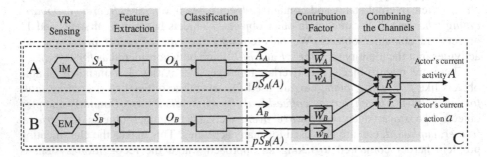

Fig. 2. The proposed activity recognition system architecture: A and B corresponds to information channels IM and EM respectively. C corresponds to a combination of IM and EM with automatically generated weights based on their contributions in recognizing individual activities.

The activity recognition system uses two information channels (refer to Fig. 2). Each information channel produces a sequence of observations that are fed into fifteen HMMs (one for each activity). For each information channel, the outputs from the fifteen HMMs are used to build an activity probability vector ($\vec{A}_A$ and $\vec{A}_B$) containing the probabilities for each possible activity. The element of the activity probability vector with the highest value gives the actor's current activity and its most probable state gives the actor's current action.

3.3 Combining the Information Channels

The two information channels are combined using activity contribution factors ($\vec{W}_A$ and $\vec{W}_B$) and action contribution factors ($\vec{w}_A$ and $\vec{w}_B$). $\vec{W}_A$ and $\vec{W}_B$ consist of the recognition precision values for each activity using IM information channel and EM information channel respectively, while $\vec{w}_A$ and $\vec{w}_B$ consist of the recognition precision values for each action using IM information channel and EM information channel respectively. The contribution factors are automatically generated from the training data. We first determine the actor's current activity by computing $\vec{R}$, the weighted sum of both the information channels using the following formula:

$$\vec{R} = \vec{W}_A * \vec{A}_A + \vec{W}_B * \vec{A}_B \tag{1}$$

Where * represents element-by-element multiplication. The element of $\vec{R}$ with the highest value gives the actor's current activity A. Once the activity is known, we determine the actor's current action by calculating $\vec{r}$ using the following formula:

$$\vec{r} = \vec{w}_A * p\vec{S}_A(A) + \vec{w}_B * p\vec{S}_B(A) \tag{2}$$

Where $p\vec{S}_A(A)$ and $p\vec{S}_B(A)$ are the vectors of state probabilities of the HMM representing the actor's current activity A for intra manipulation and extra manipulation respectively. $\vec{w}_A$ and $\vec{w}_B$ is equal to zero if their respective channel is not supportive to the activity A determined previously. The element of $\vec{r}$ with the highest value gives the actor's current action. We have not combined the two information channels before classification since we want to evaluate their contributions independently and combine them based on their contribution in recognizing individual activities. Such an approach also provides the possibility to include additional channels without affecting the overall infrastructure of our activity recognition system.

4   Evaluation

The experiments were performed by 5 subjects (none of them are affiliated to the system development team) in a virtual reality home environment[4]. 15 activities of daily living were included as shown in Table 1. The activities were performed 10 times as part of various scenarios. A scenario comprises of a few related activities performed in some sequence. We have used 7 scenarios: *lunch scenario (1)*, *lunch scenario (2)*, *coffee-break scenario (1)*, *coffee-break scenario (2)*, *baking scenario (1)*, *baking scenario (2)* and *cleaning scenario*. Some activities were common for

Table 1. List of activities and actions based on the AMPS framework [19]

Activities	Actions within individual activities
Preparing rice	Bring rice, Pour rice, Pour water, Add salt, Switch ON rice cooker, Replace rice
Preparing vegetables	Bring vegetables, Cut vegetables, Place pan on the stove, Switch ON stove, Fry vegetables in oil, Add spices and salt, Switch OFF stove
Baking cake	Bring baking dish, Switch oven ON, Add eggs, Add milk, Add sugar, Add cake powder, Place baking dish into oven, Switch oven OFF, Remove baking dish
Preparing cake	Get cake, Put cake into microwave oven, Switch ON microwave oven, Remove cake from microwave oven
Preparing coffee	Take coffee powder, Pour water into coffeemaker, Switch ON coffeemaker
Having coffee-break	Pour coffee, Drink coffee, Cut cake, Eat cake
Having lunch	Have main meal, Have dessert, Have coffee
Preparing table for coffee-break	Bring cake and coffee, Bring cutlery
Preparing table for lunch	Place mats, Bring cutlery, Bring plates, Bring juice glasses, Bring the food, Place napkins
Doing the dishes	Bring the dishes, Brush the dishes, Rinse the dishes, Wash hands
Preparing apple pie	Bring the baking dish, Bring the butter, Bring flour, Bring apples, Cut apples, Switch oven ON, Place baking dish into oven, Switch oven OFF, Remove baking dish
Preparing pasta	Get pasta, Switch stove ON, Fill casserole with water, Add salt, Set the timer and switch stove ON, Drain with the colander
Preparing pasta sauce	Place pan on the stove, Add oil, Switch stove ON, Bring onions and cut them, Place onions in the pan, Bring tomatoes and cut them, Place tomatoes in the pan, Add spices and salt, Switch stove OFF
Preparing tea	Fill casserole with water, Switch stove ON, Add tea bags, Switch stove OFF
Cleaning kitchen	Take sponge and spray, Clean the microwave oven, Clean the oven, Clean the stove, Clean the sink, Clean the table, Replace stuff and clean hands

---

[4] The subjects were initially taught how to perform activities in a virtual reality environment and then given a time period to practice in this environment. Only when the subjects were comfortable with the environment, they were allowed to perform the activities.

several scenarios like the activity of *preparing table for lunch* which is common to both the *lunch scenario (1)* and the *lunch scenario (2)*. All the subjects were allowed to perform the activities in their own way (often in many different ways).

When a subject begins performing his/her activity, each object is in the location where it was last placed in the subject's previous activities. This makes our experiments realistic compared to having a fixed initial location for each objects. Cases when the subjects dropped an object on the floor or grabbed the wrong object or performed an inappropriate object state change were also included in our dataset. A real chair was used for the subjects to perform the activities of having coffee-break and having lunch that obliged them to sit down. Subjects' body postures and locomotion within the VR environment were realistic. For instance, the subjects were not allowed to pass through a table, even though it is possible in a VR environment.

4.1 Precision, Recall and Confusion Matrix

The average *number of events* generated by IM information channel is 42 for each action, while that of EM information channel is 3.9 for each action. The *observation sequence length*s were empirically determined for individual information channels based on a trade-off between the precision and recall values. An optimal *observation sequence length* of 6 is used for both IM and EM information channels. We used the "Leave-One-Out Cross-Validation" (LOOCV) scheme to obtain the precision and recall figures. Cross-validation was used to validate our classification considering our limited, but sufficient datasets from the 5 subjects. Refer to Table 2 and Table 3 for precision, recall and confusion matrix. We define precision and recall as follows:

$$precision = \frac{TruePositives}{TruePositives + FalsePositives} \qquad recall = \frac{TruePositives}{TruePositives + FalseNegatives}$$

Table 2. Precision (P) and recall (R) in percentage (%) for each activity (Act) and action (An) using the two information channels (A and B) and by combining the two information channels (C). The last row represents global values (G) in percentage (%).

Act #	Intra Manipulation (IM)				Extra Manipulation (EM)				Combining IM and EM			
	Activity		Action		Activity		Action		Activity		Action	
	P	R	P	R	P	R	P	R	P	R	P	R
1	81	100	66	100	90	100	90	100	86	100	40	100
2	47	99	35	99	73	100	73	100	96	100	81	100
3	92	100	76	100	81	94	81	94	89	95	62	93
4	76	98	45	96	45	60	45	60	97	100	78	100
5	89	96	89	96	67	99	67	99	91	100	66	100
6	94	98	91	98	79	99	79	99	87	100	71	100
7	69	100	69	100	94	99	94	99	87	100	83	100
8	57	100	57	100	93	100	93	100	98	100	94	100
9	46	99	46	99	91	100	91	100	95	100	77	100
10	63	98	46	95	98	97	83	97	94	100	69	100
11	66	99	55	99	96	87	96	87	95	100	52	100
12	72	99	44	99	82	100	81	100	88	91	64	89
13	57	98	42	98	90	98	90	98	92	100	60	100
14	93	96	89	95	62	84	62	84	91	99	86	99
15	73	98	26	94	94	99	89	99	95	100	61	100
G	72	98	58	98	82	94	81	94	92	99	70	99

5 Discussion

Information Channels Reinforce Each Other at the Activity Level. By combining the two information channels, we obtain a recognition precision of 92% at the activity level. Such a high precision is possible due to the combination of the information channels that represent different and complementary aspects of the actor's activities. In Fig. 3, for the activity of *preparing cake*, action 2 (*Put cake into microwave oven*) and action 3 (*Switch ON microwave oven*) are recognized using IM as the information channel. This is due to the fact that the internal state of the *microwave oven* changes from *is_close* to *is_open* and then to *is_close* once again during action 2, while the *microwave oven* changes its internal state from *is_deactivated* to *is_activated* and then to *is_deactivated* during action 3. Action 4 (*Remove cake from microwave oven*) is confused with action 2 because during both these actions, similar events are generated. In this case EM provides more reliable information since <*Cake, Microwave Oven, has_left*> event is generated that is unique for action 4. Action 1 (*Get cake*) is recognized equally well using both IM and EM as information channels.

Table 3. Confusion matrix

Recognized Activities

	1	2	3	4	5	6	7	8	9	10	11	12	13	14	15
1	595	0	0	0	0	0	0	0	0	0	0	0	0	0	95
2	31	954	0	4	0	0	0	0	0	0	0	0	3	0	0
3	0	56	648	0	0	0	0	0	0	0	2	0	25	0	0
4	0	0	17	481	0	0	0	0	0	0	0	0	0	0	0
5	0	0	0	23	236	0	0	0	0	0	0	0	0	0	0
6	0	0	0	0	31	233	0	5	0	0	0	0	0	0	0
7	0	0	0	0	0	9	107	972	0	32	0	0	0	0	0
8	0	0	0	0	0	0	10	460	0	0	0	0	0	0	0
9	0	0	0	0	0	0	0	70	1351	0	0	0	0	0	0
10	0	0	0	0	0	0	0	0	204	3226	0	0	0	17	0
11	0	0	13	0	0	0	0	0	0	19	669	0	0	0	0
12	0	0	0	0	0	0	0	0	0	0	50	745	0	54	0
13	0	102	0	0	0	0	0	0	0	0	0	37	1643	0	0
14	0	0	0	0	0	0	0	0	0	0	0	0	20	209	0
15	0	0	0	0	0	1	0	0	0	0	0	0	0	68	1320

(Rows labelled "Actual Activities")

Information Channels Complement Each Other at the Action Level. At the action level, EM shows a good precision, but the recall value of 94% indicates that some actions may not be detected at all. A closer look reveals that actually 21 actions among the 15 activities are not detected even once, which is not acceptable in building a reliable activity assistive system. But by combining IM and EM information channels, the recall value is increased from 94% to 99%, there by allowing all the actions within the 15 activities to be detected at the cost of a lower overall recognition precision.

Temporal Delay in Recognizing Activities and Actions. The output of the activity recognition system may sometimes be unstable, especially around the transitions between two activities or between two actions. In order to provide a reliable assistance based on the proposed activity recognition system, the output of the activity recognition system must be smoothened which introduces temporal delays between the actual starting of an activity or action and the moment when the system makes a guess about the actor's current activity or action. An activity is recognized on an average after 30 events. At the action level, this delay varies between 7 and 24 events (13 on an average), which means that in some cases (especially if the duration of an action is short), the system may guess the actor's current action with a delay of one or two actions.

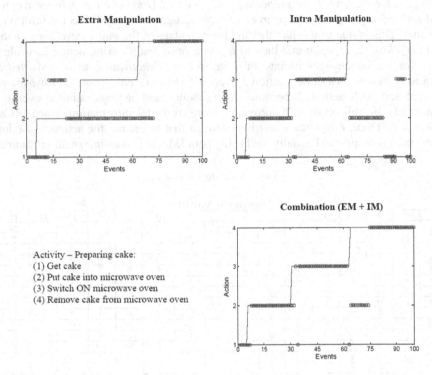

Activity – Preparing cake:
(1) Get cake
(2) Put cake into microwave oven
(3) Switch ON microwave oven
(4) Remove cake from microwave oven

Fig. 3. IM and EM information channels complement each other for activity recognition

Implications for building an Activity Assistive System. In our previous work [6], we have experimented with different information channels and have obtained an activity recognition precision of 89% among 10 activities of daily living. One main reason for building over our previous efforts by exploring complementary information channels is to recognize activities with higher precision (we have achieved an activity recognition precision of 92% among 15 activities of daily living) and sharper events that can be used for both activity recognition and in providing real-time assistance based on the actor's current activity. Examples of sharper events include *turning ON a stove* or *taking out juice packet from the fridge*. Events that are generated using EM and IM information channels are sharper compared to mere objects grabbed or released events, since EM and IM information channels contain information about a specific object's state change information. Events generated using observable space and manipulable space information channels (refer to our previous work [6]) also does not yield sharper events that can directly be used to provide assistance to the user. Even though we obtain sharper events using EM and IM information channels, there exists to some extent uncertainty and delay in recognition. To address this limitation which is inherent due to the probabilistic nature of our activity recognition system, we perform data mining on the training data and extract some events that are mandatory for each activity. Such events are referred to as mandatory events. For instance, if an actor *switches ON the stove* during the activity of *preparing vegetables* in all the training data, then *switching ON the stove* is considered to be a mandatory event. Such mandatory events are also used along with the actor's current activity and action in providing assistance to the actor.

6 Future Work

Combining IM and EM Information Channels. At present the combination between IM and EM information channels is performed based on simple weights (generated considering the individual information channels' activity recognition precision), improving the recognition precision at the activity level to 92% (see Table 3). However, the combination procedure at the action level has reduced the recognition precision from 81% (EM information channel alone) to 70% (combining IM and EM information channels). We are currently investigating the cause to this negative effect and intend to address it. At present, we have also not considered the temporal relationship between the two information channels. We intend to include such relationships and investigate the possibility of improving the recognition precision at the action level using the combination of the two information channels.

Improving the Granularity of IM Information Channel. Complex objects that can change their internal states are important information to capture in recognizing user activities. However, in our study we have used only a selected number of complex objects to avoid the necessity of too much sensing and computation in the environment. Among those selected complex objects, objects that are unique for individual activities like rice cooker, coffee maker, etc. have contributed well for activity recognition. However devices like stove and oven that are common for several activities provide less information for our activity classifier and introduce noise in recognition. This is because we sense the internal state of the stove or the oven at a coarse granularity (only on/off states). We believe that by improving the sensing of the complex objects' internal states with finer granularity, like for instance, sensing the temperature of the stove, there is a reasonable chance in improving the recognition at both the activity and the action level for many of the activities included for experimentation. For instance, the temperature of the stove changes differently during the activity of *preparing tea* compared to the activity of *preparing pasta sauce*. However, this does not mean that improved granularity always contribute to the performance improvement of recognizing activities. Further work needs to be done to compare the relationship between performance improvement and granularity of sensing the IM information channel.

Exploring the Spatial Relations between Everyday Objects. At present, the EM information uses simple relationship between the object the actor is currently interacting with and the container changes due to such interaction. However there may be some relationship between the object the actor is currently interacting with and the other objects that are inside or on the container object. Such relations will be explored in the future. Also when an object enters or leaves a container object, the internal state of the container changes, which will be considered as being part of IM information channel in the future.

Transferring to Real-World Applications. Our approach of using virtual reality as a test-bed introduces the issue of how this translates to real-world applications. Virtual-reality simulation implies that there is no noise and uncertainty in the collected signals, which is an important factor in real-world applications. As mentioned earlier, we are targeting on using passive RFID technology [20] considering its reliability in identifying the objects the actor is currently interacting with [21], [3], and [4]. Sensing EM information channel introduces many challenges including the difficulties in limiting the volume of the container object that is sensitive to EM events and in attaching RFID readers on devices like oven that might be used at high temperatures. We are aware of some passive tags that can handle high temperatures, and currently investigating on RFID readers that can handle high temperatures. Similarly there are issues that need to be solved in sensing intra manipulation information channel. However the focus of this paper is not to get too much carried away by the technology that is existing today, but instead to check the contributions of intra and extra manipulation with the assumption that sufficient technology will be available to sense these information channels in the near future. Even though the ecological validity cannot be guaranteed, our approach is a novel one and is primarily intended for guiding the development of ubiquitous and wearable computing systems capable of assisting human activities. Other issues like scalability of our approach and adaptation of our system to variations in activity patterns are discussed in [6].

7 Conclusions

In this paper we have presented a prototype activity recognition system developed based on an actor's interaction with everyday objects. Our activity recognition approach includes the objects grabbed or released information with the objects' internal state changes and their external state changes with reference to other objects. When evaluated in a virtual-reality simulated home environment: 1) activity and action recognition accuracies using EM has shown promisingly better results compared to currently dominant IM based approaches [3], [11]; 2) by combining both the information channels we have obtained a recognition precision of 92% at the activity-level among 15 activities of daily living. Our work provides an activity-aware platform for further investigations into the development of personal and user-defined activity assistive systems. As a secondary focus, we have also presented the approach of developing ubiquitous and wearable computing systems using virtual-reality simulation [6].

Acknowledgement

We would like to thank Anders Backman, Björn Sondell, Gösta Bucht, Kenneth Bodin, Lars-Erik Janlert, Marcus Maxhall, Erik Lövbom, Annabella Loconsole, and Olivier Laguionte from Umeå University, Sweden. This work is partially funded by the EC Target 1 structural fund program for Northern Norrland, Sweden.

References

1. Fishkin, K., Consolvo, S., Rode, J., Ross, B., Smith, I., Souter, K.: Ubiquitous Computing Support for Skills Assessment in Medical School. In: UbiHealth Workshop at the Sixth International Conference on Ubiquitous Computing (2004)
2. Backman, A., Bodin, K., Bucht, G., Janlert, L.-E., Maxhall, M., Pederson, T., Sjölie, D., Sondell, B., Surie, D.: easyADL - Wearable Support System for Independent Life despite Dementia. In: CHI 2006. Workshop on Designing Technology for People with Cognitive Impairments, pp. 22–23 (April 2006)
3. Philipose, M., Fishkin, K., Perkowitz, M., Patterson, D., Fox, D., Kautz, H., Hähnel, D.: Inferring Activities from Interactions with Objects. IEEE Pervasive Computing, 50–57 (October 2004)
4. Patterson, D., Fox, D., Kautz, H., Philipose, M.: Fine-Grained Activity Recognition by Aggregating Abstract Object Usage. In: Ninth IEEE International Symposium on Wearable Computers (2005)
5. Nardi, B. (ed.): Context and Consciousness: Activity Theory and Human-Computer Interaction. MIT Press, Cambridge (1995)
6. Surie, D., Pederson, T., Lagriffoul, F., Janlert, L.-E., Sjölie, D.: Activity Recognition using an Egocentric Perspective of Everyday Objects. In: UIC 2007. Proceedings of IFIP 2007 International Conference on Ubiquitous Intelligence and Computing, LNCS, vol. 4611, pp. 246–257. Springer, Heidelberg (July 2007)
7. Ward, J.A., Lukowicz, P., Troster, G., Starner, T.: Activity Recognition of Assembly Tasks Using Body-Worn Microphones and Accelerometers. Pattern Analysis and Machine Intelligence, IEEE Transactions 28(10), 1553–1567 (2006)
8. Bao, L., Intille, S.: Activity Recognition from User-Annotated Acceleration Data. In: Ferscha, A., Mattern, F. (eds.) PERVASIVE 2004. LNCS, vol. 3001, pp. 1–17. Springer, Heidelberg (2004)
9. Lee, S.W., Mase, K.: Activity and location recognition using wearable sensors. IEEE Pervasive Computing 1(3), 24–32 (2002)
10. Mayol, W., Murray, D.: Wearable hand activity recognition for event summarization. In: Ninth IEEE International Symposium on Wearable Computers, pp. 122–129 (October 2005)
11. Tapia, E., Intille, S., Larson, K.: Activity Recognition in the Home Using Simple and Ubiquitous Sensors. In: Ferscha, A., Mattern, F. (eds.) PERVASIVE 2004. LNCS, vol. 3001, pp. 158–175. Springer, Heidelberg (2004)
12. Hutchins, E.: Cognition in the Wild. MIT Press, Cambridge (1995)
13. Pederson, T.: From Conceptual Links to Causal Relations Physical-Virtual Artefacts in Mixed-Reality Space. PhD thesis, Dept. of Computing Science, Umeå university, report UMINF-03.14 (2003) ISBN 91-7305-556-5

14. Backman, A.: Colosseum3D - Authoring Framework for Virtual Environments. In: Proceedings of EUROGRAPHICS Workshop IPT & EGVE Workshop, pp. 225–226 (2005)
15. Rabiner, L.: A Tutorial on Hidden Markov Models and Selected Applications in Speech Recognition. In: Proceedings of the IEEE, vol. 77(2), IEEE Computer Society Press, Los Alamitos (1989)
16. Chen, J., Kam, A., Zhang, J., Liu, N., Shue, L.: Bathroom Activity Monitoring Based on Sound. In: Gellersen, H.-W., Want, R., Schmidt, A. (eds.) PERVASIVE 2005. LNCS, vol. 3468, pp. 47–61. Springer, Heidelberg (2005)
17. Lukowicz, P., Ward, J., Junker, H., Stäger, M., Tröster, G., Atrash, A., Starner, T.: Recognizing Workshop Activity Using Body Worn Microphones and Accelerometers. In: Ferscha, A., Mattern, F. (eds.) PERVASIVE 2004. LNCS, vol. 3001, pp. 18–32. Springer, Heidelberg (2004)
18. Lester, J., Choudhury, T., Kern, N., Borriello, G., Hannaford, B.: A Hybrid Discriminative/Generative Approach for Modeling Human Activities. In: 19th International Joint Conference on Artificial Intelligence (2005)
19. AMPS.: (as on January 2, 2007), http://www.ampsintl.com/
20. Finkenzeller, K.: RFID Handbook, 2nd edn. John Wiley and Sons, New York (2003)
21. Pederson, T.: Magic Touch: A Simple Object Location Tracking System Enabling the Development of Physical-Virtual Artefacts in Office Environments. In: Journal of Personal and Ubiquitous Computing, vol. 5, pp. 54–57. Springer, Heidelberg (2001)

Towards an Activity-Aware Wearable Computing Platform Based on an Egocentric Interaction Model

Thomas Pederson and Dipak Surie

Dept. of Computing Science, Umeå university, SE90187 Umeå, Sweden
{top,dipak}@cs.umu.se

Abstract. In this paper, we present our egocentric interaction model for recognizing and supporting everyday human activities. We explain how it allows designers of ubiquitous computing systems to view physical (real) and virtual (digital) objects as residing in one single space and how sets of objects in the vicinity of a specific human actor can be classified based on human perceptual characteristics such as what can be observed and what can be manipulated. We also propose a wearable computer architecture that is based on the egocentric interaction model which potentially could facilitate the development of Ubiquitous Computing applications by letting an operating system take care of maintaining communication with worn and instrumented sensors as well as computing devices. Finally, we present our first steps in implementing an activity-aware wearable support system for people suffering mild dementia based on the proposed model and architecture.

Keywords: Human-Computer Interaction, Ubiquitous Computing, Wearable Computing, Context Awareness, Virtual Reality.

1   Introduction

Our current user interfaces for personal computing make us less mobile than what state-of-the-art computing hardware would otherwise allow for. Miniaturization and power efficiency improvements of portable personal computers (PCs) as well as the diffusion of wireless networks has brought us to a state where all the computing power and connectivity most of us would need for a single day easily could fit into a small backpack. However, the way we have chosen to provide access to that computing power, through the WIMP[1] interaction paradigm, constraints the kind of individual human activities for which it can offer computational support. Limiting characteristics include

- the assumption that the human actor can dedicate all attention to the interaction with the virtual environment provided by the computer (e.g. does not bike or drive a car)
- the assumption that the real world environment in which the interaction takes place is always the same (quiet, in the shadow, etc.)

---

[1] WIMP — Windows, Icons, Menus, and Pointing device.

H. Ichikawa et al. (Eds.): UCS 2007, LNCS 4836, pp. 211–227, 2007.

- the assumption that input and output devices are few, and the same, at all times (i.e. screen, keyboard, and mouse)

As acknowledged widely by researchers in proactive HCI areas like Augmented/ Mixed Reality (e.g. Mackay et al. [11]); Ubiquitous/Pervasive Computing (e.g. Weiser [25]); Graspable/Tangible User Interfaces (e.g. Ishii & Ullmer [9]); Wearable Computing (e.g. Starner [21]); and Context Awareness (e.g. Dey et al. [5]), these assumptions do in general not hold, or severely limit interaction possibilities, in mobile and real-world dependent activity scenarios.

Thus, in an era where many real-world activities have become more or less PC-dependent, personal activities that for instance demand large amounts of attention to events in the real world and/or the ones better performed while on the move cannot typically make use of interactive personal computing power.[2] Wearable Computer research has tried to break free from some of the constraints in part by coming up with one-handed keyboards, head-up displays, and voice-based interaction but with little impact on the general public so far. Cellular phones/PDAs are becoming increasingly powerful but do not in any significant way extend the applicability of personal computing power due to the fact that the interaction paradigm by and large is inherited from the world of more full-grown PCs, apart from the improved portability of the hardware itself[3]. To summarize: the currently ruling interaction paradigm limits the scope of applications for personal computing. It is obvious that new alternative or complementing interaction paradigms would significantly expand the application area for personal computing systems by providing support for new activities and therefore also previously neglected user groups.

In this paper we introduce our first steps towards an egocentric interaction paradigm and show how it has helped structure and inspire our efforts in developing future applications for personal computing involving activities in the real world. The term "egocentric" has been chosen to signal that it is the human body and mind of a specific human individual that (sometimes literally, as will be shown later) acts as centre of reference to which all interaction modeling and activity support is anchored. The model is based on two conceptual corner stones: 1) a physical-virtual design perspective to enable a coherent view of domain objects residing in both physical and virtual environments, 2) a situative model of physical-virtual space for framing human object-centric activities in time and space.

The second half of the paper is devoted to the description of an envisioned wearable computer equipped with an operating system that offers modeling of basic activities in both the real and digital realms. The main motivation is that by embedding activity sensing and modeling into the operating system, developers of Ubiquitous Computing applications could be relieved from solving technological design problems that (today) frequently occur with every effort to design new task-specific UBICOMP systems. Finally, our own limited first steps towards such a wearable

---

[2] That is of course not to say that all personal activities would benefit from it.

[3] In fact, an often stressed selling-point for the most advanced cellular phones currently on the market is their ability to handle the same office-related data files as "real" personal computers. But, in other than exceptional cases, is it really an appropriate task for such small devices?

computer is presented in the light of developing a "cognitive prosthesis" for people suffering dementia, aiming at supporing patients with Activities of Daily Living.

2 Egocentric Interaction Model

2.1 A Physical-Virtual Design Perspective

Personal computing devices such as PCs, PDAs, and cellular phones play an increasingly important role in human activity. However, there are still things that most people would prefer to do "off-screen" in the physical (real) world, such as having parties, reading long text documents, or spending vacation. We argue that there exists a class of activities that are neither physical or virtual, but "physical-virtual" [15]. People frequently do parts of an activity in the physical world (e.g. proof-reading a text document under construction) and parts in the virtual world (e.g. adjusting paragraphs within "the same" document in a word processing environment). This behaviour is likely to become more common. Hence, future environments should be designed with such physical-virtual activities in mind.

The Physical World, Virtual World, and Human Activities. We have chosen to rely on the following definitions in order to model simple human activity across the physical-virtual gap:

- The physical world is the world built of and containing matter directly perceptible to humans, and whose state is defined by arrangements of such matter in places, constrained by and modified according to laws of nature, within a geometrical three-dimensional space, at any time instant partially perceptible by humans through their senses. [15]
- The virtual world is the world built of and containing digital matter (bits) that after transformation into physical phenomena becomes perceptible to humans, and whose state is defined by arrangements of such phenomena in places, constrained by and modified according to (human-designed) laws of logic, within a topological multidimensional space, at any time instant partially perceptible by humans through displays (possibly multi-modal and audio-visually up to three-dimensional) built into computational devices residing in the physical world. [15]
- Human activities are described using three levels of abstraction: activity, action and operation inspired by activity theory [12]. An activity has an objective and is comprised by a set of actions that have well-defined goals and are accomplished by largely unconscious operations.

From Input and Output Devices to Plain Direct Manipulation. The proposed physical-virtual perspective is a way to deal with the gap between the physical and the virtual world, and to facilitate the exploration of designing infrastructure for helping human actors bridging it. The assumption is that a reduced physical-virtual gap means less "friction" for physical-virtual activities, i.e. activities that involve frequent switching between physical actions (Fig. 1) and virtual actions (Fig. 2) [15].

The physical-virtual design perspective differs from more classical HCI models by explicitly ignoring input and output devices of interactive computers such as PCs,

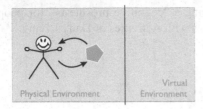 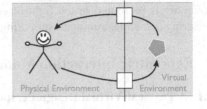

Fig. 1. Physical action: Human actor interacting directly with an object

Fig. 2. Virtual action: Human actor interacting indirectly with an object through input and output devices (the white squares) creating the illusion of direct manipulation [20]

PDAs and cellular phones, seeing them as completely transparent mediators for accessing virtual objects. In practice, this means to make no difference between the situation shown in Fig. 1 and the situation shown in Fig. 2. Taking such a stance permits the modeling of real-world and digital entities as if they were situated in the same Euclidean space, which we believe is advantageous when modeling mobile everyday computing applications where the interaction complexity wastly surpasses what can be sufficently described using a classical human-computer interaction dialogue model. Furthermore, such a view aligns well with findings in psychology indicating that expert users of tools (whether being a tennis racket or a computing device) tend to focus on the domain object they are working on (whether it is a tennis ball or an email) and forget about the details of the tool (such as the handle of the tennisracket or the workings of particular input device) itself.

2.2 A Situative Model of Physical-Virtual Space

The situative model of physical-virtual space is intended to capture what a specific human actor can see and not see, reach and not reach at any given moment in time (Fig. 3). The model is based on the physical-virtual design perspective briefly outlined in the previous section, meaning that physical and virtual domain objects are treated as being located in the same space. The model is for the emerging egocentric interaction paradigm what the virtual desktop is for the PC/WIMP interaction paradigm: more or less everything of interest to a specific human actor is assumed to, and supposed to, happen here. Although spatial and/or topological relationships between objects within a particular space (e.g. the manipulable physical-virtual space) certainly could be of interest, we have in our work so far only cared for whether an object is present in a space or not. Applying the model in this simple way generates a set of objects for each space at any given time instant.[4]

---

[4] The content of the innermost ellipsis in Fig. 3, "object manipulation", is actually not just a representation of spatial properties between the human body and a set of objects. Instead, it also provides information about the state changes to objects currently manipulated by the human actor. For reasons of simplicity we are nevertheless treating this information entity as a space unless noted otherwise.

An Example of Applying the Model to an Actor's Situation. If a glass of juice is in the right hand of a specific human actor, and an email just brought forward on the cellular phone held up in front of the same human actor's face by the left hand (see Fig. 5 left for such a situation captured in a Virtual Reality environment), both objects would be considered to reside in the object manipulation space in Fig. 3. A paper newspaper on the table just in front, and the keys in the same persons pocket would instead be modeled as inside the manipulable space. A painting on the opposite side of the table (but not the one behind the actor's back) would be in the observable space. Finally, all technically perceivable objects in the physical-virtual world which at least for the moment not happen to be perceivable by the specific human actor are regarded as situated in the world space, outside the spaces mentioned earlier.

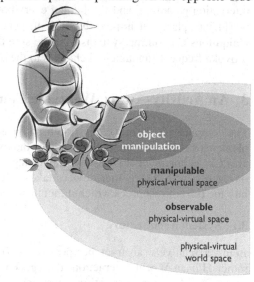

In the physical world, the border between the observable and manipulable spaces can be approximated and described in Euclidean terms: manipulable things are typically closer than things only observable and the border is somewhere in-between. This spatial relationship is

Fig. 3. A situative physical virtual space model adapted from [15]

reflected in Fig. 3. Determining a corresponding border in the virtual world is somewhat more complex and depends on situative access to input and output devices. Due to the nature of the application area towards which our current system development efforts is targeted (see next section of this paper), we have chosen to temporarily suspend the work on investigating how object manipulation and navigation should be best modeled in virtual environments (e.g. WIMP-kind) to fit into the situative space model shown in Fig. 3. However, experiences from a first attempt [15] has convinced us that it should be possible.

Using the Model for Guiding Ubiquitous Computing Application Design. We consider the borders of the observable space to define the set of objects that can possibly be part of a physical-virtual "application"[5] at any given time-instant for a

---

[5] Clarification: With "application" we mean in this context a predefined environment for supporting specific tasks like the kind of interactive software programs executed and used by end-users in virtual environments within the PC/WIMP paradigm, with the significant addition that "applications" in the egocentric interaction paradigm are imagined to potentially span the physical-virtual gap, encompassing objects residing in both the physical and the virtual world.

specific human actor. If a computing system displays information outside the observable space, it will not be noticed. If access to a desired virtual object is provided through a computing device currently outside of the manipulable space, the human actor is forced to change physical location. As it happens, this view aligns well with the WIMP/direct manipulation paradigm for virtual-world [20] interaction where successful application design as well as use very much depends on keeping the right objects "on screen" at the right time. Drawing from experience in using that interaction paradigm, and the human everyday strategy to arrange objects in the real world into places, it is probably safe to generalise and recommend to designers of Ubiquitous Computing systems to make sure that their applications do not enforce or provoke frequent fundamental changes to the observable and manipulable spaces.

3   An Activity-Aware Wearable Computing Platform

The computer platform we envision has at least two unique characteristics: 1) it complements rather than attempts to replace the existing flora of computing devices such as PCs, cellulars or PDAs, by supporting the higher-level activity in which the interaction with those other devices takes place, 2) it incorporates real-world objects into the pool of resources which it monitors and manages.

3.1   System Architecture

Being a relatively abstract perspective on future Human-Computer Interaction, or rather Human-World Interaction, the egocentric interaction model does not assume any particular implementation approach. For instance, computing and sensing technology for tracking physical activity of a specific human actor could be imagined to be either worn by the human actor herself, or be situated in the surrounding physical environment. The same goes for any computing device that provides access to the virtual world which could be both worn by their owner or ubiquitously distributed throughout the physical environment like in Mark Weiser's vision [25].

For reasons of privacy, efficiency, design complexity, feasibility, and cost, we have found an implementation approach based on wearable sensing and computing power most attractive. The basic idea is to make the wearable system as self-sufficient as possible, reducing the Pervasive Computing problem of "uneven conditioning" [18]. Information about activities performed using devices external to the wearable computing system (e.g. in the case when the human actor is using a desktop PC) need to be transmitted through some standard wireless communication protocol to the wearable computer for analysis. Complemented with the real-world object manipulation information from wearable sensors (although, depending on the application the wearable sensors probably need to be complemented with sensors instrumented in the environment), the egocentric interaction system would (at least in theory) be able to gracefully model activities across the physical-virtual gap.

The system architecture (see Fig. 4) is made up of a wearable computer offering computing power and storage space for activity-related data generated by an egocentric interaction sensor pool monitoring object-centric phenomena within the observable physical-virtual space of a specific human actor. Furthermore, the wearable computer runs an activity-aware operating system hosting both advanced physical-virtual applications developed by software developers as well as simpler programs designed by the user her/himself. Applications can incorporate the manipulation of both physical objects (e.g. an interactive item in a theme park) and virtual objects (e.g. a web page describing the same item). Explicit interaction with the activity-aware operating system (and the applications running on top of it) can be performed through user interface clients running on general-purpose devices like PCs or cellular phones. Inspired by Intel's Personal Server concept [24], the wearable computer does not provide any means for interaction itself. Implicit interaction [19] with the activity-aware operating system emerges whenever the user interacts with a physical or virtual object inside the manipulable physical-virtual space (see Fig. 5) monitored by the egocentric interaction sensor pool. We present the architecture in more detail below.

The Activity-Aware Operating System

A software system running on the wearable computer which receives and preprocesses detailed data about ongoing human activity from the egocentric interaction sensor pool, and makes the information available to high-level software applications executing on top of the operating system. The activity aware operating system also provides support for these applications whenever they need to interact with the human actor in a more explicit manner by taking the responsibilty of identifying possible input and output channels.

In contrast to how end-user interaction in virtual environments offered by current PC operating systems tend to be centered around

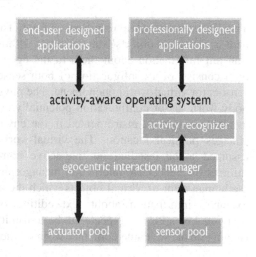

Fig. 4. Conceptual archittual of the activity-aware computing platform

(virtual) file management and tools for manipulating these files at various levels of abstraction, we imagine the proposed operating system to be centered around everyday objects residing anywhere in the physical-virtual continuum: From purely physical (such as a coffee cup) over physical-virtual (e.g. a specific newspaper manifested on paper as well as online) to purely virtual (e.g. an email). The operating system would represent all known objects as Physical-Virtual Artefacts (PVA)[6] no matter where in the continuum they happen to be situated. We believe this generalisation from "file" to PVA to paradoxally both relax and give structure to the design space for UBICOMP application developers. The relaxation comes from the relatively easy incorporation of both physical and virtual events into the applications

---

[6] A Physical-Virtual Artefact is, in short, an object having at least one representation in the physical world and at least one representation in the virtual world [15].

under development, the structure comes from a standardized view on a range of everyday physical and virtual events that by necessity has to be defined and agreed on among object and device manufacturers in order for the activity-aware operating system to handle the information.

Why include a real-world object model as low down as on the OS level? Because the world is not made up of "files" and "folders". If application designers are to design Ubiquitous Computing applications for human everyday activity support, it is best to embed mechanisms for linking physical phenomena to virtual as deep down as possible in the environment in which applications are developed. In this paper we are focusing on two components that we feel to have general applicability: a situation modelling component (the egocentric interaction manager) and an activity recognition component (the activity recognizer). Other more specific components might be needed depending on the specific application area UBICOMP developers choose as target.

The Egocentric Interaction Sensor Pool. The main purpose of this system component is to capture objects' state changes within the situative space model (Fig. 3) and transmit information about them to the egocentric interaction manager. The sensor pool consists of a configuration of both sensors for physical-world phenomena and sensors for virtual-world phenomena. The physical-world sensors are made up of a fix body-worn sensor configuration potentially complemented with a more dynamically available sensor set instrumented in the environment, changing as the human actor changes physical location. The virtual-world sensors are in fact software clients assumed to be installed on interactive computing devices and which wirelessly informs the egocentric interaction manager about object manipulation performed by the human actor on virtual objects which the specific device is making available. For example, information about text editing operations performed by the specific individual on a PC are expected to be transmitted by that PC to the activity-aware OS running on the wearable computer worn by the same individual.

The Egocentric Interaction Actuator Pool. The purpose of this component is to enable the applications running on top of the activity-aware operating system to affect the state of objects in the world space. They do this through the egocentric interaction manager, ensuring that the changes are perceived by the human actor. In analogy with the sensor pool, the actuator pool consists of both physical actuators (e.g. digital display, a light switch, or a door lock) and virtual actuators. Just like physical actuators change the state of physical objects, virtual actuators change the state of virtual objects and both kinds are treated in the same way by the egocentric interaction manager (discussed in the next paragraph). Virtual actuators are provided by client deamon processes running on external interactive computing devices, able to pop up dialogue boxes on the device's display, but also to perform more detailed actuation if application software running on the devices allow it. Furthermore, just as in the case of the sensor pool, the actuator pool is imagined to consist of a combination of both wearable and instrumented actuators.

The Egocentric Interaction Manager. This component channels and directs the major part of the communication between the human actor, the activity-aware operating system, and the surrounding physical-virtual environment. By maintaining an up-to-date high-level representation of object manipulation, the manipulable space, and the observable space (Fig. 3), it simplifies the work for other operating system components (such as the activity recognizer) as well as for applications. For instance, if an application needs to urgently inform the user about something, it can rely on the egocentric interaction manager to ensure that the information will be technically perceivable by the human actor. In this situation, the egocentric interaction manager will attempt to determine the orientation of 2D displays (belonging to the current actuator pool) in relation to the human actor's visual perception. Virtual objects shown on such a display should only be regarded as being within the observable space if the viewing angle of the display permits the objects to be perceived by the human actor. This is a special case of the tricky problem of detecting visual occlusion where objects obstruct other objects. We are convinced that the orientation of 2D displays in relation to a specific human actor's gaze is measurable using existing sensing technology although such technology is not yet widely available and used on the market today.

The Activity Recognizer. Automatic activity recognition is receiving a growing interest in Ubiquitous Computing and related research communities. Its wide applicability has motivated us to include such a mechanism in the proposed operating system. As a specific human actor changes physical and/or virtual location, objects come into and leave the observable physical-virtual space in a dynamic fashion. Inspired by situated action theory [22] and the proximity principle: "Things that matter are close. Things that are close matter." [10], we believe that the content of the observable and manipulable spaces of the model indicates the specific human actor's intent with the currently ongoing activity. The purpose of the activity recognizer is to continuously determine the ongoing activity, to store details about this activity, and to provide this information to other operating system components as well as applications on request.

Professionally Designed Applications and End-User Applications. Just like any other operating system, the activity-aware operating system will not provide any added value to a person's activities without applications running on top of it. We can only speculate in what kind of applications that could be developed using the activity-aware operating system as base. As explained in more detail in the next section, we are currently developing an everyday activity support application for people suffering mild dementia. Furthermore, just like the UNIX operating system allows skilled users (system administrators) to easily automate tasks within the domain of file processing by offering automation mechanisms at the right level of abstraction, we believe that an operating system monitoring human everyday activities on a high level could offer good support for end-users (the human actors using the system) to automate their everyday routine tasks, or at least the actions within an activity which the egocentric interaction actuator pool can affect. The paradigm of 'programming by demonstration' seems suitable due to its low learning threshold.

4 Experiences from the Development of a Cognitive Prosthesis for People Suffering Mild Dementia

We have applied the concepts discussed earlier when building a wearable "cognitive prosthesis" for supporting Activities of Daily Living. Such activities include getting dressed, preparing breakfast and activities related to personal hygiene. Dementia patients have problems in remembering to perform their everyday activities, or actions within those activities. Other problems include not being able to get started in the first place; not being able to continue after having been interrupted; or missing some operations that are mandatory for the completion of an activity. A system that

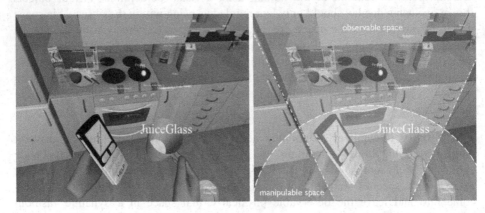

Fig. 5. A snapshot of the Virtual Reality home environment as seen by the user (left) and as seen by the egocentric interaction manager (right)

could help overcome the above mentioned problems would enable patients to stay in their home for a longer period of time, have a normal independent life, and also reduce the burden on family members and caregivers. Our long-term goal is to build a dementia tolerant home environment using wearable and ubiquitous computing technologies. By favourising the wearable approach, we hope to also open for the possibility of a future version of the system which also works outside the home. We are using a Virtual Reality environment as a test-bed in developing the cognitive prosthesis in order to 1) speed up the design (and re-design) process and 2) to compensate for the limitations with the currently available sensing technologies. A Virtual Reality model using the Colosseum3D real-time physics platform [2] is used to simulate a physical home environment augmented with an egocentric interaction sensor pool mainly consisting of wearable sensors. Fig. 5 (left) shows a snapshot of the environment. Based on the performance of the system in the VR environment presented in more detail elsewhere [23], we have also started to develop a hardware prototype in parallel with continuing the development of the cognitive prosthesis in the VR environment.

4.1 Operationalization of the Situative Space Model in Fig. 3

Observable Space (OS). It is the set of objects within a cone in front of the human actor's eyes with this cone following the head movements as shown in Fig. 6 (left). The height of the cone is limited by the walls of the indoor environment and visual occlusion is considered in determining the set of objects within this space.

Manipulable Space (MS). It is the set of objects within a hemisphere in front of the human actor's chest as shown in Fig. 6 (right). Such a shape is motivated by the fact that humans have two hands and the assumption that they manipulate objects within reach of their hands. The hemisphere follows the human actor's chest movements and the origin point represents the centre of the manipulable space hemisphere. The radius of this hemisphere is equal to the maximum distance between the origin point and a hand.

Object Manipulation (OM). When objects are manipulated by an actor, two events can be generated: grabbed event or released event. Both events include information about the object manipulated by the actor. The actor can manipulate objects with both hands. We do currently not make any distinction between the right hand and the left hand since our objective so far has been to only know what object the actor is currently manipulating and its state changes.

4.2 Implementation of the Activity-Aware Platform

To implement the complete activity-aware computing platform as shown in Fig. 4 including the activity-aware operating system is beyond our current development resources. So far, using the VR environment described earlier, we have chosen to focus our attention to components and parts of components that are of most immediate use for our aim in developing the cognitive prosthesis: the egocentric interaction sensor pool, the egocentric interaction manager, the activity recognizer, and a "professionally designed application": an ADL support application.

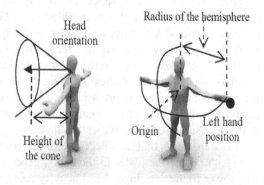

Fig. 6. Observable space (left) and manipulable space (right) as defined in the VR environment

The Egocentric Interaction Sensor Pool. The currently implemented sensor pool captures the identity of physical objects in OS, MS, and events generated by OM. It also captures simple button-pressing on a cellular phone although not in accordance with the physical-virtual design perspective since these operations are treated as being physical and the simulated cellular phone is not transmitting the manipulation of the virtual objects it shows on the display to the egocentric interaction manager. We are planning to make the sensing of interaction with the cellular phone work in accordance with the physical-virtual design perspective (e.g. that objects shown on its display would be treated similarly to real-world objects) and also to model the cellular phone display as part of an egocentric interaction actuator pool. We are also currently expanding the wearable sensor pool with a selection of instrumented physical sensors in order to improve the possibilities for providing detailed activity support.

The Egocentric Interaction Manager. The current egocentric interaction manager feeds the sensor data it receives from the sensor pool directly to the activity recognizer. We plan to modularize these components better and create a minimalistic activity-aware operating system at the same time. Currently, the egocentric interaction manager handles only input from the sensor pool. As soon as the display of the cellular phone is modeled as an actuator, the egocentric interaction manager will be enhanced with actuation control, allowing higher-level applications such as our cognitive prosthesis to display visual messages without bothering about what display device that could be the most suitable in a given situation – a decision then made by the egocentric interaction manager on the basis of the situative space model (Fig. 3) and the availability of visual actuators (display devices) in the observable space for the specific human actor.

The Activity Recognizer. Our current activity recognizer is based on a combination of Growing Neural Gas [7] and Hidden-Markov Models [17] for each activity directly mapped onto the situative space model (Fig. 3), monitoring object manipulation, the manipulable space, and the observable space. The presence patterns of objects in the different spaces are compared to previously trained patterns for the specific individual, resulting in an average recognition precision of 89% at 98% recall ability on the activity level (e.g. "setting the table for lunch"; "preparing coffee"; "frying vegetables"; "doing the dishes") among 10 trained activities within a VR-simulated kitchen environment. The precision and recall values on the action level (higher-level of detail, lower level of abstraction) which basically tries to determine what action within the same set of activities the human actor is performing (e.g. actions such as "to place the forks on the table"; "to fill the coffee maker with water"; "to turn on the stove"; "to place the plates in the sink") gives a precision of 76% and recall of 96%. The lower figures for high-detail activity recognition aligns well with findings in the literature. One problem is the high amount of general-purpose objects in kitchen environments, making object-use-based activity recognition particularly hard. We have several ideas for how the numbers can be improved and are also convinced that other environments containing a higher proportion of specialized tools and everyday objects would provide better recognition results. For more information on the activity recognizer and the evaluation of it we refer to [23].

The ADL Support Application. In order to learn about our user group, we have arranged over 10 brainstorming and interview sessions with professional dementia caregivers at the Geriatric Medicine Department at the University Hospital of

Northern Norrland in Sweden. One outcome is the fact that dementia affects patients in different ways, implying the need for individually tuned support. We have addressed this issue in part by training the activity recognizer on an individual basis (meaning in the end that the cognitive prosthesis becomes a very personal kind of tool), in part by identifying the kind of support which a majority of the patients could benefit from. The ADL support application we are currently developing intervenes when the human actor 1) has omitted to change the state of an object considered mandatory for the activity currently performed, or 2) has omitted to perform a mandatory action. An object's or action's level of "mandatoriness" for a given activity is determined based on the training data stored in the activity recognizer, resulting in a probability value. This probability value is generated automatically using unsupervised learning algorithms.

The overall design philosophy is that the ADL support application should remain completely silent as long as activities are performed as during the training phase with a certain tolerance for changes in sequence and omission of non-mandatory events. The interface modality of the intervention is decided by the ADL support application based on the current configuration of the actuator pool (e.g. what displays that are present in the observable space in Fig. 4) and based on the particual individual's abilities to perceive information in a certain modality.

Assessing the Model and the VR Design Approach

We have also conducted ethnographical studies in five households to further investigate details of everyday object manipulation and to learn about real world everyday activity. Based on a wearable video camera system capturing the environment in the direction of the subject's head (see Fig. 7), we have been able to study the dynamics of everyday object use withing the observable and manipulable spaces in the real world.

Fig. 7. A snapshot of the observable space for a human actor doing the dishes in the real world, as approximated by the area covered by a video camera lens worn on the head [3]

One result from this study is the fact that real world activities and activities performed in our VR environment differ with respect to the detail in which activities are performed [3] helping us to determine to what extent the results in the VR world is transferable to the real world.

4.3 Current System Architecture

Although most of our system development efforts have been directed towards getting an activity-aware platform to work in the VR environment, we have accounted for porting the same system to a real-world platform. Fig. 8 shows our current architecture that in principle allows us to change between running the activity support

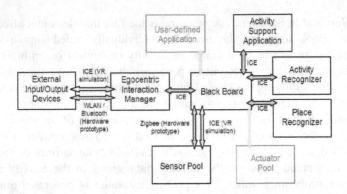

Fig. 8. The current architecture of the wearable activity-aware cognitive prosthesis. "User-defined applications" and the "actuator pool" are left for future work. The "external input and output devices" (including various kinds of visual and auditory display clients; keyboard clients, etc.) is under development.

system in the VR environment and running it in the real world by simultaneously exchanging a) the VR sensor pool with a real-world sensor pool, and b) the input and output devices simulated in the VR environment with real-world input and output devices.

5 Related Work

The idea of using computers for assisting individual human actors in everyday life is not new but has gotten increased relevance in the last 10 years because of increased capacity of mobile and wearable devices. One example is the research performed at Georgia Tech investigating the possibilities in creating an always present, context-aware "digital assistant" [21]. The egocentric view differs from their and most other similar "intelligent assistant" approaches, by focusing on detecting presence of physical (and virtual) objects rather than places or persons, for detecting and contextualizing human activity. The approaches are, of course, complementary. However, as mentioned earlier, by taking a world-neutral physical-virtual design stance, the egocentric view on interaction differs from most existing HCI modelling approaches by not seeing the state of the real world as merely context to virtual activity but an inseparable part of it. Aura [8] and Christensen and Bardram [4] have explored an activity-centered computing paradigm. Our work defers from theirs by attempting to provide support for physical-virtual activities. Philipose et al. [16] and Patterson et al. [13] explore activity recognition based on RFID-tracked object manipulation. Using the situative space model, we extend this approach by also considering the changes to the set of objects seen and to the set of objects reachable by an actor. Dey [5] proposes a framework for developing Ubiquitous Computing applications inspired by the PC/WIMP interaction paradigm and location-based services. We propose an alternative approach, centered around the human body and based on human perceptional characteristics.

6   Conclusions

We have presented an interaction model which _ealizati some of the drawbacks of the PC/WIMP interaction paradigm such as the demand for the human actor to devote complete attention to a specific computing device and the lack of computing support for activities involving everyday object manipulation. The proposed solution involves an "egocentric interaction manager" which continously monitors to what extent input and output devices are observable and manipulable for a specific user. We have also proposed a wearable activity-aware platform based on the model, as well as our first steps in implementing it for the purpose of developing a "cognitive prosthesis" for people suffering mild dementia. The main advantage of the wearable approach in designing activity-aware support is the potential independence on instrumented sensors, enabling computing and activity support literally everywhere. The proposed interaction model has proven to be successful for activity recognition in a Virtual Reality environment, motivating us to proceed with implementation in the real world. We are fully aware of the fact that the realisation of the components in the proposed activity-aware computer system faces numerous technological challenges of which we ourselves up until now have already addressed a few. However, many of these challenges are already actively addressed in isolation within areas related to Ubiquitous Computing, for instance in the shape of solutions for ad-hoc sensor networking (e.g. the Global Sensor Network middleware [1]). We see the main contribution of the work presented in this paper to be our proposal for how advances in these fields can be combined to an integrated system that has the potential of opening for new application areas for digital computing, and as a consequence, introduce the power of personal computing to new human communities beyond the classical office worker. We have also demonstrated the utility of Virtual Reality simulation as a tool for early assessment of Ubiquitous Computing systems.

Future Work. As stated in section 4, there are still several parts of the proposed activity-aware platform that needs to be developed in order to arrive a fully working cognitive prosthesis based on a sensor pool simulated in Virtual Reality. We are currently working on the implementation of these components. In parallel, we are experimenting with an RFID-based [6] sensor pool (a reader on the chest with antennas on the hands and on the chest; tags on the objects) connected to an ultra-portable PC for tracking object manipulation and the manipulable space. Such information has been reliably identified in many applications including [14], [16] and [13]. Presence of physical objects in the observable space is probably the hardest challenge but our tests in a Virtual Reality environment indicate that at least for activity recognition purposes, the manipulable space can to some extent substitute the observable space (with a reduction of 4% in activity recognition precision) [23]. With regards to sensing virtual objects in the spaces we imagine this being done by communication with the devices presenting them. The protocol and a suitable abstraction level at which the events in virtual environments (provided to the human actor by computing devices such as portable and stationary PCs, cellular phones, etc.)

are to be described and transmitted to the wearable activity aware computer is currently also an open issue.

Acknowledgements. We would like to thank Fabien Lagriffoul for developing large parts of the activity recognition component; Daniel Sjölie for developing the VR sensing infrastructure and the blackboard communication mechanism; Lars-Erik Janlert for many helpful suggestions on the physical-virtual design approach and the egocentric interaction model; Robert Bhatt for the valuable ethnographical study. We would also like to thank Gösta Bucht and Björn Sondell from the Dept. of Geriatric Medicine, as well as Kenneth Bodin, Anders Backman and Marcus Maxhall at VRlab. Final thanks go to Michel Banâtre and Paul Coderc at IRISA/INRIA, Rennes, France for supporting the initial development of the idea of a physical-virtual operating system. This work has been partially funded by the EC Target 1 structural fund program for Northern Norrland.

References

1. Aberer, K., Hauswirth, M., Salehi, A.: The Global Sensor Networks middleware for efficient and flexible deployment and interconnection of sensor networks. Technical report LSIR-REPORT-2006-006
2. Backman, A.: Colosseum3D - Authoring Framework for Virtual Environments. In: Proceedings of EUROGRAPHICS Workshop IPT & EGVE Workshop, pp. 225–226 (2005)
3. Bhatt, R.: Comparing the Performance of ADLs in "Virtual" and "Real Life" Environments. Dept. of Computing Science, Umeå university, report UMINF-06.40 (2006)
4. Christensen, H.B., Bardram, J.: Supporting Human Activities - Exploring Activity-Centered Computing. In: Borriello, G., Holmquist, L.E. (eds.) UbiComp 2002. LNCS, vol. 2498, pp. 107–116. Springer, Heidelberg (2002)
5. Dey, A.K.: Providing Architectural Support for Building Context-Aware Applications. Ph. D. Thesis Dissertation, College of Computing, Georgia Tech. (2000)
6. Finkenzeller, K.: RFID Handbook, 2nd edn. John Wiley and Sons, New York (2003)
7. Fritzke, B.A: Growing neural gas network learns topologies. In: Tesauro, G., Touretzky, D.S., Leen, T.K. (eds.) Advances in Neural Information Processing Systems, vol. 7, pp. 625–632. MIT Press, Cambridge, MA (1995)
8. Garlan, D., Siewiorek, D., Smailagic, A., Steenkiste, P.: Project Aura: Towards Distraction-Free Pervasive Computing. IEEE Pervasive Computing, special issue on Integrated Pervasive Computing Environments 21(2), 22–31 (2002)
9. Ishii, H., Ullmer, B.: Tangible Bits: Towards Seamless Interfaces between People, Bits and Atoms. In: Proceedings of CHI 1997, pp. 234–241. ACM Press, New York (1997)
10. Janlert, L.-E.: Putting Pictures in Context. In: Proceedings of AVI 2006, pp. 463–466. ACM Press, New York (2006)
11. Mackay, W., Fayard, A.-L., Frobert, L., Médini, L.: Reinventing the Familiar: Exploring an Augmented Reality Design Space for Air Traffic Control. In: Proceedings of ACM CHI 1998, Los Angeles, pp. 558–565. ACM Press, New York (1998)
12. Nardi, B. (ed.): Context and Consciousness: Activity Theory and Human-Computer Interaction. MIT Press, Cambridge (1995)

13. Patterson, D., Fox, D., Kautz, H., Philipose, M.: Fine-Grained Activity Recognition by Aggregating Abstract Object Usage. In: Ninth IEEE International Symposium on Wearable Computers (2005)

14. Pederson, T.: Magic Touch: A Simple Object Location Tracking System Enabling the Development of Physical-Virtual Artefacts in Office Environments. In: Journal of Personal and Ubiquitous Computing, vol. 5, pp. 54–57. Springer, Heidelberg (2001)

15. Pederson, T.: From Conceptual Links to Causal Relations — Physical-Virtual Artefacts in Mixed-Reality Space. PhD thesis, Dept. of Computing Science, Umeå university, report UMINF-03.14 (2003) ISBN 91-7305-556-5

16. Philipose, M., Fishkin, K., Perkowitz, M., Patterson, D., Fox, D., Kautz, H., Hähnel, D.: Inferring Activities from Interactions with Objects. IEEE Pervasive Computing, 50–57 (October 2004)

17. Rabiner, L.: A Tutorial on Hidden Markov Models and Selected Applications in Speech Recognition. In: Proceedings of the IEEE, vol. 77(2), IEEE Computer Society Press, Los Alamitos (February 1989)

18. Satyanarayanan, M.: Pervasive computing: vision and challenges. IEEE Personal Communications 8(4), 10–17 (2001)

19. Schmidt, A.: Implicit Human Computer Interaction Through Context. Personal Technologies 4(2&3), 191–199 (2000)

20. Shneiderman, B.: The future of interactive systems and the emergence of direct manipulation. Behaviour and Information Technology 1, 237–256 (1982)

21. Starner, T.: The Challenges of Wearable Computing: Part 1 & 2. IEEE Micro 21(4), 44–52, 54–67 (2001)

22. Suchman, L.: Plans and situated actions: the problem of human machine interaction. Cambridge University Press, Cambridge (1987)

23. Surie, D., Pederson, T., Lagriffoul, F., Janlert, L., Sjölie, D.: Activity Recognition using an Egocentric Perspective of Everyday Objects. In: UIC 2007. Proceedings of IFIP 2007 International Conference on Ubiquitous and Intelligent Computing, Hong Kong, Springer, Heidelberg (July 11-13, 2007)

24. Want, R., Pering, T., Danneels, G., Kumar, M., Sundar, M., Light, J.: The Personal Server: Changing the Way We Think about Ubiquitous Computing. In: Borriello, G., Holmquist, L.E. (eds.) UbiComp 2002. LNCS, vol. 2498, Springer, Heidelberg (2002)

25. Weiser, M.: The Computer for the 21st Century. Scientific American 265(3), 66–75 (1991)

mCube – Towards a Versatile Gesture Input Device for Ubiquitous Computing Environments

Doo Young Kwon, Stephan Würmlin, and Markus Gross

Computer Graphics Laboratory, ETH Zurich
8092 Zurich, Switzerland
{dkwon,wuermlin,grossm}@inf.ethz.ch
graphics.ethz.ch

Abstract. We propose a novel versatile gesture input device called the mCube to support both desktop and hand-held interactions in ubiquitous computing environments. It allows for desktop interactions by moving the device on a planar surface, like a computer mouse. By lifting the device from the surface, users can seamlessly continue handheld interactions in the same application. Since mCube is a single completely wireless device, it can be carried and used for different display platforms. We explore the use of multiple sensors to support a wide range of tasks namely gesture commands, multi-dimensional manipulation and navigation, and tool selections on a pie-menu. This paper addresses the design and implementation of the device with a set of design principles, and demonstrates its exploratory interaction techniques. We also discuss the results of a user evaluation and future directions.

1 Introduction

Everyday objects and our environments themselves are getting enriched with computer systems [17]. Computer graphics and display technologies have transformed our environments to windows connecting the physical and the virtual world. In recent years many researchers have recognized the value of such ubiquitous computing environments and studied to develop more natural and intuitive alternatives for interaction techniques.

In this context, the use of gestures has emerged as an attractive solution for more intuitive communication between human and machine. For instance, gestures have been widely studied to control graphical objects in various displays namely desktop monitors [9,12], tabletop displays [7], large wall displays [5], and immersive VR displays [22]. Gestures are also actively employed for eyes-free interactions in pervasive, mobile and wearable computing domains [3]. Using gestures, users control appliances and physical conditions of environments such as lights [19]. Gestures are added to commercial video game consoles [14,1].

As the purpose of using gestures is getting diverse, a variety of devices have been proposed for gesture inputs. For instance, computer mice and tablet pens are adapted for stroke-based gesture inputs [9]. Glove based input devices are utilized to capture detailed hand and finger movements for hand gestures [22]. In addition to these commercial devices, several prototypes of input devices have been developed by investigating multiple sensor technologies [14,19,5] . However, while these devices have been

H. Ichikawa et al. (Eds.): UCS 2007, LNCS 4836, pp. 228–239, 2007.

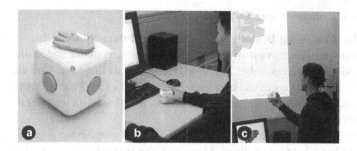

Fig. 1. (a) The mCube prototype device for combined desktop and hand-held interaction. (b) Desktop interaction on a planar surface. (c) Hand-held interaction in the free-space.

successfully tailored for special tasks and specific displays, it is still an open issue to make a gesture input device more versatile such that interactions can be more fluent in a ubiquitous manner in different applications and displays.

In this paper, we propose a versatile gesture input device called mCube which allows for combined desktop and hand-held interactions (Figure 1). We combine visual and embedded sensor technologies to acquire gesture information for robust recognition of a wide range of gestures as well as for multi-dimensional manipulation and navigation. The current prototype has a cube shape, and includes accelerometers, digital compasses, buttons, an IR sensor, and a potentiometer. Sensor data is collected and processed with a microcontroller and transferred via Bluetooth wireless communication. 3D positional information of the mCube is obtained by means of an attached LED, which is captured by multiple cameras and processed using computer vision algorithms.

Our ultimate goal is to minimize the use and learning of additional input devices, and to improve the work flow of interactions. Using the mCube, users can perform gesture commands, virtual object manipulation and navigation, and tool selections on e.g. a pie-menu. Particularly, users can switch between desktop positioning and hand-held positioning on the fly, yielding a high degree of freedom for appropriate interactions. The mCube is a single completely wireless device so that the user is not burdened by wires or additional devices and he can freely move between different display platforms.

In the following sections, we describe the mCube device with a set of design principles for a versatile gesture input device (§2). We explain the system implementation and its core algorithms for computing orientation and position of the device (§3). Then, interaction techniques of the device are demonstrated showing the capabilities of the mCube (§4). We conclude with a summary of a user evaluation (§5) and directions for future work (§6).

2   mCube – A Novel Versatile Gesture Input Device

In this section, we describe our approach to build a versatile gesture input device. First, we describe a set of design principles and solutions. Then we introduce our prototype device, called mCube with its hardware design and sensor configuration.

2.1 Design Principles and Solutions

Support for Combined Desktop and Hand-held Interactions. Ubiquitous computing environments can consist of computer controlled systems and multiple displays
namely desktop monitors, table top displays, and wall displays. Considering potential spatial configurations of the user and displays, we categorize interactions into two
groups (*desktop interaction* and *hand-held interaction*) based on whether the interaction
takes place on a flat surface or in free space.

As one of the main principles, a versatile gesture input device should support both
desktop and hand-held interactions. Moreover, the transition between them should be
possible without additional operation requirements. Thus, users can instantly choose
the best interaction for the current applications and displays. For this purpose, we use
a cube form which has been widely used for the development of input devices in both
interaction groups [11,14,15,8]. A cube form affords users to intuitively grab, move,
and rotate both on a flat surface and in free space [16]. For an automatic transition, the
device exhibits a IR reflective light sensor on the bottom so that it can automatically
reconfigure with respect to contact with a surface.

Support for Wireless Operation. A versatile gesture input device needs to be completely wireless so that the user can carry the device to another location and operate it
freely in space. To achieve this goal, the main challenging problem is to track the 3D
position of the device. We use cameras and detection algorithms from computer vision.

The visual sensor approach relies on the accurate detection of relevant features which
is a challenging task under varying illumination and environmental conditions. Moreover, it is not a-priori clear if the required tasks for a versatile gesture input device can
be accomplished given their inherent level of inaccuracy. Due to these reasons, we use
a bright color LED which provides focal brightness on the captured images, thereby
achieving easier and more robust tracking.

Support for Multifunctionality. A generic and versatile input device should support
multi-functional operations so that the user does not have to change the input device
between different tasks. We identify a set of required operations for a versatile gesture
input device: gesture commands, navigation, manipulation of virtual objects, and tool
selection.

The use of gesture commands has been motivated for various purposes such as appliance control in smart environments [19] and game control [14,1]. A gesture input
device is required to provide enough features to discriminate between different gesture
commands. For this, we combine visual sensors and embedded sensors with a proper
feature extraction methods.

We compute 6-DOF information combining the visual and embedded sensor data
so that the device can be used to manipulate and navigate virtual objects. Manipulating virtual objects requires a certain degree of precision, which can be challenging to
achieve with a vision-based approach. We facilitate this problem by using a bright color
LED. Finally, for efficient tool selection, we allow the user to control e.g. a pie-menu
by rotating a top handle attached to the cube.

Support for Design Variations and User Definable Ergonomics. These days, many
commercial electronics such as MP3 players and mobile phones are designed

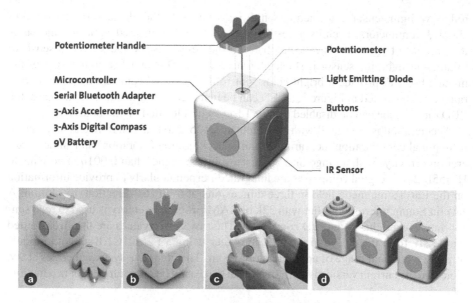

Fig. 2. (Top) Hardware configuration of the mCube. The device includes multiple sensors such as accelerometers, digital compasses, four buttons, a rotary potentiometer, an infrared (IR) distance sensor, and one color LED. In addition, it contains a micro-controller for acquisition, a Bluetooth transmitter, and a 9V battery power supply. (Bottom) The top handle can be easily replaced with other designs according to the user's preference. (a) A flat style top handle using the hand metaphor. (b) A vertical style top handle using hand metaphor. (c) The operation of the vertical style top handle with both hands. (d) Top handle design alternatives using different metaphors.

considering the user's desire to change the appearance and ergonomics of the device. We also consider these issues as a principle of a versatile gesture input device.

2.2 mCube Hardware Design and Sensor Configuration

Based on the proposed design principles and solutions, we developed the prototype device mCube. The mCube consists of two units: a *body* and a *top-handle*. The body is a cube with an edge length of 6 centimeters as shown in Figure 2. For the top handle, various designs can be provided so that users can choose according to preference for design, application, and ergonomics. For instance, by attaching another top handle in an upright position (Figure 2b and c), the mCube can be easily re-configured for two-handed interaction.

The mCube is designed to sense various events (button clicks, handle rotation, and surface contact) and the physical manipulation of the device (translation, rotation and tilt). We labeled the six sides of the body with top, bottom, front, back, left, and right.

We attach a button to each side face of the body such that the user can intuitively use them, mapping the button/handle direction to the user direction. A potentiometer is located under the top side, and senses the rotation angle of the top handle which is connected to the mCube body through a rotary shaft. On the bottom side, an IR reflective light sensor is located to sense the distance to the planar surface from 0 to about 3 centimeters. It emits a small beam of invisible infrared light and measures the amount of light that is reflected back to the sensor. Since the sensor is sensitive to ambient light, the sensor is shielded. One color LED is attached to a corner of the mCube body to provide a bright color spot in the acquired camera images at a wide range. As illustrated in Figure 2, a LED can be installed to top-handles. In this case, the LED on the cube can be disabled using a LED switch located on the bottom side.

Acceleration is measured with two Memsic 2125 2-axis accelerometers attached in orthogonal configuration measuring dynamic acceleration (vibration) and static acceleration (gravity) with a range of $\pm 2g$ at a resolution higher than $0.001g$. Two Hitachi HM55B 2-axis digital compasses are integrated perpendicularly to provide information on the Earth's magnetic field in three dimensions at 6-bit (64-direction) resolution. A Javelin Stamp micro-controller with 32k of RAM/program memory is used to read sensor data using delta-sigma A/D conversion. The raw sensor values are then transmitted wirelessly from the device to the host computer using a F2M01C1 Bluetooth module offering a nominal range of approximately 100m. The complete system operates at 9V. Note that the current version is a prototype that can easily be miniaturized for production.

3   System Implementation

In this section, we give a brief overview of the mCube system setup and the core software modules for computing the rotational and positional information of the device. We also explain the extraction of gesture features from the combined sensor data.

3.1   Overview

The overall system consists of a pair of video cameras (USB or Firewire), the mCube device, a computer with active Bluetooth, and display devices (projectors and/or monitors) (Figure 3). In our current prototype setup, two firewire cameras are used to acquire the range of operation at 30 frames per second. The acquired images are processed to determine the 3D position of the mCube LED (§3.2). Synchronously, the mCube acquires the data of the embedded sensors at a sample rate of 60 Hz and transfers the data to the host computer over the Bluetooth network. On the host, the sensor data is directly read from a communication port using the *java.comm* library. In the preprocessing stage, the acquired data amplitude is scaled using linear min-max scaling. The visual features are derived from the sensor data with appropriate up-sampling in order to match the frequency of the embedded sensor data and low-pass filtering to remove noise.

3.2   Computing the Rotational and Positional Data

We acquire the rotational data of the device combining the values of the compasses and accelerometers. The main idea is to take the output of the accelerometers as pitch and roll, and use the output of the digital compasses to compute the yaw. To get appropriate yaw information from the digital compasses, we use the accelerometer data to compensate for the erroneous compass data. This technique is widely used in hand-held electronic compass applications. We refer to [10] for details on the computation.

Fig. 3. A prototype setup with a pair of video cameras, the mCube device, a desktop monitor, and a large display wall for wall projections

As mentioned earlier, tracking the 3D position of the device using cameras is a challenging task because lighting and background conditions can change over time. We use a bright color LED for faster and more robust tracking. A focal brightness provides relatively robust tracking results even for small-scale movements in indoor environments. Moreover, using different color LEDs allows to track several devices at the same time for multiple users.

We developed a simple vision tracking algorithm to find the pixel positions within a certain color and brightness range. To compute the 3D position of the marker, we employ conventional triangulation from a pair of calibrated cameras [21], [13].

3.3   Extraction of Gesture Features and Rotational Invariance

In our context, gesture features should be robust and also invariant with regard to translations and rotations [4]. Such gesture features can be achieved by combining accelerometer data and visual features from the cameras [2].

For visual features, we tested a variety of invariant features derived from the visual sensor, including angular velocity, curvature, and velocity. However, all of these features have limited reliability and do only work for larger and longer gestures. The main reason for this lack of robustness is the differential nature of these features including computations of the first and second derivatives. This leaves us with the relative Cartesian positions (rx, ry, rz) computed with respect to the start position of the gesture. The relative position is translationally invariant, but cannot compensate for rotations. This type of invariance is achieved by adding data from the accelerometers to the extraction.

4   Interaction Techniques

In this section, we describe an exploratory set of techniques intended to investigate as thoroughly as possible the design space of mCube interactions. Some of these techniques can be selected and optimized for any application that seeks to use the mCube.

4.1   Switching Between Desktop and Hand-Held Interaction

As described earlier, the mCube uses the affordances of cube shape which can be operated on a flat surface and in free space. To facilitate this operation, we program the mCube to automatically recognize the current interaction mode based on the contact between the device and the surface of the table using the embedded IR sensor. If the value is lower than a desktop threshold (1 cm) for a certain amount time (2 sec), the interaction mode is changed to desktop interaction.

Using this feature, users can optimize the interaction for the required task in the current application and display setup. For instance, for manipulation tasks requiring more precise control, users can use desktop interactions minimizing the hand tremor which can be caused by the lack of fixed support in hand-held interaction. Alternatively, users can choose hand-held interactions to perform direct 3D inputs and operations in free space.

4.2   Top Handle-Based Mode/Tool Selection

The mCube allows users to switch between different modes or select a tool on a pie-menu by simply rotating the top handle. The main idea is to use the highly intuitive operation of the pepper caster which we use almost every day to grind and scatter pepper on our dish. During this operation, we usually hold the bottom part and rotate the top part without any substantial previous learning. The main benefit is that users can use this handle during other operations. For instance, during navigation or manipulation of virtual objects, users can choose different tools such as rendering modes (wireframe or shaded rendering) or texture and color styles of the model without interfering with the positional control of the device.

We use the top-handle to define the device mode. We defined three necessary modes: an *idle* mode for power saving, a *recognition* mode for gesture recognition and a *pie-menu* mode for selecting different tools. Figure 4-b illustrates an example of a pie-menu with twelve icons. During rotation of the top handle, the widget is displayed and the designated sub menu is highlighted depending on the direction of the handle as shown in Figure 4. Different numbers of icons can be used by dividing the circular region of the top handle into a corresponding number of sections.

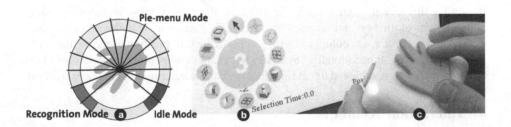

Fig. 4. (a) Three modes of the device controlled with the top handle: recognition mode, pie-menu mode, and idle mode. (b, c) In the pie-menu mode, users can select a tool with a modified pie menu by rotating the top-handle. The circular region of the pie-menu is divided into 12 regions for 12 icons of the pie-menu. The number 3 in the center of the pie menu indicates that hand-held interaction is currently activated.

4.3   Examples of mCube Gestures for Command Inputs

We designed a multipurpose set of gestures with the mCube exploring the intuitiveness and interoperability of the mCube in desktop and hand-held applications.

Gestures for Desktop Interactions. For desktop interactions, we designed a set of gestures which are suitable using a *glass metaphor*: pouring water in three directions (front, left, and right), twirling and rotating in CCW and CW as illustrated in Figure 5-a. These gestures can be easily learned because of their familiarity and intuitiveness from the operation of a real glass. To perform the glass gestures, users place the mCube on a surface and then perform the gestures by lifting the device from the surface. This simple initialization motion greatly disambiguates the recognition based on the IR-distance value for each gesture.

Gestures for Hand-held Interactions. One of the common tasks of hand-held interactions is to select a physical or virtual object using a pointing gesture and control it with subsequent gestures [19]. For this purpose, we designed a set of hand-held gestures targeting the commonly used actions on appliances, e.g. rotating the handle to turn on/off and change the volume (up/down).

In addition to the previous simple gestures, more complex 3D spatial gestures can be performed using the mCube. While simple gestures can be recognized with a heuristic approach which looks for simple trends or peaks in one or more of the sensor values [19], for complex gestures, we need advanced pattern matching techniques. Various recognition algorithms are proposed using statistical pattern matching techniques

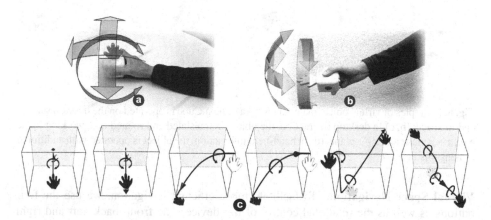

Fig. 5. (a) Examples of desktop gestures. A user is performing gestures on the desktop surface: pouring-left, -right, -front, and rotating-CW, -CCW. (b) Examples of hand-held gestures. A user is holding the device in the air and performing gestures: pointing-up, -down, -right, -left, and rotating-CW, -CCW. (c) The 3D spatial gesture examples with a box style 3D gesture volume. The line indicates the trajectory of the gesture and the end of the gesture is presented as an arrow. The hand symbol indicates the direction and rotation of the mCube using black for a palm-down position and white for a palm-up position. The 3D gestures are increasing in complexity from left to right.

[18,4], and multiple sensors are combined to provide better discriminating gesture features [2]. Even though their explanation is considered outside the scope of this paper, it is assumed that the combined gesture features of mCube will improve the recognition and enable a larger gesture space. It is also important to consider human variability exhibited in 3D spatial gestures due to the difference in user performance [14]. During our developments, we found that the illustration of 3D spatial gestures plays an important role in minimizing the human variability and improving the recognition rates. Figure 5c illustrates examples of our 3D gesture diagrams for the mCube device.

4.4   Multi-dimensional Manipulation and Navigation

Virtual Object Manipulation. In desktop interaction, the object is controlled in the same way as a computer mouse. We implemented a similar implicit clutching using the IR distance sensor. For instance, when the user lifts up the device, the movements of the device do not affect manipulation. Users can also rotate the virtual object by physically rotating the device which is not possible using a conventional computer mouse as shown in Figure 6.

During hand-held interaction, the device is operated in space mapping the horizontal and vertical movement of the device to the corresponding object position. Therefore, users can directly move, rotate and tilt the object in any direction for 3D manipulation (Figure 6d). An explicit clutching technique is used with the right button of the mCube similar to other commercial 3D input devices.

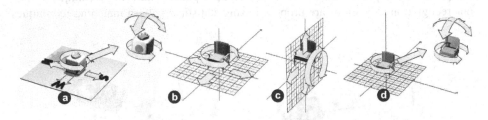

Fig. 6. Examples of virtual object manipulation: (a) The mCube is operated on the desktop surface and in space. (b, c) In desktop interaction, the object is translated and rotated on a working plane e.g., $x-y$ plane and $x-z$ plane. (d) In hand-held interaction, the object is operated with additional dimensions in space.

Virtual Space Navigation. To facilitate more efficient navigation, we use the four buttons as well as the rotational control of the device. The front, back, left and right buttons are used to control the movement of cameras. This idea is inspired by the *Cubic Mouse* which successfully utilizes a cube shape as an intuitive physical proxy of virtual objects in navigation purposes [8].

As illustrated in Figure 7, we implemented two navigation schemes: *examine viewer* to control a 3D virtual object like a 3D trackball and *walk viewer* to navigate through 3D virtual space with a walking metaphor. In the examine viewer, the rotational control of the mCube is used to rotate a virtual trackball. The virtual camera is located outside of the model pointing to the center of the model. The rotational movement of the device

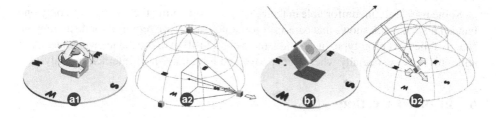

Fig. 7. Examples of virtual space navigation: examine viewer and walk viewer. (a) In the examine viewer, the virtual camera is rotated around the scene pointing to the center while manipulating the mCube. To zoom in and out, the front and back buttons are used respectively. (b) In the walk viewer, the virtual camera is moved and oriented based on button clicks and the orientation of the mCube.

is mapped to a virtual camera angle. The front and back buttons are used for zooming in and out, respectively. In the walk viewer, users can look in a certain direction while moving in another direction similar to the walking navigation in real world.

5   User Evaluation

We conducted a user evaluation to determine perceived exertion and movement characteristics when the mCube is used in desktop and hand-held interaction. We invited six participants who have strong backgrounds in computer science and computer graphics. Each participant was given a demo of how the system and interaction techniques work. Then they practiced all implemented functions. All users got used to the system after short practice (about 15 minutes).

The top handle was easily understood and performed well. All participants felt comfortable when rotating the top handle in both desktop and hand-held interactions. As we intended, they could select a tool on the pie-menu during other operations such as navigation and manipulation. Specially in a large screen display, using the pie-menu with the top handle, users can minimize the use of cursors which might be difficult to precisely control therein. Some users stated that they could remember the item locations on the pie-menu and rotate the top handle even without looking at the widget. We expect that this can be a powerful mechanism minimizing the cognitive loads during interaction and may be an interesting topic for a more extensive user experiment.

To explicitly test the user capabilities of desktop and hand-held interactions and switching between them, we performed a simple 3D docking task. Each subject was asked to perform several recurrences of the same task to locate one cube to another cube positioned at different positions in 3D. Between the recurrences, users were asked to perform the same tasks alternately in both interaction modes. During this task, users can easily return to desktop interaction by putting the mCube onto the table and lifting it up for further hand-held interaction. As we expected, in the hand-held interaction, we clearly noticed that fine positioning was hard to accomplish even with the intuitive 3D operation in the air. Almost 50% of the task completion time was taken for the final placement. These problems are mainly due to trembling of the user's hand and further caused by the well-known fatigue problem in hand-held input devices [20].

Some users felt uncomfortable in their grip when operating the mCube with only one hand. This feedback shows that careful ergonomic studies are required for designing the shape of the next prototype. In addition, the weight (140 g) of the device was considered still a bit heavy especially when users performed long hand-held interactions only.

6   Future Directions

The mCube is a promising prototype to understand the capabilities and limitations of a versatile gesture input device. We intend to perform a profound usability study to assess potential user acceptance of a versatile gesture input device with various target applications.

We also investigate the design variations to gain deeper insights into the perceptual issues in interacting with this class of input devices. Figure 8 shows a ring style mCube called *cubeRing* designed to be wearable on the finger. The cubeRing is designed with a highly unobtrusive form which minimizes a fatigue problem while keeping the required design principles for a versatile gesture input device. For instance, the flat bottom surface of the cubeRing provides a stable operation on the desktop surface, and the unique combination of a ring with a cube provides comfortable grip during the use in both the desktop and hand-held interactions.

To realize the small size, we use a coin size MICA dot module which is designed around a stacked configurable circuit board architecture, with a high-bandwidth transceiver and a general microprocessor, and a sensor board [6]. The cubeRing is equipped with two color LEDs one on the top side and another on the bottom side to enable robust tracking even with a hand rotation.

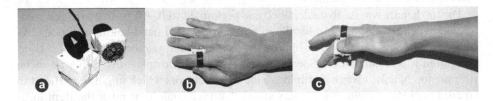

Fig. 8. (a) The cubeRing design with an adjustable finger ring on the top, and a small cube on the bottom. The cubeRing can be worn in the index finger, and operated on the desktop surface (b) and in hand-held position (c).

7   Conclusion

In this paper, we proposed a novel versatile gesture input device called mCube which supports various types of gesture inputs in desktop and hand-held interactions. We defined a set of design principles and solutions for the developments of a versatile gesture input device, and introduced our first prototype which integrates all necessary sensors. Combining visual and embedded sensor data has been proven to be useful for developing a versatile gesture input device supporting robust features for gesture recognition. We demonstrated a variety of interaction techniques namely tool selection, gesture commands, navigation, and manipulation which can be useful in a wide range of applications.

Acknowledgments. This work was carried out in the context of the blue-c-II project, funded by ETH grant No. 0-21020-04 as an internal poly-project.

References

1. Wii, http://wii.nintendo.com/
2. Brashear, H., Starner, T., Lukowicz, P., Junker, H.: Using multiple sensors for mobile sign language recognition. In: Fensel, D., Sycara, K.P., Mylopoulos, J. (eds.) ISWC 2003. LNCS, vol. 2870, Springer, Heidelberg (2003)
3. Brewster, S., Lumsden, J., Hall, M.B.M., Tasker, S.: Multimodal 'eyes-free' interaction techniques for wearable devices. In: Proceedings of CHI 2003, pp. 473–480 (2003)
4. Campbell, L.W., Becker, D.A.: Invariant features for 3-d gesture recognition. In: Second International Workshop on Face and Gesture Recognition (1996)
5. Cao, X., Balakrishnan, R.: Visionwand: interaction techniques for large displays using a passive wand tracked in 3d. In: Proceedings of UIST 2003, pp. 173–182 (2003)
6. Crossbow Technology, http://www.xbow.com/
7. Epps, J., Lichman, S., Wu, M.: A study of hand shape use in tabletop gesture interaction. In: CHI 2006 extended abstracts, pp. 748–753. ACM Press, New York (2006)
8. Frohlich, B., Plate, J.: The cubic mouse: a new device for three-dimensional input. In: Proceedings of CHI 2000, pp. 526–531. ACM Press, New York (2000)
9. Quill Jr., L.: a gesture design tool for penbased user interfaces (2001)
10. Kionix: Handheld Electronic Compass Applications Using the Kionix KXM52 MEMS Tri-axis Accelerometer, http://kionix.com/App-Notes/app-notes.htm
11. Laerhoven, K.V., Villar, N., Schmidt, A., Gellersen, G.K.H.: Using an autonomous cube for basic navigation and input. In: Proceedings of ICMI 2003, pp. 203–210 (2003)
12. Malik, S., Laszlo, J.: Visual touchpad: a two-handed gestural input device. In: Sharma, R., Darrell, T., Harper, M.P., Lazzari, G., Turk, M. (eds.) ICMI, pp. 289–296. ACM, New York (2004)
13. OpenSource Computer Vision Library. Intel Corp., http://www.intel.com
14. Payne, J., Keir, P., Elgoyhen, J., McLundie, M., Naef, M., Horner, M., Anderson, P.: Gameplay issues in the design of spatial 3d gestures for video games. In: Extended abstracts in CHI 2006, pp. 1217–1222 (2006)
15. Rekimoto, J., Sciammarella, E.: Toolstone: Effective use of the physical manipulation vocabularies of input devices. In: Proceedings of UIST 2000, pp. 109–117 (2000)
16. Sheridan, J.G., Short, B.W., Van Laerhoven, K., Villar, N., Kortuem, G.: Exploring cube affordance. In: Proceedings of Eurowearables 2003 (2003)
17. Weiser, M.: The world is not a desktop. Interactions 1(1), 7–8 (1994)
18. Westeyn, T., Brashear, H., Atrash, A., Starner, T.: Georgia tech gesture toolkit: Supporting experiments in gesture recognition. In: Proceedings of ICMI 2003 (2003)
19. Wilson, A., Shafer, S.: Xwand: Ui for intelligent spaces. In: Proceedings of ACM CHI Conference on Human Factors in Computing Systems, pp. 522–545. ACM Press, New York (2003)
20. Zhai, S.: User performance in relation to 3d input device design 32, 50–54 (1998)
21. Zhang, Z.: Flexible camera calibration by viewing a plane from unknown orientations. In: Proceedings of Computer Vision 1999, pp. 662–673 (1999)
22. Zimmerman, T.G., Lanier, J., Blanchard, C., Bryson, S., Harvill, Y.: A hand gesture interface device. In: Proceedings of CHI 1987, pp. 189–192 (1987)

uPackage – A Package to Enable Do-It-Yourself Style Ubiquitous Services with Daily Objects

Takuro Yonezawa[1], Hiroshi Sakakibara[1], Kengo Koizumi[1], Shingo Miyajima[1], Jin Nakazawa[1], Kazunori Takashio[2], and Hideyuki Tokuda[2]

[1] Graduate School of Media and Governance, Keio University
[2] Faculty of Environment and Information Studies, Keio University,
5322, Endo, Fujisawa, Kanagawa 252-8520, Japan
{takuro,skk,mics,jino,jin,kaz,hxt}@ht.sfc.keio.ac.jp

Abstract. This paper explores a suitable service model for realizing domestic smart object applications and proposes a software and hardware package called *uPackage* to support this model. By attaching a tiny wireless sensor node to users' belongings, users can augment the object digitally and take the object into various services such as status monitoring or preventing lost property. The system provided by uPackage supports users to install and manage such smart object services; it enables users to digitally associate sensor nodes with daily objects, manage the associated information and sensor data, and create various smart object applications without professional skills. Initial demonstration to children indicate that the service model provided by uPackage is easy understandable and increases users' acceptance of the wireless sensor node technology.

1 Introduction

To realize a ubiquitous computing environment, technologies such as computers, sensors and networks needs to be more integrated and easy to use. Especially, small sensor nodes equipped with various types of sensors such as thermometers, accelerators, or illuminometers have enormous potential to create context-aware services that assist a variety of human activities. Our life is filled with everyday objects, and we often have troubles with them (e.g. lost property). In order to achieve the ubiquitous computing environment, it is important to take everyday objects into ubiquitous services. Sensor nodes, when attached to everyday objects, enable us to gather real-world information as context. Recently many researchers are focusing on ubiquitous services with these smart objects [4] [11]. With smart objects, users would be able to enjoy the privilege of ubiquitous technology anytime anywhere in their lives.

The motivation behind our research is the lack of a suitable model to deploy and use smart object services in the home or office. Successful installation of smart object services requires a three-step process: 1) attaching sensor nodes to objects, 2) making semantic associations between the sensor nodes and the objects, and 3) configuring each application to a preferred setting. Yet, previous research on smart object services has not focused on the critical issue of how to create these configurations easily. Existing research on the services may not have paid attention to the configuration issue as it

H. Ichikawa et al. (Eds.): UCS 2007, LNCS 4836, pp. 240–257, 2007.
© Springer-Verlag Berlin Heidelberg 2007

simply assumed that all of these smart objects are pre-configured at the time of ship-ment and therefore users do not need to make semantic associations for themselves: all they are expected to do is only adjusting each application to their own liking. Yet, this assumption implies that the users should buy and use pre-configured products only. If that is the case, we cannot make smart objects out of many ordinary (i.e., not pre-configured) products that already exist in our daily life. Instead, we have to call on experts to configure the settings or overcome numerous technical obstacles on our own. Either way, smart object services will end up too costly to be deployed in home or office settings.

Unlike these previous studies, our research does not make these assumptions. Rather, our purpose is to advance research in such a way that smart object services can be deployed in everyday settings without being confined to the use of pre-configured products, relying on experts for configurations, or expecting users to possess special technical expertise. In other words, our goal is to create system architecture for satis-fying following three characters: (i) *Flexibility*: users can leverage daily objects which exist in their surroundings; (ii) *Extendibility*: not only programmers but also non-expert users can create simple applications on demand; and (iii) *Ease of deployment*: non-expert users can deploy and use smart object services in their home or office.

To achieve this goal, we present a hardware and software suite called "uPackage" (see Figure1). uPackage contains sensor nodes (uParts [3] developed by TecO), a tool to associate sensor nodes and daily objects with a camera, a base server that handles sensor data and associated information between sensor nodes and daily objects, and a simple development tool for end-users to create their own services. In addition, we designed and implemented several prototype applications based on uPackage, such as object status viewer, a burglar-proof service, a reminder services that prevents lost prop-erty and a remote monitoring service for the elderly living alone.

The rest of the paper is organized as follows. Section 2 describes DIY smart ob-ject service model and overview the elements of uPackage that realizes the service model. Section 3 details two main systems in uPackage, called uAssociator and uGate-way. Section 4 describes application framework and introduce example applications, and Section 5 presents two experiences using uPackage; demonstration to children and usability test. Section 6 describes related work, and finally Section 7 concludes the pa-per and discusses directions for future work.

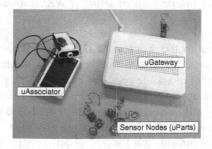

Fig. 1. uPackage components

2   uPackage – A Package to Realize Do-It-Yourself Style Smart Object Services

In this section, we introduce overview of uPackage system. At first, we present service model that uPackage provides. Secondly, we show uPackage's system overview before further system details.

2.1   DIY Smart Object Service Model

uPackage provides a service model for realizing Do-It-Yourself(DIY) style of smart object services. It supports both bootstrap and management of smart object services. As Beckmann argued in [2], it may be difficult for end-users to form conceptual service model of ubiquitous computing applications as the applications are often highly distributed and break the familiar paradigm of desktop-based human-computer interaction. Therefore, it is necessary to present understandable service model that commonly-adapts a range of smart object services.

Before introducing our service model, the application domain that we target should be made clear. Applications based on uPackage is acquired by changing the state of computer or information appliances to support our daily life according to the change of daily objects' status. Thus, applications requires following three steps: 1) sensing, 2) processing, and 3) actuating. As an example, we show an application scenario below.

– *Scenario: Smart Caregiver Application*
  Smart Caregiver is a smart object service that takes care of an elderly living alone. To use this service, the user first needs to register household items that the monitored persons frequently use. This registration is conducted by 1) physically attaching a sensor node to an item, 2) digitally associating the sensor node and the item, and 3) loading the association information into the service. After these operations the service starts monitoring how these items are being used. This usage information is obtained by monitoring the item's movement. After a while, family members or caretakers should be able to tell, by the extent to which the usage of a certain object (e.g., a mug) deviates from the usual pattern, if something unusual might have happened to the monitored. The service exports the item's usage status (i.e. activities of the monitored person) on a WEB page. This enables remote caregivers to have access to the information by using a WEB browser in their PCs or cell phones.

The major requirement in the scenario is DIY style of service usage; non-expert users must be able to register their preferred belongings to preferred services. Therefore, the service model that uPackage provides goes through the following process in common: A) installing an application to the user's PC, B) attaching a sensor node to a user's belongings, C) digitally association the sensor node and the object with camera, and D) use services (see Figure 2). The relationship of which object each sensor node is attached to is a critical information for any smart object services, so that the easy association inevitably leads to the DIY smart object service model. uPackage system supports association between sensor nodes and objects by using a spotlight-and-camera

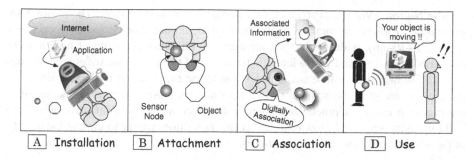

A | Installation   B | Attachment   C | Association   D | Use

Fig. 2. DIY smart object service model that uPackage provides

association tool. Details of the technique are described later in this paper. A great advantage of this model is that, by attaching a sensor node, household items instantly start interfacing physical activity of the user, and can participate in various services. Since different people may use a range of different items in their homes, this advantage is important to adapt the service to each person's life. Our model corresponds to the existing desktop-based application model; get software from a CD or through the Internet, install it, and use it. The difference between our model and the traditional model is that users can choose their belongings (i.e., not smart object) to participate in applications, attach sensor nodes to the objects, and digitally associate them.

2.2 uPackage System Overview

To realize DIY smart object service model, we developed the uPackage system based on TecO particle sensor network technology. Figure 3 shows the overall configuration of uPackage. uPackage system is built by four components - sensor nodes, uAssociator, uGateway and the user's PC. Each component is connected by applicable network - sensor network, wired or wireless LAN. We describe each of the components below in turn.

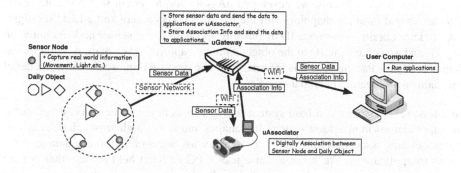

Fig. 3. Overall of uPackage's system

Sensor Nodes: We use uParts as sensor nodes in uPackage system. The reason why we choose uParts is that they are small enough to be mounted on personal effects (their size is 10x10mm), with wireless communication, enabling the setup of high density networks at low cost and with a long life time. Out of these reasons, we especially paid attention to the cost because we consider cost is the most important factor. Since our target users are at home or small offices with non-professionals, it is not adequate to leverage expensive equipments and complicated operations. Our distinctive point is to build up many services in low cost. Under this condition, we try to elevate the quality of the services, and take root in our society.

User's PC: uParts have limited computation power only enough to transport sensor data for reducing the cost. Thus, application softwares are implemented on high performance machines such as desktop or laptop PCs. We believe using user's PC for application platform is reasonable because our target is at home or office, not outdoor or battlefield, where one or more PCs exist at present.

uAssociator: As mentioned in previous section, it is necessary for realizing DIY style of smart object service to provide easy association method. Association between a sensor node and an object requires two operations 1) identification of sensor node ID and 2) entry of relationship between sensor nodes ID and the object information. To enable end-users to realize easy association, the following problems need to be solved:

1. **Difficulty in identifying the sensor node ID:** Sensor nodes have no display on which their IDs can be shown. This makes it highly difficult for non-expert users to accurately obtain the sensor node ID of interest. Consequently, the users are forced to rely on professional identification tools or simply estimate the ID based on the sensor data packet sent by the node to the network. Either way, the procedure could be highly inhibiting to end-users.
2. **Difficulty in containing the cost of manual mapping:** Even after the sensor node is successfully identified, users still need to feed the association information to the system manually. In fact, the users have to repeat this cumbersome feeding task every time they mount a sensor node on an object.

To solve these problems, we developed uAssociator, a system which enables easy, interactive and intuitive mapping with the use of a USB camera and a LED spotlight. uAssociator obtain sensor node ID by flashing spotlight to the sensor node mounted on object, and associates the ID to the object's image captured by camera. All of applications based on uPackage use this information. The next section, we describe the detail mechanism and feature behind uAssociator.

uGateway: uGateway is a base system which connects sensor network, uAssociator and applications in uPackage system. It manages and stores both sensor data from sensor nodes and associated information created by uAssociator, and these data are provided to applications. We assume that a user's PC or hand held device, that are the platform for applications and uAssociator in uPackage system, are often turned off. In other words, these devices does not suit for storing sensor data and associated information, because these data are required asynchronously with the devices. The cope with the storing data, we chose a wireless access point for the host to store data. Since it is turned on continuously, it suits base system in uPackage system. In addition, this is able to provide network infrastructure for PCs which are exploited by uAssociator and applications in home or office. For these reason, uGateway have following hardware requirements: wireless access point function, receive sensor data function, storage to store sensor data and associated information, and computational power.

We implemented uGateway on a Linux-based wireless access point. It mounts a sink node for a uPart wireless sensor network system. We describe uGateway's software and protocols for communication with uAssociator and applications in the next section.

3 Technical Design

This section describes the design and implementation of uPackage's components: uAssociator and uGateway. We first describe the details of uAssociator, then we show that of uGateway.

3.1 uAssociator

uAssociator enables users to associate sensor nodes with daily objects in home or office with the help of digital camera. Our first prototype system utilizes a USB camera and spotlight device, which are connected to a PDA. In addition to this configuration, Bluetooth-enabled digital cameras and cell phones, which entail camera units these days, can be used for the purpose.

Interaction. Figure 4 shows the basic interaction using our first prototype system. After attaching sensor node to an object, for successful association, users only need to (1) direct the camera to the node and the object, (2) flash the spotlight on both for a second, and (3) turn off the spotlight. The uAssociator system recognizes the targeted sensor node ID, and associates it with the image of the object obtained from the camera. When uAssociator succeeds association, it gives sound feedback to users. After that, the user can take advantage of various applications.

To this extent, uAssociator requires no expert knowledge or skills. Users only need to keep in mind that whatever object they flash spotlight on will be associated with the sensor node mounted on them. As such, uAssociator enables association through a simple and intuitive interaction.

Fig. 4. uAssociator's Intection: user turns a spotlight on and snaps a photo of sensor-attached everyday object, then sensor-object associated image is created and able to be used for applications

How to express the physical object in the digital world to combine with sensor node ID is an important discussion point. The various expression forms of the object are conceivable such as the object's name, attribute, or property. Ideally, the expression form should fulfill the following two conditions: 1) it is naturally understandable for human, and 2) it is useful for realizing various applications. As described above, uAssociator uses the object's image as the target to associate with sensor node ID. Generally, human beings recognize the object through visual organs and shape an impression in their brain, then understand the object's name or property by combining the impression with their memory [17]. It is difficult to identify what object is like only from its name or attributes. For example, a word "cup" cannot express which particular cup is represented. Although the cup's attributes, such as shape and color, could be input on association by the users, it is impractical to force them to do so for a number of his belongings. Therefore, the use of images to indicate objects is practical and intuitive.

Meanwhile, we also see names or attributes of the objects as important information to develop wide range of applications. Many researchers have made efforts to extract digital information of physical objects automatically. For example, research on computer vision developed several techniques to extract objects' information from their images (e.g., the content-based image retrieval system [1]). Though they can work well for small number of objects under specific conditions, there are still no method applicable under a generic condition. The limitation of uAssociator is that it can't obtain object meta-information. However, uPackage system focuses on the advantages of using objects image more than disadvantages of unusing objects' meta-information. One purpose of this paper is to show that only using the images of the objects enable us to develop a wide range of applications actually. Examples of these applications describes in the latter section.

Sensor Node Identification Algorithm. uAssociator, when spotlight is flashed on an object, identifies a particular sensor node mounted on the object from many sensor nodes in a network. The system runs on a PC to which packets from all sensor nodes including their ID and sensor data are transmitted through sink nodes. It monitors the illuminance to detect that the values from a sensor node indicate highest for a given time. When the system detects the condition (i.e., spotlight is flashed on the sensor node), it starts the association procedure.

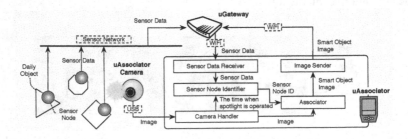

Fig. 5. System architecture of uAssociator

The detail of this algorithm is as follows. The uAssociator system monitors both the time T, at which the user turns on or off the spotlight camera unit, and $S_T = \{s1, ..., sn\}$, the set of sensor nodes that meet a certain condition described below. When a user turns on a spotlight at $T1$, the system obtains a set of sensor nodes S_{T1}, where the illuminometer value of sensor node $s_j \in S_{T1}$ $(1 \leq j \leq n)$ starts indicating maximum in $T1 < t \leq T1 + N$. Oppositely, when the user turns off the spotlight at $T2$ $(T1 < T2)$, it obtains another set of sensor nodes S_{T2}, where the illuminometer value of sensor node $s_k \in S_{T2}$ $(1 \leq k \leq n)$ finish indicating maximum in $T2 < t \leq T2 + N$. If the element count of product set $S_{T1} \cap S_{T2}$ is one, the system determines that $s \in S_{T1} \cap S_{T2}$ is the sensor node on which the spotlight is flashed by the user. If the element count is two or more, the system determines the identification is failed. Allowed time N is provided to cope with packet sending interval of sensor nodes and network latency from the time when the user spotlight a sensor node to the time when the computer receives the packet from the node. The value of N is calculated by $N = 2i$, where i is the average packet arrival interval of the latest five packets.

System Architecture. As illustrated in Figure 5, uAssociator system consists of the following five modules implemented with JAVA. First, the **Sensor Data Receiver** receives sensor data from uGateway. We describe protocol for communication with uGateway in the next section. Second, the **Sensor Node Identifier** identifies a particular sensor node illuminated by the camera's spotlight. This module utilizes the sensor node identification algorithm we described above. The third module, the **Camera Handler**, obtains the time when the user operates camera, and captures the object's image when the user turns off the camera's spotlight. If the sensor node ID is successfully obtained in the sensor node identification module, Fourth module, the **Associator**, associates sensor node ID and object image as associated information called **Smart Object Images**. Finally, the fifth module, the **Image Sender**, sends Smart Object Image to uGateway.

Let us describe the detail of Smart Object Image. Smart Object Image is formatted in JPEG. As such, it can be handled as a normal JPEG image in other applications. Our extension to this JPEG image is done in the header field. Associated information (e.g., the sensor node ID or completion time of association) is stored in an XML format as a part of the standard EXIF header in the JPEG file. Sample metadata of the Smart Object Image are shown in Figure 6. Applications can extract the association information from the image through our XML schema. This XML schema of Smart Object Image is defined by the DTD shown in Figure 7. The DTD is composed of two parts: 1) information about the sensor node, 2) completion time-stamp. The first part, information about the sensor node, contains a sensor node's type and ID. This information enables

```
<?xml version="1.0" encoding="UTF-8" ?>
<!DOCTYPE association_info SYSTEM
"AssociationInfo.dtd">
<association_info>
    <sensor_info>
        <type> uPart </type>
        <id> 1.2.3.4.0.1.0.12 </id>
    </sensor_info>
    <timestamp> 1159523569317 </timestamp>
</association_info>
```

Fig. 6. Sample meta-data using XML

```
<?xml version="1.0"?>

<!ELEMENT association_info (sensor_info, timestamp)>

<!ELEMENT sensor_info (type, id)?>
<!ELEMENT type (#PCDATA)>
<!ELEMENT id (#PCDATA)>

<!ELEMENT timestamp (#PCDATA)>
```

Fig. 7. DTD for Smart Object Image's XML

applications to handle the sensor node while realizing smart object services. The second part of the DTD, the time-stamp, indicates when Smart Object Image was created in the UNIX time. This information is used for managing various versions of smart object images.

3.2 uGateway

uGateway plays a two important role in uPackage system. First, uGateway relays sensor data from sensor network to both applications and uAssociator. In addition, it stores sensor data to database for applications which require sensor data history. Second, uGateway relays Smart Object Image from uAssociator to applications. This enables uPackage system to manage uniform association information. Figure 8 shows system architecture of uGateway. Sensor data from sensor nodes and Smart Object Image from uAssociator is processed by **Sensor Data Receiver** and **Smart Object Image Receiver** respectively. When these data are required from applications, **Sensor Data Transfer** and **Smart Object Image Transfer** transmits data respectively. Both the sensor data and Smart Object Images are stored to the database in uGateway.

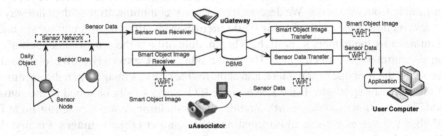

Fig. 8. System architecture of uGateway

uGateway Protocol for Communicating with Applications and uAssociator. Figure 9 shows a time space chart when an application or uAssociator receives sensor data from uGateway. Since uPackage system tries to reduce users' operation const, uGateway supports discovery function not to make users aware of configuration such as IP address or port setting. To recieve sensor data, applications or uAssociator sends UDP broadcast called *uGateway discovery message* at first. Figure 10 shows the message format. The first 32 bit is assigned to store IP address of applications or uAssociator, next 16 bits for *type*, and the last 16 bit for *port*. The definition that can be set to *type* field is listed in Figure 11. This field is used to distinguish the sender of *uGateway discovery request*. *port* is set a port number to receive an acknowledgement message from uGateway. In case of *uGateway discovery ack*, IP address field is assigned an address of uGateway, port is a port number to communicate with applications or uAssociator. This port is used for receiving sensor data request (by both applications and uAssociator), smart object images request (used by applications) and smart object images upload (by uAssociator).

In case of receiving the sensor data, *sensor data request message* is sent to the port number which is set at *port* field in *uGateway discovery ack* message. Then, the

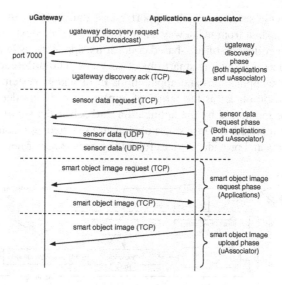

Fig. 9. Time space chart between uGateway and applications or uAssociator

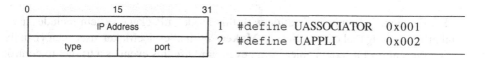

Fig. 10. uGateway discovery request message format   **Fig. 11.** Discovery message type definition

sensor data is sent to the applications or uAssociator using UDP periodically. uGateway sends the sensor data for 5 seconds. Therefore, applications or uAssociator needs to re-send *sensor data request message* within 5 seconds, if more data is necessary. There is *method* field in *sensor data reqest message* that indicates how to receive sensor data. When REALTIME(0x001) is set, the sensor dat a which uGateway receives from sensor network is periodically push to applications or uAssociator. In contrast, when HISTORY(0x002) is set, applications need to send more messages (SQL request) to pull a certain range of data that applications require.

4 Applications

In this section, we show applications in uPackage system. Firstly, we describe application framework in uPackage system. After that, we propose some of example applications with uPackage.

4.1 Application Framework

Like today's desktop-applications, applications in uPackage system run on the user's PC. Figure 12 shows conceptual architecture of applications in uPackage system.

Applications provide services which support user's daily life by using Smart Object Images and sensor data from uGateway. As most common context-aware applications are described as a collection of rule-based conditions, applications in uPackage system adapts *if-then* rule for providing smart object services. The difference between common context-aware applications and applications in uPackage system is that users can choose any domestic object as the target of applications. Users decide which smart objects should be monitored by the application and select the smart object image by using GUI of the application. Once smart objects are selected, applications monitor the objects' sensor data and provide services following each *if-then* rules.

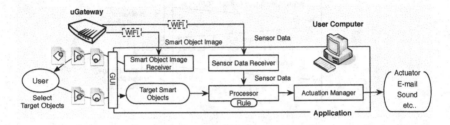

Fig. 12. Conceptual architecture of applications in uPackage system

For developing simple application with this model, uPackage system includes a visual programming tool called **uServiceMaker**. With uServiceMaker, users can visually define the status of a certain object as an event and use this event as a trigger to control various actuators such as alarm or e-mail. An event consists of sensor type (e.g., temperature, light or movement), threshold and threshold type. Threshold types are "and above", "and below", and regional threshold (e.g., from 10 to 20). With these elements, the user can define an event like "If temperature is equal to 20 or above 2". As actuators, uServiceMaker provides smart object image viewer, sound player, e-mail function and simple telnet function to control information appliances (e.g., light or TV). uServiceMaker has two modes: the edit mode and the execution mode. In the edit mode, uServiceMaker provides a GUI editor to create services (see Figure13) for users who do not have knowledge on programming. On this editor, Event, Action, and their relationship are represented as figures, and users can edit rules with these figures. In the execution mode, uServiceMaker changes these figures into if-then rules and evaluates the rules with sensor data. If the sensor data fits an Event's threshold, uServiceMaker invokes the Action that is connected with the Event. For example, a smart light service can be created with this application; when someone takes a seat on the chair in front of a desk, a movement sensor mounted on the chair detects the person's motion and turns on the light on the desk.

4.2   Example Applications

Let us describe some application ideas with uPackage system. In the following, four of prototypes are presented: 1) uViewer, an object status viewer, 2) uAlert, a burglar-proof service, 3) uReminder, a reminder service that prevents lost property, and 4) uCare, a remote monitoring service for the elderly living alone.

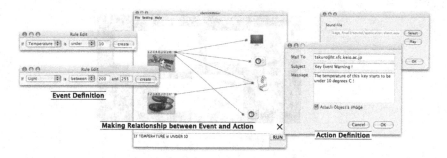

Fig. 13. uServiceMaker: user can visually define the status of a certain object as an event and use this event as a a trigger to control various actuators

uViewer: The first application, uViewer, assists a user in monitoring his or her personal belongings even when these objects are out of sight. It reports the changing status of the objects visually with images created by uAssociator (see Figure 14). For instance, when an object moves, its image also moves. This visual presentation of the object status enables the user to intuitively understand the object's whereabouts. In addition to this basic service, uViewer is capable of presenting the history of a particular object's status. With this type of information, the user can tell how frequently the object is being used. All in all, uViewer extends the users' ability to manage their personal belongings.

uAlert: uAlert helps prevent valuables (e.g., keys) from removed drawer by someone. It keeps track of the illuminance and movement of valuables to be monitored and takes actions accordingly. When the illuminance of a registered object continues to indicate 0 for 30 seconds, uAlert assumes the object is stored in a dark place such as a drawer and starts monitoring the object's status. After that, if the object moves and its illuminance goes up, uAlert concludes that the object is removed from the drawer and sounds an alarm. At the same time, a verbal warning and an image of the removed object are sent to the user's mobile device by e-mail. The use of object images in the alarm increases intuitiveness of this service.

uReminder: The third example of the services, uReminder, is also designed for the context of personal effects management. It assists a user by reminding them of their belongings they tend to leave behind. To use uReminder, the user needs to register two types of objects: 1) objects that should be moved when the user leaves his/her home (e.g., front door or shoes); and 2) objects that should not be left behind (e.g., a wallet or key). Either type of the objects can be registered to uReminder through graphical interface. If the former type of object moves while the latter type does not, uReminder judges that the user left behind the latter kind of object. Then, uReminder notifies the user of the forgotten item by sounding an alarm and displaying the object's image on a monitor near the user.

uCare: With uCare, an elderly living alone can be monitored remotely. In order to use this service, the user first needs to register household items that the monitored persons frequently use. Then uCare starts monitoring how these items are being used. This usage information is obtained by monitoring the object's movement. After a while,

Fig. 14. uViewer, a simple object status viewer; it reports the changing status of the objects visually with images. In addition, it shows objects' status history using the chart.

family members or caretakers should be able to tell, by the extent to which the usage of a certain object (e.g., mug) deviates from the usual pattern, if something unusual might have happened to the monitored.

Note that these applications indicates notable fact that even with such image-centric association assisted by uAssociator, the applications is possible to offer a wide range of services; there is no need for these applications to know the identity of physical objects because the user is only required to visually recognize the object by its image.

5   Experience

5.1   Demonstration to Children

Demonstration at a symposium "What will you do in ubiquitous computing environment?" in Aomori showed us children's impressions of our system. The event was held to excite children's creativity by demonstrating various technologies of ubiquitous computing. After the demonstration, children cooked up and made a presentation of some application ideas through their group discussion. More than a hundred of children who are the sixth grade of elementary school participated in the event. We introduced technology of sensor nodes and the concept of our system, and demonstrated association using uAssociator and some applications (see Figure15). Most of the children seemed to understand and enjoy our system. In the group discussion, many groups proposed various unique applications using our system such as "if secret diary which mounts sensor node is removed from drawer, alert by sounds" or "if a brush is not moved after a meal, tell the child to brush his teeth". From this experience, we confirmed the mental model of our system is easily understandable even for children.

5.2   Usability Test

This section evaluates usability of uAssociator following to the 5 indicators [13] - *Learnability*, *Efficiency*, *Memorability*, *Error Handling* and *User Satisfaction*. We experiment usability test to evaluate intuitively of uAssociator operation. The participants are 13 students(participants A-M) who are novice users of uAssociator (participants A-I) and experts users(participants J-M) who have a lot of experiences of using uAssociator. The experiment was performed in a room where every fluorescent lights

Fig. 15. Demonstration to children

are turned on. As an experimental setup, uAssociator camera, μPart and a cup to attach μPart are placed on the desk. At first, we did simple orientation that contains the purpose of experiment, how to use uAssociator and note of experiment. Next, participants performed 20 times of association task with uAssociator. After completing the test, we ask the participants of novice users to fill out our questionnaire which includes free comment field. We measure each time until association succeeded. Each recorded time contains following operation - participants pick up camera, direct and spotlight the camera to the object, and finished the association. The questionnaire is based on the Likert scale [10].

Figure 16 shows average time to success association according to the number of operation. Figure 17 shows the time of maximum, minimum and average of each participant to success association. Table 1 shows the statements and results of questionnaire. Users indicated their degree of agreement for each statement on a 1-5 scale (1 = strongly disagree, 2 = partly disagree, 3 = neither agree nor disagree, 4 = partly agree, 5 = strongly agree).

Learnability. Regardless of computer skills, every participant used uAssociator only with short orientation. The average rating of the questionnaire "It was very easy to learn how to use this system." was 4.62. From this result, we consider that non-experts can conduct uAssociator in their practical environments without experts' help.

Efficiency. Regardless of the number of operation, the participants could perform association operation within 5 seconds (see Figure 16). Identification of sensor node and feeding association information manually using a computer GUI could require much more than 4 seconds to input sensor node ID and the object's image through keyboard. Therefore, this result shows high efficiency of uAssociator interaction.

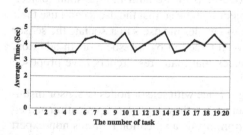

Fig. 16. The number of operations and average time for successful association

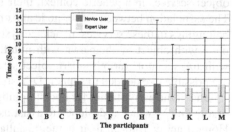

Fig. 17. Maximum, minimum and average time for successful association

Table 1. Result of questionarie

Question about using this system:	1 2 3 4 5	Average
Q1: It was very easy to learn how to use this system.	0 0 0 3 6	4.67
Q2: Using this system was a frustrating experience.	5 2 0 2 0	1.44
Q3: This system is very pleasant to work with.	1 0 3 1 4	3.78

Memorability. uAssociator is such a simple interaction that the participants could learn use of uAssociator. After a month from this experiment, we asked participants how to use of uAssociator. All of them remembered the operation of uAssociator. This shows that uAssociator is a highly memorable interface.

Error Handling. Figure 17 shows that participants succeeded the association task in average 4 seconds. However, there were some cases that exceeds 10 seconds. These errors were due to the packet losses of sensor nodes. This error might have effect to the result of questionnaire "Using this system was a frustrating experience." In contrast, there were no error which caused by participants' mal-operation. One problem of the current implementation of uAssociator system is that, on errors, it does not provide users with feedback about the reason of the errors. Some participants mentioned in the free comment field in the questionnaire that they want such a feedback mechanism.

User Satisfaction. The average ratings of the questionnaire are 4.03. To calculate the average rating, the rating of the negative question (Q2) is reversed. The value 3.6 is known as a better estimate of "neutral" or "average" user satisfaction. Therefore, the user satisfaction with our system is better than average. As participants' free comments, we could see many positive comments such as "it's easy to use" or "interesting". In addition, there were some comments that it is useful to realize this system with cell phones. Meanwhile, some participants seem to concern about security and privacy. Because if the status of their belongings are monitored by someone, it could be used for crimes. We should reflect these feedbacks to the future system.

6   Related Work

There are many related works about smart object such as MediaCup [4], DigiClip [6], MAX [18] or Sentient Artifacts [7]. While they have proved the usefulness of smart object services in a generic context, their focuses is to use built-in type smart object. The association between sensor node and object is static so that the users can't use their belongings in these services. uPackage system enables the users to associate the sensor node with object by their own with intuitive interaction by uAssociator. In addition, with uAssociator, various smart object services that many researchers have proposed are possible to extended to support DIY style.

One of the early studies for bootstrapping service with sensor nodes is Sensor Installation Kit [2], which is designed to assist users when they deploy an application named Home Energy Tutor in their home. Installation of this application requires non-expert users to accurately attach sensor nodes to appliances. The Kit guides users through this process as it contains a set of predefined association information. While this guide greatly helps non-expert users to install sensor nodes correctly, they cannot attach a sensor node to an appliance if it is not predefined in the Kit. Thus, it cannot apply to association for a hundred of daily objects. Meanwhile, Pervasive Association [14] focuses on automatic association. The Pervasive Association project proposes a two-step procedure to obtain a name of an object. In the first step, the system recognizes how an object is used (e.g., pulled, turned around or pushed) by analyzing the history of sensor data obtained from the sensor node on the object. In the second step, the system determines the object's name by its usage after looking it up in a special name-usage dictionary. However, it is difficult to assume every objects only with limited sensors mounted on sensor node. Moreover, if it takes long time to assume the object, it is not appropriate to register users' belongings to the application immediately. Additionary, names of those objects may be accurately identified, but only as general nouns (e.g., book), not as proper names (e.g., "War and Peace"). In other words, with this method, it is still impossible to identify an object with total accuracy. In contrast, uAssociator enables users to recognize what the object is correctly due to the use of images. In addition, uAssociator provides instant association.

Let us describe more research related to association. To enhance the RFID method, some researchers employed both light and radio frequency. FindIT Flashlight [12] and RFIG [15] are examples of these combined techniques. Both techniques expose light - which contains some coded patterns - to an RFID with a light sensor. Then, the RFID, which is also equipped with an LED light, returns the RFID [12] or the RFID with its location information [15]. With the help of these functions, users can easily find items they need. These techniques are very similar to our approach to sensor node identification in that both make use of light as the medium. The major difference between these two methods and ours is that FindIT Flashlight and RFIG require more preparation; they require special implementation on sensor nodes. However, if RFIG's technique can be applied to association, it realizes association between multiple sensors and objects simultaneously. This is because RFIG uses combination of light (projector) and camera as same as our approach.

In addition, there are many techniques for identifying devices such as using radio frequency [5], using synchronous movement [16, 9], using both radio frequency and movement [8]. However, these methods have some disadvantage compared to our approach using light. For example, using radio frequency lacks general versatility. Since sensor nodes of the same type emit the same radio frequency, we cannot use more than one sensor nodes of the same type with this method. This could be a major obstacle when all different sensor nodes co-exist in an environment. Similarly, using IrDA or buttons also has a disadvantage of limited versatility. The problem here is that these methods cannot be used with sensor nodes if they have no IrDA or button. The use of light, on the other hand, increases universality of the system since most of the currently available sensor nodes contain illuminometers.

7 Conclusion

Providing a suitable model to deploy smart object services is one of the key challenges to realize ubiquitous computing environment in homes or offices. This paper presented our solution called uPackage system. It is a package that contains tiny sensor nodes, uAssociator that enables users image-based association easily, uGateway that manages sensor data and association information, and a simple visual programming tool called uServiceMaker. uPackage has the following three-folds. First, it enables daily objects to participate in various applications with the help of uAssociator. uAssociator realizes simple and powerful interaction that enables non-expert users to specify a particular object and a sensor node for association without using classic PC interfaces like a keyboard. Second, it provides application framework for programmers to design and implement context-aware applications easily. In addition, uServiceMaker enables end-users to create their own application. Third, it can be deployed easily; uGateway, a base system in uPackage, is implemented on a wireless access point so that the users can deploy without complex knowledge. We have shown these features in this paper by describing the design and implementation, proposing a range of services built with uPackage, and evaluating it through experiments.

Finally we suggest two directions for future research. One is the extension of the association method, incorporating object recognition technologies. uAssociator can be extended to use object recognition techniques to support services that cannot exist without having smart object information in texts. We have not confronted with such situations so far to realize a range of smart object services. However, since uAssociator uses images of objects as association targets, it can be used as a basis to apply the object recognition techniques such as text extraction or content-based image retrieve techniques [1]. Object recognition techniques are not limited to the above two methods, but no matter what technique we may choose, it cannot be the best way for identifying various objects. Thus, it may be more realistic, at least at present, that we will combine these technologies and try to develop the best-effort object recognition system. Second is to support privacy-protection mechanism in uGateway. Current uGateway sends sensor data to any application without authentication. In home environment, there are some users who don't want to reveal their belongings' status. To support privacy protection, we should design an applicable privacy-protection model and integrate it with the uPackage system.

Acknowledgements. This research has been conducted as part of Core Research for Evolutional Science and Technology of Japan Science and Technology Agency, and Exploratory Software Project supported by information technology promotion agency, Japan.

References

1. Antani, S., Kasturi, R., Jain, R.: A survey on the use of pattern recognition methods for abstraction, indexing and retrieval of images and video. Pattern Recognition 35(4), 945–965 (2002)
2. Beckmann, C., Consolvo, S., LaMarca, A.: Some assembly required: Supporting end-user sensor installation in domestic ubiquitous computing environment. In: International Conference on Ubiquitous Computing, pp. 107–124 (2004)
3. Beigl, M., Decker, C., Krohn, A., Riedel, T., Zimmer, T.: μparts: Low cost sensor networks at scale. In: International Conference on Ubiquitous Computing, Demonstration (2005)

4. Beigl, M., Gellersen, H.-W., Schmidt, A.: Mediacups: experience with design and use of computer-augmented everyday artifacts. Computer Networks 35(4), 401–409 (2001)
5. Brunette, W., Hartung, C., Nordstrom, B., Borriello, G.: Proximity interactions between wireless sensors and their application. In: ACM international conference on Wireless sensor networks and applications, pp. 30–37. ACM Press, New York (2003)
6. Decker, C., Beigl, M., Eames, A., Kubach, U.: Digiclip: Activating physical documents. In: International Conference on Distributed Computing Systems Workshops, vol. 03, pp. 388–393 (2004)
7. Fujinami, K., Nakajima, T.: Sentient artefacts: Acquiring user's context through daily objects. In: UISW 2005. The 2nd International Workshop on Ubiquitous Intelligence and Smart Worlds, Nagasaki, Japan (December 2005)
8. Gellersen, H., Kortuem, G., Schmidt, A., Beigl, M.: Physical prototyping with smart-its. IEEE Pervasive Computing 3(3), 74–82 (2004)
9. Hinckley, K.: Synchronous gestures for multiple persons and computers. In: ACM symposium on User interface software and technology, pp. 149–158. ACM Press, New York (2003)
10. LaLomia, M.J., Sidowski, J.B.: Measurements of computer satisfaction, literacy, and aptitudes: A review. International Journal of Human-Computer Interaction 2 (1990)
11. Lamming, M., Bohm, D.: Specs: Another approach to human context and activity sensing research, using tiny peer-to-peer wireless computers. In: International Conference on Ubiquitous Computing (2003)
12. Ma, H., Paradiso, J.A.: The findit flashlight: Responsive tagging based on optically triggered microprocessor wakeup. In: International conference on Ubiquitous Computing, pp. 160–167. Springer, London (2002)
13. Nielsen, J.: Usability Engineering. Morgan Kaufmann Publishers Inc., San Francisco (1995)
14. Okadome, T., Hattori, T., Hiramatsu, K., Yanagisawa, Y.: Project pervasive association: Toward acquiring situations in sensor networked environments. International Journal of Computer Science and Network Security 6(3B) (2006)
15. Raskar, R., Beardsley, P., van Baar, J., Wang, Y., Dietz, P., Lee, J., Leigh, D., Willwacher, T.: Rfig lamps: interacting with a self-describing world via photosensing wireless tags and projectors. In: ACM SIGGRAPH 2004 Papers, pp. 406–415. ACM Press, New York (2004)
16. Rekimoto, J.: Synctap: synchronous user operation for spontaneous network connection. Personal Ubiquitous Comput. 8(2), 126–134 (2004)
17. Warren, C., Morton, J.: The effects of priming on picture recognition. British Journal of Psychology 23, 117–129 (1982)
18. Yap, K.-K., Srinivasan, V., Motani, M.: Max: human-centric search of the physical world. In: international conference on Embedded networked sensor systems, pp. 166–179. ACM Press, New York (2005)

DroPicks – A Tool for Collaborative Content Sharing Exploiting Everyday Artefacts

Simo Hosio, Fahim Kawsar, Jukka Riekki, and Tatsuo Nakajima

Department of Electrical and Information Engineering, University of Oulu, Finland
Department of Computer Science, Waseda University, Japan
{simo.hosio,jukka.riekki}@ee.oulu.fi,
{fahim,tatsuo}@dcl.info.waseda.ac.jp

Abstract. Emergence of social web services like YouTube[1], Flickr[2] etc. is constantly transforming the way we share our lifestyles with family, friends and colleagues. The significance of specific contents can be enhanced if shared with the right person, at right location and time. This paper explores this contextual social content sharing mechanism and presents DroPicks that utilizes augmented everyday artefacts as containers for digital information. Many everyday artefacts are immobile, which implicitly restricts contents stored to a location. Such indirect, contextual sharing has advantages over direct communication mechanisms (E-mail, SMS, IM...) as it provides the content in correct context, seeking minimal attention. Considering the lightness of social contents, we argue that our approach is appropriate, as it does not seek immediate attention, but rather offers the content in the background.

1 Introduction

One of the direct implications of the convergence of ubiquitous technologies (like proliferation of wireless internet, short-range radio connectivity, high-end personal devices etc.) is the improvement of peoples' social communication. Internet, E-mail, Short Message Service (SMS) and Instant Messaging (IM) are now integral part of our lives through cell phones, PDAs, Internet Terminals, and Laptops. In addition, social Internet services like YouTube [1], Flickr [2] etc. have provided us with the opportunities to share our lifestyles with our families, friends and colleagues in a new and fascinating way. The meaning and utilization of social contents like photos, video clips or messages can be greatly improved if context information is attached to them. For example: Sharing a funny video clip from YouTube in the coffee room's display in the office might have a greater effect than sending it through email to all colleagues. Previous works on so-called "electronic graffiti" like Stick-e Notes [3] or Place-its [4] allow users to leave an electronic message/reminder for themselves or others associating location context, for example: "There is a better Ramen shop three blocks away". Usually these systems depend on a dedicated location repository and network infrastructure available in the interested locations and they do not consider the social applicability of the contents, e.g. with whom the content should be shared and when. In this paper we have explored this particular aspect of sharing ambient

H. Ichikawa et al. (Eds.): UCS 2007, LNCS 4836, pp. 258–265, 2007.

information in a contextual manner with our families, friends and colleagues in a timely fashion exploiting sentient artefacts.

Sentient artefacts are everyday artefacts, like a chair, a desk, a door, a cup, etc. augmented with various kinds of sensors and actuators that suit their appearance and primary functionalities. So far we have utilized these augmented artefacts e.g. as context providers or for providing ambient feedback [5, 6, 7, 8]. An interesting property of some of the everyday artefacts is their binding to a specific location. For example, a meeting table in the office room or a refrigerator in the coffee room etc. These artefacts are suitable as a container for containing indirect content sharing, eliminating the requirement of any positioning infrastructure. We present DroPicks, a tool that allows sharing social content utilizing sentient artefacts and Internet terminals. User can touch a designated artefact to share content with someone or with a group. Here by content, we mean the metadata that describes an actual content, for example: URL of a video clip. Once the content is dropped to an artefact, it provides ambient clue(s) to the intended persons to pick the content. Figure 1 below illustrates some use cases of DroPicks.

(a)   (b)

Fig. 1. DroPicks in action: At the left user picks up content using internet terminal and augmented desk in his personal space while. In the next photo he leaves something behind to a common area augmented display.

DroPicks makes it easy to share contents and has advantage over direct communications like SMS, IM and E-Mail because of its contextual location-centric sharing characteristics. In addition, DroPicks offers the contents in the background unobtrusively, offering the content to only interested people, which is not possible with direct communications (There is no way to block a specific SMS or E-mail from trusted senders based on the content priority). Furthermore, DroPicks can be used as a location-aware personal reminder. Our initial user evaluation shows that DroPicks is quite promising, especially because of its intuitive utilization of location specific artefacts. However, there were mixed comments on its overall affectivity over the direct communications. Rest of this short paper is organized as follows: Section 2 summarizes the usage, requirements and design considerations of DroPicks. In section 3 we present the application itself in detail. Following sections, 4 and 5, provide implications with some related work and discussion and conclusions of DroPicks.

2 Use Cases and Design Principles

DroPicks has four use cases. Each of these cases has some requirements that we needed to fulfill while constructing DroPicks application:

Creating a content item from web content requires a comfortable method for acquiring this item from a normal web environment.

"Physical" dropping and picking of a content item needs augmented artefacts which are capable of communicating and storing digital data. Furthermore, a tangible interface between devices and artefacts has to be provided.

Usage of personal reminders with sentient artefact relies on a way to create these reminders easily and artefacts capable of notifying accordingly.

Dedicating the content to an appropriate recipient and remote deployment of content needs support for browsing and selecting from available users and sentient artefacts.

Considering the use cases presented above, we decided three primary design principles to follow in DroPicks:

Simple interaction. To appeal to a user in the first hand, the system must be as pleasurable to use as possible. Besides offering an easy way to create and view content, the system aims to mimic physical drop and pick as closely as possible.

Ambient feedback. In order to be noticed from environment and to increase interaction between users and sentient artefacts, visual and audio based feedback should be provided. When dealing with sentient artefacts, one should somehow feel the difference between a regular artefact and an augmented one.

Privacy enabled sharing of content. The system has to support the sharing of content with the right person in a secure way, i.e. not exposing the content to unintended recipients. We need to support sharing in *one to one* and *one to many* sharing.

3 The DroPicks Application

As shown in Figure 2, DroPicks utilizes two components, Internet terminals and Sentient Artefacts:

As the terminals for DroPicks we are using Nokia N770 Internet tablets. Internet tablets are aimed primarily for Internet browsing. We see these devices as a rich and interesting platform for prototype applications because of their relatively cheap price, suitability for fast developing and comfortable user interface.

Sentient Artefacts are augmented everyday artefacts capable of performing additional functionalities beyond their primary role. For example: A mirror can be augmented to act as an ambient display in addition to its primary role of reflecting image. Augmenting everyday artefacts and using them for various ubiquitous computing tasks have been widely discussed and researched in [5, 6, 7, 8]. Many of these artefacts, e.g. a couch in the living room or a refrigerator in the kitchen, are static in nature and thus associated to a specific location. This particular property gives us an implicit advantage of augmenting these artefacts for location specific services. In DroPicks, we have used sentient artefacts as location specific container for lightweight social communications.

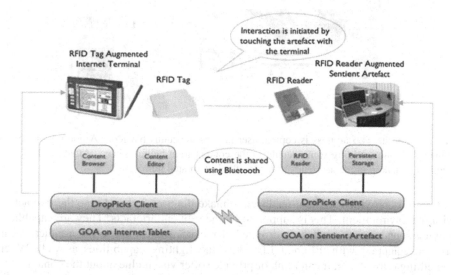

Fig. 2. Architecture of DroPicks. GOA middleware handles group management and RFID is utilized for initiating the Bluetooth communication sequences for sharing contents using internet terminals and augmented artefacts.

DroPicks shares so called *content items*, lightweight data objects that carry metadata with it. The mandatory part of a content item is the recipient specification; either whole group of a single member of a group. An item can contain URL(s), recipient, human readable name, a free description and some tags, i.e. keywords describing its content. Besides this, content item can also consist of a simple timed calendar note with a message. If nobody picks the content for a time specified by the host artefact, it will be deleted automatically. Also, the artefact can specify a pick limit for an item. After being picked stipulated times, it is automatically deleted.

In order to support simple interaction, DroPicks provides a status bar icon for the user interface of N770 device (Figure 3). This way, when user is browsing the web and finds an interesting page, he only has to copy the address and click the icon. Immediately, a pop up window is provided to choose the receiver and provide further information if desired. Clicking ok finishes the item creation. For providing a tangible interface we utilize RFID technology. This method has been researched and found to be an effective and convenient way to access various services in the environment in e.g. [9]. RFID is used to trigger the interaction between internet terminal and the artefact while the actual communication, handshaking, negotiating on the device mode (drop/pick) etc. is done through Bluetooth. We have avoided Bluetooth for triggering purpose due to time-consuming discovery phase. The model is described in detail in [10]. Items picked get stored automatically in the local device, thus giving the user a firm choice of viewing the item right away or just collecting it for later usage.

Fig. 3. After the web address is copied, user presses the status bar icon. A pop up window is launched to allow adding some details to the content item being created. After finishing, the terminal is in drop mode and ready to deploy the just created item.

DroPicks provides ambient feedback to make the user feel and note the interaction with the environment. This is supported by the sentient artefacts. They are capable of playing sounds when an item is dropped or picked. Depending to the artefact, it can also be equipped with different LED kits and lighting capabilities as well. When something is available, it can blink or provide softer visual clue about the content.

In DroPicks content items are shared for one or many recipients that belong to the same group of content creator (Figure 4). Identifying users and managing the groups in the environment is enabled by a simple middleware called GOA. It handles all user related managing as well as privacy by handshaking and recognizing the users. Both the internet terminal and the sentient artefacts run GOA. When dropping or submitting an artefact, it contains recipient information. After the device makes a request, artefact returns an item if the requestor is allowed to obtain it. Each user of the systems has a unique identifier which is generated the first time they run GOA.

Fig. 4. User interfaces of DroPicks: views for displaying group environment and local content items. Through UI the user can e.g. create, delete, drop and edit items.

4 Implications

We performed an informal user trial with 10 participants aging from 25 to 29, all of them technical students and thus capable of understanding new technologies and systems and providing valid feedback. After introducing and demonstrating DroPicks, we let the users create and share contents freely.

In general, DroPicks got quite a deviated response. Definitely the main concern noticed was the difficulty to understand the overall concept of using sentient artefacts as digital memo boxes. Many of the testers misunderstood it or did not see the difference to instant messaging, e-mail and similar already available communication ways. The user interface issue seemed to rise also often. The internet tablet itself and DroPicks did not offer as convenient way to browse and create content as we hoped it would do. Users were already accustomised with their PCs or mobile phones which they use everyday for communications.

Users proposed that we should provide support for full synchronization with sentient artefacts and sharing full content instead of a URL. Also there was seen a need for categorizing the content stored. DroPicks was considered a useful system when dealing with privacy restricted use cases. It allows deploying personal memos in a public space. The system would also be free to use, since there wouldn't be any data packet costs over a commercial network. Avoiding physical notes and paper was considered a good thing also. Linking the digital content with physical artefacts was also an interesting and fresh functional aspect to testers.

Some of the ideas of DroPicks have been researched before. NuggetMine [11] is very similar to our concept of sharing metadata among group members. They provide a visual interface centered on desktops to share and browse small self-contained information among the group members utilizing a central server. DroPicks supports mobility and is independent of any centralized repository. In addition DroPicks' background appearance makes it more suitable for social contents. Forget-me-not [12] and Place-Its [4] are two of the earlier efforts to support location aware personal reminders. Stick-e Notes [3] project is perhaps the closest to our approach of tagging artefacts with digital notes as it explored the post-it metaphor as digital world rather than real world using GPS enabled PDA. DroPicks differs from these by being independent of any location-sensing infrastructure and utilizing only augmented artefacts for associating content with location, thus eliminating e.g. the need for GPS. However, DroPicks only works in Indoor facility unlike the above systems where coverage is broader.

5 Discussion and Conclusions

In the following, we discuss about characteristics of combining sentient artefacts and groupware into DroPicks and draw conclusions of the research done. Also limitations of DroPicks are addressed.

Privacy is one of the major concerns when considering notes, memos or any content. Take e.g. a post-it note: you cannot leave a personal message to someone's desk. With DroPicks we support personal messages which are tied to a location and context. When connection is established between the terminal and the artefact, the first thing done is handshaking where the identities of the participants are confirmed, thus enabling targeting the items.

Location restricted content sharing is introduced by utilizing sentient artefacts. Using sentient artefacts as location restricting element is not only highly accurate, but provides new and different kind of context information. The characteristics of each artefact can tell something about the type of content stored in it. Consider a normal household for example. With current technology it is possible to recognize someone's location in the house and build services accordingly as proven in many research projects. Sentient artefacts, on the other hand, make it possible to go a step further. They allow us to associate appropriate content with appropriate items with similar association or role. Content item stored on someone's workspace is most likely different by its nature than the one stored in a fridge or a night desk. Over time, a possible situation would be that certain type of content would find own home among our everyday objects in our house. It isn't hard to imagine a common area in a student dormitory equipped with augmented artefacts. People visiting there could share favorite entertainment online by leaving content items on the couch or shelf. This offers us the benefit of targeting the content to a narrower target group and reducing the overhead of sharing content to a group. Compare e.g. to posting an e-mail to whole company's e-mail list, out of which maybe only a fraction is interested in it.

Despite successfully working in our test environment, DroPicks realizes some limitations. As a pure P2P system, DroPicks does not have a centralized server or infrastructure to support functionality among different networks. Thus, it has to be run in the same network in order to e.g. support discovery of remote artefacts. Also, since DroPicks runs on Internet terminals, not all the advanced web functionalities are available. Furthermore, DroPicks depends on sentient artefacts which are primarily nonexistent in domestic environment.

We presented DroPicks, a sophisticated tool that utilizes groupware and sentient artefacts for sharing content in a collaborative environment. DroPicks shares content items that are designated for one or more recipients. We did not aim to share heavyweight content, but rather metadata or a personal memo. With the help of sentient artefacts, we achieved accurate location and contextual restriction for our content sharing scheme.

An informal user study was performed to gather feedback and ideas on the overall concept. We learned that the system's purpose was quite hard to understand, and it was hard to differentiate DroPicks from instant messaging or e-mail communication. Also, the interface was recognized to be somewhat too clumsy. However, many positive things could be found in DroPicks, such as using it when privacy is an issue and the nonexistent usage costs. It avoids the usage of physical memos and allows the user to narrow the target audience by the means of location restriction and utilizing sentient artefacts.

We have a lot of ideas and suggestions for improvement of DroPicks. Another aspect that we are investigating is the expressiveness of an artefact, i.e. how an artefact can be understood to have such storage features by the end users? We hope to address this and improve the system beyond current limitations in the future.

References

1. YouTube homepage:(accessed May 2007), http://www.youtube.com/
2. Flickr homepage:(accessed May 2007), http://www.flickr.com/
3. Brown, P.J.: The Stick-e Document: A Framework for Creating Context-Aware Applications, vol. 8(2&3), pp. 259–272. Electronic Publishing, Cologne University (1996)
4. Timothy, S., Kevin, A.L., Gunny, L., Ian, S., James, S., William, G.G.: Place-Its: A Study of Location-Based Reminders on Mobile Phones. In: Beigl, M., Intille, S.S., Rekimoto, J., Tokuda, H. (eds.) UbiComp 2005. LNCS, vol. 3660, pp. 232–250. Springer, Heidelberg (2005)
5. Kawsar, F., Fujinami, K., Nakajima, T.: Augmenting Everyday Life with Sentient Artefacts. In: sOc-EUSAI 2005. Proceedings of the joint conference on Smart objects and ambient intelligence: innovative context-aware services: usages and technologies (2005)
6. Kawsar, F., Fujinami, K., Nakajima, T.: Exploiting Passive Advantages of Sentient Artefacts. In: Youn, H.Y., Kim, M., Morikawa, H. (eds.) UCS 2006. LNCS, vol. 4239, pp. 270–285. Springer, Heidelberg (2006)
7. Fujinami, K., Kawsar, F., Nakajima, T.: AwareMirror: A Personalized Display using a Mirror. In: Proceedings of Pervasive Computing 2005, pp. 315–332 (2005)
8. Kawsar, F., Fujinami, K., Nakajima, T.: A lightweight indoor location model for sentient artefacts using sentient artefacts. In: Proceedings of the 2007 ACM symposium on Applied computing, ACM Press, New York (2007)
9. Riekki, J., Salminen, T., Alakärppä, I.: Requesting Pervasive Services by Touching RFID Tags. IEEE Pervasive Computing 5(1), 40–46 (2006)
10. Salminen, T., Hosio, S., Riekki, J.: Enhancing Bluetooth Connectivity with RFID. In: Proceedings of IEEE International Conference on Pervasive Computing and Communications, pp. 36–41. IEEE Computer Society Press, Los Alamitos (2006)
11. Goecks, J., Cosley, D.: NuggetMine: intelligent groupware for opportunistically sharing information nuggets. In: Proceedings of the 7th international conference on Intelligent user interfaces, pp. 87–94 (2002)
12. Lamming, M., Flynn, M.: Forget-me-not: Intimate Computing in Support of Human Memory. In: Proceedings of FRIEND21 1994, International Symposium on Next Generation Human Interface, pp. 125–128 (1994)

Place Recognition Using Multiple Wearable Cameras

Kyungmin Min, Seonghun Lee, Kee-Eung Kim, and Jin Hyung Kim

Korea Advanced Institute of Science and Technology,
373-1 Guseong-dong, Yuseong-gu, Daejeon, Korea
{kmmin, leesh, kekim, jkim}@ai.kaist.ac.kr

Abstract. Recognizing a user's location is the most challenging problem for providing intelligent location-based services. In this paper, we presented a real-time camera-based system for the place recognition problem. This system takes streams of scene images of a learned environment from user-worn cameras and produces the class label of the current place as an output. Multiple cameras are used to collect multi-directional scene images because utilizing multiple images yields better and robust recognition than a single image. For more robust recognition, we utilized spatial relationships between the places. In addition that, a temporal reasoning is incorporated with a Markov model to reflect typical staying time at each place. Recognition experiments, which were conducted in a real environment in a university campus, showed that the proposed method yields a very promising result.

Keywords: context recognition, place recognition, image understanding, wearable computing, hidden Markov models.

1 Introduction

Recognizing the situation of a user is an important problem for context aware intelligent services. Depending on the service to be provided, a user's context can be defined in various ways, such as location, current activity, physical state, and so on,. Among these, place information (a labeled location such as classroom, lobby, corridor, etc.) can be useful to provide various services such as mobility aids for the visually impaired [1], spatially-based notes and memory aids [2]. It can also be used as a basic feature to recognize high level contexts such as the user's current activity. For example, if we know a user is in a classroom, we may assume with high likelihood that he is attending a lecture.

Approaches for place recognition can be grouped into three categories; using a Global Positioning System (GPS), using Radio Frequency Identification (RFID) tags pre-attached on target places, and using sensors worn by the user. However, GPS has limited precision and only indoor availability. The RFID is also limited in the sense that we need to deal with the high setup cost of attaching a large number of tags in various places. Therefore, the approach based on user-mounted sensors is being actively pursued. Many kinds of sensors, such as microphones [3], accelerometers [4], and cameras [5] [6], can be used in this purpose. However, the image data from cameras is the most informative.

H. Ichikawa et al. (Eds.): UCS 2007, LNCS 4836, pp. 266–273, 2007.
© Springer-Verlag Berlin Heidelberg 2007

In this paper, we focus on developing a camera-based place recognition system. The goal of our system is to recognize the user's current place in real time when the user navigates in a known environment with attached cameras.

Even though images contain rich information, it is hard to utilize the information efficiently because the images are usually degraded by motion blur, change of illumination, and several other factors. Previous approaches used only one camera capturing images in the front direction [5] [6]. However, these approaches are subject to incorrect recognition whenever the front-directional image (i.e, the single source of information) is degraded by noise or does not contain unique features of a certain place.

To make the inference process more robust, temporal reasoning was adopted in a number of previous studies. It uses sequences of visited places up to the previous time to recognize the current place. It was modeled often with the 1st order Markov assumption [5] [6]. This modeling makes the computation simple by assuming only the first preceding place affects the current place. However, this assumption is not usually correct in the problem of place recognition.

In this paper, we propose two additional features to make up for the weak points of the previous camera-based approaches. The basic idea of each approach is as follows. The first one is to use multiple directional scene images obtained by using multiple cameras instead of single. With this, our system is able to recognize places more correctly. The second feature is to use information of staying time at a certain place for better temporal reasoning. In addition to the relationship between previous and current places, this temporal reasoning approach allows us to utilize better the map knowledge of target environment and, therefore, yields more robust recognition result.

The paper is organized as follows. Section 2 briefly describes the overview of the place recognition system and Section 3 explains the method of constructing the transition model. We validate in Section 4 the proposed method through the experiments conducted in the real environment and conclude in Section 5.

2 Place Recognition System Overview

The goal of the place recognition system is to determine the most likely current place from given image streams up to the current time. Our recognition system consists of learning module and recognition module. The learning module learns the transition probability and observation probability from the environment at the system development stage. The transition probability is the probability that the user moves from one place to another which is based on a given sequence of visited places up to the previous time step. The observation probability is the probability of a certain image to be observed in a given place. These two probabilities are combined as Hidden Markov Model (HMM) where the hidden nodes represent the user's place, the observation variables represent the captured image, and links represent the transition probabilities between nodes.

The recognition module performs real-time classification based on the models constructed by the learning module. The recognition module consists of a wavelet-based feature extractor and HMM-based classifier. The feature extractor uses the wavelet image decomposition method known as steerable pyramid [7]. By applying the steerable pyramid on the input image frame with four orientations and four scales, we got 16 decomposed images. To capture global image properties, we divided each decomposed image into 4x4 cells and take the mean of the feature values in the cell. Therefore we obtained 16 features per decomposed image and a total of 16x16=256 features per input image frame. By the principal component analysis, we finally obtained 80-dimensional feature vectors.

The observation probability for each directional image, $p(z_d|Q)$, is estimated with Parzen window method, a well-known non-parametric probability density estimation method. We used a Gaussian as the Parzen window function and the window size is obtained from several trials. With an assumption that every direction image is independent to each other, we obtain the observation probability of a set four images by multiplying the individual probabilities.

Then our recognition problem can be formulated as finding the maximal a posteriori probability place given image sequences with the trained HMM. Let Q_t denote the place label at t and $z_{1:t}$ denote image up to time t. Then, a posteriori probability is formulated as follows:

$$P(Q_t = q \mid z_{1:t}) \propto p(z_t \mid Q_t = q)P(Q_t = q \mid z_{1:t-1})$$

and   (1)

$$P(Q_t = q \mid z_{1:t-1}) = \sum P(Q_t = q \mid Q_{1:t-1})P(Q_{1:t-1} \mid z_{1:t-1})$$

where $p(z_t|Q_t=q)$ represents the observation probability of image z at place q at t and $P(Q_t=q|Q_{1:t-1})$ represents the transition probability to reach q. Since we already learned the observation probabilities with Parzen window method as described above, we only required to model the transition probability in order to solve this equation and obtain the posteriori probability.

3 Transition Modeling

In many problems using hidden Markov models, transition probability is learned from sample data because system designers usually do not have enough prior knowledge to construct the correct transition probability table. However, in the place recognition problem, the prior knowledge of the location of each place allows to clearly decide whether it is possible to move from current place to another. Therefore, we can build a robust model by determining transition probability along the prior knowledge rather than learning from sample data.

The probability of transition from the current place to the next place is determined by the possibility of the transition. The probability is set to zero when the next place is impossible to move from the current place. We assume that transitions to places reachable from the current place are equally likely.

To decide the validity of transition, we consider two kinds of constraints. First one states that a place transition can be occurred only between adjacent places. We call this constraint 'spatial constraint'. The second constraint states that to move to another place from current place, one must stay in current place at least some time periods. We call this constraint 'staying time constraint'.

In the next chapters, we will explain the concept of the constraints and discuss how to apply these constraints for solving this problem.

3.1 Spatial Constraint

In the real world, it is impossible for a user to be in a classroom just after appearing on the roof of the building. This is because there is a spatial constraint in the place transition. This means that within one time step, the user can either stay in the current place or move to adjacent place, but cannot move to non-adjacent places. To make the transition probability include this constraint, the neighborhood information between every pair of places is required. This information can be represented efficiently by using a graph structure, which is called place transition graph. It is defined as an undirected graph such that its nodes correspond to places and edges exist only between adjacent places.

Figure 1 shows an example of inferring the user's place using the spatial constraint. The map composed of lobby, corridor, lab and bathroom (Figure 1 (a)) is represented as the place transition graph (Figure 1 (b)). Then, even in the case that the current image features does not give enough information to decide whether the user is located in the corridor or the bathroom, the system could correctly decide the current place as the corridor by using the spatial constraint. (If the user was in the lab in the previous time step, he cannot be in the bathroom now because the lab and the bathroom is not connected) (Figure 1 (c)).

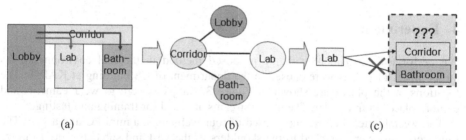

(a)   (b)   (c)

Fig. 1. Example of inference based on spatial constraint

3.2 Staying Time Constraint

As it is impossible to move between non-adjacent places directly, it is also impossible to move to a far place in a short time. For example, we can think of a situation that the user appears at 1st floor, stairs, and 2nd floor in 3 continuous time steps. If we only focus on the moving path, the path of '1st floor $\rightarrow$ stairs $\rightarrow$ 2nd floor' has no problem. However, in the real world, the situation is impossible because the staying time in stairs is too short to move from 1st floor to 2nd floor.

To summarize, it is impossible to move to a place and immediately move to another place again. In other words, it is possible to move to another place only after staying more than certain time periods in the current place. We will call this minimum staying time. After constructing a table of minimum staying time, we can decide invalid moving paths by comparing the staying time in a moving path to the minimum staying time.

Figure 2 shows an example of inference considering the staying time constraint. The table of minimum staying time (Figure 2 (b)) was constructed from the map of places (Figure 2 (a)). In this example, it is hard to distinguish lab and bathroom only with current image data and spatial constraint. However, by considering the staying time that the user came from lobby to corridor and stayed in 3 time steps, we reject the bathroom because the staying time is shorter than the minimum staying time in 'lobby → corridor → bathroom' path. And because the minimum staying time is longer than the minimum staying time of 'lobby → corridor → lab' path, we can select lab as the current place (Figure 2 (c)).

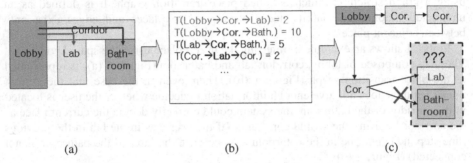

(a)   (b)   (c)

Fig. 2. Example of inference based on staying time constraint

4 Experiment

We performed experiment with the proposed method in the real environment. As target place, 11 places were chosen in the department of CS building at KAIST. The locations of the places are shown in Figure 3. Subjects were to wear cameras and explore places in free order. The image streams are used for training and testing.

The wearable test bed was composed of four web-cams, a mini PC and a vest. The four web-cams were attached to the shoulders of the vest and subjects were to move wearing the vest. This system allowed us to acquire images under realistic conditions while the user navigates the environment. In this way, 12,606 images for each direction, a total of 50,424 images were collected from six different subjects. 2~3 images per second were captured, and the size of each image was 320x240. We collected six image sequences from six subjects. We trained and evaluated the system by using 6-fold cross validation.

To analyze the effect of using multiple cameras, we evaluated the system twice; with using only one camera and with using four cameras. Similarly, to analyze the effect of considering two types of constraints in temporal reasoning, we performed evaluation for three cases; using no temporal reasoning, considering spatial constraint only, and considering both constraints. Figure 4 shows the recognition rate of the six experiments which differs in number of cameras used and types of constraints considered.

As we expected, using four cameras gave higher recognition rate than using only one. We could also find that considering more constraints in temporal reasoning gives higher recognition result. The proposed approach with four cameras considering both of the constraints recognized 90.91% of images correctly.

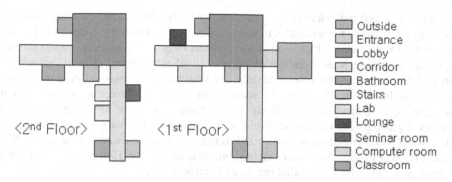

Fig. 3. Target places

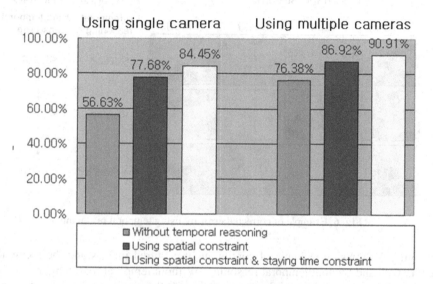

Fig. 4. Experimental result

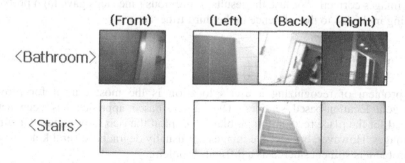

Fig. 5. Examples of corrected error by using multiple cameras

We confirmed the effect of four cameras by taking some examples from the data set. Figure 5 shows the examples of corrected misrecognition by using four direction cameras. In the case of bathroom images, when only the front image was used, the system recognized it as a seminar room instead of a bathroom. This is because the front direction scene image is common scene which can be observed in seminar room as well as bathroom. However, the scene images of other directions contain unique features of a bathroom, so the likelihood of bathroom is the larger than any other places. By comparing the sum of likelihoods of each image, bathroom got the highest likelihood and recognition was corrected. Images of stairs showed similar result. With only the front image, the system misrecognized it as outside. However, the result was corrected as stairs by considering the four direction images.

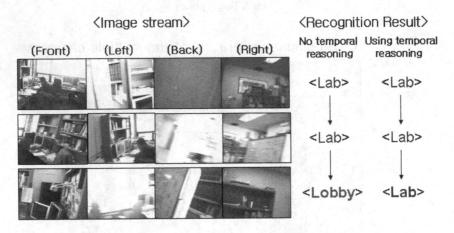

Fig. 6. Example of corrected error by using temporal reasoning

Figure 6 shows an example of continuously captured images and the recognition results with and without temporal reasoning. Without temporal reasoning, recognition result was incorrect in the third time step, though the results in the first and second time step were correct. However, with temporal reasoning, the system recognized all three images correctly because the results of previous time steps gave high probability of being in the lab to the inference in the third time step.

5 Conclusion

The problem of recognizing a user's location is the most crucial for providing intelligent location-based services. The camera-based approach has been actively pursued for the place recognition problem to exploit the rich information contained in the images. However, because the images are usually degraded several kinds of noise, the problem is still considered as a difficult problem.

In this work, we propose efficient methods for camera-based place recognition. In the proposed method, multiple cameras are used to collect multi-direction scene images. By using multi-direction images instead of single image, the system can recognize the place even if some images have insufficient information.

For more robust recognition, we utilized spatial relationships between the places. In addition that, a temporal reasoning is incorporated with a Markov model to reflect typical staying time at each place

Recognition experiments were conducted in 11 places in the real environment with both the previous method and the proposed method. The proposed approach recognized 90.91% of images correctly.

Acknowledgements

This research is supported by Ubiquitous Computing and Network (UCN) Project, the Ministry of Information and Communication (MIC) 21st Century Frontier R&D Program in Korea.

References

1. Loomis, J.M.R., Golledge, R.G., Klatzky, R.L., Speigle, J.M., Tietz, J.: Personal guidance system for the visually impaired. In: 1st annual ACM conference on Assistive Technologies, pp. 85–90. ACM Press, New York (1994)
2. Rhodes, B., Starner, T.: Remembrance agent: a continuously running automated information retrieval system. In: 1st International Conference on the Practical Application of Intelligent Agents and Multi Agent Technology, pp. 487–495 (1996)
3. Clarkson, B., Mase, K., Pentland, A.: Recognizing User Context via Wearable Sensors. In: 4th IEEE International Symposium on Wearable Computers, pp. 69–74. IEEE Press, Los Alamitos (2000)
4. Lee, S., Mase, K.: Activity and Location Recognition Using Wearable Sensors. Pervasive Computing 1(3), 24–32 (2002)
5. Torralba, A., Murphy, K.P., Freeman, W.T., Rubin, M.A.: Context-based vision system for place and object recognition. In: 9th IEEE Int'l Conf. on Computer Vision, vol. 1, pp. 273–280. IEEE Press, Los Alamitos (2003)
6. Li, F., Kosecka, J.: Probabilistic Location Recognition using Reduced Feature Set. In: IEEE Int. Conf. on Robotics and Automation, pp. 3405–3410. IEEE Press, Los Alamitos (2006)
7. Simoncelli, E.P., Freeman, W.T.: The steerable pyramid: a flexible architecture for multi-scale derivative computation. In: IEEE Int. Conf. on Image Processing, vol. 3, pp. 444–447. IEEE Press, Los Alamitos (1995)

Compact Data Format for Advertising and Discovery in Ubiquitous Networks

Pavel Poupyrev[1], Yoshihiro Kawahara[1], Peter Davis[2], and Hiroyuki Morikawa[1]

[1] Research Center for Advanced Science and Technology, The University of Tokyo
4-6-1, Komaba, Meguro-ku, Tokyo 153-8904, Japan
{pavel,kawahara,mori}@mlab.t.u-tokyo.ac.jp
[2] ATR Adaptive Communications Research Laboratories
2-2-2 Hikaridai, Keihanna Science City, Kyoto 619-0288, Japan
davis@atr.jp

Abstract. In this paper, we describe a packet data size minimization method designed specifically for advertising and discovery in ubiquitous networks. The minimization is effective for achieving superior discovery performance characteristics such as discovery time and power consumption. The proposed method for data packet size minimization is based on indexing of advertisement text. In the method, dictionaries and indexed data are stored separately, i.e. dictionaries are stored on a server and indexed data is stored on ubiquitous wireless devices, and the same dictionaries are shared among all users. We evaluate an average packet data size and dictionary size for three indexing methods: regular indexing, category indexing and attribute indexing; and show that these methods achieve data packet sizes which are about two and three times smaller than raw data packets and zipped packet data sizes respectively. Also, we show that category indexing allows users to be less dependent on the infrastructure.

Keywords: discovery system; service discovery; compact data format.

1 Introduction

Advertising and discovery [1] of information and services are essential elements of ubiquitous networks. Currently, a number of service discovery systems [21], [22] have been developed to provide an ability to discover and control services in proximity. Some systems allow a user to download a control panel to manage states of the service such as controlling illumination level in a room. These systems usually run on top of a TCP/IP protocol stack that assumes resource-rich devices, for instance personal computers or PDAs.

Other types of information discovery include systems for peer-to-peer social networks [2]-[7] which have recently received great attention. These systems use wireless computing devices which perform a limited set of functions including beacon transmissions and user alerts with LED blinks and sound beeps. One of the pioneer devices for information discovery in a social network is the Japanese Lovegetty [4]

H. Ichikawa et al. (Eds.): UCS 2007, LNCS 4836, pp. 274–289, 2007.

which allows a user to specify one of these tasks: 1) go out to eat, 2) go to karaoke, and 3) ready to do anything. When profiles of two proximate devices match, users are notified about the discovery.

In our laboratory, currently we are developing a similar type of discovery system with a wider scope of scenarios, such as accommodation search, product location, recipe discovery [6, 7]. For example, in the accommodation scenario, a wireless device is placed at the entrance of the apartment building for rent. The device constantly emits information that includes data such as the number of rooms, monthly payment, pets, etc. When a user comes in proximity he is automatically alerted if his preferences match to the received broadcast. In such scenarios, the number of wireless devices can be potentially large. Large amounts of information broadcast over a wireless channel will negatively affect discovery time and power consumption due to long transmission times and high collision rates.

In this paper, we present a method for data packet size minimization. The main principles of the method are 1) indexing advertisement text data, 2) the separation of dictionaries and indexed data and 3) sharing dictionaries among all users. In particular, the dictionaries are stored on a server while indexed data is stored on wireless devices. The compact data format preserves the ability of the device to perform matchmaking between the contents of a received advertisement and the preferences held in a discovery filter on the device.

We consider three methods for data indexing called regular indexing, category indexing and attribute indexing. We perform comparison of these methods using real data from Google-base; and show that the category indexing is the most favorable method. The category indexing method is most favorable because it allows a small dictionary and partial replication of the dictionary to a wireless device so that a mobile user becomes less dependent on infrastructure. Finally, we provide comparison of data packet sizes for the indexing methods with pre-processed and compressed data packet sizes. Throughout this paper, we define pre-processed data as the raw text data entered by a user, before it is modified to a compact data format. We show that the category indexing method provides significant data packet size minimization that is two times smaller than the data packet size received with zip compression and three times smaller than of the pre-processed data packet size.

The paper is organized as follows. Section 2 provides related works. In Section 3, we will describe the discovery model in ubiquitous networks. In Section 4, we will present the method for data size minimization. In Section 5, we perform an analysis of the proposed method and section 6 concludes our paper.

2 Related Work

An RFID system [14] is one example of a system in which data minimization makes it possible for a reader to discover a large number of tags within a short time. A good example of RFID tag format is an Electronic Product Code [15], or EPC, which is a globally-unique identifier. To ensure that each EPC is unique, EPCglobal (the organization driving standards for EPC) assigns each company a unique manager number. Each company is then responsible for assigning the other fields required by the encoding format being used. The main difference between tag format and our proposed format is that we use attribute-based data that makes it possible to perform matchmaking at the wireless device. In case of RFID systems, the matchmaking is done at the server that requires a user to be connected to the infrastructure every time when matchmaking is necessary.

A Bloom filter [16], [17] is a vector method for space-efficient membership queries. A system described in [18] proposes using Bloom filters for service discovery where a single vector stores a number of services. Due to its poor scalability, the Bloom filter is not appropriate for information discovery in large-scale ubiquitous networks. In order to decide the filter size the number of possible values must be known in advance. Since information in service discovery is dynamic, this makes usage of the Bloom filter difficult.

Bluetooth SDP [19] defines another format for service discovery in personal area networks. It is used mainly by professional developers who decide its format based on data size efficiency. In contrast, our method provides a general algorithm for converting data entered by a user to the compact data format.

Other service discovery systems such as those described in [21], [22] do not target issues of data size minimization. The main reason is that they operate on top of TCP/IP protocol stack which usually requires sophisticated hardware characteristics of the computer including large wireless bandwidth, memory and fast computing processors. If we want to use wireless devices which are resource-constrained we cannot afford using formats such as XML.

Another approach is to use compression tools such as zip utility [13] or XML document compressions [23]-[25]. The disadvantage of using compression tools is that they require additional computational power on resource-constrained wireless devices. Furthermore, we will show in the evaluation section that zip utility does not provide superior minimization results compared to the proposed method. In addition, XML compression tools fail to provide better compression because they obtain higher compression due to the XML document structure, i.e. indexing tag name values which usually have high occurrence. The ideal data size for discovery in ubiquitous networks is usually a few hundred bytes. Therefore, XML compression tools will not gain extra compression compared to data packet sizes obtained with zip utility.

3 Discovery System Overview

3.1 Discovery Model

Consider the scenario in which a user seeks recipes advertised by wireless devices, which include short range radio transceivers, controllers and data storage. In the recipe scenario, advertising devices are either installed in public places, such as cafes, book stores, or carried by mobile users in their pockets. Recipe advertisements stored on devices contain information such as recipe title, cuisine type and ingredients. Other mobile devices are pre-configured with recipe preferences using one or more recipe attributes.

The discovery model consists of five modes: 1) data initialization, 2) wireless data exchange, 3) data matchmaking, 4) discovery alert, and 5) data access.

First, both advertiser and discoverer perform *data initialization* of a wireless device for either advertisement or discovery. Considering the recipe scenario, one user configures a wireless device to advertise available recipes and another user configures a device with recipe preferences.

Second, after the data has been initialized, the *wireless data exchange* process begins with wireless devices sending either queries or advertisements over a wireless channel. There are two types of discoveries: push type and pull type. The first type is when a user configures a device to broadcast advertisements and the latter is when a user broadcasts a query. The discovery type selection is done during initialization mode.

Third, the *data matchmaking* process matches all received broadcast packets with the locally stored data. When a wireless device receives a query, a matchmaking engine compares it with locally stored advertisements. Similarly, when a wireless device receives an advertisement, the matchmaking engine compares received advertisements with locally stored preferences. Thus, the matchmaking engine provides a function that takes an advertisement and preferences as parameters, and returns a comparison result in the form of a true or false value.

Fourth, in the *discovery alert* process, if a matchmaking function returns a true result after comparison, a wireless device locally saves the discovered information and notifies the user about discovery using audio or visual effects.

Fifth, in the *data access* process, after the user is notified about the discovery, the user accesses detailed information about the discovered resource and makes a decision whether to contact the advertiser or not.

3.2 System Components and Their Functionality

The main component in the advertising and discovery system is a wireless device. We developed a prototype wireless device called Buoy (Fig 2). It consists of two modules: wireless and add-on modules. The wireless module comprises of 110 mAh

Fig. 1. Buoy: wireless advertising and discovery device

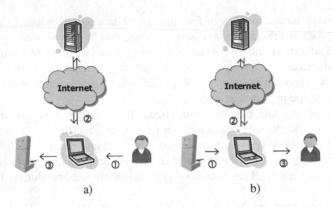

Fig. 2. Discovery modes: a) data initialization mode and b) data access mode

rechargeable battery, a Chipcon CC1000 wireless chip, Atmel ATmega 128L microcontroller, and 315 Mhz antenna. The add-on module includes button, two LEDs, buzzer and Infrared port. It is important to note that the user does not need to have any additional devices, such as a cellular phone or PDA, during discovery. However, the device can also be equipped with other interfaces that allow it to be used in conjunction with a personal computer or a cellular phone.

There have been previous proposals for advertising and discovery methods. For example, [9] proposes the introduction of proxies, which gather information about available services from neighboring wireless devices. To discover a service, a mobile user queries a proxy which provides a user with a list of services. The disadvantage of such a solution is that it requires costly installation of proxies in public places and poses maintenance issues. Other solutions, such as [10] and [11], suggest distribution of service information so that nodes cache services of the neighboring nodes in its local database which allows a user to discover services from nodes other than a source. Solutions based on service caching require extra memory and computational power for caching algorithms.

In general, any heavy computation on resource-constrained wireless devices should be avoided. Hence, in our discovery system, we assume a primitive wireless device such as Buoy which performs simple computations including data matchmaking, notification alerts, and data broadcasts. In our discovery model, we use infrastructure only in the following modes: data initialization and discovered data access. We believe that pre-configuring wireless devices using infrastructure provides a more powerful solution since a server has sufficient computing power and large data storage.

During data initialization mode, a user enters data for discovery or advertisement using a personal computer, PDA or cellular phone. The client device has two communication interfaces (Fig. 2a): one is to connect to the server through the Internet and another is to exchange data with a wireless device. The entered data is sent to the server which converts it to the compact data format. Then, the compact data is sent back to the client computer and passed to the wireless device for storage in its local database. After a wireless device is initialized, it can discover or advertise itself without assistance from infrastructure or client computer. The user will be alerted with when a device discovers information that matches user preferences.

During data access mode, the user accesses detailed information at the server. This is necessary because compact data used by wireless devices does not contain full information about the advertised item. – it contains only information necessary for matchmaking. For example, information such as images and contact information is not included in the packet. Connection of the wireless device to the client computer is necessary should the user decide to obtain more information (Fig. 2b). After the discovered reference ids are downloaded from the wireless device to the client computer the user retrieves detailed information from the server using those ids (Fig. 2b).

In general, usage of servers is inconvenient since it requires a node to be connected to the infrastructure. However, the minimization method requires a wireless device to be connected to the infrastructure only during data initialization and data access modes, which is usually occasional. Most of the time devices operate autonomously sending/receiving packets and perform matchmaking without relying on any infrastructures.

4 Data Minimization

We assume that pre-processed data has a structured format similar to that used in other service discovery systems to describe a service [21], [22]. The structured format is specified with its attributes – each attribute is represented with its name, type and value.

The data minimization is based on the following three principles: 1) indexing of text data on word basis, 2) separate storage of dictionaries and indexed data, and 3) all users using the same dictionaries. The assignment of indexes on the basis of words, instead of a set of characters, is motivated by the fact that it is necessary to perform matchmaking of advertisements and filters. Therefore, wireless devices compare word indexes only. Using words for indexing purpose is acceptable because users usually specify a search query with keywords instead of a set of characters. Dictionaries are stored on the server while indexed data is stored on wireless devices. This is because wireless nodes can perform matchmaking using only indexed data, independent of dictionaries. It is important that conversion of text data is accomplished using common dictionaries for all users, otherwise matchmaking will not be possible.

A simple example of data conversion to the compact data format is presented in Fig. 3. The pre-processed data shown in Fig. 3a represents a recipe advertisement and its compact representation can be seen in Fig. 3b. The pre-processed data contains category name, attribute names, types and values. These are each converted to numbers in the compact representation.

It is important to note that indexing of category name, attribute names and attribute types is different from indexing of attribute values. For example, the attribute value "beef curry" is represented by two indexes, one for each word. On the other hand, attribute names are assigned a single index for each representation.

category: recipes		
name	type	value
title	text	beef curry
cuisine	text	indian
course	text	main
expired	date	07/1/1

⇨

category id: 266		
name id	type id	value
1	3	1, 2
2	3	3
3	3	4
4	4	356

a)   b)

Fig. 3. Data format a) pre-processed data and b) compact data

There are a number of different methods for indexing. In the example in Fig. 3, a single dictionary is used to assign indexes to all words within "recipes" category. We call this method *category indexing*. There are two other methods for text indexing called *regular indexing* and *attribute indexing*. The regular indexing uses only a single dictionary for all categories. The attribute indexing uses a single dictionary for each attribute. In the analysis section, we will evaluate these methods in terms of average data packet size and dictionary size.

4.1 Text Type Conversion

Indexing of category, attribute name and attribute type is straightforward. However, before indexing attribute value the text must be modified. This is because text can have characters, such as punctuation characters, which are not used in the matchmaking process. For example, a user must be able to query data such as "(soup)" and "soup" equally. In other words, these values must use the same index of the word "soup". In addition, we separate words which represent a combination of characters and digits. For example, the text "soup23" will be divided in two words "soup" and "23" so that a user can query the text by using the index of the word "soup".

Before assigning indexes to words in the text we modify text as follows. First, all text is converted to the lower case letters. Second, characters other than English characters and digits are replaced by spaces. Then, all words which are a combination of digits and English characters are separated by spaces. Thus, the text includes only words which consist of either only English characters or digits. The following flowchart shows an example of the procedure for modifying the text "Thin-crusted pizza (pt2)" before indexing:

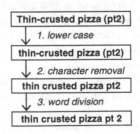

The text is indexed by extracting each word separated by spaces. The conversion of text is done in the following way. First of all, a word that consists only of digits is not added to the dictionary. Otherwise, the length of the word is compared with the length of the maximum index of the dictionary. If the index size has the same length as a word, the word is not added to the dictionary. If a word already exists in the dictionary, its frequency counter is increased by one. Otherwise, the word is added to the dictionary and assigned the incremented maximum index of the dictionary.

For example, words from "thin crusted pizza pt 2" will be added to the dictionary as follows:

word	index	frequency
...		
pizza	391	6
...		
crusted	697	2
...		
thin	1494	1

In the example, the word "thin" is a new word which has not been previously added. Therefore, the word "thin" is allocated the incremented maximum index in the dictionary. On the other hand, two words, "pizza" and "crusted", have been previously added to the dictionary. Hence, their frequency counters are increased by one. The word "pt" is not indexed because the maximum index that is equal to 1495 requires two bytes of memory that is the same length of word "pt". Also, the word "2" is not added to the dictionary because the word is a number.

After indexes are assigned to the words, the text value can be represented in compact format using the indexes. For example, the representation of "Thin-crusted pizza (pt2)" text will be as follows:

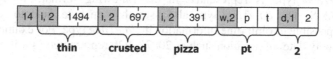

The first byte represents the length of the whole text value. The length byte is always one byte long that allows having the text value of 255 byte long. The rest of the data contains words of the text – each word consists of a *parameter byte* and a word value. The parameter byte includes information about the word length and word type. The word type is a format in which a word is stored. There are three possible word types: index, word and digit types. For example, the word "thin" has an index type, the word "pt" has a word type and "2" has a digit type. Therefore, the first two bits of the parameter byte represent a word type and the other six bits represent the length of the value. As a result the compact data size of the text "Thin-crusted pizza (pt2)" is fourteen bytes long compared to its original size of twenty four bytes.

It is important to emphasize that restoring indexed data to its original format is unnecessary because indexed data is used only for matchmaking between an advertisement and a filter. In other words, indexed data loses original contents but preserves matchmaking capabilities. If a user needs the original data it can be accessed on the server.

4.2 Other Type Conversion

Besides text type, we also allow other types such as *Boolean*, *int*, *float*, *intUnit*, *floatUnit*, *dateTime* and *dateTimeRange*. These types are the same as the ones used in Google-base [12]. Instead of storing them in text format, we store them in binary representation.

We use variable data length for most types so that data format includes one byte field which represent the length of the value. Variable length gives the benefit of having large data size up to 255 bytes.

The *int* type is represented by two fields: one byte length field and binary integer value. The sign of integer is represented by the first bit in the first byte of the value. For example, the value 275 has the following format:

2	275

The *float* type is represented by two parts: an integral portion and a fractional portion. Each of this part is represented by one byte length field and its value in the similar way to the integer type. For example, a *float* value of 5.275 will have the following representation:

1	5	2	275

intUnit and *floatUnit* types include value and unit name. In order to preserve more memory space, we also convert unit names to indexes. For example, "5.275 hours", assuming that "hours" has an index equal to seven, will have the following representation:

1	5	2	275	1	7

The *dateTime* type is represented in the following format: YYYY/MM/DD-HH:MM:SS.MS. The *dateTime* type also uses the one byte field to represent the length. It is possible to omit time information in *dateTime* type. For example, this type can contain only date information such as 2007/03/20 represented as follows:

4	2007	3	20

Finally, *dateTimeRange* is stored as a combination of two values of *dateTime* type.

There are a number of other efficient ways of defining data formats. But we will show in the evaluation section that attribute data of these types do not significantly affect data packet size. In particular, we will show that indexing of text type attribute presented in Section 4.1 is most important for achieving significant data minimizations.

4.3 Data Packet Format

An example of data packet format is presented in Fig 4. The first byte is an info byte which contains information about three settings:

1. Whether the packet is an advertisement or query;
2. Whether the packet must be broadcast;
3. The number of sub-categories.

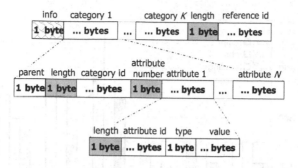

Fig. 4. Data packet format

The first two bits of the info byte represent the first two settings while the other six bits represent the third setting. The third setting is necessary to allow having tree-structured data in the packet that includes a top category and sub-categories.

After the info byte, the packet contains data of each category/subcategory. Each category block has the same format which includes the following data fields: parent, category id, attribute number and attributes. The parent field represents the parent id of the category. In case of the top category, this value equals zero. The category id consists of one byte length and id value. Finally, an attribute number represents the number of attribute values. Consequently, each attribute includes an attribute id which consists of one byte length and value. Other parameters of the attribute include its type and value in which the type field has length of one byte and the value field has the format described in the earlier subsection. The rest of the packet includes information about reference id used for resource look-ups at the server. Similarly, the reference id is defined as one byte length field and its value.

It is important to note that here we consider only the format for advertisement packets. The query packets will have different format. In particular, values of attributes will have additional information on operators such as "<", ">", "=", etc.

5 Analysis

In this section, we present evaluation of average data packet size for the described indexing methods and we compare average data packet sizes with pre-processed data and compressed data sizes. In addition, we will analyze cost of using infrastructure and cost of running compression tools on resource-constraint wireless devices.

5.1 Data Packet Size

Since results for the average data packet size heavily depend on data content, we perform evaluation using real data. In our analysis, we use real data retrieved from Google-base [12] that contains attribute-based data used for searching web content in the Internet. Google-base associates a number of attributes with a web page available on the Internet. New items can be easily added to the Google-base database through either Google user interface or customized software developed with Google-base API.

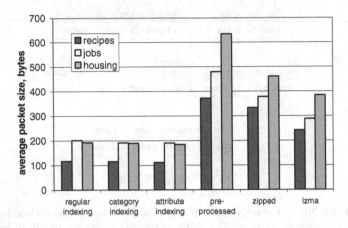

Fig. 5. Average data packet size of individual category for 1) regular indexing data, 2) category indexing data, 3) attribute indexing data, 4) pre-processed data, 5) zipped data and 6) lzma-compressed data

We used Google-base data because it provides similar data sets used for discovery in ubiquitous networks. An interesting characteristic of Google-base is that it allows having unlimited number of attributes for the specific category – giving a user freedom to define new properties for an existing category. Using Google-base API, we downloaded 50,000 items for each of three categories including "recipes", "jobs" and "housing". The data types in our system have the same data types as those used in Google-base. However, Google-base defines two additional types *url* and *location* which are omitted from our analysis. This is because *url* type provides unnecessary information which is not used in matchmaking process while *location* type is unnecessary since a wireless device broadcasting data locally has location defined implicitly by its transmission range.

In our first experiment, we evaluate average data packet sizes for the three indexing methods: regular indexing, category indexing and attributes indexing. In addition, we evaluate average data packet sizes for pre-processed data, zipped data and *lzma*-compressed data. In Fig 5, we can see results of average data packet size for all cases. We can see that the difference in average data packet size for different indexing methods is insignificant. For example, category indexing and attribute indexing methods provide improvements of only 2% and 4.5% respectively compared to the regular indexing. The word index size is related to the number of dictionaries that a method uses. A larger number of dictionaries allow a smaller index size. For example, the attribute indexing uses a larger number of dictionaries, which results in smaller index size compared to the other methods. However, we can see from the results that using smaller indexes does not provide significant improvement on data packet size. To evaluate packet sizes for pre-processed data, we represented each advertisement as text which includes a category name, a number of attributes and reference id as follows:

category;
name1,type1,value1;
name2,type2,value2;
...
reference_id;

To evaluate average packet size of compressed data we use two compression utilities, *zip* and *lzma* [13]. Using these utilities we compressed the pre-processed data by setting compression ratio to the maximum level to achieve maximum compression results.

In Fig 5, we can see that indexing methods provide the smallest packet data size compared to the pre-processed and compressed data. The average packet size for any of indexing methods is almost three times smaller than the pre-processed packet data size and twice smaller than zipped packet data size. Also, we observed an interesting fact that zip utility does not achieve compression gain for pre-processed data sizes smaller than 350 bytes. In fact, compression of smaller data results in larger data sizes. On the other hand, *lzma* utility achieves compression gain for data packet sizes above 50 bytes.

We achieved such compression results since advertisement data downloaded from Google typically contain a lot of text data. We evaluated the occurrence of data types in Google-base represented in Table 1:

Table 1. Data Type Occurrence

	text	int	dateTime	others
recipes	77%	12%	10%	1%
jobs	84%	6%	8%	2%
housing	70%	13%	5%	12%

We can see that on average 77% of attributes have text type. That means that other types such as *float* and *int* do not really affect the overall data packet size. In particular, data in the table shows the importance of indexing text values in order to achieve smaller data packet sizes.

5.2 Indexing and Compression Method Costs

In the previous subsection, we compared average data packet size for different methods. It is also important to compare the cost of methods since they have different requirements on the systems. For instance, indexing methods require presence of a server which performs indexing while compression method does not rely on the server but requires extra computational power from a wireless discovery device. Hence, we discuss cost of using infrastructure and cost of using compression tool on resource-constraint devices such as Buoy.

The disadvantage of using infrastructure is that a user must be connected to the infrastructure to configure a wireless device for discovery or advertisement. Users initializing their device create workload on the server. However, the workload is negligible due to two factors including: 1) we assume that device initialization is infrequent and 2) the average size of advertisement is about 500 bytes, which will not

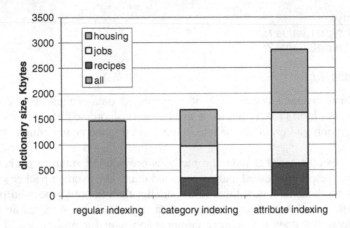

Fig. 6. Dictionary sizes for three methods 1) regular indexing, 2) category indexing and 3) attribute indexing

create heavy workload on the server even with a large number of users initializing their devices. Therefore, we focus on how a user can avoid using infrastructure and so increase usability of the system. In particular, a simple method is to replicate dictionary data on the mobile user device. That would be possible only if dictionaries provide relatively small sizes so that a user can create an advertisement or a filter without contacting the server.

Fig 6 presents dictionary sizes for three methods. We can see that dictionary sizes for regular indexing and category indexing have about the same size. On the other hand, the dictionary size for attribute indexing is almost twice as large as dictionary size for regular indexing. The reason for this is that attribute indexing uses a larger number of dictionaries (a single dictionary for each attribute) that, in turn, results in a larger number of repeated words. In comparison, category indexing and regular indexing have almost the same dictionary size, which shows that dictionaries of category indexing have fewer numbers of repeated words. Therefore, regular indexing or category indexing are favorable methods for a service discovery system because they provide small dictionary sizes. Comparing the category and regular indexing methods, we recommend using category indexing because this method allows partial dictionary replication according to user preferences. For example, if a user wants to discover only "recipes" advertisements the user replicates only the "recipes" dictionary to his mobile device in the case of the category indexing method. The "recipes" dictionary size for category indexing is about 350 bytes (Fig 6). On the other hand, if the system uses regular indexing the user must replicate the whole dictionary which has much larger size that is 1.5 Mb. The current mobile devices have sufficient memory to store dictionaries for category indexing and regular indexing methods. For instance, PDAs and cellular phones have memory over 16-32 Mbytes. It is important to note that the replication method will not work when a user tries to specify a word which is not in the dictionary. In this case, a user must connect to the infrastructure so that the server allocates an index to the new word.

We also evaluated the cost of using compression tool on a wireless device such as Buoy. To do that, we downloaded a source code written in C for *lzma* compression utility [13] designed specifically to work on portable devices such as PDA and compress data which has small data sets of about a few hundreds of bytes. We could see that *lzma* provides better compression results than zip. For the Buoy device, we implemented only the decompression function since decompression can be done on the cellular phone or PDA. Decompression on Buoy is important since the Buoy device upon packet reception should decompress received packet and perform matchmaking. Since Buoy runs service discovery software which requires 43 bytes of memory we added decompression functionality to it. After completion of the program with decompression capability, the program size became 57 bytes, giving an increase of 14 Kbytes. This program fits on the ATMega 128L processor which provides 128 Kbytes of flash memory. However, we could not run simultaneously service discovery software and decompression functionality because they require a total of 6.5 Kbytes of memory (3 Kbytes for service discovery software and 3.5 Kbytes for decompression). Since ATMega 128L has only 4 Kbytes of RAM, in order to understand the decompression speed we removed the service discovery software. Our experiments with data decompression on the Buoy device showed a decompression speed of about 24,000 bps. For example, if Buoy receives a packet of 305 bytes, then the decompression will take 102 milliseconds. This gives quite long decompression time which may result in missing some packets in device-crowded areas.

6 Conclusions

In this paper, we described a data packet size minimization method for advertising and discovery in ubiquitous networks. The method is based on three principles: 1) text type data indexing, 2) storing dictionaries and indexed data separately and 3) sharing the same dictionaries among all users. We described three indexing methods which include regular, category and attribute indexing. We outlined a compact packet data format used by wireless devices to advertise and discover information in ubiquitous networks.

In order to evaluate the average data packet size and dictionary size for different indexing methods we used Google-base data represented by attribute-based descriptors. The results showed that the difference in average data packet sizes among indexing methods is insignificant. Also, we presented a comparison of the average data packet sizes with pre-processed data and compressed data. The results showed that indexing methods provide reduction in data packet sizes by two and three times compared to pre-processed and zipped packet data sizes respectively. We also analyzed cost of infrastructure and cost of using a decompression tool on resource-constrained devices. We showed that it is possible to make the system to be less dependable on infrastructure by replicating dictionaries on the mobile devices. We also showed that decompression tool requires extra resources such as RAM and processing time to decompress data. Since additional RAM increases the cost of the device as well as power consumption during decompression we believe that using the indexing method to represent data for service discovery will provide better performance compared to using compressed data.

Acknowledgments. This work was supported by the Ministry of Internal Affairs and Communications.

References

1. Akyildiz, I.F., Weilian, S., Sankarasubramaniam, Y., Cayirci, E.: A survey on sensor networks. IEEE Commun. Mag. 40(8), 102–114 (2002)
2. Borovoy, R., McDonald, M., Martin, F., Resnick, M.: Things that blink: computationally augemented name tags. IBM Systems Journal 35(3-4), 488–495 (1996)
3. Borovoy, R., et al.: Meme tags and community mirrows: moving from cnferences to collaboration. In: Proc. of ACM Conf. Computer Supported Cooperative Work, pp. 159–169 (1998)
4. McCrone, J.: You buzzing me? New Scientist, 20–23 (2000)
5. Laibowwitz, M., Gips, J., Aylward, R., Pentland, A., Paradiso, J.A.: A sensor network for social dynamics. In: Proc. of Conf. on Information processing in sensor networks, pp. 483–491 (2006)
6. Poupyrev, P., Davis, P., Morikawa, H.: TinyObj: A Framework for Service discovery in Ubiquitous Environments. In: Dourish, P., Friday, A. (eds.) UbiComp 2006. LNCS, vol. 4206, Springer, Heidelberg (2006)
7. Poupyrev, P., Sasao, T., Surawatari, S., Davis, P., Morikawa, H., Aoyama, T.: Service Discovery in TinyObj: Strategies and Approaches. In: Gellersen, H.-W., Want, R., Schmidt, A. (eds.) PERVASIVE 2005. LNCS, vol. 3468, pp. 34–39. Springer, Heidelberg (2005)
8. Madden, S., Franklin, M.J., Hellerstein, J.: TAG: A tiny aggregation service for ad-hoc sensor networks. In: Proc. of 5th Simposium on Operating Systems Design and Implementation, pp. 131–146 (2002)
9. Klein, M., Konig-Ries, B., Obreiter, P.: Service Rings - a Semantic Overlay for Service Discovery in Ad Hoc Networks. In: Mařík, V., Štěpánková, O., Retschitzegger, W. (eds.) DEXA 2003. LNCS, vol. 2736, pp. 180–185. Springer, Heidelberg (2003)
10. Chakraborty, D., Joshi, A., Finin, T., Yesha, Y.: GSD: A novel groupbased service discovery protocol for MANETS. In: MWCN 2002. Proc. of 4th IEEE Conf. on Mobile and Wireless Communications Networks, pp. 3165–3182 (2002)
11. Ratsimor, O., Chakraborty, D., Tolia, S., Kushraj, D., Kunjithapatham, A., Gupta, G., Joshi, A., Finin, T.: Allia: Alliance-based service discovery for ad-hoc environments. In: Proc. of ACM Mobile Commerce Workshop, pp. 1–9 (2002)
12. Google-base (2007), http://base.google.com/
13. 7-zip compression tool (2007), http://www.7-zip.org/
14. Finkenzeller, K.: RFID Handbook. John Wiley & Sons, New York (1999)
15. Sarma, S., Brock, D., Engels, D.: Radio Frequency Identification and the Electronic Product Code. IEEE Mag. Micro 21(6), 50–54 (2001)
16. Bloom, B.: Space/time tradeoffs in hash coding with allowable errors. CACM 13(7), 422–426 (1970)
17. Broder, A., Mitzenmacher, M.: Network applications of Bloom filters: A survey. In: Proc. of the 40th Annual Allerton Conference on Communications, Control, and Computing, pp. 636–646 (2002)
18. Sailhan, F., Issarny, V.: Scalable Service Discovery for MANET. In: PerCom 2005. Proc. of Third IEEE Int. Conf. on Pervasive Computing and Communications, pp. 235–244 (2005)

19. Bluetooth Consortium, Specification of the bluetooth system core version 1.0b, Service Discovery Protocol (1999)
20. Avancha, S., Joshi, A., Finin, T.: Enhanced service discovery in Bluetooth. IEEE Computer 35(6), 96–99 (2002)
21. Sun micosystems, Jini architecutre specification 2.0 (2003)
22. Guttman, E., Perkins, C.: Service Location Protocol (1999)
23. Liefke, H., Suciu, D.: XMill: An Efficient Compressor for XML Data. In: Proc. of the ACM SIGMOD Intl. Conf. on Management of Data, pp. 153–164. ACM Press, New York (2000)
24. Min, J.-K., Park, M.-J., Chung, C.-W.: XPRESS: A Queriable Compression for XML data. In: Proc. Int. Conf. of Management of Data, ACM SIGMOD, pp. 122–133 (2003)
25. Tolani, P.M., Haritsa, J.R.: XGRIND: A query-friendly XML compressor. In: ICDE 2002. Proc. of 18th Int. IEEE Conf. on Data Engineering, pp. 225–234 (2002)

A Media Access Protocol for Proactive Discovery in Ubiquitous Wireless Networks

Pavel Poupyrev[1], Peter Davis[2], and Hiroyuki Morikawa[1]

[1] Research Center for Advanced Science and Technology, The University of Tokyo
4-6-1, Komaba, Meguro-ku, Tokyo 153-8904, Japan
{pavel,mori}@mlab.t.u-tokyo.ac.jp
[2] ATR Adaptive Communications Research Laboratories,
2-2-2 Hikaridai, Keihanna Science City, Kyoto 619-0288, Japan
davis@atr.jp

Abstract. A MAC protocol is proposed for proactive discovery in which wireless devices periodically broadcast packets containing presence or service information. The protocol is based on Framed Aloha and is designed to allow discovery of all neighbors within a specified time using the minimum broadcast rate. Numerical simulations are used to show that the protocol is able to assure specified discovery time in distributed networks with random topology.

Keywords: MAC protocol, discovery, Framed Aloha, ubiquitous networks.

1 Introduction

The use of short-range wireless transmissions for local sensing and discovery [1] is a basic function in ubiquitous networks. It is an ongoing technical challenge to achieve good performance of short-range wireless transmissions in ubiquitous network environments with various application requirements and increasingly large numbers and varieties of devices. Hence it is important to design and develop MAC protocols which are tuned to the needs of emerging new classes of applications.

In this paper we propose a protocol which is designed for efficient discovery in ubiquitous networks. Discovery in ubiquitous networks constitutes a common problem in which users want to discover resources and services within their vicinity as they move from one place to another [2]-[6]. One application scenario for the proposed protocol is shop advertising in which devices installed in shops broadcast discount information, which may also include discount coupons. Another application scenario is a friend-finder application in which users discover broadcasts from nearby friends corresponding to entries in their address books. In these scenarios, devices which are physically close-enough to receive the local radio transmissions automatically check the broadcast data to see whether it matches the user's criteria. If it does, the user is alerted about the discovery. In these scenarios, it is important to assure time-bounded discovery of neighbors.

H. Ichikawa et al. (Eds.): UCS 2007, LNCS 4836, pp. 290–297, 2007.

In the design of the protocol, the discovery time parameter is considered to be a key parameter. The discovery time parameter is the time within which a node should discover all its neighbors with high probability. Another key consideration of the protocol design is to make the packet transmission rate as low as possible. The reason for this is that power saving is an important requirement for battery-operated devices in ubiquitous networks. Power savings can be realized if nodes use lower packet transmission rates, since they can send fewer packets and they can spend more time in sleep mode. However, the actual discovery time can be largely affected by the number of transmitting devices. A method is needed to reliably determine the minimum transmission rate which can assure a specified discovery time. Previous works have analyzed packet collisions to find an optimum transmission rate which provides the fastest discovery time [7]-[10]. However, these works have not targeted issues of determining the minimal transmission rate to provide discovery *within a given time* in *distributed networks*.

This paper proposes a new protocol for discovery within a given time in distributed networks based on Framed Aloha [7]-[10] in which the time is slotted and grouped in frames. We present an algorithm for determining a frame size which allows discovery within a given time, considering packet collisions. The algorithm uses a formula for frame size which depends on neighbor density. The formula is derived assuming a compact network where all nodes are within transmission range of each other. We also show that by using the maximum number of neighbors among neighbors as the density parameter, the protocol works well in non-compact, distributed networks with random topology.

The paper is organized as follows: In Section 2 we provide an overview of the protocol. Section 3 presents evaluation results for compact and distributed networks respectively. In Section 4 we discuss related works.

2 Protocol Design

In this section we describe the proposed protocol and the derivation of the frame size formula which is used to dynamically adapt the packet broadcast rate to ensure the performance of the protocol is satisfactory in networks with varying node density.

The protocol is based on Framed Aloha [7]-[10] in which the time is slotted and grouped in frames. The basic procedure for transmitting a packet in each frame is summarized as follows: 1) update neighbor density parameter D, 2) update frame size m, 3) choose random slot, and 4) transmit packet.

Fig. 1 shows an example of the use of the protocol by three nodes A, B and C. Each node broadcasts one packet once in every frame. The slot is chosen randomly in each frame. When nodes accidentally chose the same slot, their broadcast packets collide and are lost. Hence it may take more than one frame to successfully transmit and receive one packet for each node. We make the following assumptions: 1) the broadcast data fits into one single broadcast packet, 2) each node repeatedly broadcasts the same data, 3) all nodes are synchronized (time slot synchronization), 4) values of two key control parameters, discovery time and assurance probability, are common to all nodes.

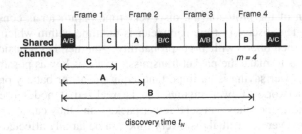

Fig. 1. An example showing discovery of broadcasts from *N=3* nodes (A, B, and C) using Framed Aloha with frame size *m=4* slots

The selection of frame size *m* is based on three parameters: the density parameter *D*, the assurance level α, and the specified discovery time *T*. The values of parameters α and *T* are constants and predefined in the system and the parameter *D* is variable. The *discovery time T* represents the time required to discover all neighbors with probability greater than the value of the *assurance level* α. The introduction of assurance level α is important because of wireless collisions. The assurance level α is formally defined as a cumulative distribution function $f_\alpha(N, T, m) = P(t<T: N, m)$ which represents the probability for the time *t* of a single discovery event in a compact network to take a value less than or equal to *T* when the number of neighbors is *N* and the frame size is *m*.

It is important to note that this paper considers only local discovery based on direct broadcasts. That is, nodes do not relay information broadcast by other nodes.

We also note that in this paper we do not consider the issue of synchronization of time slots. One method to synchronize slots is to use GPS. This is expected to become increasingly more practical as GPS devices become cheaper. Considerations of synchronization and analysis of its effect on discovery are left for future work.

2.1 Density Determination

The parameter *D* represents the density of the transmitting nodes in the network. In the case of compact networks, this simply corresponds to the number *N* of active neighbors within wireless transmission range. More generally, it is taken to be N_{max}, the maximum value of *N* for a node and its neighbors. In following sections, we will describe a practical procedure for estimation of the parameter *D*.

Fig. 2a presents an example of the compact network case topology in which all nodes are within transmission range of each other. The parameter *D* in compact networks is just the number of neighbors *N*. The procedure for obtaining the number of neighbors *N* is as follows: each node includes its unique id in the header of the packet, which it transmits repeatedly. Upon a packet reception, a receiver extracts the sender id from the received packet and adds it to a list of neighbors. It is also important for a node to detect missing nodes – nodes which are not any longer neighbors. A node is considered missing if no packet is received from the node within time interval T_d. A node must keep track of the last packet reception time to remove corresponding id from the list when T_d expires.

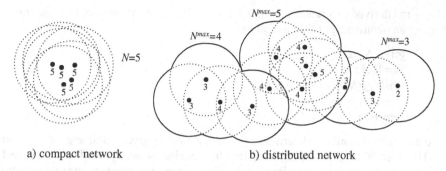

a) compact network   b) distributed network

Fig. 2. An example of a) compact network when $D=N$ and b) distributed networks when $D=N_{max}$ (numbers next to dots correspond to the number of neighbors of the node including the node itself)

In a distributed network (Fig. 2b), the use of the number of neighbors N for the parameter D will not always provide adequate discovery time performance. This will be shown in the following experimental result section. We will show that using N_{max}, the maximum number of neighbors among immediate neighbors for the value of the parameter D, instead of the number of neighbors N, will achieve better performance with respect to discovery within a given time in distributed networks. In order for nodes to be able to determine the value of the parameter N_{max}, each node must include its id and the number of its neighbors in the packet.

In a distributed network, it is possible that different nodes could determine different values of N_{max}. We define a group of nodes which use the same parameter N_{max} as a network segment. Fig. 2b shows an example of a distributed network multiple segments. Solid lines in Fig. 2b show the boundaries of network segments in which nodes use the same parameter N_{max}.

2.2 Frame Size Determination

In this section, we discuss how to determine the frame size m from the specified values of discovery time T_{slot} (measured in slots), assurance level α, and the number of neighbors N. Considering the case of a compact network where $D=N$, we derive the assurance level function f_α (N, m, T_{slot}) and then we present an algorithm for determining the frame size m using this function.

A rigorous analysis of assurance level is possible with Markov chain and combinatorial apparatus [7], [8]. However, these approaches are not suitable for real-time control due to its calculation complexity. Therefore, we introduce an assumption which allows us to obtain approximate expressions which simplify calculation. The assumption is that the probability of receiving a packet is independent of the transmission states of other nodes. This assumption allows us to calculate the assurance level function $f_\alpha(N, m, T_{slot})$ as follows:

$$f_\alpha = \left(1 - \left(1 - \left(1 - \frac{1}{m}\right)^{N-1}\right)^{\left\lfloor \frac{T_{slot}}{m} \right\rfloor} \left(1 - \frac{(T_{slot} \bmod m) \times (m-1)^{N-1}}{m^N}\right)\right)^N \quad (1)$$

Using the derived assurance function $f_\alpha(N, m, T_{slot})$, we can now obtain the frame size using an iterative algorithm as follows:

> **given** N, α, T_{slot}
> $m = \lceil 1.42\ N \rceil$
> **while** $f_\alpha(N, m+1, T_{slot}) \geq \alpha$
> $m = m + 1$
> **return** m

The algorithm iteratively determines the frame size for given parameters N, α, and T_{slot}. The algorithm first determines the frame size which provides the fastest discovery time using the approximation $\lceil 1.42N \rceil$, where the brackets mean round-up to an integer value. In the while loop, the frame size m is increased while the assurance level determined by the function $f_\alpha(N, m+1, T_{slot})$ is not smaller than pre-determined assurance level α. In the algorithm, we use the approximation $1.42N$ to determine the frame size for minimum discovery time. The approximation is obtained from equation (1) by finding the frame size m when derivative $\partial T/\partial m$ equals null.

3   Performance Evaluation

In this section, we evaluate the performance of the protocol in compact and non-compact distributed networks, using numerical simulations. To present our numerical results, it is more convenient to measure discovery time in seconds rather than in slots. Hence, instead of using the parameter T_{slot} we will replace it with the parameter T/t_{slot}, where T is the discovery time measured in seconds and t_{slot} is the slot length defined in seconds. In this paper, the slot length will be 10 milliseconds. We present results for one case, namely, when the discovery time T equals 4 seconds ($T=4$ sec).

3.1   Performance in Compact Networks

In this section, we evaluate the performance of the protocol in compact network. In Fig. 3a, we can see discovery time results consist of two regimes: 1) when the discovery time of 4 seconds is achievable and 2) when it is not. The discovery time is achievable for small number of nodes, however with increase in the number of nodes, it becomes impossible to achieve the desired discovery time. When this happens, according to the proposed algorithm, nodes use the frame size which achieves the fastest discovery time. For example, it is possible to achieve discovery of 4 seconds when the number of nodes is between 2 and 24 nodes. When the number of nodes becomes larger than 24 nodes the discovery time of 4 seconds becomes impossible and nodes select the frame size to achieve the fastest discovery time which increases with the number of nodes.

Fig. 3b presents frames sizes selected by nodes to achieve discovery time of $T=4$ seconds presented in Fig. 3a. In Fig. 3b, we can see that to achieve the given discovery time, nodes must decrease their frame sizes when the number of nodes increases. The frame size decreases from 402 slots for 2 nodes down to 35 slots for 24 nodes. However, when the number of nodes in the network becomes greater than 24 nodes the frame size linearly increases. This is because a network with a larger

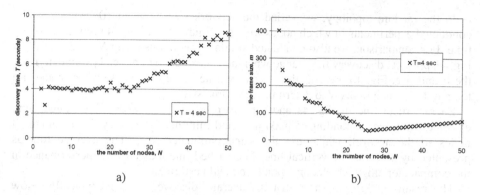

a)   b)

Fig. 3. a) simulation results for the discovery time in a compact network and b) the frame size in a compact network obtained with the iterative algorithm for assurance level $\alpha=0.99$

number of nodes becomes too congested. Further decrease in frame size will result in exponential growth of discovery time. Therefore, in order to reduce network congestion and to achieve the fastest discovery time, we have to reduce the network load by increasing the frame size.

We comment on the detection of missing nodes. It is necessary to choose a suitable value of parameter T_d for detection of missing nodes. In this paper, we use $T_d = T$ that is a single discovery time interval, since a node receives at least one packet from each neighbor during time T with high probability when the assurance level is 0.99.

3.2 Performance in Distributed Networks

In this section, we evaluate discovery performance in a distributed network. Unlike compact networks (Fig. 2a) in which all nodes use the same value of the parameter N to determine their frame sizes, in distributed networks, the network can split into multiple segments (Fig. 2b) with different values of density parameter N_{max}. This causes some uncertainties in the discovery time at the segment borders where nodes use different values of N_{max} for frame size determination.

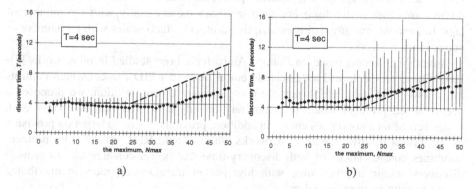

a)   b)

Fig. 4. The discovery time when a node uses a) the parameter N_{max} and b) the number of neighbors N, to determine the frame size in a distributed network

In the random topology, we varied the network size between 10-200 nodes. We conducted experiments in which nodes were configured to provide 4 second discovery time. For comparison, we also conducted similar simulations using N instead of N_{max}. Fig. 4a presents discovery time range when nodes use the parameter N_{max} to determine the frame size. Fig. 4b presents the discovery time range in the case where nodes use the number of neighbors N to determine the frame size.

Each vertical line in Fig. 4a and Fig. 4b represents discovery time range, with extreme values corresponding to maximum and minimum discovery times among all nodes in the network which use the same parameter N_{max}. The average time is presented by a dot on the vertical line. The dashed line indicates the performance in the compact topology which corresponds to ideal performance.

The results in Fig. 4a show that the average discovery time is typically below the ideal discovery time which is represented by the dash line. On the other hand, the results in Fig. 4b show that if nodes use the number of neighbors N to determine the frame size the average discovery time will exceed the ideal discovery time. From these results, it is clear that the method which uses the parameter N_{max} to determine the frame size in a distributed network with random topology provides better performance compared to the method which uses the number of neighbors N.

4 Related Work

Various systems, including Wi-Fi [11] and Bluetooth [12], have mechanisms for service discovery as higher level protocols. Bluetooth provides connection-oriented communication, meaning that a device must connect with another device before it can "discover" another node in the sense of getting profile information. The disadvantage of the higher level discovery protocols is long and variable discovery time - up to 18 seconds for two Bluetooth devices [13].

A RFID tag reader discovers wireless tags in its reception range. There are two categories of protocols for tag discovery which include deterministic and adaptive. In deterministic protocols, tags broadcast their ids with fixed rate. The discovery time analysis of deterministic Aloha-based protocol for active RFID tags is described in [14]. The disadvantage of deterministic protocols is that they do not scale with the number of nodes – the discovery time increases exponentially with the number of tags. In contrast, our protocol is an adaptive protocol which scales with the number of nodes in the network.

Adaptive protocols based on Framed Aloha have been studied in other works [7]-[10]. These protocols use a dedicated central node (a RFID reader) which controls transmissions of neighboring tags. In comparison with our solution, we proposed a decentralized protocol which does not rely on any dedicated central node – each nodes acts as an autonomous entity. In addition, previous solutions target on provision of the fastest discovery time in networks with a single RFID reader. Our protocol combines considerations of both discovery-time and power-consumption to provide discovery within a given time with low packet transmission rates in distributed networks with varying node density.

5 Conclusion

In this paper we have developed a new MAC protocol specifically designed for efficient discovery in networks with varying node density. The protocol supports discovery using the minimum packet broadcast rate which can achieve a specified discovery time. To the best of our knowledge, we are the first to develop a protocol which provides the time-bounded neighbor discovery in distributed networks. It is expected that this protocol could support a wide range of discovery applications. The discovery protocol is based on Framed Aloha. Each node determines the frame size using knowledge of the maximum number of neighbors among neighbors. We evaluated the performance of the protocol in various network topologies, and confirmed that the proposed protocol provides adequate discovery time performance in compact networks and random distributed networks.

References

1. Akyildiz, I.F., Weilian, S., Sankarasubramaniam, Y., Cayirci, E.: A survey on sensor networks. IEEE Comm. Mag. 40(8), 102–114 (2002)
2. Zhu, F., Mutka, M.W., Ni, L.M.: Service discovery in pervasive computing environments. IEEE Pervasive Comp. 4(4), 81–90 (2005)
3. Helal, S., Desai, N., Lee, C., Verna, V.: Konark - A service discovery and delivery protocol for ad-hoc networks. In: Proc. 3rd IEEE Conf. on Wireless Commun. Netw., New Orleans, USA, pp. 2107–2113 (March 2003)
4. Poupyrev, P., Kosuga, M., Davis, P.: Analysis of wireless message broadcasts in large ad-hoc networks of PDAs. In: Proc. 4th IEEE Conf. on Mobile and Wireless Commun. Networks, Stockholm, Sweden, pp. 299–303 (September 2002)
5. Poupyrev, P., Sasao, T., Saruwatari, S., Davis, P., Morikawa, H., Aoyama, T.: Service discovery in TinyObj: Strategies and Approaches. In: Proc. Workshop on Pervasive Mobile Interaction Devices, Munich, Germany, pp. 19–24 (May 2005)
6. Nidd, M.: Service discovery in DEAPspace. IEEE Personal Commun. 8(4), 39–45 (2001)
7. Vogt, H.: Efficient object identification with passive RFID tags. In: Proc. Conf. on Pervasive Computing, Zurich, Switzerland, pp. 98–113 (April 2002)
8. Zhen, B., Konayashi, M., Shimizu, M.: Framed Aloha for multiple RFID objects identification. IEICE Trans. Commun. E88-B(3), 991–999 (2005)
9. Schoute, F.C.: Dynamic frame length Aloha. IEEE Trans. Commun. 31(4), 565–568 (1983)
10. Wieselthier, J.E., Ephremides, A., Michaels, L.A.: An exact analysis and performance evaluation of Framed Aloha with capture. IEEE Trans. Commun. 37(2), 125–137 (1989)
11. Wireless LAN Medium Access Control and Physical Layer Specification IEEE Standard (August 1999), http://www.ieee.org/
12. Bluetooth SIG. In specification of the Bluetooth system (2005), http://www.bluetooth.com/
13. Sedov, S., Preuss, C., Cap, M.H., Timmermann, D.: Time and energy efficient service discovery in Bluetooth. In: Proc. 57th IEEE VTC Conf., pp. 418–422. IEEE Computer Society Press, Los Alamitos (April 2003)
14. Zhen, B., Kobayashi, M., Shimizu, M.: The reading of transmission-only active RFID tags. Int. J. on Comp. and Applications 27(1), 10–19 (2005)

Mobility Helps Data Delivery in Disruption Tolerant Networks

Kaoru Sezaki[1], Niwat Thepvilojanapong[2], and Yoshito Tobe[3]

[1] Center for Spatial Information Science, University of Tokyo
4–6–1 Komaba Meguro Tokyo 153–8505 Japan
sezaki@iis.u-tokyo.ac.jp
[2] Department of Information and Communication Engineering, University of Tokyo
7–3–1 Hongo Bunkyo Tokyo 113–8654 Japan
wat@acm.org
[3] Department of Info. Systems and Multimedia Design, Tokyo Denki University
2–2 Kanda-Nishikicho Chiyoda Tokyo 101–8457 Japan
yoshito_tobe@osoite.jp

Abstract. Sensor networks using mobile robots have recently been proposed to deal with data communication in disruption tolerant networks (DTNs) where an instantaneous end-to-end path between a source and destination may not exist. In such network scenarios, a node should move to deliver data to the destination. In this paper, we study adaptive formations of mobile robots based on the knowledge of network topology held by each node. Different node formations are applied when nodes have neighboring, clustering, or perfect information of network. Node formations also depend on traffic patterns, e.g., single and multiples packets per event. We introduce a straight line formation called pipeline for delivering multiple packets continuously. The benefit of controlled mobility in DTNs is validated through the ns–2 simulation tool by comparing with the ideal cases.

Keywords: routing, mobile sensor networks, disruption tolerant networks, mobile robots, evaluation, simulation.

1 Introduction

As technology rapidly advances, diverse sensing and mobility capabilities will become more readily available to devices. Once mobility becomes feasible, we fully expect that large systems of mobile autonomous agents performing various important tasks will soon follow. Of course, communication will be an essential function of these *Mobile Sensor Networks (MSNs)*. The objective of this paper is to explore the capability of such networks using controlled mobility to help data delivery.

One can envision many settings where mobility may potentially be used to improve network communications. One such scenario is a long term deployment of self-organizing mobile sensors designed to intercept or record, and then report

H. Ichikawa et al. (Eds.): UCS 2007, LNCS 4836, pp. 298–305, 2007.
© Springer-Verlag Berlin Heidelberg 2007

as much data as possible. One promising scenario is the use of sensing robots to conduct difficult or dangerous tasks that cannot be done by human beings. The movement of mobile robots is a key consideration in constructing an efficient network and performing sensing adaptive to important events in a wider area. Sensor networks that employ mobile robots have recently been proposed to conduct more efficient sensing tasks in disruption tolerant networks (DTNs) [1,2] where an instantaneous end-to-end path between a source and destination may not exist. Path disruption could exist because tiny-sized devices cannot offer very long radio range. In such network scenarios, a node should move to deliver data to the destination.

This paper extensively studies *WISER (Wireless Interactive SEnsing Robot)* protocol [3], and then validates the benefit of mobility through simulations. One of the major features of WISER is the criteria for selecting between physical movement and wireless transmission for data transfer at each hop. WISER determines the formation of mobile sensing nodes depending on available information about network topology. Unlike the movement in mobile ad hoc networks (MANETs), a node moves intentionally to transfer data. Although an end-to-end path does not exist, a WISER node can control not only its movement but also the mobility of other mobile sensors to make communication both feasible and efficient. Such explicit collaboration of nodes makes data transfer in partitioned networks possible.

The remainder of the paper is organized as follows. Section 2 introduces some related work. Section 3 describes problem statement. Section 4 articulates the WISER protocols. Section 5 evaluates the benefit of mobility through simulations. We conclude our work in Section 6.

2 Related Work

GPSR [4] is a geographic routing that uses location information to decrease overhead of route discovery. GPSR uses greedy forwarding at each hop by routing each packet to the neighbor closest to the destination. However, any location-based routing (LBR) protocols do not work well in DTNs. To solve the problem of LBR protocols, previous works exploited mobility when nodes meet each other by chance, i.e., natural and uncontrolled movement. Epidemic routing [1] that relies on the theory of epidemic algorithms is a routing protocol for intermittently connected networks. Similarly, moving objects in [5] move randomly and disseminate data across disconnected static nodes by trying to distribute data to all nodes. In [6,7], randomly moving humans and animals act as data mules and collect data opportunistically from sensor nodes when in range. Such approaches are orthogonal to our work which exploits controlled movement.

Message ferrying [2] uses non-randomness movement which is known by other nodes to help deliver data. Goldenberg et al. [8] also exploits controlled mobility to improve communication performance. The Infostations model [9] of wireless ad-hoc networks aims to provide trade-offs between delay and capacity of these networks by providing geographically intermittent connectivity. Fall [10] proposed the Delay Tolerant Network architecture to solve the internetworking issues in scenarios where partitions are frequent and a connected path between message senders and receivers may be not present. This approach relies on routing mechanism presented in detail in [11].

3   Problem Statement

We consider a sparse sensor network where end-to-end path is not available for all pairs of nodes in the network. A node or robot composes of sensing and moving components, and it is called mobile robot, mobile sensor, or sensor node throughout the paper. The mobile robot is also equipped with a short-range wireless communication interface (RF). Each node identifies its location by using GPS or other means of positioning systems. The location of sink node or data collector is known in advance, while the location of other nodes can be obtained by beacon messages. Our study divides knowledge of location information into three levels. First, *neighboring information* is location information of all neighboring nodes. Second, *clustering information* means location information of all nodes in a cluster, where the cluster means a group of nodes that can reach each other using multi-hop, wireless communication. Third, *perfect information* is location information of all nodes in a network. We propose different protocols to cope with each level of location information.

We consider two traffic models in our study. First, each node generates one packet per event in a *single-packet model*. The event may be warning, notice, or any sensed data detected in tracking systems, intrusion detection, etc. Second, a node reports sensed data periodically for a fixed period of time in a *multiple-packet model*. Actually, sensing data may not fit into a single packet and need fragmentation in this model. The protocol for each level of location information is further divided into two cases according to our traffic models.

4   Data Delivery Protocols for DTNs

4.1   The WISER Protocol

Single Data Packet. Basically, a node uses the *greedy forwarding (GF) scheme* [4] whenever possible. In particular, next hop is a neighboring node geographically closest to the destination D. If the GF scheme fails, the node moves towards D for a distance of its communication range (r). After its journey, the node discovers new neighbors and decides the next hop based on the GF scheme. The process of moving r meters is repeated until the GF scheme is valid. After transmitting data to the next hop, the node moves back to its original position.

Multiple Data Packets. Data delivery within a cluster uses the GF scheme. When the GF fails, nodes form a straight line formation called *pipeline* between partitioned clusters. In particular, current node X, which is the node geographically closest to destination D in the cluster, moves towards D to check the

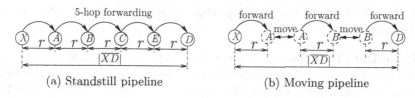

(a) Standstill pipeline   (b) Moving pipeline

Fig. 1. Robots construct a pipeline collaboratively

number of potential *helper-nodes* (m). X then calculates whether m is enough to construct a *standstill pipeline* (Fig. 1a) by using the following inequality: $m \geq |\overrightarrow{P_D} - \overrightarrow{P_X}|/r - 1$. If m is enough (the inequality is true), we use minimum number of helper-nodes, i.e., $m = |\overrightarrow{P_D} - \overrightarrow{P_X}|/r - 1$, where each helper-node is separated equally as shown in Fig. 1a. After deciding the helper-nodes and their positions, X requests the helper-nodes to move to the defined position during its journey back to the original position. Therefore, the total delay (Δt) of the first packet using the standstill pipeline composes of communication ($|\overrightarrow{P_D} - \overrightarrow{P_X}|(d + s/b)/r$) and moving ($2|\overrightarrow{P_D} - \overrightarrow{P_X}|/v$) delays, where d is transmission delay, s is packet size, b is bandwidth, and v is node velocity. However, it costs only communication delay for the second and following packets.

If the number of helper-nodes (m) is not enough, we introduce a *moving pipeline* (Fig. 1b). Helper-nodes need to move forth-and-back to get, carry, and forward data packets. Each node should move forth-and-back the same distance. The total delay excluding round-trip movement (helper-node discovery) of X also composes of communication ($(m + 1)(d + s/b)$) and moving ($|\overrightarrow{P_D} - \overrightarrow{P_X}|/v - r(m + 1)/v$) delays.

4.2   The WISER/c Protocol: Beyond Neighboring Information

Single Data Packet. Each node calculates a minimum-hop path in its own cluster by using Dijkstra's algorithm. A temporary destination in the cluster is the node geographically closest to the destination. The time (Δt) needed for a packet traversing k hops from a current node to the temporary destination is $\sum_{i=0}^{k-1}(d + s/b)$. Assume transmission ($d$) and propagation ($s/b$) delays are equal for the same-sized packet at any wireless link, the total delay becomes $k(d + s/b)$.

Because wireless communication is prone to loss, nodes should include loss rate when determining a path. Let $(1 - p)$ be the probability that a packet loses when being delivered to the next hop. If the packet loses, the sender retransmits the packet until it is successfully delivered to the next hop. The expectation value of one-hop delay from node i to node j is $E[\Delta t_{ij}] = \sum_{k=1}^{\infty} p_i(1 - p_i)^{k-1}(k\Delta t_{ij}) = \Delta t_{ij}/p_i$. Therefore, the delay taking link quality into consideration is $\Delta t = (d + s/b)\sum_{i=0}^{k-1} p_i^{-1}$.

When the next hop does not exist (i.e., the packet arrived the temporary destination), the temporary destination uses the same procedures as the WISER protocol (Sect. 4.1) by moving r meters towards final destination. Instead of using the GF, it selects the next hop whose cluster is geographically closest to the destination.

Multiple Data Packets. A node uses the same algorithm as the single-packet scenario to discover the next hop within a cluster. If the next hop does not exist, the node also applies standstill or moving pipeline as the WISER protocol. However, the pipeline is created between the current node and the node in the next cluster that is geographically closest to the destination.

4.3   The WISER/p Protocol: An Ideal Case of Data Delivery

Single Data Packet. A node (says X) uses the same algorithm as WISER/c to forward data within a cluster. If the next hop does not exist, the node uses a *greedy moving* scheme. In particular, the node moves in the direction towards the next-hop node (N) which satisfies two conditions: (i) N must be geographically closest to itself and, (ii) N must be closer to the destination than itself. It stops at the edge of N's communication range. Actually, the node stops after passing the communication border for a short distance (δ). If the next hop does not exist, i.e., no any node satisfies the above two conditions, the destination will be the next-hop node.

However, if there are at least two movements when a packet is sent from a source to a destination, the node uses divide-and-conquer method to achieve minimal movement. For example, if A must move towards B ($|\overrightarrow{P_B} - \overrightarrow{P_A}| - r + \delta$), and then E must move towards F ($|\overrightarrow{P_F} - \overrightarrow{P_E}| - r + \delta$), the node compares a direct distance from A to F ($|\overrightarrow{P_F} - \overrightarrow{P_A}| - r + \delta$) with the two-step movement ($|\overrightarrow{P_B} - \overrightarrow{P_A}| + |\overrightarrow{P_F} - \overrightarrow{P_E}| - 2r + 2\delta$), and chooses the shorter one. As usual, the total delay from a source S to a destination D composes of communication ($(d + s/b)\sum_{i=0}^{k-1} p_i^{-1}$) and moving ($\sum_{\forall j}(l_j - r + \delta)/v$) delays, where ($l_j - r + \delta$) is a distance of the jth movement.

Multiple Data Packets. The protocol is based on the single-packet algorithm described above. However, when wireless transmission is not possible, WISER/p agent creates a pipeline between the current node and temporary destination in the next cluster. The current node moves and sends a request message to the node that follows greedy moving scheme, i.e., the node that is closest to itself and, closer to the destination than itself. After sending the request message, it moves back to its original position and starts forwarding data packets.

5   Performance Evaluation

We used the ns–2 simulation tool to run a number of simulations so as to validate the benefit of intentional mobility. We compared WISER and WISER/c with the ideal solution, WISER/p.

Table 1. Packet delivery ratio and delay

Scenario	Packet delivery ratio			Delay (seconds)			Messages/energy (KB/J)		
	WISER	WISER/c	WISER/p	WISER	WISER/c	WISER/p	WISER	WISER/c	WISER/p
I	100%	100%	100%	6.92	5.21	2.24	3.21	6.12	13.93
II	100%	100%	100%	4.42	3.81	1.45	4.25	4.80	13.45
III	96%	99.73%	100%	4.94	1.82	1.35	7.11	15.00	25.95

5.1 Simulation Environment

50 mobile sensor nodes were randomly placed in a 180 m by 180 m square region. Each node had fixed radio coverage of 25 m, the bandwidth of 19.2 kbps, and moved with a speed 10 m/s. 30 random sources sent 36-byte data packet(s) to randomly chosen destination(s). Receive power dissipation (395 mW) was nearly 60% of transmit power dissipation (660 mW) [12]. Another key ingredient of our simulation setup is the cost of mobility. We chose to use a distance proportional cost model, $P_m(d) = kd$, where d is distance and k is 1 J/m [8].

The simulation scenarios varied the number of packets per event (single and multiple) and the number of destinations (single and multiple) as follows.

• **Scenario I** – Each source generated single packet per event. Every packet destined to the only destination in the network.

• **Scenario II** – Each source generated single packet per event as the first scenario but the destinations of generated packets were randomly chosen.

• **Scenario III** – 25 sources generated single packet per event, while other five sources generated ten packets per event. All packets destined to the only destination in the network.

• **Scenario IV** – All are the same as Scenario 3, except the pipelining scheme is turned off.

Performance metrics are packet delivery ratio, end-to-end delay, and delivered messages per unit energy.

5.2 Simulation Results

Simulation results of Scenario I, II, and III are shown in Table 1. First we consider packet delivery ratio to study the correctness of the protocols. Three WISER protocols deliver 100% in Scenario I and II where single packet is generated per event. As some sources generate multiple packets per event (Scenario III), 4% and 0.3% of the originated packets are dropped by WISER and WISER/c, respectively, while WISER/p can deliver all generated packets. Because helper-nodes in WISER and WISER/c move longer than those of WISER/p, some packets were dropped if queue is full. After the simulations finished, some packets were still on the way to the destination. Those packets are another cause of loss.

Next we consider end-to-end delay used by the protocols. For all of three scenarios, delays of WISER/p are shorter than those of WISER/c, which in turn are

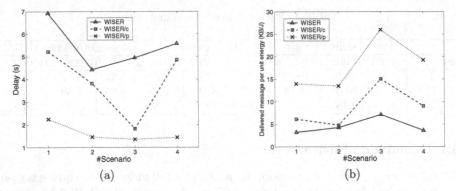

Fig. 2. Impact of pipeline: (a) delay; (b) delivered messages per unit energy

shorter than those of WISER. This is because WISER protocol exploits physical movement of node as a mean of data transfer the most, followed by WISER/c and WISER/p, respectively. The reason behind this fact is that WISER/p has knowledge of the entire network while WISER/c knows only the nodes within the cluster and WISER has only information of neighbors. Hence WISER/p can discover shorter-delay paths compared to the paths decided by WISER/c and WISER. Since mobile nodes in WISER and WISER/c move in a similar way, i.e., they move towards destination for r m, the delays do not differ so much. However, the trend of results in Scenario III is different where the delays of WISER/p are a little bit shorter than those of WISER/c when delivering continuous data packets, while WISER takes more than two times to deliver the packets in the same scenario. In this scenario, WISER/p and WISER/c have more helper-nodes than WISER to construct pipeline, thereby, moving pipeline happens frequently in WISER comparing to WISER/p and WISER/c. Because moving pipeline takes longer time than standstill pipeline to deliver the data, the delays of WISER are much longer than those of WISER/p and WISER/c.

Finally we study energy-efficiency of each protocol by considering how much data can be delivered per unit energy. Because physical movement consumes much more energy than wireless communication, WISER/p which employs less movement than WISER/c and WISER is the best energy-efficient protocol, followed by WISER/c and WISER for all scenarios. The reason can be explained in the same way as the results of delay discussed above.

Impact of Pipeline. We study the effectiveness of pipeline by comparing Scenario III and IV. When the pipelining scheme is turned off, all protocols use more time to deliver packets (Fig. 2a) because a node must move multiple round-trips between its current position and destination or next hop. Energy consumption is also higher due to more movements (Fig. 2b). We conclude that the pipelining scheme increases the performance of the protocols in terms of end-to-end delay and energy efficiency because node movement decreases.

6   Conclusions

WISER protocols allow network partitioning and utilize controlled mobility of nodes as a means of data transfer in addition to wireless transmission. Mobile sensors in WISER protocols move adaptively according to traffic models and the knowledge of network topology. A node establishes a session for stream data and instructs other mobile robots to construct standstill or moving pipeline as a bridge connecting partitioned networks. We used the ns-2 network simulator to study the performance of WISER protocols in many aspects. Simulation results demonstrated the benefit of physical movement, i.e., 100% or nearly 100% of the originated packets were correctly delivered. Perfect data delivery could not be feasible, if prior schemes (e.g., [4]) were applied. Explicit collaboration of robots to deliver stream data also reduces latency and energy dissipation.

References

1. Vahdat, A., Becker, D.: Epidemic routing for partially-connected ad hoc networks. Technical Report CS-2000-06, Duke University (July 2000)
2. Zhao, W., Ammar, M., Zegura, E.: A message ferrying approach for data delivery in sparse mobile ad hoc networks. In: Proceedings of MobiHoc, pp. 187–198 (May 2004)
3. Thepvilojanapong, N., Tobe, Y., Sezaki, K.: Impact of intentional mobility in sparse sensor networks. In: Proceedings of SenSys, pp. 286–287 (November 2005)
4. Karp, B., Kung, H.T.: GPSR: greedy perimeter stateless routing for wireless networks. In: Proceedings of MobiCom, Boston, MA, USA, pp. 243–254 (August 2000)
5. Beaufour, A., Leopold, M., Bonnet, P.: Smart-tag based data dissemination. In: Proceedings of WSNA, pp. 68–77 (September 2002)
6. Shah, R.C., et al.: Data mules: Modeling a three-tier architecture for sparse sensor networks. In: Proceedings of SNPA, pp. 30–41 (May 2003)
7. Jain, S., et al.: Exploiting mobility for energy efficient data collection in sensor networks. In: Proceedings of WiOpt (March 2004)
8. Goldenberg, D.K., Lin, J., Morse, A.S.: Towards mobility as a network control primitive. In: Proceedings of MobiHoc, pp. 163–174 (May 2004)
9. Small, T., Haas, Z.J.: The shared wireless infostation model: a new ad hoc networking paradigm (or where there is a whale, there is a way). In: Proceedings of MobiHoc, pp. 233–244 (June 2003)
10. Fall, K.: A delay-tolerant network architecture for challenged internets. In: Proceedings of SIGCOMM, Karlsruhe, Germany, pp. 27–34 (August 2003)
11. Jain, S., Fall, K., Patra, R.: Routing in a delay tolerant network. In: Proceedings of SIGCOMM, Portland, Oregon, USA, pp. 145–158 (August 2004)
12. Intanagonwiwat, C., Govindan, R., Estrin, D.: Directed diffusion: a scalable and robust communication paradigm for sensor networks. In: Proceedings of MobiCom, Boston, Massachusetts, USA, pp. 56–67 (August 2000)

Author Index

Lecture Notes in Computer Science

Sublibrary 3: Information Systems and Application, incl. Internet/Web and HCI

For information about Vols. 1– 4380
please contact your bookseller or Springer

Vol. 4605: D. Papadias, D. Zhang, G. Kollios (Eds.), Advances in Spatial and Temporal Databases. X, 479 pages. 2007.

Vol. 4602: S. Barker, G.-J. Ahn (Eds.), Data and Applications Security XXI. X, 291 pages. 2007.

Vol. 4601: S. Spaccapietra, P. Atzeni, F. Fages, M.-S. Hacid, M. Kifer, J. Mylopoulos, B. Pernici, P. Shvaiko, J. Trujillo, I. Zaihrayeu (Eds.), Journal on Data Semantics IX. XV, 197 pages. 2007.

Vol. 4592: Z. Kedad, N. Lammari, E. Métais, F. Meziane, Y. Rezgui (Eds.), Natural Language Processing and Information Systems. XIV, 442 pages. 2007.

Vol. 4587: R. Cooper, J. Kennedy (Eds.), Data Management. XIII, 259 pages. 2007.

Vol. 4577: N. Sebe, Y. Liu, Y.-t. Zhuang, T.S. Huang (Eds.), Multimedia Content Analysis and Mining. XIII, 513 pages. 2007.

Vol. 4568: T. Ishida, S. R. Fussell, P. T. J. M. Vossen (Eds.), Intercultural Collaboration. XIII, 395 pages. 2007.

Vol. 4566: M.J. Dainoff (Ed.), Ergonomics and Health Aspects of Work with Computers. XVIII, 390 pages. 2007.

Vol. 4564: D. Schuler (Ed.), Online Communities and Social Computing. XVII, 520 pages. 2007.

Vol. 4563: R. Shumaker (Ed.), Virtual Reality. XXII, 762 pages. 2007.

Vol. 4561: V.G. Duffy (Ed.), Digital Human Modeling. XXIII, 1068 pages. 2007.

Vol. 4560: N. Aykin (Ed.), Usability and Internationalization, Part II. XVIII, 576 pages. 2007.

Vol. 4559: N. Aykin (Ed.), Usability and Internationalization, Part I. XVIII, 661 pages. 2007.

Vol. 4558: M.J. Smith, G. Salvendy (Eds.), Human Interface and the Management of Information, Part II. XXIII, 1162 pages. 2007.

Vol. 4557: M.J. Smith, G. Salvendy (Eds.), Human Interface and the Management of Information, Part I. XXII, 1030 pages. 2007.

Vol. 4541: T. Okadome, T. Yamazaki, M. Makhtari (Eds.), Pervasive Computing for Quality of Life Enhancement. IX, 248 pages. 2007.

Vol. 4537: K.C.-C. Chang, W. Wang, L. Chen, C.A. Ellis, C.-H. Hsu, A.C. Tsoi, H. Wang (Eds.), Advances in Web and Network Technologies, and Information Management. XXIII, 707 pages. 2007.

Vol. 4531: J. Indulska, K. Raymond (Eds.), Distributed Applications and Interoperable Systems. XI, 337 pages. 2007.

Vol. 4526: M. Malek, M. Reitenspieß, A. van Moorsel (Eds.), Service Availability. X, 155 pages. 2007.

Vol. 4524: M. Marchiori, J.Z. Pan, C.d.S. Marie (Eds.), Web Reasoning and Rule Systems. XI, 382 pages. 2007.

Vol. 4519: E. Franconi, M. Kifer, W. May (Eds.), The Semantic Web: Research and Applications. XVIII, 830 pages. 2007.

Vol. 4518: N. Fuhr, M. Lalmas, A. Trotman (Eds.), Comparative Evaluation of XML Information Retrieval Systems. XII, 554 pages. 2007.

Vol. 4508: M.-Y. Kao, X.-Y. Li (Eds.), Algorithmic Aspects in Information and Management. VIII, 428 pages. 2007.

Vol. 4506: D. Zeng, I. Gotham, K. Komatsu, C. Lynch, M. Thurmond, D. Madigan, B. Lober, J. Kvach, H. Chen (Eds.), Intelligence and Security Informatics: Biosurveillance. XI, 234 pages. 2007.

Vol. 4505: G. Dong, X. Lin, W. Wang, Y. Yang, J.X. Yu (Eds.), Advances in Data and Web Management. XXII, 896 pages. 2007.

Vol. 4504: J. Huang, R. Kowalczyk, Z. Maamar, D. Martin, I. Müller, S. Stoutenburg, K.P. Sycara (Eds.), Service-Oriented Computing: Agents, Semantics, and Engineering. X, 175 pages. 2007.

Vol. 4500: N.A. Streitz, A.D. Kameas, I. Mavrommati (Eds.), The Disappearing Computer. XVIII, 304 pages. 2007.

Vol. 4495: J. Krogstie, A. Opdahl, G. Sindre (Eds.), Advanced Information Systems Engineering. XVI, 606 pages. 2007.

Vol. 4480: A. LaMarca, M. Langheinrich, K.N. Truong (Eds.), Pervasive Computing. XIII, 369 pages. 2007.

Vol. 4473: D. Draheim, G. Weber (Eds.), Trends in Enterprise Application Architecture. X, 355 pages. 2007.

Vol. 4471: P. Cesar, K. Chorianopoulos, J.F. Jensen (Eds.), Interactive TV: A Shared Experience. XIII, 236 pages. 2007.

Vol. 4469: K.-c. Hui, Z. Pan, R.C.-k. Chung, C.C.L. Wang, X. Jin, S. Göbel, E.C.-L. Li (Eds.), Technologies for E-Learning and Digital Entertainment. XVIII, 974 pages. 2007.

Vol. 4443: R. Kotagiri, P. Radha Krishna, M. Mohania, E. Nantajeewarawat (Eds.), Advances in Databases: Concepts, Systems and Applications. XXI, 1126 pages. 2007.

Vol. 4439: W. Abramowicz (Ed.), Business Information Systems. XV, 654 pages. 2007.

Vol. 4430: C.C. Yang, D. Zeng, M. Chau, K. Chang, Q. Yang, X. Cheng, J. Wang, F.-Y. Wang, H. Chen (Eds.), Intelligence and Security Informatics. XII, 330 pages. 2007.

Vol. 4425: G. Amati, C. Carpineto, G. Romano (Eds.), Advances in Information Retrieval. XIX, 759 pages. 2007.

Vol. 4412: F. Stajano, H.J. Kim, J.-S. Chae, S.-D. Kim (Eds.), Ubiquitous Convergence Technology. XI, 302 pages. 2007.

Vol. 4402: W. Shen, J.-Z. Luo, Z. Lin, J.-P.A. Barthès, Q. Hao (Eds.), Computer Supported Cooperative Work in Design III. XV, 763 pages. 2007.

Vol. 4398: S. Marchand-Maillet, E. Bruno, A. Nürnberger, M. Detyniecki (Eds.), Adaptive Multimedia Retrieval: User, Context, and Feedback. XI, 269 pages. 2007.

Vol. 4397: C. Stephanidis, M. Pieper (Eds.), Universal Access in Ambient Intelligence Environments. XV, 467 pages. 2007.